THE LONGEST KISS

THE LIFE AND TIMES OF
★ DEVIKA RANI ★

THE LONGEST KISS

KISHWAR DESAI

HarperCollins *Publishers* India

First published in 2020

This edition published in India by HarperCollins *Publishers* 2022
4th Floor, Tower A, Building No. 10, Phase II, DLF Cyber City,
Gurugram, Haryana –122002
www.harpercollins.co.in

2 4 6 8 10 9 7 5 3 1

Copyright © Kishwar Desai 2020, 2022

P-ISBN: 978-93-5629-477-6
E-ISBN: 978-93-5629-478-3

The views and opinions expressed in this book are the author's own and the facts are as reported by her, and the publishers are not in any way liable for the same.

Kishwar Desai asserts the moral right
to be identified as the author of this work.

All rights reserved. No part of this publication may be reproduced, stored in a retrieval system, or transmitted, in any form or by any means, electronic, mechanical, photocopying, recording or otherwise, without the prior permission of the publishers.

Typeset by Jojy Philip, New Delhi - 110015

Printed and bound at
Thomson Press (India) Ltd

This book is produced from independently certified FSC® paper
to ensure responsible forest management.

For Mallika,
brave, brilliant, beautiful

Devika Rani (1908–1994)

CONTENTS

Author's Note	ix
Prologue: 15 May 1933, London	1
1. Bombay Talkies, 1945	8
2. Himansu, 1922	25
3. The Light of Asia, 1925–26	42
4. Like a Demon in Hell, 1926–1929	61
5. Devika, 1927–1930s	82
6. A Monument to Love, 1927–1930s	100
7. Trouble in Berlin, 1929–1932	121
8. Karma: A Twist of Fate, 1930–1933	145
9. Himansurai Indo-International Talkies Ltd, 1930s	173
10. Bombay Talkies, 1930s	193
11. 'A Broken, Unwanted Thing,' 1934–1939	216
12. The War Within, 1930s	251
13. Life Without Himansu, 1940s	279
14. Devika's Revenge, 1940s	303

15. Dazzling Devika! 1944–45   333
16. Breaking Free, 1944–45   357
17. Curtain Call, 1944–45   393

Epilogue, 1945–1994   423

Select Bibliography   437
Filmography: Devika Rani, actress   438
Acknowledgements   440
About the Author   443

AUTHOR'S NOTE

This book has its origin in a fortuitous incident. I was at the National Film Archives of India (NFAI) around fifteen years ago for some research, and preoccupied with my thoughts, when I stumbled and almost fell over some film reels lying haphazardly on the floor. They turned out to be films produced by Himansu Rai, some of which featured Devika Rani. Curious, I requested to be allowed to watch the films, which included some silent films.

I was stunned at the high visual quality and the confidence with which the films were made way back in the 1920s and 1930s, and with Devika's acting. It has always surprised me that we do not talk more about the globalisation of early Indian cinema. Why do we not celebrate the fact that Himansu's films were made with an international crew, and that his early, silent films were shown in Europe and America, something contemporary filmmakers crave to do but rarely achieve? Nor do we remember Devika's first film, which had its debut in London, where every critic raved about her. I was intrigued enough to want to write about both of them as well as Bombay Talkies, the studio they set up. With the generous help of the staff at NFAI, I gathered all the material I could find there. And so began the journey which took me all over the world, not just India, which is partly why this book took so long to put together.

Writing the book was a process of discovery, and sometimes very challenging. I met the Dietze family, who said that they were the grandchildren of Himansu, from Mary Hainlin. (I have written about Himansu and Mary's relationship in the book, but not about the Dietze family, as they went public with their claim after Devika had died. The timeline for my book ends with her death.) We had many interesting and friendly meetings in India and Australia. But then, fate or karma intervened—and I found, on my own (guided, no doubt, by Devika's determination) the real core of the book: Devika's personal and professional letters and papers, containing exciting new information that had not been seen for 80 years. Despite all the hurdles, I had miraculously discovered authentic source material, much of it in her handwriting, relating to all aspects of her life. It was the luckiest break ever. After all those years of trying to find credible material, I had struck gold.

This book draws mainly on that primary source material, piecing it together to form the main narrative. It has been a slow and excruciating process, as only extremely brief online biographies, full of inaccuracies, were available about both Devika and Himansu. Even photographic exhibitions centred on her had gaping holes—or incorrect statements. There was no ready record or source that I could use to form the structure. The narrative had to be created from scratch, from the thousands of papers and letters, personal and official, that I had collected over the years.

Had it not been for the COVID induced lockdown, I could not have had the uninterrupted time to be able to spread the papers all over the house, to read and put them into a proper context and sequence. Though I had started writing the book nearly a decade earlier, the papers required an intense and careful forensic scrutiny, which previously I could only manage in short bursts. All the documents, more than 4,000 of them, running into over 8,000 pages, had to be examined over and over again. These included Devika's letters, Himansu's letters, and other correspondence, as well as detailed records of board meetings. There was correspondence between Himansu and Sir Chimanlal Setalvad, the resignation letters of Ashok Kumar and others at Bombay Talkies, letters from media

AUTHOR'S NOTE

persons such as Baburao Patel, the acerbic editor of *Filmindia*, and the piece de resistance—the letters introducing Dilip Kumar (then Yusuf Khan) and Raj Kapoor (then Ranbir Raj Kapoor) to Devika. There were also details of the numerous court cases, intrigues and financial debacles faced by Devika and Himansu. All these became my main source of information, as also the letters written by Svetoslav—though those will probably become another book.

Apart from all this, there were the interviews I had conducted with the families and friends of the main protagonists and a large number of film reviews, media articles and films. To put the narrative in context, I referred to books on the period, which are listed in a separate bibliography.

But the most important focus of this book remained Devika's letters, from which I learnt about her very successful but painful life and the abuse she silently suffered for so long. From these letters emerges the story of a young woman surviving in a deeply patriarchal industry mainly through her brilliance and hard work. She considered herself a professional working woman, but an intensely private one at the same time—and her life and experiences are documented here for the very first time. I hope I have been able to capture some part of her gutsy and determined fight against those who wanted to destroy her, her career and her legacy built over the two decades that she worked in cinema.

I do not go into the details of her life after she married Svetoslav, because by then she felt she had won her battle, and had moved on to a different life. Nor does this book cover the story of the claimants to her property and legacy, who appeared on the scene after her death. Had she been alive, as with everything else, I have no doubt that the 'Bengal tigress' would have fought them and won.

I have used extracts from the letters and documents, verbatim as far as possible. Devika's personal letters have been very lightly edited, as she wrote very long epistles, with a non-stop flow of connected ideas and experiences. The letters are not reproduced in the exact sequence in which they were written. Most of them (especially those written by Devika) are from the 1940s and speak of her family and early life, her life with Himansu and, later, her struggle at Bombay Talkies.

While using extracts from letters in the early chapters, I have not mentioned the exact date on which they were written, as that may have been confusing for the reader. But in all the later chapters which deal with the 1940s, the dates are given, as the events and descriptions are in a contemporaneous time frame.

Another supportive source of material was the memoirs of Niranjan Pal, *Such Is Life*, especially for the early years when he and Himansu first met. I referred to the original book shared with me by his family, and not the later editions.

The conversations between characters in the book are obviously all from my imagination—that is the only part where I have allowed myself a bit of literary licence. More importantly, I have tried to correct many of the myths and unfounded rumours which were repeated over and over again about Devika, Himansu, Niranjan, Sir Richard Temple, Ashok Kumar and many others who were involved in the setting up and running of Bombay Talkies. I am grateful for this opportunity to set the record straight.

I hope this book will be of help to others who care to study this very important phase in Indian cinema, with its passion, idealism and entrepreneurship, in the days before it became a business like any other.

I do also hope that I have managed to establish who Devika Rani really was. A rebellious and unusually talented and beautiful woman, a great actress and studio head who changed the course of Indian cinema in many ways, despite her intense personal suffering. A pioneer, then and now.

Kishwar Desai
October 2020

Courtesy Rashid Ashraf

PROLOGUE
15 May 1933, London

It had been a warm though cloudy summer's day, and those strolling down to Hyde Park were attracted by the large, intriguing poster displayed above the cinema hall at the Marble Arch Pavilion.

They could not help but stop, mesmerised by the picture of a very beautiful, dark-eyed Indian woman gazing out at them. Behind her were painted palaces and tigers. Emblazoned across the poster was the film's title—*Karma*. At the theatre's entrance, lords and ladies dressed in finery were alighting from carriages and automobiles, eager to see the film produced by this new Indo-British-German collaboration.

The interest was more among those who had already served in the far reaches of the British Empire—they remembered with a deep nostalgia the hot and humid climes, the vast array of riches, maharajas and maharanis, the blinding colours, the fiery tastes, and the variety of songs, sounds and music. How would this film, in black-and-white, capture it all? Undoubtedly, it was a unique experiment—but would it succeed? Theatrical productions and silent films had tried to recreate 'India' with some success for European audiences, but this was a first for the newly born 'Talkies'.

The crowd of spectators grew appreciably in size as the evening drew on. A few policemen on duty had to move them from the

BUCKINGHAM PALACE

25th May, 1933.

Dear Sirs,

    I beg to acknowledge your letter of May 22nd, addressed to Sir Clive Wigram, and to inform you that its contents have been submitted to the King.

    I much regret that it will not be possible to comply with your request that the film "Karma" should be shown before Their Majesties in the near future. At the same time I am to assure you of the King's interest in the details connected with its production.

                         Yours truly,

The Managing Directors,
  I & B.P.Ltd., London
        and
  H.I.T., Ltd., Bombay.

cinema's entrance to create a narrow passage, walking through which could be spotted Lord and Lady Irwin, Lord and Lady Hoare, Lord Snell, Sir Pheroze Sethna, Sir Forbes Robertson and other well-known British aristocrats. A soft ripple of recognition would go through the spectators when they recognised someone. It had been rumoured that His Majesty King George V and Queen Mary would also attend, but by now the expectations had died down.

    It was already close to 9.30 p.m. and the crowd was getting restless. But their curiosity kept them rooted to the spot. Why were so many well established personalities interested in this particular Talkie? There were no famous actors in it, and yet they had counted more than four hundred attendees.

A few of the watchers knew that some reviews were already out and they were all quite favourable, especially about the film's heroine, Devika Rani, who could be seen pouting prettily in the poster over Oxford Street. The critics who had seen an advance show were impressed by her beauty and diction. The *Evening Star* had pronounced that it would be difficult to find anyone lovelier than her.

In fact, the reviewer for the *Evening Dispatch*, F.R. Buckley, would go on to write:

> I say quite frankly that this is a picture well worth seeing. Its technique has faults but on the other hand its photography and composition (in certain scenes) have extraordinary merits. It must be remembered that I review films quite brutally from the point of view of the population who pay to enter and who don't care to hear economic speeches as explanations.

And then he added bluntly, 'I liked the snakes and the elephants and what there was of the tiger.'

The 'brutal' Buckley would also be impressed both by Devika Rani and by the number of celebrities attending another show in Birmingham:

> Incidentally, the 9.15 show last evening was graced by the presence of The Lord Mayor (complete with chain of office) and by a charming speech by Miss Devika Rani....
> I met her....
> She sets a record by being even prettier off the screen than she is on.

There were many who would have agreed with him, and certainly, given the very flattering comparisons with famous Hollywood actresses, Devika Rani, the heroine of *Karma*, had truly arrived. Like many other papers, the *Birmingham Post* also raved about her 'lovely features, and lustrous eyes and her graceful movements'. Not only did the *Times* and the *Manchester Guardian* agree, her debut was noticed all over the world, especially in the colonies in Asia. The bedazzled media advised Hollywood to sign her up as she was the new Dolores del Rio. There were few positive mentions, however, of Himansu Rai, the producer and hero of the film.

Devika looked and sounded refreshingly sophisticated and modern. It was also a pleasant surprise for many to see an Indian couple kissing passionately on screen. Or rather, Devika kissed Himansu, while he lay supine on the ground, ostensibly close to death from a snakebite. This sensual abandonment made Devika intriguing for the viewer, as it so absolutely contradicted her virginal and rather traditional saree-clad looks. The kiss, the longest for any Indian actress, lasted for nearly two minutes—but many thought it was five.

Right now, at the entrance of the Marble Arch Pavilion cinema hall, the dark, good-looking Himansu stood with the petite Devika by his side, anxious but delighted that his hard work of gathering an elite audience had paid off. He greeted everyone individually, telling each person that he hoped they liked the film. It was the first time in the short history of Indian cinema that an Indian producer displayed the temerity to open his film in the heart of London, and invite the who's who of British society to watch. The fact that the guests had arrived in hugely gratifying numbers was a possible tribute to his powers of persuasion and self-belief. Some of them had, of course, heard about his previous successes in silent cinema, such as *The Light of Asia* and *A Throw of Dice*. A few had seen him on stage at the West End, in *The Goddess*. But none of them had heard of Devika Rani before.

Devika, draped in a silk saree, with her hair parted in the middle and tied in a low knot at the nape of her neck, looked every inch the princess of Sitapur she had portrayed in *Karma*. Even more so than the real-life Indian princess Sudha Rani of Burdwan, who played the role of Devika's loyal friend. Sudha was not gifted with the beauty or natural insouciance Devika displayed even at the age of twenty-five.

Devika turned to Himansu, her eyes welling with unexpected tears of happiness. She was, despite her calm exterior, overwhelmed by the response. To have the cream of London turn out in this way was astonishing. But she still had some doubts about the outcome—the film had an entirely Indian cast. Would that upset the audience?

'I hope they like it,' she murmured, a very slight tremor in her usually steady voice revealing her anxiety.

Himansu squeezed her hand in reassurance. 'Don't worry, darling. When they see you on the screen, they'll be bowled over,' he whispered back to her. Between them passed a look of love and commitment. They would make their mark on cinema, come what may.

As the evening progressed, it became clear that though both Himansu and Devika had their time on the screen, it was she who stole the show. There was pin-drop silence whenever she appeared, and even the ladies in the audience, usually so critical, nodded approvingly when she sang. However, when Himansu spoke there were a few loud whispers, and even an occasional—quickly shushed—titter at his broad Bengali accent compared to her clipped though dulcet tones.

Devika was thrilled at the applause for her performance but felt a twinge of apprehension looking at Himansu. His face, still handsome at forty-one, was impassive. If he was upset, he did not show it. Perhaps he had prepared himself for it. Besides, she told herself, if the film succeeded, it would be because of him. This was his dream, and she must reiterate that to him later today. He must not get upset with her. He was her Svengali, after all. She was here only to do his bidding. Nothing must spoil this magical moment.

At last—at last she had shown the world that she, Devika Choudhuri, till recently a nobody in the large Tagore household, could become an international star. She was confident that the newspaper headlines the next day would reiterate this once more. So what if her family disapproved of her career and her husband? Devika had learnt early to ignore them. She was on her way to fame and fortune. No one, *no one*, could stop her now. As she walked to the stage to accept a floral bouquet and gave a short, confident speech for the waiting BBC team, she kept thinking, *things can only get better*.

Aloud, she praised Himansu's dedication, making it clear that her successful debut was only thanks to him. As she spoke, she saw his expression change and lighten up. Both of them graciously accepted the accolades from the lords and the ladies, the knights and the dames. They were the first Indians to be so honoured in the heart of central London.

Who could have ever imagined that?

Letter from Devika to Svetoslav

She is so scarred my dearest, been beaten, been starved, been made to work and work without consideration, been crushed mentally, but God has saved her from being broken. She said to God, I will do everything to the best of my ability, and I will do so cheerfully, so that I may prove to you I am living my life as a religion, but you must, sometime, give me happiness, real, true happiness.

Bombay, 1945

1

BOMBAY TALKIES, 1945

Devika burst out laughing.

What an odd expression: 'Russian Roast'! Svetoslav would not be amused to be described as a 'Russian Roast' by the 'People of India'. After all, he was the son of the former Russian aristocrat, artist and intellectual Nicholas Roerich, and a famous artist in his own right. She read the anonymous letter carefully.

> Well, Mrs Devika Rani
> Couldn't any indian satisfy you?
> Does your conscience allow you to marry
> a Russian Roast?

She had seen that handwriting so many times before—and had dismissed the letters as from some crazed fan. But now she felt uneasy. Who was he? Her fans could be from both within and outside the industry. Would he turn out to be dangerous and wreck her delicately planned exit from Bombay Talkies?

Or was there a more innocent and amusing answer to the question of his identity? After all, he was a prolific, obsessive letter writer, who appeared to follow her closely. Sometimes he seemed to know more about her than she did herself. She knew the author was a man because of the jealous fashion in which he questioned her, often sounding angry and upset, even possessive. Why had she smiled at someone at a party or why was she linked to a particular actor in a specific film?

Most of the unsigned letters, however, were about her personal life. Lately, he never tired of reminding her that at the age of thirty-seven she should behave 'respectably'. If she wanted to re-marry, she should choose an Indian and not a Russian. She had belonged once to Himansu Rai, the great filmmaker. As his widow, she should preserve his legacy. The 'Russian Roast' would destroy it.

She was resigned to the fact that she could never please this demanding, moralistic monster. Nor did she care about his threats and harsh criticism, often combined with sexual overtones, written in a spiky, uneven handwriting. In the past fifteen years, ever since she began working in the film industry, she had been through so much that her mind was far more resilient and alert than her fragile looks suggested. She could not—would not—be crushed. Especially not at this moment when she was consumed by the threat of losing everything—her reputation, her money, the studio, perhaps even Svetoslav—if her plans did not come to fruition.

She lit a cigarette and read through the letter once again, slowly. How much did he know? Her relationship with Svetoslav was a jealously guarded secret. Very few people knew about their impending marriage, though there were occasional hints and speculation in the gossip columns. Had someone seen them together?

That day on the beach, for instance. They had been holding hands and watching the sunset. No one was around. They had taken care to drive to a secluded part of Juhu beach, where the palms hid them from view.

He had pulled her into a tighter and tighter embrace, unwilling to be restrained. Nor did she want him to stop. He had kissed her and she had allowed him to. He had pushed her silk saree up, up her legs, till his fingers reached 'madam', his own quaint word. She had been parched for that touch, the rough fondling that she had almost forgotten. Her normal reticence abandoned, she had become reckless, leaning into him, her own hands spreading over her 'friend'.

It was another little euphemism they had invented, useful for their personal correspondence. World War II was underway and he knew that the British censors checked his mail, wanting to know what he and his family, the high-profile Roerichs, were up to. Devika was sure the meanings of their love words were quite clear. But like everything else about her relationship with Svetoslav, these codes were fun. And fun was not an element she had associated with sex for a long time.

There had been more formality than fun in her marriage with Himansu. Even fear. Yes, there had been moments when she had been afraid of him.

The passion had receded very quickly, within a couple of years. Was that what made him so cruel? Certainly, he had loved her in his own way, but he had also been very matter-of-fact about their relationship and their sexual life—though, towards the end, it had become a nightmare. Especially when he became sick and she had to isolate him from the outside world, hiding the reality of what was happening to him. But the distancing had begun in their early years together, and continued as they got busy making films, setting up their production house, this very studio, Bombay Talkies. She was a partner but also an actress, a set designer, a production assistant— all rolled into one. They were constantly on the move, as a team or separately. With Svetoslav, everything was far more relaxed because he was a gentle romantic, a dreamer, a philosopher.

Had she ever felt like this before? Everything about her seemed to glow these days. Everyone told her so. She remembered briefly her time with Najam in Calcutta. That was the only other time she had felt this exhilarated. But no, she must focus on the present and forget the past. Svetoslav was so pure and intense, he may not even want to know about any of that.

She wondered if someone had followed them that evening. Svetoslav had warned her about the possibility often enough, though that day it was he who forgot the rules. And later in the car, the dark night covering them comfortably, they had undressed each other with the passion of teenagers. She wanted to see his cool blue eyes on fire as he examined her, his 'brown fellow', kissing her breasts till she ached for him. Knowing they would be separated for a while, she felt the urge to have him remember her with her dark hair open, and the sweat on brown and white skins mingling. That night they belonged to each other. The actress and the artist.

Could someone have seen them? Was there an element of blackmail in this letter? The wretched 'People of India' maniac was now threatening to burn Bombay Talkies down! She had dealt with threats before, and if the enemy was in front of her, she could handle him. But not if he was hidden behind a scrap of paper. It was so frustrating.

She decided to remain calm, smoking steadily and thinking it all through. She felt she could brush all this away because soon, very soon, she was leaving this life forever. She could deal with this abuse for a few days more. It made her feel almost triumphant over this persistent stalker who had written her hundreds of letters, criticising her, hurting her, humiliating her. But now his power over her was slowly ebbing away. The game would soon be over.

She got up and walked to the window. She stood there with the letter in her hand, leaning slightly against the wall, facing the room. She knew Amiya would be dropping in this morning and with the light flooding in behind her, she made a pretty picture, with her sleeveless blouse and the saree draped sinuously around her. Of course it was wrong of her to tease Amiya, but this way, she knew his anger would dissipate quickly. She had never pretended with him, and she would not pretend now. Once she walked out of his life, she wanted him to remember her as beautiful but unattainable. After all, he loved her and she was marrying a 'Russian Roast'. This time, the words did not make her laugh. The eyes that audiences all over the world loved to gaze into, magnified a hundred times on the screen, were clouded with worry.

She had been concerned that these anonymous letters from the 'People of India' could be from someone she knew well. The writer seemed like an educated person; she speculated that he injected a few deliberate errors of spelling and grammar into his sentences to keep her guessing about his identity.

She read through the letter once more.

> Well, Mrs Devika Rani
> Couldn't any indian satisfy you?
> Does your conscience allow you to marry
> a Russian Roast?
>
> Take it if you don't
> Divorce Svetoslav
> You will find
> Bombay Talkies
> Mansions into ashes
> upto Sept 15
>
> We don't say
> why you marry? No.
>
> You can but with
> any Indian.
>
> Mr Himansu Rai's
> soul is abusing you

The writing was in capital letters, though sometimes he wrote in a scrawl, probably deliberately disguised and distorted. Was this really what people thought of her? Another desperate middle-aged actress, over-the-hill, trying to marry anyone she could? Made worse, in her case, by the fact that she was a widow.

She blew smoke through the window while staying out of view of anyone lurking outside. If visitors to the studio saw her, they would be shocked. She knew they sought in her the characters she played on screen—the innocent village woman, the virginal bride. In her well-cut blouse, her thin waist still the span of a man's two hands, the damning cigarette dangling in her fingers, she could be mistaken for the stereotypical, seductive vamp played by some of the B-grade actresses she hired for her films.

There was a timid knock on the door. Guruswami, her secretary—or Swami as everyone called him—a perpetually worried man, came in and averting his eyes, placed a few more letters on the table. She had taken him into confidence about Svetoslav a few days ago, along with one of her most trusted colleagues, Sachin Choudhuri, because they were bound to find out anyway. But he did not have to look like she had dealt him a mortal blow! She asked him to bring her a cup of tea, and then sat down at her desk once more while he scurried out, looking more troubled than usual.

She could understand his concern. He, like many others, was not just worried about her eventual exit but about the turmoil taking place right now in the studio, the change of guard, and the possible further exodus to Filmistan, the rival studio which many of her so-called loyalists had set up together. After all that she had done for them, how could they be only concerned about themselves? Or could it be that some of them were upset about her leaving—just because she had been nice to them, they thought they had a special bond with her?

She sighed. How else could a woman get any work done? Surely they must know that, or did they really think she cared about them, with their oily skin and bad breath? Some of them had not even completed school, and yet had reached startling heights in the film industry. All because of her. Could they really imagine she was interested in them? No, for her it had always been the soft-spoken men like Amiya—till Svetoslav Roerich came along.

She looked at the clock across the room. Amiya was late today. Perhaps he was sulking as well. Though he was usually quite respectful towards her, he did occasionally behave as though he thought he deserved better. Surely he had not forgotten all that she had done for him? She had even helped him during his illness.

All right, that was also because she needed a companion whom she could trust, and he understood her dilemmas. Her worry about

Bombay Talkies. Her fear that she would have to keep the business going because there may be no escape for her. She had built up her team of managers, producers, directors, music composers. Sachin and Hiten Choudhuri, Amiya Chakrabarty, Anil Biswas, Dilip Kumar, and now Raj Kapoor. Intelligent and understanding men. All willing to do anything for her.

But all that was before Svetoslav. Besides, she had to be realistic. Amiya may be ready for romance in penury, but she was tired of struggling and never being very rich. She still had to work every day, even though she was a founder, a partner, a manager at the studio. She deserved a little bit of rest, a tiny bit of happiness. Why couldn't Amiya see that? He was more intelligent than the others. Of late, she had become fearful of him too—their last meeting had not been very pleasant.

And what was to be said of Sir Richard Temple? She'd had to jump through hoops to get Himansu's shares back from him, while he professed undying affection for her. At the age of sixty! Heavens, her list of so-called admirers was long—and any of them could be writing these sexually charged notes to her.

Annoyed, Devika waited for Swami to bring the tea as she looked through the fresh lot of letters. She had instructed Swami to bring all her letters opened and neatly placed in a pile, with the envelopes attached. She would then write a response to them in her large scrawl, in red pencil. After Swami had typed them out, she would sign each letter. It was a process that meant every letter was replied to and a copy archived in the appropriate file. She felt it was a very British thing to do; she had learnt it from Himansu. You never knew what or who could be useful, he used to say. It was important to answer each letter and to archive them all. Even the abusive ones.

Now, to her intense and growing irritation, she found another letter which was clearly written under a pseudonym. She almost tore it up. And then stopped herself. It might have some information.

Luckily, it was in Bengali. That meant Swami would not have been able to read it. Or could he have got someone to read it out to him? Was that why he looked more morose than usual? A faint flush crept up her neck and face as she scanned this new missive.

At one stage, such open adulation was what she had lived for. She still enjoyed it, because that's what made money at the box office. And Himansu had trained her to handle it well when he had first built her up into a star.

It's the sexual power you have over men, he told her, when she faced the camera for the first time. That's what will bring them to the cinema halls. Not the acting. And he was right. Her genteel looks made her the princess in the tower. She was the reward at the end of the battle—and the film. She looked untouched and innocent, and that's why everyone wanted to possess her.

She read through the Bengali slowly because she had half-forgotten the script, thinking all the while that if it was not too embarrassing, she could share it with Amiya. Her eyes skimmed rapidly over the letter which was in four parts. Bits of the sentences burned into her.

To
Mrs Devika Rani
Ex Wife of Himansu Roy
Of Bombay Talkies

Till date I have been worshipping you like a Goddess—and I will continue doing that till the end of my life. Though I knew you wanted to get married despite being a widow and even though I lusted after you, I never had the courage to speak up. I never knew that your standards have fallen so much. Why did you choose an outcast, a foreigner, an old man with a grey beard as your life partner—why this extreme step [by] a famous artist? This is suicide. Did you not have any other choice?...

Life is ephemeral and not well defined, even then no one gives enough value to it—that is my sorrow. Though my thoughts don't have much value, according to me in real life husbands and wives should be compatible in every way, specially with respect to their age and social values. I have no clue whether marriage is for sexual satisfaction or not—that should be confirmed by someone who is married. And in any case you are an expert in this—because you are attempting it openly the second time. Maybe your mindset is different from ordinary people. We are unable to accept your second marriage to this bearded esteemed Russian artist.

It will be better if this sexual pact is for a small tenure. Looking at your age it seems like a very short tenure.

His tone was angry, and surprisingly personal.

In this life you ditched me, but in the next life I will not allow you to run away. Will you not be cursed a little because you have completely destroyed my precious life? If there is a God you will be punished, you surely will be. I have the right to be upset with you. Even I will sell myself but not to an outcast. I will throw myself at the feet of God and you will be responsible. Before the final goodbye I will try to see you once but I don't know if I will be able to manage the time.

Interesting. He was going to kill himself, he said. Foolish man. Didn't he know that since she had no idea who he was, she would never find out?

I have nothing to give to you—but my only wish is that you should have a happy life. If you have done this to fulfil the needs of your sensual youthfulness, then it is wrong and if this step was for the greed of money, even then it is wrong—you have enough ill-gotten wealth. Money is not everything in life. We don't require more than we need. Money is the root of all evil. It is behind this ongoing world war. I know I will not get a reply from you. If I have hurt you or written anything wrong please forgive me because as it is I don't have much of life left in me.

(To be continued)
The Beard Moustache Edition
Shri Rabindranath Sanskara

'The Beard Moustache Edition...to be continued, indeed. And then using the poet's name. What a fraud!' Devika murmured to herself.

Yet, she also felt flattered that even now, at almost forty, she could make men want to possess her. It was especially reassuring because the earnings from her new film, *Hamari Baat*, were not particularly good, though the film had got excellent reviews.

No, she would not hide the letters away. She would show them to Svetoslav. In case he thought that leaving this world of films was easy for her, or if he ever took her for granted. He should know how much she had to suffer, how much she had to endure in order to be with him. And how much men still desired her. She knew that at her age the best aphrodisiac for any man was to know that he was the victor among many competitors. She gathered together the two letters and rang the bell for Swami.

'Please file them under "anonymous" and send them home for Mr Roerich to see,' she said to him. Swami was startled out of his depression.

'But madam,' he began. Then, remembering recent events, he stopped abruptly and picked up the letters. Who was he to say anything to her? Mrs Rai would always be an enigma.

Amiya walked in just as Swami was making his way out. Looking at him, she smiled. He was looking very handsome today. Specially chosen clothes. In another world, another time, it might have worked.

But of course, she told herself, it was she who had spotted his talent, pulled him up from canteen clerk to script writer to director. He had many, many reasons to be grateful to her.

In the past he would have sat down, gazed at her, told her how beautiful she was, and after a while, in the middle of the conversation, almost absent-mindedly, put his hand over hers. Just lightly, as long as no one else was around. They had shared a lot. He knew how much she had suffered after Himansu's death. The rumours, the trouble with the insurers, the rebellion in the studio.

He had supported her, been by her side, even staying at her home when she needed someone with her to get through the night. It had been very worthwhile, but now she had to move on.

'Good you came. I was getting worried.'

He sat down, and even though the doctors had told him to cut down smoking, lit a cigarette. 'You know I've been thinking of leaving, probably before you go.'

'Don't do that. How will it help? In any case, my departure will make things easier for you. No one will insinuate that you are…'

'You are the reason I am still here,' he cut in swiftly.

His humility hurt her more than aggression could. She remembered when they had driven to Panchgani, the cool air making them both forget the heat and humidity of Bombay. He was still recovering from his illness, but his skin had lost its usual pallor.

He had often told her how much he cared for her. But, knowing about his tuberculosis, she wasn't sure she wanted to reciprocate. She had already nursed one very ill man and did not want to go through the experience again. It had brought her close to breaking point. Besides, if there was a scandal, as there was bound to be, and they had to quit the studio, how would he support her? She had tried it once, ten years ago with Najam, and learnt an invaluable lesson. If nothing else, as Himansu Rai's widow, she was respected.

He looked over her shoulder at the photograph of Himansu behind her. 'Do you miss him at all? Won't you feel bad leaving all that you built together? It's like abandoning a child, isn't it?'

His words reminded her uncomfortably of the anonymous letters in the morning. But as always, her expression remained gentle and sweet. Only her words were tinged with a slight bitterness. And only the most careful listener would have picked up the nuances.

'So it's not because of me but because of him that you don't want me to leave? Because I was the great Himansu Rai's wife and now his widow? What if I were to tell you that your hero was not the man you thought he was?' She remembered the letter she had written to Svetoslav last night. Perhaps she was being too direct about what she had been through, but she needed to express some of the feelings she had buried away.

'Perhaps I need to leave this...this man far, far behind. You know that better than anyone else.'

Amiya was not shocked. He had seen her suffer when Himansu was alive. But he had also seen her perform an aarti with a diya and fresh flowers every morning in front of Himansu Rai's photograph, demonstrating to the world her respect for him as the founder of Bombay Talkies as well as her dead husband. A pair of Himansu's chappals lay below the photograph and in front of everyone, her head demurely covered with a saree, she touched them to her forehead. Every day. She was the perfect Bengali widow mourning her husband's death. But it was also a strong symbolic gesture which gave her dominance in the studio and made him an eternal presence. By being respectful towards Himansu, she transferred some of the respect onto herself. Those who were grateful to him now felt obligated to her. It was a clever move, he realised. As a film director, he understood the power of imagery and melodrama only too well.

Yet, as she spoke, Devika's eyes shone with tears. Or was it anger?

Amiya wanted to lean across and comfort her. The fragile Devika, the falling apart Devika. Or was she an iron rose? She looked as though a gust of wind would blow her away, but he knew she was tougher than most people imagined her to be.

'All these years you have publicly shown him nothing but respect, even after his death. Why do you want to change the script now when you are leaving?'

'I want you to know the truth, and I don't want you to think I am betraying anyone. Just last night I was remembering some of the things that happened between him and me. Remember that German woman who claimed she had his illegitimate child? My god, how difficult that time was for us, the stress of completing *Karma*. The other films he made, they were not all great hits either. The problems over money, and then...' She stopped abruptly. The memories made her restless. Had she said too much?

She got up and walked over to the window again. Could she really talk about how Himansu had treated her? She had hinted to Amiya often enough—but never the whole story, the details. She tried to remember the words she had written to Svetoslav, how Himansu had hit her, over and over again, how she had bled and had fainted... somehow it was difficult for her to admit that she had been a victim. She had wanted everyone to think she had an enchanted life. And yet... she could not even call him Himansu like any wife would. No, it was always Mr Rai in public and Rai otherwise.

She had tried to explain in that letter all the agony and brutality that had accompanied the making of the films. Of course, she could never complain about it, or let the bruises show in public, because it would have diminished her stature. She would have become a pathetic creature in need of help instead of being a star, the envy of all, married to a great film producer.

She had tried to explain to Svetoslav the claustrophobia of their studio life, of how hard she had worked, in fourteen films out of the twenty-seven that Bombay Talkies had made thus far. And that, unlike what everyone said about her, she was not 'a great artist'. And that, truthfully, at least three of her films, especially *Janma Bhoomi* which was made in 1936, were not outstanding. It was not always possible to deliver a great performance given the terrible circumstances under which they had to work.

She wrote, remembering all the humiliation she had endured, and which no one else knew about:

> I was ill, 102, 103 fever and I was unhappy—also dearest I was used to Mr Franz Osten, our German director and our German cameraman. They knew how to take work out of me, they were very kind to me and never got angry or were unkind. Janmabhoomi, during Mr Osten's time, was not nice. I was very bad in that—I don't know why but Rai was angry always and when I saw his face I used to get frightened. I thought he would give me the usual thrashing for not doing good work, my spirit was cowed. But dearest, I never showed him I was frightened,

I behaved quite gay. And I was ill too then, I had malaria and if an artist however small is frightened dearest, you can well understand nothing comes—no inspiration. Luckily Mr Osten bought lots of sweets in the middle of the picture and he gave me some every morning, with nice flowers, on a small tray, and when I entered, he used to joke and laugh with me and take an interest in my hair, dress, and face and eyes & smile. He was really wonderful! He [was] old & very good & strict. This helped me and I am happy to tell you I did very good work in those scenes—one can actually see the marked difference, which of course helped the picture. Up to the 1939 declaration of war, I worked [on films] one after another like a <u>slave</u> with rest of 2 or 3 pictures in 2 or 3 months, we started in '34, & in other pictures. Rai made me train artists. I had to dress them too and do <u>all</u> the dances, design and get everything ready—he used to just come and pass my work. He never said a nice thing, we were satisfied, if he passed it. I remember him coming to my dressing room once & shout at me before I went on stage, and take my thick script & hit me left and right on me face shouting 'What do you think you are <u>paid</u> for? What do you mean by giving such a <u>rotten</u> close up? What do you think you are <u>paid</u> for?' And he went on and on till I dropped and fainted. Blood came from my nose, I remember but I stood until I fainted—I never fell until I lost consciousness (your Bunny was never a coward dearest, she never moved—she always stood erect and looked him straight in the eyes, not a <u>sound</u> either, not a <u>cry</u> and a <u>still</u> face). That's what annoyed him—and then he would leave me like that & I would wake [up] or some servant, I had one faithful one, he picked me & gave me some brandy & ice (he protected me!!). Once he hit Rai with a stick poor fellow & Rai could not dismiss him because he came from my old home & mother knew of him & if he went back it would be a scandal! But why do I talk of the dreaded past?? Perhaps because I saw those photos. All my misery & suffering perhaps came up with each one of the incidents. Anyway dearest I am not sorry in the <u>least</u> and I am glad in a way I was able to stand it and I am not bitter, but love

God more!! And dearest what a reward God has given me!! <u>Our</u> love—you!! You!! You!! Oh my dearest most <u>perfect wonderful god like husband</u>!! Is any suffering too much if one can attain <u>such great happiness</u>?

the Picture, up to 1939, — the declaration of war — I worked — one after another, like a slave, with rest of 2 or 3 pictures 2-or 3 months, only from 38-end + one 39 — we started in 34, + in other pictures Rai made me train artists, I had to dress them b/c + do all the designs + get everything trendy — he used to just come + pass my work — he never said a nice thing, we were satisfied if he passed it — I remember his coming to my dressing room once + shout at me, before I went on the stage — + take my thick script + hit me left + right on my face, shouting, "what do you think you're paid for?, what the hell do you mean by giving such a rotten close up, what do you think you are paid for." and he went on until I dropped and fainted — blood came from my nose, I remember — but I stood dear + until I fainted — I never fell unless I had lost consciousness, thats what annoyed him — + then he would leave me like that — + I would wake or some servant I had one faithful one, he peeked me + sent me Brandy + ice — (he protected me!!) once, he hit Rai with a stick poor fellow — + Rai could not dismiss him because he came from my old home — + mother knew of him + if he went back it would be a scandal —! But why do I talk of the dreaded past?? perhaps because I sent those photos — all my misery + suffering perhaps came up with each one + the incidents — any way dearest Sam

* Your funny way — never a curse — I was saying about eyebrow, eyes — the eye, not a certain mole — she always

57, DADISHET RD.,
MALAD—B. B. & C. I. RLY.

She wanted to tell Amiya some of this. But something held her back. Would he be able to take it? She hadn't told anyone. Not even her mother, who sometimes guessed what she had been going through behind that cool, unruffled persona.

She turned to look at him. How much did he know? And now that she was leaving, was it safe to tell him everything? Would he be able to accept that his idol, Himansu Rai, had been violent towards her? He had only seen him lash out at others. Or that she, Devika, was susceptible and vulnerable in ways that he may not have understood earlier? Yes, she had stood by Himansu while he made his films and set up Bombay Talkies, but at what price? And had she truly become an avaricious, over-ambitious, hard-hearted woman and yes, perhaps even a murderer, if you listened to gossip—or read the letters from the 'People of India'?

'What do you mean? Please don't speak in riddles.' Amiya got up, his hands reaching for her. She shook her head and pushed his hands away lightly before moving back to the desk.

She had kept so many secrets that it was difficult to know where to begin. And frankly, she wasn't even sure if, as she left this business of filmmaking and joined Svetoslav in his Himalayan abode, any of it was even important anymore. Also, she had to remember Amiya's condition—there was no need to put any extra strain on him.

She switched on her brightest smile and said, 'Why are we so glum today? These are my last few weeks here, let's celebrate. Why don't you drop by this evening for a drink and let's relax?'

Amiya smiled back at her, but his eyes did not light up. He had the look of a drowning man casting about for help from a rapidly receding shore.

Letter from Devika to Svetoslav

The worst of all is my education dearest. I know absolutely no facts and figures, no education at school, never learnt, I played all the time, only did subjects I liked, others just before the exams, studied and got through....Heavens, I really am shocked at myself and you my dearest will find out really my lack of education—how in the world you feel I can be useful to you, I can't imagine, but I have one thing which may be hopeful. It is that I have a burning desire to be better and to learn. There is some hope therefore...with that I shall catch up in some small degree to your expectations and I can remember too. If you, through your love, know my limitations and still have the desire to make something of me.

Bombay, 1945

2

HIMANSU, 1922

Devika was just fourteen years old, a pretty young girl studying in a British boarding school by the time Himansu was in London, making a name for himself.

At thirty, he was a confident, handsome man. They did not know each other at the time, though within eight years they would meet and change Indian cinema forever. While she was struggling to find her feet in a strange culture, he had already created a small stir at the West End.

On a drizzling wet morning, he walked swiftly from Aldwych Theatre into a restaurant off Charing Cross road, with a bunch of newspaper clippings in his hands. He had extremely good news to give his friend, Niranjan Pal, who had written the play, *The Goddess*. Or at least that is how Himansu, ever the gregarious hustler, would put it.

No one gave him a second glance, despite his dark skin and black hair revealing his nationality, setting him apart from those around him. Perhaps it was something to do with his self-confidence, his Savile Row suit, or maybe his good looks, but he seemed very much at home in what was definitely an expensive and very White establishment. He could pass off as a swarthy Italian—not that many of them were to be found in this part of London, either.

Flashing his trademark smile at the waitress, he ordered a pot of tea as he sat down (it would have been difficult to guess that he could barely afford it) and almost immediately pulled out the review pages of the different newspapers that had been given to him by Guy Bragdon, the producer of *The Goddess*, the play he was acting in these days. The smile spread further over his face and his excitement was apparent.

As he began to read, he knew his luck had finally turned. There was a huge difference between the response to this play and those he had acted in previously. Of course, the more caustic critics, such as the *Sunday Times*, still complained about the 'quaintest of English'. The *Era* was less polite, and stated that 'the pronunciation of English was a little precarious'. But there was plenty of praise as well. The *Daily Telegraph* said *The Goddess* 'carried away the audience by a performance touched with profound pathos and extreme beauty'.

The *Times* was even more emphatic. 'It is an admirable drama with a powerful story and a great deal of very subtle characterisation.' The *Sunday Times*, despite its criticism about the language, did concede that it had not seen anything 'more fascinating in a theatre for a long time past'. Really?

As he went through the reviews, he felt elated. He had glanced through some of them before, but now, seeing them all together convinced him all over again that this was a breakthrough. He wanted to shout, to announce it to everyone in the restaurant. Instead, he poured himself a cup of tea and quickly began to make a list of things he had to do. When Niranjan joined him, they would discuss what looked like a pretty hopeful future.

Bearing in mind that a monetary bonanza may arrive sometime in the future, a significant development during this post-war period, he decided he would order some scones as well. So what if he couldn't afford them just now? Himansu never allowed a financial crunch to cramp his style. If you act like you have money, he always said, money will come.

The waitress who came up to take his order of buttered scones remembered who he was, and gave him a special look. She had seen him come by often with other actors and actresses. He had always noticed her. But for a change, Himansu was too preoccupied to respond.

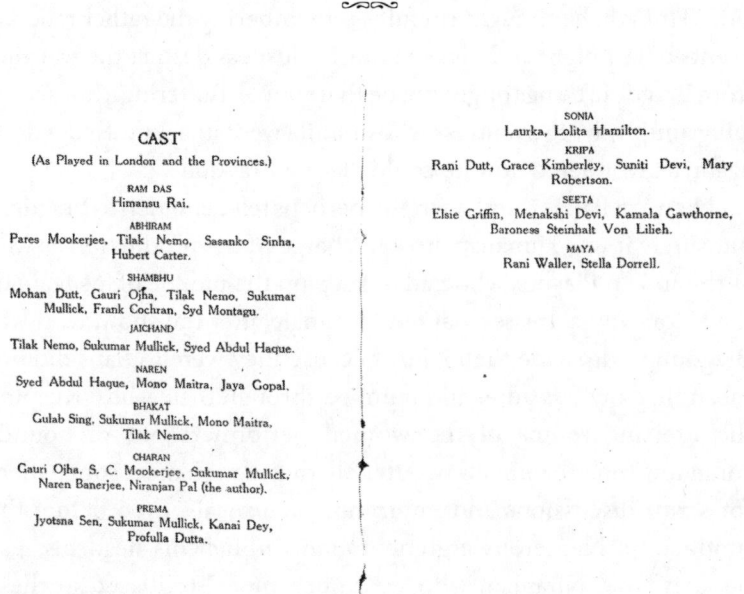

CAST
(As Played in London and the Provinces.)

RAM DAS
Himansu Rai.

ABHIRAM
Pares Mookerjee, Tilak Nemo, Sasanko Sinha, Hubert Carter.

SHAMBHU
Mohan Dutt, Gauri Ojha, Tilak Nemo, Sukumar Mullick, Frank Cochran, Syd Montagu.

JAICHAND
Tilak Nemo, Sukumar Mullick, Syed Abdul Haque.

NAREN
Syed Abdul Haque, Mono Maitra, Jaya Gopal.

BHAKAT
Gulab Sing, Sukumar Mullick, Mono Maitra, Tilak Nemo.

CHARAN
Gauri Ojha, S. C. Mookerjee, Sukumar Mullick, Naren Banerjee, Niranjan Pal (the author).

PREMA
Jyotsna Sen, Sukumar Mullick, Kanai Dey, Profulla Dutta.

SONIA
Laurka, Lolita Hamilton.

KRIPA
Rani Dutt, Grace Kimberley, Suniti Devi, Mary Robertson.

SEETA
Elsie Griffin, Menakshi Devi, Kamala Gawthorne, Baroness Steinhalt Von Lilieh.

MAYA
Rani Waller, Stella Dorrell.

His topmost priority now would be to coalesce the Indian Players, the group of actors presently engaged to perform in *The Goddess*, into a more formal arrangement. Perhaps Aunty Mabel would have to be consulted again. Mabel Palit was well connected with the Indian community. She was the daughter-in-law of Sir Tarak Nath Palit, a successful barrister from Bengal, as well as a philanthropic educationist.

There were others he could consult as well. London had a few enterprising women like Mabel, mostly from Bengal (Mrs P.K. Ray and Mrs P.L. Roy among them), who were the backbone of all India related activities, discussions and drama. Through their vast network among the community, they rustled up speakers, costumes, make-up artistes and even actors. And it was Aunty Mabel who had cast Himansu in the lead role of Ram Das in *The Goddess*—the proverbial lucky break. Since it was through her contacts that the actors had been brought together, it was important to keep her on his side. Though, he thought ruefully, remembering the rather raucous events of last night and his own boisterousness despite the warning from Bragdon, things might not be that simple. Buttering a hot scone, left grumpily by the waitress whose smile went unacknowledged yet again, he wondered how he could placate Bragdon.

Niranjan Pal, as the playwright, perhaps felt beholden to Bragdon, but surely it was Himansu, now in charge of the production as well as the Indian Players, who had to keep up the morale of his team. If the actors and actresses wanted to mingle after the show, who was Bragdon to dissuade them? Just because they were Indians did not mean that any less adrenalin pumped through their veins. Keeping the dressing rooms of the women performers out of bounds somehow took the fun away. After all, they had to meet somewhere for script discussions and impromptu rehearsals, even before the production. Numerous arguments ran through his head because he knew that Niranjan, who was much more straitlaced in these matters, might still be worried that Bragdon had threatened to quit.

Himansu was quite clear in his mind. With or without Bragdon, the show would go on. And if they had to tour extensively, they would need better budgets and (perhaps) more discipline. Indian Players comprised a mixed bag of professionals, but the majority of them were students. They would have to withdraw from their other activities, and he would have to make it worth their while. Of course, for many of them, the positive response to the play thus far was enough. But touring the English countryside in the cold and the rain, in uncertain circumstances, would be very different, and mere adulation from the audience might not be enough to sustain their enthusiasm.

Perhaps they would be motivated if he told them that they could, buoyed by this success of more than sixty shows (starting at the Duke of York, then Ambassadors Theatre, and finally at Aldwych), take the play to India. A paid trip back home! That would be an excellent incentive for them. For him, too, it would be a befittingly satisfying homecoming though an expensive one. He could also finally tell his parents that their cherished dream of him becoming a barrister was over. He was moving into a completely different career; it was something they had known, but kept quiet about, though the insecurity of it all made them nervous.

They had every right to be concerned, because ever since Himansu had been lured into stage performances, he barely had time to practise law. Instead of sending them money, he was constantly asking them for funds. They had been reluctant to send him abroad for this very reason, and the results were apparent to all.

Following his arrival in London just a few years earlier, he, along with other Indian students, began working, almost immediately, with the theatre impresario Kedar Nath Das Gupta, putting up shows mostly based on the works of Rabindranath Tagore or Sanskrit classics such as *Sakuntala*. The shows were performed in mainstream arenas and well attended.

Das Gupta, a determined Bengali, not only pushed for an understanding of Indian culture in England, but had also created a social hub for Indians there. He offered them an opportunity to bond with one another in a strange land ruled by a government against which many of their friends and family were fighting back home in India.

It was a paradox which brought them closer to one another, and often even closer to the London liberals and Indophiles, of whom there were quite a few. The more the Indian nationalists rebelled against the Raj, the more interest and sympathy the Indian diaspora seemed to arouse among the liberal British in England. Several cultural and academic circles and associations had sprung up around this time, such as the Theosophists, the Royal Asiatic Society and the India Society, creating and encouraging intellectual interaction. For those Indians who were privileged enough to enter this space, it was a heady experience, for here they encountered not racism but curiosity. The only criteria for success appeared to be that Indian writers within these hallowed groups had to stick to the exotic, and not venture into British themes. As long as they remained within those parameters, they were treated as near equals, and their enterprises found funders. Das Gupta had already discovered this creative intellectual hunger in the British elite, and many like Himansu and Niranjan were beginning to mine it.

And so Das Gupta could nurture, almost by default, a substantial number of talented Indian students and professionals who were in England in the 1920s and 1930s, and who were interested in the performing arts. When spotted, they would be roped in by keen-eyed ladies like Aunty Mabel.

Like many among the Indian diaspora, Das Gupta too had a chequered past in India, which included campaigning against the Partition of Bengal in 1905. He was forced to flee the country and came to London seeking safety, as well as a law degree. While he would have been arrested in India, in London he could find the time and space for theatre and poetry. After graduating in 1911, he formed the Union of East and West, which was supported by many British worthies such as the explorer Lt Col Sir Francis Edward Younghusband, as well as the author H.G. Wells. It was also a time when orientalism and the search for alternate spiritualities were becoming popular among the elite. To further the cause of India and its rich heritage, Das Gupta founded the Indian Art and Dramatic Society in 1912, based at 14, St Marks Crescent. Perhaps unsurprisingly, it attracted many White actors willing to play Indians, such as Sybil Thorndike, who memorably enacted the eponymous role in *Sakuntala*, the English adaptation of Kalidas's play by Das Gupta.

Himansu, Niranjan and a few other Indians performed in Das Gupta's projects, from where they developed their basic self-confidence on stage. When they met for *The Goddess*, it was this common love for theatre that pulled the two men together. They were almost the same age, and yet, they could not have been more different in their upbringing and outlook.

Himansu's father Hemendranath Roy was a zamindar with some land in Manikganj, Bengal. Hemendranath was educated and cultured, but eccentric compared to his brothers, as he set up businesses and then hived them off, usually without a profit. In the process, he sold his land to set up a woollen garments factory. And when that did not work out, he went on to establish the Victoria Hotel in Pune. According to family lore, he gave away both these businesses to the managers, without making any profit or even recovering his own investment.

Hemendranath's other four brothers were fairly successful professionals and one of them, J.N. Roy, was a particularly wealthy, well-established barrister. He sent his son, Arjan Ray (who later became a famous architect) to study law in England. Another brother was a well-known gynaecologist, whose wife was an inspector of schools. For this 'illustrious' and Westernised family, sending children abroad, usually to study either law or medicine, was almost a tradition.

In Himansu's case, his parents were initially hesitant about sending him away. He was their only son, and his mother, Sarat Sukumari Roy, felt more secure with him by her side. But Himansu, who had other ideas, eventually managed to prevail upon his parents. Of his five sisters, Chinmoyee, Himani, Anjali, Sagar and Subrata, the older four would soon be married and settle into their own homes. Only the youngest, Subrata or Lilu, remained single for a long time, and was the closest to her brother, even staying with him upon his return to India ten years later.

From his father, perhaps, Himansu inherited a desire to try the more difficult path, and yet he remained fond of the good life. And so, after his arrival in London ostensibly to complete his law degree, he ended up spending more time at the theatre and at Das Gupta's Indian Art and Dramatic Society, than at the courts. The other problem was that he thought of himself as something of a lady-killer. There was little doubt that women too were charmed by his ambition and his dark looks—a finely chiselled nose, large eyes and sensuous lips. Though he did not know this as yet, his flirtatious manner would almost lead to an early end to his artistic career.

Niranjan, on the other hand, came from a much more conflicted past, and had been brought up without the comforts that Himansu took for granted. Not only had he lost his mother at an early age, he was the son of Bipin Chandra Pal, one of the famous triumvirate of Indian revolutionaries, the other two being Lala Lajpat Rai and Balgangadhar Tilak, together known as Lal, Bal, Pal. Bipin Chandra Pal was, initially, an absentee father (he would eventually suffer a mental breakdown, as well as a stint in jail), often leaving the young Niranjan with his stepmother in Calcutta. She was loving, but had few resources to provide to her own children or Niranjan.

At the turn of the twentieth century, Bengal was at the forefront of the rising anti-British movement in India, and it was only natural for those with a sense of patriotism to be drawn towards it. As was Niranjan. And so it happened that, while still a teenager, in the first decade of the 1900s he was forced to accompany his father to London (somewhat like Das Gupta) to escape possible arrest in Calcutta where he had, in a moment of passion or mistaken zeal, attempted to snatch the gun of a Scotsman travelling in a tramcar.

Niranjan's family was already on the radar of the British in Calcutta, as his father was one of the leaders of the freedom struggle. Even before the arrival of Mohandas Karamchand Gandhi in India, Bipin along with his cohorts had started the movement for boycotting Western clothes and asking for Purna Swaraj, or full independence. Though Bipin Chandra Pal was to become an outspoken and severe critic of Mahatma Gandhi, the British continued to keep him under surveillance.

This was also a time when young men like Niranjan were being indoctrinated and signed up for what would eventually become a mass rebellion. At this stage, especially in Bengal, it was a fairly violent movement and freedom fighters could be sentenced to extremely harsh punishments, including death. Arguing with a representative of the Raj would have meant swift incarceration, especially after Niranjan, desperate for martyrdom, sent an anonymous note confessing his 'crime'.

Even in London, attempts to insulate him from the freedom struggle and encourage him to study medicine would prove to be futile, given the volatile environment. Almost immediately, Niranjan came under the influence of students and other members of the Indian community who were trying to wage a battle for India's freedom on British soil.

Initially he stayed at India House, which was at Cromwell Avenue, at the top of Highgate Hill. It was here that he met the controversial freedom fighter, Vinayak Damodar Savarkar, whom he was to describe as 'dynamic' and 'completely fearless'. 'Veer' Savarkar led the Free India Society which, as Niranjan would find out, was used to send out leaflets to India with information on how to make bombs alongside guns and ammunition, which were often packed into false-bottom suitcases.

This was not the secure haven Niranjan's father had hoped to bring him to. Sooner or later, the British police, which kept a watchful eye on India House, would discover what was going on, and undoubtedly some people would go behind bars.

Following the assassination in 1909 of Sir Curzon Wyllie, political ADC to Lord Morley, by Madan Lal Dhingra, a student and Savarkar acolyte, Niranjan found himself unable to support the use of violence as a means of attaining India's freedom. And his inability to help Savarkar escape from jail convinced him to take his career in medicine more seriously.

The murder of Sir Curzon meant stricter rules in England for the resident Indian community. The magazine that Niranjan's father published from London was shut down. This may have been the trigger for Bipin Chandra Pal's reported mental breakdown. After returning to India, the revered freedom fighter faced severe penury and jail.

All this brought the twenty-year-old Niranjan's academic pursuits to a halt, and he began to think about earning an income in London. After attempting a variety of careers including that of a cook and a wine clerk, he began volunteering with Das Gupta, who by then had set up his theatre society. Mingling with theatre experts such as William Poel, founder of the Elizabethan Stage Society, inspired him to start writing plays. Under Poel's guidance, one of the first plays he wrote was *The Light of Asia*, based on the Edwin Arnold poem on the life of Lord Buddha. The play went on to be staged at the Royal Court Theatre by Das Gupta, though all the characters, barring two (one of whom was played by Niranjan) were performed by British actors. The actor, director and manager Clarence Derwent played Buddha, and the blonde film and stage actress Ruby Miller was his consort, Gopa. Shades of brown were liberally dabbed to give them an Eastern look. The play would eventually become the inspiration for a spectacular film, but that was still in the distant future.

The fact that British actors found his play substantial and satisfying was a major reassurance for Niranjan. In those days, he was just honing his skills and was greatly thrilled at the reception of his play, though he earned nothing from it. Das Gupta must have thought that giving the young Indian students a break and a chance to display their talent to the British was reward enough.

Niranjan now launched himself as a playwright and also began looking for work in cinema, mainly as a scriptwriter. While randomly sending out his scripts to producers, he was able to interest Charles Urban, a film producer and director who was also renowned for his documentary, educational and scientific films. Urban had developed one of the first motion picture colour systems and patented it, and that brought him a substantial income. He was heading the Natural Colour Kinematograph Co. Ltd in London when he was persuaded to convert *The Light of Asia* into a film. The crew and the money had all been arranged but unfortunately, in 1914, war broke out and the film was shelved.

Undeterred, Niranjan, now only twenty-five years old, continued to make progress on his own script-writing and film production work. A full-length silent feature film, *The Faith of a Child*, was produced based on his story, depicting the Indian troops in the UK. He and Thornton produced it for the not very well-known Kent Film Co. and, unusually, he even managed a healthy profit from it though he lost the money fairly soon in a vanity production. But at least, thanks to his own creative efforts, in the difficult years during the First World War he carried on working, and writing more and more for the London stage.

Disappointingly, filming *The Light of Asia* seemed like a doomed project, although he persisted with it, even getting permission from Edwin Arnold to use the title of his poem for the prospective film. He then went to Germany to follow up on an offer made by the Emelka Konzern studio. The studio had agreed to produce the film, on one condition—a guarantee that the production costs in India would be taken care of. Niranjan did not have the money, but fate was conspiring to bring him closer to the person with whom he would finally make the film.

One evening, in a restaurant in Piccadilly, he accidentally met the chief dramatic director of Selwyn Theatres (with offices in New York, Chicago and Philadelphia), Guy Bragdon. The very next day, he invited Bragdon for a taste of real Indian curry at his home. Over dinner, he presented the scripts of his plays to him, and Bragdon's eye was caught, not by *The Light of Asia* but by *The Goddess*.

Bragdon wanted to show the script first to the theatre owner and Conservative party politician, Sir Alfred Butt. Though Butt had rejected the script when Niranjan had sent it to him earlier, this time, thanks to Bragdon's enthusiasm, he accepted it.

Initially staged as a matinee at the Duke of York Theatre, *The Goddess* garnered a great response, to the satisfaction of both Butt and Bragdon. It had been a highly risky venture for them because of its all-India cast—a first for professional theatre. Not only were the Indian accents a cause for concern, all the actors were amateurs. On the plus side, it was cheaper to produce and they must have hoped that as there were no established British actors in the play for unfair comparisons to be made, the British press would be slightly less scathing.

As Himansu liked to tell his largely female fans, he had to thank Sir Alfred's friend, the rather hard-to-please Lady Mackenzie, for the opportunity to play the lead role in the play. Lady Mackenzie had been asked to critique the show for authenticity as she had actually been to India and was thus considered an expert on the 'natives'. She was adamant that West End actors would simply not be able to reproduce the Indian look or demeanour. Better than that, she suggested, why not put together a matinee performance by Indians and let the British actors watch and pick up the nuances to perfect their own performances? Bragdon liked the idea and began to train his raw recruits, who barely had any idea of professional theatre.

At the end of this story, Himansu would wink at his spellbound audience. That is how his career began. The rest was history.

The production, which included popular Indian music, was so well received that it shifted from the Duke of York to play at the Ambassadors for three months, and then at the Aldwych Theatre for another two. Himansu stole the show in the lead role of a Hindu temple priest who manipulates the blind faith of the worshippers leading eventually to a tragic denouement.

The Goddess, inspired by Tagore's story *Bisarjan*, basically presented Indians as gullible and superstitious, and likely to be exploited. This image of poverty-stricken Indians suffering a drought, enacted by very well-educated sons and daughters of India's elite was not perceived as ironical or demeaning. In fact, since anti-British political narratives were firmly discouraged, the only conflict shown on stage had to be confined to Indian society itself. It was this stereotypical presentation of India that British theatre-goers and reviewers were most comfortable with. The portrait of an illiterate and poor society made the British feel, yet again, the full weight of the White man's burden, ruling over these poor natives who were stuck in the dark ages. It also drew an effective veil over some of the unpalatable truths arising out of British brutality, especially post the Jallianwala Bagh massacre in 1919.

Niranjan and Himansu, both looking for an entry into the closed mainstream world of performing arts, quickly imbibed the formula. The once revolutionary Niranjan had already seen that some of his best plays in which he portrayed the 'British' way of life were mocked by the reviewers. The message was clear—stick to the exotic.

He had been thrilled to be given an advance royalty by Sir Alfred of £750 for *The Goddess*, and now realised that he could earn more if he followed the unwritten rules of what Indians could and could not write. He could safely succeed as long as he continued to write about stereotypes or by packaging another very saleable commodity—religion—as he had done in *The Light of Asia*.

Himansu also understood the formula only too well. Swiftly, following the theatrical success of *The Goddess*, he cut a deal with Sir Alfred that they would divide the profits of any future productions between them. Both sides were content, and now Himansu only had to make a roadmap for the way forward.

※

Which is what he was doing, sipping his tea, in the restaurant near Aldwych. Once again, he shuffled the reviews like a gambler with a pack of cards, mentally preparing what he had to tell Niranjan.

Looking up, he saw the familiar tall figure lope towards him. They shook hands with the vigour of two men who were about to sip champagne from a golden chalice, rather than tea in plain white cups.

'Well, is our fortune turning? Shall I cross your palm with silver?' asked Niranjan, giving his friend a quizzical look. He had grown quite fond of Himansu, though at times he appeared to be nothing more than a self-obsessed rogue.

'Look at the response!'

Niranjan glanced through the clippings, quietly pleased.

'Tea?'

Himansu signalled to a waitress, who came up quickly to take their order.

'So what's the news?' asked Niranjan.

'Some good news and some bad.'

'First the bad news.'

'Bragdon won't direct us anymore. He says the incident was reprehensible.'

Niranjan couldn't hide his dismay.

The previous night, after the performance, some of the male actors had walked into the dressing rooms of the actresses. It was the usual high-spirited behaviour after a successful show. Both Himansu and Niranjan had seen it happen in other productions as well. There was unruliness that could not be restrained, but it did help the production if the artistes were allowed to be free with one another. The argument was that if kept apart and not allowed to interact, the natural flow of dialogue and their body language would be restricted and the stiffness would show on stage. But this also led to a few liaisons, frowned upon by some in the Indian community. The evening had ended in a sharp exchange of words with Bragdon.

'So is he leaving us?' Niranjan asked, remembering how upset Bragdon had appeared.

Himansu shrugged and placed another piece of paper on top of the reviews.

'And now for the good news. The Indian Players are heading to the countryside. We'll tour Manchester, Leeds and a few other places with *The Goddess*. And I've just signed this agreement, which means I get £6000 to organise it all... and you will get your royalties, as always.'

Niranjan almost dropped the cigarette he was trying to light. He felt a sharp stab of envy. It was his play, but the lion's share was being taken by Himansu. But then he quickly composed himself, realising that much of the money coming in would be spent on production costs as well as travel and stay.

'Held up a bank?'

'Four or five of them—went to these big guns who have businesses in India.'

Conscious that they might be overheard, he leaned forward and spoke in Bengali. 'These are people who have stakes in India, and for their businesses they could do with some good publicity. You know how it is. I told them they should encourage greater understanding between the East and the West...the bosses of Shaw Wallace, Bird & Co., Jardine and Skinner, McLeod & Co. They are all supporting us. And the next stop after this is India. We have to take the Indian Players there.'

Himansu's enthusiasm was difficult to resist. Niranjan found himself smiling and together they walked out into the drizzle, convinced that the grey clouds were behind them and London was ready to embrace them with enthusiasm.

In reality, the next few months of touring did not bring in as much money as they had hoped. And much of the capital raised by Himansu went into the day-to-day expenses.

There were other problems too. Bragdon's warning about male actors entering the women's dressing rooms may well have had a catastrophic effect, as fewer Indians came forward to act. But the ever-resourceful Himansu managed some European recruits who were willing to darken their skin for the show.

The experience of handling the entire production would prove to be very useful to Himansu later, when he launched himself into the world of cinema. However, the next step now was to try to take the play to India. He was convinced it would be a huge success. Unfortunately, his profligate lifestyle had already thrown the group's finances into dire straits, and he knew it would be difficult for him to pay for his passage home, but he was determined to go.

Letter from Devika to Svetoslav

In my life I have never asked <u>anyone</u> for <u>anything</u> for <u>myself</u>. I could not—it never came out of my mouth nor could I ever even suggest that I wish for a thing when it really concerned <u>me</u>. This has been my definite rule or habit in my life. I developed it from the age of 11, when I was locked up for asking for eggs for my breakfast at the private boarding school I first was in, in England. They not only refused me, but they said for bad manners I was to be separated from the well mannered girls for two days. I was kept in a room alone, on bread and water, and then a teacher came to me and she made me write a letter of apology to the headmistress, that I was sorry. I am ashamed to say I refused to do so. I said I had done nothing wrong. I just felt hungry and wondered if they could give me eggs, and also only for that day. When I was adamant on that issue, they let me out, but made me write on the Blackboard 200 times 'I will be good, I must not question my superiors'. This in due turn was shown to my class and I had to stand near the Teacher to be punished. Three old maids ran that private school and somehow after my prayers I thought, well, these are foreign people, I am an Indian girl and I should do nothing that puts Indian girls in a bad light— and I should try my best for this. Strange at such a small age I should think like that. I was again locked up for one day when I asked in Bible class, why Solomon had so many wives. Which made all the girls laugh. I wasn't making fun. I really was surprised when I was asked by the teacher what made me ask such a question. I said, I don't know, but I thought all good people like my father had one wife—it was at this that *the girls laughed again, and for insulting 'God Almighty' as it was put, I was locked up. But I was released by my old friend the Vicar of the place. He was a wonderful man and secretly would give me sweets, and a tip of two shillings every time he came to examine us. I stood always top in Bible class, 99 or 100 out of a 100—and he later taught me the Bible. I left that place after two years and then was very happy in my public school. There I met and had really fine friends. But all my wishes, I kept to myself, I never really asked for anything, and that has gone on and on...*

Bombay, 1945

3

THE LIGHT OF ASIA, 1925–26

The latter half of the 1920s were a struggle for both the young Devika and the much older Himansu, each in their own sphere.

Now nearly seventeen, Devika had not forgotten the lessons on self-reliance that she had imbibed while studying in a private school in England. From the age of eleven, she had been the outsider there, and her rebelliousness, or even natural curiosity, were not appreciated. She was harshly disciplined and locked up once, with just bread and water, when she asked for eggs for breakfast. This episode, as she later said, made her resolve never to ask for anything again. In class, too, she was made to feel an ignoramus, and she could not tolerate the sniggers each time she asked a simple question. She decided that as an Indian in an alien culture, it was her duty to maintain her dignity. A highly intelligent and sensitive girl, she became even more independent, relying on her wits for survival.

Years later, she would wonder how she could have become so adamant about self-reliance at such a young age—but it was a trait she continued to display for the rest of her life. She concluded early in her life that if she depended on anyone else, disappointment would ensue. Unlike other girls her age, she wanted a professional career which could satisfy her creativity, and sustain her financially. If it meant that she had to leave home and both her parents in India once again and stay alone in England, she would do so, and face any difficulties that would come her way. It was an unusual decision which, while supported by her father, would estrange her from her mother. Her rebellious nature was recognised in the family—and one of her maternal uncles would even affectionately address her as 'junglee' or the wild, untamed one. A very beautiful girl whose soft-spoken demeanour hid her iron will, she did not allow anything to stop her from pursuing her dreams. She thought becoming an architect would be a good idea, and was actively exploring ways to achieve that goal in London.

Meanwhile, Himansu was facing his own battles. He had found that nothing he wanted to achieve came to him easily—he always had to struggle hard to reach his goal. But like Devika, he had learnt early to rely on himself. The only difference was that he was not shy of persuading others to support him, and if he wanted something, he would move heaven and earth to get it. This was something she would learn from him, many years later.

At the end of his travels with the play across the UK, Himansu had made very little profit, so he decided to raise money for the 'Indian' production to go to India. As always, it was an ambitious plan.

It began with a wager with Biren De, his personal assistant during the performance of *The Goddess*. (Biren, as Niranjan Pal was to recollect in his biography, *Such Is Life*, was employed with the waterworks department in Glasgow and later became the chief engineer of the Calcutta Corporation.) Himansu was to travel as a deck passenger on the ship back home—it was all he could afford, but it was also, as everyone knew, well-nigh impossible for him to tolerate discomfort for any length of time. Biren bet Himansu would not travel deck-class and was convinced he would win the bet, though he needed someone to verify that Himansu did indeed suffer the journey. He would have to be monitored carefully.

And so a sporting member of the Indian Players, Jayagopal Pillai, became the ombudsman who would travel with Himansu to verify whether he stuck to the terms of the bet. The duo took a train to Naples from where they were to board the ship, but upon reaching they found that not only had they missed the ship, their luggage had sailed away without them! The two checked into a hotel that nestled luxuriously within the Bay of Naples, offering fabulous views of Mount Vesuvius and the Isle of Capri. From the Excelsior Hotel, ensconced in silk and with wine on call, Himansu sent a telegram home, urgently asking for money, without revealing to the hotel staff that their two new guests had neither money nor a change of clothes.

In Calcutta, his family must have sighed with despair and put together what they could for the favourite son. But when the money arrived, it was just enough to cover the hotel bills. Ultimately, Himansu took three months to reach India. It is unlikely that the long-suffering Pillai would have stuck around to experience more extenuating circumstances.

❦

Upon arriving in India, Himansu spent little time in Calcutta as his purpose was not to be with his family but to gather resources for the play. He wanted to cash in on the success of *The Goddess* while it still mattered to those who had invested in it in London.

It promised to be a heartbreaking enterprise, but Himansu refused to give up. Putting on his three-piece suit like an armour before battle, he looked every bit the gentleman who was 'foreign returned'. As an actor, he already knew that perception was important, and that presenting himself as a successful impresario would open doors. And indeed, he was received fairly warmly by Indian potentates and businessmen. But no one was interested in a play in English about starving villagers. Besides, apart from a few cities like Calcutta, Bombay and Shimla, proper theatres were hard to find.

Disappointed, Himansu toured the larger cities, following the money trail. It was only his faith that something would turn up that kept him going in spite of all the refusals he faced. He went through all the reviews he had carefully preserved following the success of *The Goddess*, trying to figure out how he could persuade investors that they would be missing out on a great opportunity by not supporting the play. Then he wondered, instead of promoting the story of the play, should he promote Niranjan, the playwright, who had also written scripts for cinema? Cinema seemed to be far more of an attraction in India than theatre. And come what may, he was determined not to go back to England empty-handed.

Perhaps he could speak to someone interested in films, he thought. He knew that film production houses were springing up in Calcutta, Bombay, Lahore and far-flung Burma, but he was certain that they would all be on the lookout for funding, just like him. It was unlikely that they would be handing out money. It might be better, then, to spread the net a little wider and look for people who were in professions other than filmmaking. He could tap them for investment in the same manner in which he had roped in British business houses with interests in India. Maybe he could get high-profile professionals and businessmen who might want to expand in Europe to come on board. His half-a-dozen years in England had made him aware of the importance of wealth and manners, and he found the lack of both in the Indian cinema industry disturbing. But there were a few potential investors he could approach, who were more sophisticated than the rest.

While on the hunt for funding in Lahore and Delhi, Himansu met Sir Moti Sagar and his son, Seth Prem Sagar Jain. Sir Moti Sagar was an influential lawyer and a former justice of the Punjab High Court, who had recently been appointed the vice-chancellor of Delhi University. Theirs was a wealthy family with interest in education and culture. Just the kind of partners Himansu was looking for.

Using every bit of his charm, he described to the father and son duo the huge possibilities that lay ahead, if only they would repose their trust in him. Seth Prem Sagar Jain, a member of the Royal Asiatic Society in London, was familiar with some of the names that Himansu casually dropped, of actors and directors; Himansu took care to mention only the more famous ones. Impressed with his loquaciousness and passion, the Sagars invited him for a more detailed discussion. The possibility of a partnership between England and India for exploiting the possibilities offered by theatre seemed to intrigue them.

∽∾∽

Sharp sunlight glazed the desk as they sat together to review the proposal in Sir Moti Sagar's office. It was an unlikely meeting of minds. The father and son belonged to the Jain community, which was known to be abstemious, while Himansu made no secret of his profligacy, though he tempered it with professionalism. He was earnest and persuasive as he spread out the photographs and reviews—carefully snipped off at the right places, containing only the praise—before them. They went through the lot, nodding their heads each time they came across a name they recognised.

Just as it was important for Himansu to impress them with his references and contacts, it appeared equally important for the former judge and his son to let him know that they had travelled the world. The father mentioned that he had been to the theatre and appreciated the good things of life in London. It was a rare pleasure for him to meet a man as knowledgeable as Himansu, he said. Prem Sagar was particularly pleased that Himansu knew members of the Royal Asiatic Society, of which he too was a member.

'You will find, Mr Rai, there is not too much happening in theatre in India,' said Sir Moti, slowly twirling the heavy silver paperweight, crafted in Sheffield, on his desk. 'It will be difficult for a troupe to move around. And especially if the actors are men and women from the upper classes, the children of the elite of India and are well educated. It might be acceptable for them to perform in England, but not here.

'The problem is that in our country it is the women from not very respectable backgrounds, you know, the tawaifs, who perform in front of an audience. Acting is not something people from good homes would get into. If you bring these Indian actors and actresses here, be aware that they will become outcasts from their own communities. It could be taken as a very serious offence, you know.'

'But in Bengal, at least, Gurudev has changed things. Theatre is not looked down upon any more,' Himansu pointed out, remembering the almost worshipful treatment of Rabindranath Tagore, especially after he had won the Nobel prize just twelve years earlier. His plays were performed everywhere; his songs were even being sung in temples!

Prem Sagar shook his head regretfully. 'All this has had a limited impact. The influence of Bapu goes beyond that of Gurudev. Besides, given the widespread impact of the freedom movement, there is a good chance you will encounter a lot of resistance, especially if it is a troupe from England, you know. We are all going swadeshi here, old chap!'

Himansu smiled to himself at the deliberate English twist at the end of the sentence. Clearly, the problem was Mohandas Karamchand Gandhi (affectionately called Bapu by many and disliked by others such as Niranjan's father, Bipin Chandra Pal), who had brought a sharp focus to the freedom struggle. Gandhi, despite his years in England, frowned upon anything that did not contribute to the freedom movement. Himansu realised that unless poetry, music, painting, fed the spirit of nationalism, it was considered to be reprehensibly self-indulgent. All energy had to be directed, in a peaceful way, towards swaraj.

He could see the money wafting away along with his cigarette smoke, out of the window. Of all the businessmen he had met so far, he felt that Sir Moti and his son understood him and were interested in his work. So how could he convince them?

'Don't you think we need some enlightened entertainment in India too? There is little for either the discerning few or for the masses,' he emphasised.

Sir Moti nodded, almost seeming to read Himansu's mind.

'I agree we must do something about that. We should look at profiting from entertainment, but in a more modern fashion. Have you thought about this new craze for moving pictures? Our friends tell us that despite the ravages of the war, cinema in Europe, especially France and Germany, is doing quite well. I am sure it's the same in England now. We too have quite a lot of interest in it, here.'

Himansu felt a tug of relief that the conversation was, at last, moving in the right direction, but he wondered how he could capitalise on it.

'Have you managed to see some of the new films in India?'

Himansu shook his head.

'I only remember what I saw before I went to England. Dadasaheb Phalke's *Raja Harischandra* and so on. But, of course, I have seen cinema in England. My partner, Niranjan, wrote a full-length feature film for the Kent Film Company nearly ten years ago. It drew a full house when it was shown on Regent Street at New Gallery Cinema. It was called *The Faith of a Child*. It even featured Indian troops who fought in the World War. As you saw from the clippings, he has done quite a few more.'

Prem Sagar looked impressed and pointed to a picture of Charles Windermere, who had acted in another production with which Niranjan had been associated.

'Now, if we could get someone like him to act for us,' he pronounced, 'it would be very exciting. So do you have some ideas for a moving picture with you?'

Having prepared himself in advance for this very question, Himansu opened the file with the script of *The Light of Asia* and handed it over with a flourish.

'Actually, this film idea has been with us for almost ten years. It's about the life of Lord Buddha. It was also staged as a very successful play in London. Then the war broke out in 1914, and the film project came to a standstill.'

Though Himansu had not known Niranjan at the time, he had heard the story often enough. Sir Moti began turning the pages. It was obvious he was impressed with the details. Few Indian films began with a well-planned written script—most were only vague notions in the head of the producer or the director.

'And then, following the war?'

'One more attempt was made through a production house set up in 1920 for the purpose of making the film. Sir Walter Lawrence took a lot of interest in it.'

'Yes, yes, I know of him. Indian Civil Service, posted in Kashmir. Wrote a book about it.' Prem Sagar was anxious to reveal his own knowledge.

Himansu did not bother to suppress his smile.

'That's right. Well, he introduced Niranjan to Colonel Gabriel, who got very excited about the project and set up the British and Oriental Films Limited, with Lord Meston as the chairman. I am sure you know him too. He was the governor of the United Provinces.'

By now, Sir Moti was feeling entirely comfortable. These were all honourable men, according to him. Anything they recommended could not be bad. The paperweight spun a little faster in his hand.

Himansu hesitated before passing on the next piece of information. 'There was a lot of support for the project, but Lord Meston insisted that the company should make films about the life of the British in India, and not about Indians, or the Buddha. Basically, he wanted propaganda. And so we had to shelve it once more.

'But the good part is that even after all this, a German studio, Emelka Konzern, is still very interested. All they want from us is that the production costs in India are covered, and we provide the artistes. They will provide everything else—the technicians, cameras, everything. Including post-production.'

Sir Moti liked the sound of this. It was precisely the kind of international production he was interested in. Through his contacts in Europe, he had heard about the Munich based Emelka Konzern, with Peter Ostermeyer as the producer and Franz, his older brother, as the director. He recollected that it had been launched as a full-fledged studio in 1918 at the height of the war, and it had survived.

Himansu confirmed that the studio was considered quite modern as specialised departments for film production, such as editing, filming and so on had been set up under one roof. Of course, the two brothers had also been making films for a while.

'And if there was a chance of someone helping with the production of this film, how much would it cost the Indian company?'

Himansu had been busy making the calculations while he listened to Sir Moti. Perhaps it would be prudent to ask for a little more rather than a little less. From his conversations with other producers, he knew roughly how much people were prepared to invest. To be associated with a film was alluring, and this after all was an international production, so the figure had to be equally substantial and worthy.

'I was thinking of around… £6,000?'

Sir Moti, who was mentally prepared for a larger sum, immediately rang the bell and asked for his accountant to come in. The production was eminently suitable as it was an international one, with German and British partners. It would put the Indian partner at the same level, which was a very welcome thought.

'The happy coincidence is that I am in the process of setting up a company just for film production. I did not say anything because I had no idea you were so well prepared and had so much experience in the field.' He looked very pleased and nodded appreciatively. His son did the same.

Wisely, Himansu did not correct him. The skilled actor that he was, he had silently slipped into the persona of a successful producer. It was not difficult since he already looked the part.

'So, my dear Mr Rai, your arrival is fortuitous. But if we participate in the venture, I don't think we would invest more than £5,000. Is that acceptable? Even that is quite a lot, because in India you could probably make two films with that amount.'

Himansu wasn't going to quibble. This was going far better than he had expected.

'I will get one of our men, Pandit Sharma, to work with you when you are here and also to deal with Emelka Konzern in Germany. Meanwhile, we will draw up a contract for the film.'

Unlike other producers in the film business who came from varied backgrounds and relied on verbal agreements, being financed by a former judge meant that everything would be bound in legal tape, signed and delivered.

'My company, the Great Eastern Corporation Ltd, will be based here in Delhi. In the contract, I suggest we say that you will produce the film jointly with Emelka and us. I think it will be good if you can give us a production schedule to show, tentatively of course, how the money would be spent. After that we can give you a letter of credit. How does that sound?'

Himansu tried hard not to look or sound too eager. He continued to smoke his cigarette.

'To be honest, I have some other people interested in the venture,' he said as thoughtfully as any judicious producer weighing his options would, 'but nothing would make us happier if both of you were to join us for this production. You have a certain sensibility which will work for all of us. I promise you, sir, you will recover all your money. The sooner we begin, the better it will be.'

'Shall we sign tomorrow?' Sir Moti asked, ignoring the cautionary look on his son's face.

'Certainly! I was only waiting for this. I will have to head back to England post haste to start the work.'

The two men shook hands and Himansu exited, excited and relieved. At last he could return to London with his head held high. There was no need to feel any more that he was close to ruining his reputation. He couldn't wait to tell Niranjan. He would book a berth on the next available ship, once he had collected the letter of credit. Thanks to his experience with theatre, he knew he could quickly draw up a proposal for Sir Moti.

Right now, all that mattered to him was how quickly the project could begin. He already imagined the opening scenes. They were to be set in the present day, and would have English tourists in India asking questions about the Buddha, while the rest of the story would be narrated in a flashback. The contemporary scenes could be shot very easily in the older part of Delhi, near the Red Fort and Chandni Chowk. It would be wise to display the grandeur of India. They could use the backdrop of the Jama Masjid and other important monuments, even though these were Mughal structures and not connected to the Buddha's life. The idea was to showcase the exotic, and do everything possible to attract the British and European audiences. Besides, these opening scenes did not require actors, and so the more helpful officials and a few others could be easily obliged by including them on screen as 'tourists'. Himansu, as usual, was already trying to find ways to smoothen the path ahead.

Tomorrow he would discuss the location shooting with Sir Moti Sagar and his son, to see if they could suggest some nearby palaces for those crucial scenes between Gopa and Siddharth as well as the other courtiers. Perhaps no farther than Jaipur. Going to Nepal, where the Buddha was born, was out of the question. He would need some introductions for help with the production, but he had no doubt that once he and Niranjan came back to India, accompanied by their German crew and technicians, all doors would open. Despite the recent enmity during the war, Britain and Germany were eager to make commercial progress. And unlike the way Indians were treated in India, foreigners would have everything done for them. And quickly.

He, like Niranjan, was surprised that the same people, and this was especially true of the English, who were so open and friendly in London, became haughty and distant when they came to India. In India, he had to negotiate overt racism and still maintain his self-respect. Once upon a time, he could do it instinctively, but after his years in London, he found it very difficult to accept that he was essentially a second-class citizen in his own country. He not only had to establish his own superiority somehow, but he also had to be liked by everyone while doing that. He especially wanted to be appreciated by Sir Moti Sagar, and anyone else who would invest in his film.

One key decision still had to be made. Who was to enact the role of the Buddha? He fervently hoped that everyone would conclude soon enough that he was the best person for the job. It would depend on how well he played his cards.

With his present mission accomplished, and armed with the precious letter of credit on Lloyds Bank, Himansu left for England. He couldn't wait to tell Niranjan about his big breakthrough.

⌒⌒

The journey by ship had never seemed slower to Himansu as he pored over the script and thought about the various actors they would need for the film. Now that Sir Moti was involved, he would come for the shooting, particularly in Rajasthan. His son Prem Sagar had already been appointed the organising director of the company. Though Himansu had given them a tentative production schedule, they were looking forward to the final one, which could only be worked out once the entire crew reached India.

Comfortable in his new role of a film producer, away from the censorious eyes of Niranjan, Himansu found that most of the women on the ship to whom he offered both compliments and roles in equal measure, were ready to succumb to his charms. Quite by accident, and sheer tenacity, he had found his forte. Now all that remained, he thought, as he leaned against the railings on the deck, gazing upon the sea with his latest conquest by his side, was to ensure that the film was a success.

It would be a huge hit, he dreamt. Bigger and better than any film ever made before. At thirty-three, he felt he had to make his mark now. Time was running out. He did not want to suffer the same fate as his father—despite an ability to dream and to make things happen, he had been unable to create any lasting wealth or legacy.

'Someday I will make sure you get a leading role in my film,' he murmured to the girl whose name, thanks to the many glasses of wine, he had forgotten.

The girl nodded excitedly. They exchanged addresses in England and Himansu promised he would be in touch. And at that moment he actually meant it. After all, she had been a wonderful companion, ignoring her parents and the rest of her family, seeking him out to share confidences or play a game of cards. She had shrugged off the cold and disapproving looks from her family and other passengers, excitedly telling them that he was a famous Indian film producer. He looked wealthy, had expensive tastes and had promised to give her an important role. It was one of the many promises he would not be able to keep.

⁓⁓

When he reached London, Himansu did not immediately check into Kensington Palace Hotel where, in keeping with his old desires and new position, he had meant to stay. Instead, he rushed to Paddington, impatient to share his news with Niranjan. He had decided against sending a wire in advance, thinking that the discussion would be better done face-to-face, since it was now about a film project, quite different from the stage tour they had planned.

He found that Niranjan's house was in darkness. He was hesitant about ringing the bell because he knew Niranjan had got married not long ago and was now a father. He did not want to wake up the whole family. Wondering what to do, he crept to a nearby window where he could see that one light was still on, and gently knocked on it. After a few moments, the door opened cautiously.

To his surprise, a young woman stood there. Though obviously Indian, she was neither Lily, Niranjan's wife, nor someone he had met before. She was petite, and even with her tousled hair and a dressing gown wrapped around her, one could not miss the fact that she was beautiful, with her fine features and hypnotic dark eyes. She stared at Himansu, and from her faint smile, he thought she knew him, while he stood gazing back at her, at a loss for words.

'Sorry to disturb you, but is Niranjan at home?' he asked finally, in a voice that was little more than a whisper. Over her shoulder, he could see a pillow and a thick quilt laid out on the sofa, so she was definitely a house guest.

'Yes,' she said, quite composed for someone who had just been woken up at a late hour by an unknown man. 'He's upstairs. I'll just call him. Who should I say is here?'

Why was she smiling like that? Was there something on his face? Unusually for him, he felt discomfited. She was laughing at him. He was sure of that. He noted that her voice was clear, with a surprisingly British accent. She did not sound like the Indian women he normally interacted with, in London. Who could she be?

There was a sound behind her, and she turned around with relief writ large on her face. Niranjan was coming down the stairs. Perhaps worried about the fact that she might be misunderstood, she spoke quickly, in Bengali, 'I heard a sound and opened the door. I have no idea who this is.'

Noticing her frown, Niranjan laughed and said, 'This is my good friend Himansu Rai.'

Then he called out to Himansu, 'When did you arrive? And why are you creeping around like a thief at night? Come in and shut the door, for god's sake. This is Devika Choudhuri. Daughter of Dr M.N. Choudhuri, Surgeon-General in Madras. Old family friend. Recently returned to London.'

The girl looked at Himansu curiously. She could not have been more than seventeen years old, but something about her made Himansu, who was used to good looking women, glance at her frequently. She was far too young for him, but her dark eyes challenged him to speak to her.

'You will not believe the adventures that I have had in India,' he said to Niranjan. 'I just got into London, and came straight here. Perhaps we could sit somewhere and talk.'

Upstairs, he could hear a baby crying.

Devika flicked a mocking glance at Himansu and then said to Niranjan in that soft, confident fashion, 'Colin has woken up. Perhaps I should go upstairs and help Lily?'

Himansu, realising he was fast turning into a villainous rouser of sleeping children, quickly asked Niranjan, 'There is so much to talk about, shall we go to my hotel? I have a great offer to discuss with you, one which will solve all our problems. But there is little time to waste!'

Catching the underlying excitement in Himansu's voice, Niranjan turned apologetically to his house guest.

'I'll change quickly and go out with Himansu. I'd be very grateful if you could help out, in case anything is needed.'

While Niranjan went upstairs, Himansu sat down on the nearest chair and lit a cigarette. She looked too young to be offered one.

'I must seem mannerless to you. Apart from the baby upstairs, I've woken you up as well. That's two babies, not one,' he said, turning on the charm and smiling at her through the smoke, lounging at the foot of the staircase. 'You know who I am, but I still don't know who you really are.'

'The first thing you should know is that I am not a child, and the second thing is that I know quite a lot about you,' she responded. 'From your cousin Pramode.'

Pramode was studying to be an engineer. Himansu wondered what he had told her, because she seemed to be looking at him with a little more curiosity than was warranted.

'As I said, you have such an advantage over me! I am intrigued by the presence of a beautiful, mysterious woman in Niranjan's home. It's rare!'

She laughed, looking delighted. Both at being called a woman and at his slightly flirtatious manner of speaking.

'I'm here to study architecture. I'm staying with Niranjan till I find a place of my own. And in my spare time, I work for Elizabeth Arden. I do make-up for old ladies—earn some pocket money.'

Himansu was genuinely interested. Very few Indian girls her age would be thinking of anything beyond finding a husband. She was indeed very beautiful and had a lovely, rich voice.

'Have you lived here long?'

'As you know now, my father's a doctor, and for a while he was at St Thomas's hospital. He's gone back to India now. After school here, I went to Europe. I don't think going back to India for good is an option right now. It would be very boring.'

The Indian girls that Himansu knew, even in the theatre world, rarely showed this kind of determination. She seemed young, but Himansu was growing interested. Her desire to be noticed was evident. She was making statements that she knew would get his attention. Did she want to be an actress? The words were on his lips, but he hesitated. Rarely did girls from 'decent' backgrounds want to be on screen. She might even feel insulted if he asked her. But before he could discover more about her, Niranjan appeared on the stairs.

With evident reluctance, Himansu rose and put his coat on again. He tipped his hat to Devika and said, 'I do hope we will meet again!'

She smiled prettily, 'Certainly.'

As the men walked to Kensington Palace Hotel, Niranjan shook his head.

'Can't even leave you alone with a child without you trying to make a pass at her.'

Offended, Himansu said, 'A pass? At her? Are you mad? I was curious—she is a nice looking girl, and we are now in the movie business...'

'Leave her alone. Besides, I think your cousin is interested in her.'

That explained her curiosity about him. She must have been trying to understand how the two cousins could be so different. Himansu tried to console himself, hoping she would remember him. But something about her kept troubling him. That dark, open hair, her glowing skin, the naïveté that was contradicted by the invitation in her eyes. He could not forget her face, and the way she stood before him, completely at ease. For someone so young, she didn't seem the least bit overwhelmed, conversing in the middle of the night with someone much older than her.

Throughout that night, as he spoke to Niranjan about the upcoming film and the adventures he had undergone procuring the money, he tried to bring her up in the conversation, but Niranjan was firm. This girl was off limits.

'She's in my care and she is sixteen years younger than you are. Pick someone less defenceless. And there are two more reasons. Pramode may not like it, and secondly, she is related to Rabindranath Tagore. He is very fond of her. She is his great-grand-niece. I don't want your blood on my hands, so just don't…'

Himansu got the message.

⌒⌒

The next day they left for Germany to present their case to Emelka. During those few weeks in Munich, Niranjan and he settled the terms for *The Light of Asia* with Emelka Konzern. The thrill of his first film contract meant that Himansu had to celebrate—with the Frauleins.

They were in post-war Germany, and among the women he met was Mary Hainlin, the daughter of a seamstress, who probably liked the attentions of the handsome Indian producer and actor. What Mary did not know was that Himansu had no intention of allowing anything to get in the way of his ambition. They spent some pleasant days and nights together, but very soon, he would have no place in his life for her, or for any of the other German women who became fond of him.

These pleasant encounters also became a means of raising funds. While chatting up the Fräuleins he met, he was able to borrow money or get a room to stay. His smooth manner, his good looks, and now his claim to making a film paved the way.

And so it was that he borrowed a grand sum of 3,500 German marks from Marie Lolgen, who lived in Hanover. He signed a contract with her dated 19 December 1926, giving his address as Himansu Rai of Nawagram, Manikgunj, Dacca, India and also 19, De Vere Gardens, London. He said the money would be used to produce the film *The Light of Asia* in France and Belgium. He would also 'pay an interest of twenty-two per cent per annum each month and repay capital and interest at the earliest possible moment out of all my income from now on, at the latest on 1st August 1927'.

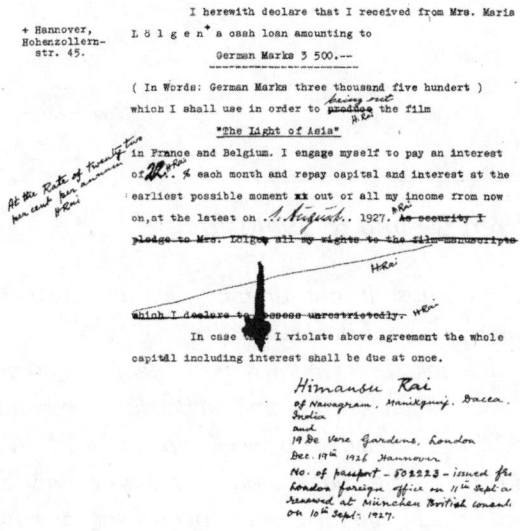

At a later date, he changed a few elements of the contract, replacing the word 'produce' with 'bring out', as obviously, by that time, the film had already been made as an Indo-German production. It was something that Himansu was aware of even as he signed the original contract saying that he would produce the film in France and Belgium. Even if this was a fantasy he secretly harboured, or if he took the money on a false pretext, it is interesting to note that he was able to persuade Mrs Lolgen and several others to part with their money without any body of work to support his claims. Like all ambitious producers, he knew how to get his work done. And right now he was completely focused on making his career in cinema. He knew, too, that Devika Choudhuri was the sort of woman he should pursue. If Mary Hainlin or Marie Lolgen or any others thought they had a future with him, they were mistaken.

He had already forgotten them by the time he left for London.

Letter from Devika to Svetoslav

I was lucky because in my summer vacations (in London) I was an apprentice in Elizabeth Arden.

I did this for three months each year. I got paid 35 shillings a week then when promoted because they said 'I was intelligent'?! I got 2 pounds a week, tips are lots!! With this cash dearest I used to have good time with all my Chelsea friends and I used to go the theatre, opera—or save and have a good dinner!

It was lots of fun, and I had a grand time lifting the chin of a Duchess, putting foam baths for a loose old society woman. This was in Bond street…so we got all Piccadilly & Whitehall & off shoots from the palace. They gave me tips dearest, sometimes of 5 pounds and sometimes 2/6!! I enjoyed it and learnt lots about make-up, massage etc., so in my work here I was able to at least do some little looking after my skin—or it would have been much worse than it is!

Bombay, 1945

4

LIKE A DEMON IN HELL, 1926–1929

When you are on your own, the only way forward is to beg, borrow or bamboozle your way through. As a friend said, Himansu was working like a 'demon in hell' to achieve the impossible.

But no matter how hard he worked, he could not forget Devika. London had a close-knit community working in the creative arts, and Himansu was nothing if not opportunistic. And once he made up his mind, he was persuasive and unstoppable.

He wondered if Devika could be asked to come on board for his first film, but he knew that Niranjan would veto the idea. How could she, a Tagore, act with the tawaifs who performed the female roles in Indian cinema? The problem was, even as he worked on *The Light of Asia* day and night, he could not get those smouldering eyes or that innocent face out of his mind.

Devika stood out from the crowd. If not as an actress, could she be a set designer with her aptitude for architecture, or help with the costume design or make-up? He was old enough to be her father, but her rebellious personality, her desire to be different—to reject the life that awaited her in India—made her even more attractive. Even if she bore the legacy of a Tagore connection, she sought her own identity. In this, she was a kindred spirit.

If work on the film was not so demanding, he might have spent time persuading her, but he knew that while it was Niranjan Pal who had got the commitment from Emelka, it was his own hard work that would ensure the film got made. For the time being, he would need to move on without Devika.

Thanks to Niranjan, Emelka was now firmly on board, and they were able to get technicians, such as the director Franz Osten, who would become a good friend over a period of time. The team had been told to leave soon for India as the owners of the Great Eastern Film Corporation, Sir Moti Sagar and his son, were getting impatient and wanted the shooting to begin as soon as possible.

The speed with which Himansu operated made people comment, even in the early years, that one day he would be a 'star'. Articles about him began appearing in the European, especially German, press. These would increase in number as he became better known and made a few more films. Between 1925–27, when he went frequently to Germany while making his initial silent films, *The Light of Asia* and *Shiraz*, his friendships with women, which had previously followed a pattern of being short-lived and intense, now began to lose steam. He neither kept in touch with past friends, nor did he demonstrate any desire for making fresh ones. He became more and more focussed only on those relationships which could support his increasingly passionate dream of creating high-quality international cinema on Indian themes, and eventually setting up a studio. He was only in touch with women such as Marie Lolgen who could in some way help in making this dream a reality.

In practice, this meant that people he had been close to in the past often learnt only from the press that he had been in town. This obviously led to some heartbreaks, and complaints from women who may have believed they had his affection.

He ignored the pleading for a continuation of some friendships, which perhaps he had outgrown, as reflected in this letter from Bonn. This letter was written after *The Light of Asia* and his second silent film *Shiraz* had been made. Mariam, the writer of this plaintive note, clearly had a special attachment for him.

Something that pains me is that you did not write to me, telling you were in Germany. Why? You promised me the time when we both were in Paris, that whenever you came to Germany, you would come & see me in Bonn. Are you so very occupied, that no time remains for an old friend like me? You see, dear, I thought there was sort of companionship between us two: the result of spending many an hour together under not altogether happy circumstances.

What I want to know before all, is how you are. I do hope so very much that physically you are quite fit. And apart from that, I am pretty sure you are making your way—or better still you are a star already. Please tell me, if your work is satisfactory & what plans you have for the future....

I saw 'Das Grabmal Einer Groben Liebe' [Shiraz, 1928]. I am sure I will not be able to express my proper feelings & ideas about it. A fact is, that I was deeply moved by the wonderful way of your giving life to the hero of the drama...

She then requested him to come and spend a week with her, her mother and her sister, so that they could talk about the 'old days'. There is no doubt that Himansu, while looking for funding and furthering his own career as an actor, had turned into somewhat of a heartbreaker. And now, as a full-time actor and producer, he had no time to pursue or revive any past romances.

Besides, the environment was competitive and he was not the only Indian seeking funds and partners abroad. Jamshedji Framji Madan, a Parsi entrepreneur who had made his fortune in Parsi theatre in the dying years of the nineteenth century, had set up the Elphinstone Bioscope Company, which grew into a full-fledged production house making feature films. Within two decades, the studio he set up was reputed to be earning more than half of the box-office revenue in India. He listed Madan Theatres Ltd on the stock market in 1919 and hired Italian directors, Eugenio de Liguoro and Georgio Manini. The first silent feature film from Bengal, *Billwamangal*, was made by Madan Theatres in 1919, and the later *Indrasabha*, made in 1932, was a Talkie with over seventy songs. Madan had good connections abroad, and back in India, some of the people he had hired for his films were working for other studios as well. While Himansu was launching his own career as a filmmaker, young J.J. Madan, following in his father's footsteps, was scouting for fresh pastures and partners abroad. This added an edge and an urgency to Himansu's hunt for investors.

All seemed to be going well—until Mary Hainlin informed him that she was pregnant.

For once, Himansu's confidence was shaken. He knew that strict laws prevailed for the maintenance and upkeep of children in Germany, in particular. The First World War had left behind a legacy of unwed and young, widowed mothers. The country had to take care of them.

Despite such misgivings, he left Munich; his film was still his topmost priority. Mary had a baby girl, and to underline the child's parentage, she called her Nilima. Himansu paid for the childbirth and occasionally sent her money.

He got busy with casting for the film, and very soon Mary became just another problem in the life of the busy producer and actor. A few members of the film crew remembered talk of 'trouble' in Germany, but no one knew what it was. Other friends in Europe, such as Shambhu Dutt, appeared to know, and asked Himansu about Nilima but didn't get much response.

Some, like Niranjan, thought Mary and Himansu were married, but that is unlikely as Himansu never spoke of Mary as his wife, and referred to her as Miss Hainlin in all his correspondence. In none of Mary's letters did she refer to him as her husband either. Nor was there any mention of a wedding.

Under pressure, and unsure how to deal with the situation, Himansu promised Mary some more money whenever she wrote to him about the upkeep of the child, and from her letters it seemed he did not visit her or the child for at least a couple of years. Fortunately for him, she appeared to have also decided, with some reluctance, that pursuing him was a pointless exercise. So, for the moment at least, she let him be.

Other issues required Himansu's attention. For instance, there were serious misunderstandings sometimes between the German team and the two Indians, as neither side understood the other's language well. But still, the work got off to a flying start. Franz Osten, the director who was to become Himansu's friend and partner, were to sail for India on 26 February 1925, along with cameramen Willi Kiermeier and Josef Wirsching, and the German comedian and interpreter Bertl Schultes, to start work on the film. As decided, the production money had been raised in India while Emelka provided all the technical support, including the all-German crew.

On the face of it, Niranjan and Himansu were now partners in the making of *The Light of Asia*, but Niranjan did not hide his impatience with Himansu's lifestyle. He was critical of Himansu's dalliances, as he himself was much more conservative in these matters. He was married and the father of a young son. Why couldn't Himansu settle down too? And why didn't he control his libido? Throughout their early partnership, Himansu's affairs, most of them with women whom Niranjan considered unsuitable, remained a contentious issue between them. Nor did Niranjan trust Himansu with finances.

He stood now at the door of Himansu's hotel room. They were back in London, and he was still reeling from the impact of Himansu's latest bombshell, though he had suspected as much from their discussions in Germany.

'What do you mean the money is finished? It was meant to pay for everyone's passage to India!'

Niranjan could not help wondering if Mary Hainlin had been the recipient of some of Himansu's generosity. But he controlled his temper. It was too close to the start of production. The crew was ready to leave, all the contracts had been signed. The immediate tasks included finding locations where they would shoot, as well as a local cast.

A solution had to be found. Niranjan braced himself and entered the room. To his surprise, a packed suitcase lay on the side of the bed. Following his gaze, Himansu picked up his overcoat and shrugged into it.

'Where are you going?'

Himansu raised his eyebrows.

'We have a film to produce, casting to be done. Obviously, I am heading for India.'

'And what about the Germans? Who brings them?'

'You do. I've already dropped a hint to Emelka. I think if you delicately point out that passage has to be paid for everyone, you will find a positive response. You know that Osten, in any case, is very keen on this film. So the money shouldn't be a problem. I'll go on ahead and prepare the way.'

Niranjan hid his irritation. He had asked Himansu to request Sir Moti Sagar for more money, but he had refused. He figured Himansu had got his own ticket and would leave without a second thought. And he also realised that the sooner one of them left for India to handle the logistics, the better it would be. He fell silent, for the sake of their film.

Persuasion was not Niranjan's forte, writing was. He had already realised that between them, Himansu was the doer. He could only hope that when he knocked on Emelka's door, it would not be too embarrassing.

As it happened, everything went smoothly. Emelka paid for the team's passage to India. Once the filming was done, the reels would be brought back to Germany. All the post-production would be done at the Emelka studios in Munich. The studio could already see that there would be a good return on their investment.

When the team arrived in India, there was no time to think, as they plunged into choosing the cast. Himansu had lined up all the extras and had chosen a spectacular location in Rajasthan. But the main roles, of Gautama Buddha, his wife Gopa, and his parents, were still to be decided. From Himansu's evasive replies, Niranjan had begun to suspect that he was not keen to actually find anyone to play the lead role of the Buddha. And he was right.

Himansu's efforts at keeping everyone on his side paid off, and even the discerning Franz Osten approved of him playing the lead. And eventually, though there was nothing austere or Buddha-like about him, Niranjan, too, had to admit that he played the part very convincingly. Those who had seen him as a heartless hustler or Casanova could be forgiven for wondering if there was a new seriousness in Himansu now that he had found his métier? Again they would have been correct—because it was through the making of *The Light of Asia* that Himansu discovered that he wanted to act and produce, and the dream of having his own production house had begun to take concrete shape.

The search for the other actors took the team from Bombay to Delhi, and finally Calcutta. The sticking point was the female lead to play Siddhartha's wife, Gopa. The Germans were keen on a slim, international-looking actress, and none of the available, rather plump women from dubious backgrounds, would do. They wanted an actress who radiated the elegance of a princess. But the problem, as Himansu knew, was that no woman from a respectable family would agree to be seen on screen.

The desperate Germans were now thinking of sending a cable home and bringing an actress from there. This was one of the advantages of silent cinema—with no dialogues to deliver, the actors could be sought globally.

Even advertisements published in newspapers in India did not have the desired impact. Though the team ended up spending over ₹10,000 on them, they got nowhere. And advertisements published in the Calcutta papers did not attract even a single applicant.

Then one day, a young Anglo-Indian girl called Renee Smith dropped in for an audition, accompanied by her mother. The teenager was a slip of a girl, and the Germans were rather concerned at her youthful appearance. But she had a certain swan-like grace, and they were impatient to begin their shoot. To their relief, once she was draped in a saree, she acquired a distinctly regal air. Niranjan was concerned that Himansu might take too much interest in the girl, but whether it was the change in Himansu or the constant presence of her mother, no untoward incident took place. Much of the credit for his increasing lack of interest in flirtatious behaviour would go, later, to his devotion to Devika.

Renee, with her new and demure Hindu name of Seeta Devi, went on to become a rather fine actress and featured in several films—not just those produced by Himansu but by other studios too, including Madan, in Bengal. Her mother, Mabel Dyer, was a shrewd negotiator and managed to get some payment for herself as well, as a chaperone. Seeta Devi's first silent film made her into an international star. She would earn more than ₹500 a month, which was more than what most actresses earned at their peak at the time.

Himansu was able to re-engage Seeta Devi when he shot his later films, including *Shiraz* and *A Throw of Dice*, right up to the proposed *Vasantasena* in 1928.

The Light of Asia was shot within a month, thanks to German efficiency and Himansu's determined charm. The locations were in Rajasthan, far away from Kapilavastu in Nepal, where the Buddha was born. Each frame was opulently composed at Amber palace, and it was obvious already that the director Franz Osten and cinematographer Josef Wirsching were creating a stereotypically exotic location, on an epic scale. Osten followed the script closely, only getting confused sometimes when he couldn't understand certain words. It was an international production where communication was key, and so, along with his other responsibilities, Himansu had to ensure that the crew was not overwhelmed by the heat and the dust, and the barriers of language. He also used the opportunity to learn about production and to hone his own thoughts about what sort of cinema did well abroad. He understood well by now that once you were successful overseas, you could easily make it big in India, too.

As work began, the importance of the shooting script, rarely used in Indian studios, became apparent. Gradually, through careful and economical use of their time and resources, they were able to create the grandeur that foreign audiences were likely to appreciate. Every scene was discussed before the shoot took place and in keeping with the style prevalent in Germany at the time, realism was adhered to. No sets were created, nothing was constructed, though much thought was given to costumes and, as the story dealt with royalty, the headgear. As Himansu came from a theatrical background, he was able to hire designers quite cheaply, and he soon realised their importance, especially in a period film.

Perhaps due to its scale and magnificence, *The Light of Asia*, which supposedly advocated austerity and a simple life, would eventually cost more than ten times the average film of the time. The costs increased at every stage. But Himansu decided not to think about all that right now.

Right now he had to concentrate on convincing his producers, especially Sir Moti Sagar, that he was worth every penny as an actor. Or every paisa. Not only did he have to impress everyone with his histrionics, he also had to ensure that Sir Alexander Muddiman (who was the member for Home in the British government of Lord Reading) was sympathetic, as it was through his good offices that he had managed to get permission to shoot in Jaipur.

⁓⌇⌇⁓

Now finally in Rajasthan, with the shooting well into its second week, even Niranjan was impressed with the progress.

The day's work was over, and as he sat with a glass of whiskey in his hand, admiring the scene from the sprawling Amber Fort, set high on a hill some 11 km outside Jaipur, he felt like a king. The sixteenth-century fort had been built by Raja Man Singh and had nothing to do with the Buddha, but it was a grandiose mix of Hindu and Mughal architecture, with red sandstone and white marble. It also offered enough vistas for creating large-scale shots, which Osten and Wirsching were keen to film. And there was enough room for the thousands of elephants and horses and humans that Osten was keen to line up.

'How did you manage it? This is perfect, and the maharaja seems to have opened his doors for us. Someone has obviously told him that he should help us,' Niranjan commented.

Himansu was removing his make-up after a very long day in the hot sun.

'Glad you appreciate the effort.' Himansu was not above lacing his words with irony. He knew Niranjan struggled to give him any credit. Fortunately, business or creative partners did not have to be best friends.

'It's a combination of things actually,' he added. 'I had told Muddiman that this would be an important way for the British to counter the Germans. If everything went smoothly, how well it would reflect on the Empire, especially since there is so much unrest elsewhere—they saw the point in that. And besides, cooperation between the Indians and the British is a key element in this. Good publicity!'

What Himansu did not tell Niranjan was that he was also hoping to build a solid British connection for his next film. It was astonishing that there were European, especially German, French and Italian collaborations, but a full-fledged British collaboration was still a distant dream for Indian production houses. Perhaps the master-slave relationship in India made it difficult to evolve the sort of equal footing that was required for film collaborations. And yet, how wonderful it would be if the British decided to support him, thought Himansu. It would send out an important message—that the British were interested in building a film industry to rival the one in Germany. Himansu would reveal this eventually, but right now he was just tying up all the loose ends.

'Did you meet Lord Reading?' Niranjan asked.

'I had already written to him before starting—and Sarojini Naidu, whom you know, is also supporting us.'

'The president of the Indian National Congress?'

'Exactly! She wrote to Lord Reading about the Buddha, the apostle of peace. A timely reminder.'

Niranjan poured himself another drink.

'And let's not forget that it's all based on Edwin Arnold's poem, after all. Very British,' he said triumphantly.

Of the two, it was Niranjan who felt unsettled in India because he had spent seventeen years in London by now. His greatest admiration was reserved for the British in England, who he said were far more straightforward than the 'wily' Indians. Himansu, on the other hand, was able to negotiate his way in both countries.

Franz Osten drifted in, exhausted from poring over the shooting script. They were in a small tented area on one side of the fort, a temporary room where the cast and crew could gather for discussions or make-up sessions. Boxes and cupboards at one end contained all the costumes and jewellery. Everything was labelled, with sketches, so that nothing would be inadvertently left out and continuity lost. There was a Germanic precision to all this that appealed to Himansu.

Osten was excited that the filming was going so well. He spoke quickly in his broken English, conveying the importance of the next scene to be shot. It was a difficult one, and could get out of hand. They could see that people from the neighbouring villages were already arriving for the shoot, though it was to take place only the next morning. They needed spectators for the scene, and word had been put out. But it looked like there would be far more people than were required. Osten, however, was thrilled. The more the number of people, the grander the scene. No German film could come close to this. He had already planned the camera angles.

'Tomorrow we have...the fight...the tiger and the elephant.'

Himansu almost laughed, looking at his face. The usually cool German, slim and dapper, freshly bathed after sweating over the scenes in the day in which thousands had participated, looked flushed once more.

Niranjan, who had sat down to light a cigarette, leapt to his feet. It was time he asserted himself. Everyone had forgotten that this was his film, too, his idea!

'This is preposterous. I thought we had cut that scene.'

'Sir Moti is very keen. Perhaps we could consult him?' Himansu stripped down to his vest and then pulled a loose shirt over it. It was too hot to wear a suit. He tried to divert Niranjan with a mention of the main financier who had been lusting for a blood-bath with the animals. Nothing Jain or Buddhist about it.

Frustrated, partly at Himansu's insouciance but mostly at the blatant crowd-pulling tactics, Niranjan grabbed the shooting script from Osten's hands. The director turned visibly pale, his enthusiasm ebbing.

'If you don't agree, I will tear up the script,' Niranjan said threateningly. Osten was bewildered. Why would Niranjan want to axe such a fascinating and important scene? Where in the world could you film wild animals like this? They were simply bringing the natural beauty of India to the viewers!

Himansu lit a cigarette, wondering if Niranjan had misunderstood the commercial angle to their cinema. People paid money to see a film; no one was doing charity work. But he refrained from speaking.

Niranjan was still complaining about the inappropriateness of bloodshed in a film about the Buddha. And the older and more experienced Osten was looking increasingly grim. Here he was, miles from his studio in Germany, and the scriptwriter wanted to wreck the entire production. Even though Osten understood very little English, he knew the problems that would ensue if Niranjan followed through with his threat. He raised his hands and, unconsciously, a pleading tone crept into his voice.

'No, no...don't tear it...we will...cancel. Cancel. Finish.'

The fight between the elephant and the tiger was eliminated but, despite Osten's reassurances, certain scenes of violence were still built into the film. However, this seemingly trivial argument was to have long-lasting ramifications. Niranjan did not forget or forgive this moment where he had been challenged by the German director. It would lead to a serious rupture a decade later—and eventually break what had become a historic partnership between him, Himansu and Osten.

Once the shooting was completed, Himansu headed back to Munich with the rest of the team, while Niranjan stayed on in India to try and revive interest in *The Goddess*. The reason he proffered for this was that the actors Himansu had brought together for the film had been left high and dry. They had no work following *The Light of Asia*.

He persuaded a Jaipur-based businessman, M. Khajulall, who provided 'tour agents' and 'film management experts' and who had organised the costumes for the film, to invest in the play. Enchanted by the idea of supporting these actors who had come all the way from England, Khajulall paid them between ₹100 and ₹1,250, and the play was staged in Calcutta's Empire theatre. It was a H way from Rajasthan, and the play's profits were meant to be shared. But Khajulall was too much of a businessman and the actors were concerned about their payments. And thus, when Khajulall began counting the number of attendees per show, (before he made any payment to the actors) the contract broke down.

Interestingly, it was Himansu who kept up his connections with Khajulall, and even though payments were erratic, he continued supplying costumes and providing support to Himansu's films. Often, he would be forced to write to Himansu asking for pending payments, as did so many others. To be perpetually in debt was the birthright of all film producers and this was one of the main reasons that Himansu later became interested in creating a public limited company. Perhaps then the constant struggle to raise funds would be over.

A few years later, in 1931, Khajulall cabled Himansu in Berlin, saying that his daughter was getting married and that he was 'penniless'. For further emphasis, he added that he was sure Himansu's love for his daughter, Manphooli, would 'induce' him to remit the amount he owed him. He added that in case he did not send the money, Khajulall would 'arrange' something in the expectation of receiving the money.

Such threats, blandishments and cajoling for money would soon become a regular part of Himansu's life. As he became better known and more successful, people assumed that he had become wealthier. But thanks to his desire to live well, any money he earned was spent like water, although the bulk of it was ploughed back into cinema, his first love.

All through this period, he remembered Devika with affection—and now that he was back in Europe to edit *The Light of Asia*, he could revive contact with her. And she too was keen to meet him.

The Light of Asia was well received in Germany, Sweden and even as far away as New York. Himansu was certainly among the first Indian filmmakers to have a film reviewed in New York, and he took the trouble to go there as well.

MOVIE REVIEW
The Light of Asia (1925)
THE SCREEN
By MORDAUNT HALL.
Published: May 12, 1928

The magnificence of the Rajahs of two thousand years ago is dealt with in "The Light of Asia," a pictorial story of the life of Gotama Buddha, which was presented by the Film Guild last night at Carnegie Hall, where it will be shown again tomorrow afternoon and evening. It was produced in India about four years ago by the Himansu Rai Group in collaboration with the

Emelka Producing Company of Munich, with a cast of high-born Hindus. Although the photography is poor, with peculiarly undesirable tinting, and the acting of little consequence, it is a picture that has some interesting episodes, particularly those depicting the pomp and ceremony of the potentates, the queer superstitions of the poor, the poetic passages, the rivalry for the hand of a Princess and the unfailing note of sincerity in all the scenes.

Himansu Rai, an Oxford graduate, who impersonates Gotama Buddha, is chiefly responsible for the direction, or, at least, for the supervision of the scenes as they were filmed. The timing of the movements of the players is praiseworthy, but it is evident that they dodge the camera lens, which is only a fault when the players are as palpably nervous as they are in this subject.

In the beginning there are the gorgeously decked elephants, with tusks ringed with silver and gold. The narrative is a little vague in the early passages, but after Gotama Buddha is introduced as an adult, it is told fairly smoothly.

Buddha is the son of King Suddohodhanna and Queen Maya. The young man at first evinces displeasure when a hunting cheetah is dispatched after a deer. Here it seems as though the humanitarian spirit of Buddha might have been brought out without having him fondle the dying deer. As he does so, the cheetah is driven away in solid comfort.

Then there is a tournament which is quite absorbing, due chiefly to the exotic character of the events. The suitors for the hand of Princess Gopa at first essay their dexterity with the bow and arrow, shooting blindfolded at drums, which are sounded for them so that they know at which mark they have to aim.

Subsequently Buddha learns that there is sickness in life and that people must die. He is confronted with the misery of the poor, and during a storm is supposed to be told from the heavens that the time has come for him to choose between the luxury, ease and power of a ruler or go forth without friends or wealth to minister to the sick and the poor. Buddha elects to abandon his palace and his consort. This stretch has been pictured with reliance on its atmospheric quality, but it is hardly imaginative. There are moments when, because of an attempt at something akin to suspense, the scenes bring to mind Longfellow's "Evangeline," not in its theme, but in the Princess Gopa's search for Buddha.

Buddha gives his necklace of precious stones to a beggar in exchange for the old man's clothes. He wanders through the wilds, discouraging the natives who torture themselves.

It is set forth on the program that the Himansu Group is indebted to the Maharajah of Jaipur for his "co-operation in providing the priceless settings, costumes, his retinues of retainers and his troops of elephants, camels and horses."

The Legend of Buddha.

THE LIGHT OF ASIA, with Sarada Ukil, Rani Bala, Himansu Rai, Seeta Devi, Profulla Kuma and Dyanananda, produced by the Himansu Rai Group in collaboration with the Emelka Producing Company of Munich; Songs of the Inner Spirit, with tambura accompaniment; introduction by Mr. Govil; Hindu temple dance. At Carnegie Hall.

Though the review in *The New York Times* was far from laudatory (and full of spelling mistakes, where the names were concerned) it did suggest that Himansu was getting noticed. Side by side, Himansu, ever the self-publicist, did not hesitate to embellish his degrees. With each interview, he improved upon his education and sounded more cosmopolitan. Was it a deliberate spin or a genuine mistake? Suddenly, Himansu, who had come to England to become a solicitor, acquired a degree from Oxford and became a man of means. He certainly looked the part, and he did not deny it. The entire cast became 'high-born Hindus'. All this was very important for the image Himansu wanted to create of himself—of being one among equals.

But the very real problem that Niranjan and Himansu now faced was that while the film had been completed, they were likely to make little money from it. They had no control over the final negotiations with Emelka, as the Great Eastern Corporation had sent their managing director, Pandit Sharma, to negotiate with them and Sharma was convinced that a lot of money was at stake. One lakh rupees had already been spent on the film and Pandit Sharma thought that the revenue should be several hundred times that amount, at least.

Emelka finally managed to get the upper hand by suggesting a 60:40 sharing of the collections. And there was no minimum guarantee. Niranjan and Himansu tried to convince Sharma that it might be more profitable to conduct an outright sale of the negatives, for £20,000, than to stress on sharing of profits. But suspicious of their intent, Sharma refused to listen to them. According to Niranjan, Pandit Sharma was duped by Emelka through the judicious use of wine and women. Perhaps Sharma was not accustomed to being feted thus. And in those days certainly, the very fact that a European woman was willing to spend time with him was enough to weaken the resolve of the strongest Indian man. In any case, Emelka stood to gain, for they knew exactly how and where the film would be exhibited in Europe.

Whichever way it was calculated, Himansu and Niranjan got no meaningful profit from the film. It was nothing short of a disaster. Once again, they fell to wondering how they could ensure distribution in Britain, where the film had no takers. They requested Emelka for a sub-agency commission on a 60:40 basis, to get the film released in London. They were to get the lion's share this time, but they couldn't drum up any interest in the film. Everyone they approached seemed to feel the storyline of a prince who turned into a pauper would not appeal to viewers. They could not, on their own, afford the £1,500 required to screen the film at London's Philharmonic Hall for two weeks. An angel investor came up with the money—and getting a theatre became the easy part. The challenge now was to get an audience to see it.

Then Niranjan had a brilliant idea. And, with Himansu, he hatched a plan to screen the film for King George V and Queen Mary.

Niranjan first approached the high commissioner for India in London, Sir Atul Chatterjee, and tried to convince him of the importance of a command performance for the film. Sir Atul was doubtful since it was a commercial venture, but Niranjan wrote to the king explaining the significance of an Indo-British production, especially in the present conditions. He gave a heart-rending account of the difficulties they had faced in making and later exhibiting the film.

It was a moment of exultation when the two of them received an invitation to screen their film on 27 April 1926 at Windsor Castle.

The event turned out to be every bit as overwhelming as they had imagined, but it had its comic touches. They wore evening suits that they had acquired after a visit to a pawn shop. No longer casually dressed, and despite the holes in their socks that they tried to keep hidden, they tried to look like they dined at Windsor every day of the year. It was an unforgettable experience, being ushered into the Waterloo Chamber, with over five hundred guests waiting to see the film 'in pin-drop silence'.

However, when the lights were turned on, it was clear that the exploits of the Buddha were not fascinating enough for His Majesty, who had fallen asleep. But Queen Mary showed them the kindness of a private audience, during which she praised the film and wished it were in colour.

Whatever the reaction of the royal couple, the required publicity had been generated. The moment the news spread of the screening at Windsor Castle, crowds started gathering at the Philharmonic Hall and queues began to wind around Great Portland Street where the theatre was situated. It was an apt venue for the screening—exotic travel films were often shown there, sometimes accompanied by music and even a lecture, and so audiences were used to a touch of the unusual.

The impact of the screening by 'Royal Command' was felt even in Europe. In London, amusingly, the manager of the Philharmonic Hall expressed anxiety about not having a 'house-full' board. Nothing could stop the audiences, it seemed. Not even the general strike for a week, between 3 May and 13 May 1926. During those dark days, people found solace in watching films.

The Light of Asia ultimately ran for ten months and was chosen by the *Times* in London as one of the ten best films of the year. It continued to do well despite the fact that Charlie Chaplin's *Gold Rush*, MGM's *Ben Hur* and Douglas Fairbanks's *Thief of Baghdad* were also running at the same time.

Another burst of publicity arrived in a more unexpected fashion.

It was while watching the film, rather 'forlornly', that another idea struck Niranjan. He turned to Himansu and asked him to fix a meeting with the makers of Dunlop tyres. Himansu was mystified for a moment, then a smile flashed across his face.

'Remember the scene in which a tram crosses in front of Jama Masjid? The tram carries an advertisement for Dunlop Tyres. Usually, it is a complete distraction and people laugh. But can't we monetise it somehow?' Niranjan wondered.

'You mean, tell Dunlop that it's an advertisement?'

'Yes, why should it be free? They should pay for it!'

It made perfect sense to Himansu. After all, it was already in the film and it was being screened all over Europe. Surely some sales would have resulted from it.

To their surprise, the company was more than willing to give a small compensation to them, not for the advertisement but, as the chairman of the company Sir Eric Geddes said, for the 'good work' of 'bringing to the West a glimpse of your culture'. The directors at Dunlop decided to give them a cheque of ₹10,000, or around £1,000, which was much more than the £100 that Niranjan had hoped for. Even more helpful was the fact that the company held a press conference about it, which got the film more publicity.

Close on the heels of the film's success, there was an effort by some Indian royals to come together to form an Indo-British combine to promote cinema. News reports were published about grand plans to raise at least one million pounds in capital to fund film productions. Unfortunately, the scheme became controversial before it could take off. The egos of each maharajah and potentate had to be satisfied. Niranjan found, to his annoyance, that when the maharajah of Alwar wanted to see *The Light of Asia*, he expected a special box to be made at the theatre. He could not (or would not) understand that the film advocated against inheriting the mantle of royalty.

Even the Aga Khan withdrew from the venture, which was a huge blow for Himansu, who had been working through all his contacts to create some kind of stable route for funding. However, the experience gave him enough incentive to think of launching his next production, *Shiraz*. *The Light of Asia* may not have made them millionaires, but it certainly had opened many doors.

And now, as an established film producer and actor, Himansu could approach Devika again. And maybe even get her to work with him.

Letter from Devika to Svetoslav

When I was 17 or so, you have no idea how nice and simple I was then. I remember...compared to the real modern smart type of girls now, how simply we were brought up & how lovely it all was. I was however very fortunate in Europe. As a child I had wonderful friends, in England, France, Italy, Switzerland, Austria, you know, a good type and a large number to know and choose from. Many have now died or gone somewhere. No trace of them on the continent. Count Mario also was one of them, he was a boy then, quite nice, but I didn't care for him much, he was too funny with girls, he always expected everyone to fall for him...he asked me once why I was so 'goody goody'. I told him that by that he probably meant 'Why don't I fall for him?' He got very red & said you Hindus are very rude...we were quite good friends otherwise. This was in Straza on the lake...yes a long time ago!

Bombay, 1945

5

DEVIKA, 1927–1930s

Himansu had not forgotten the girl he had met in Niranjan's house. Niranjan had insisted that she was only a child, but Himansu had responded to her as he would have to any attractive woman. She had not forgotten him either. Devika Choudhuri may have looked petite and girlish, but she was gifted with a razor-sharp wit and a steely determination. After meeting Himansu, she found herself rethinking her plan of studying architecture, and turned her mind to cinema instead. It seemed like an exciting new area, and the glamour appealed to her. But it was still a new medium, and she wasn't sure if she should be on screen or work behind the scenes. She knew that her mother was unlikely to approve of either option.

Devika had come to England to complete her education in architecture and find a lucrative job—or find a good match. In any case, she wanted to continue living here. Middle-class girls like her who had studied abroad were unlikely to get the kind of jobs they wanted in India. Being in England, away from her parents, did not make her struggle any easier, but her natural elegance and confident demeanour made many feel that she belonged to the Indian aristocracy. She liked the lifestyle this gave her access to, even if she could not really afford it. And so she made some pocket money working as a freelance make-up artist to supplement her income. This may not have been the life her parents would have chosen for her, but they could not afford to send her very much by way of extras, given the cost of educating her and her brothers.

Because she had lived between England and Europe most of her life, Devika's connection with her country of birth was somewhat tenuous. She had gone to school in England and travelled in Europe with her father when he could afford it. This was the life for her, she had decided early. How she would manage it on her own was largely dependent on the kind of work that came her way—or if she found the right person to settle down with. Devika had one quality that would serve her well—she was willing to take a risk, a quality she inherited from her father, who loved to gamble when he could, and who believed in destiny.

Despite belonging to the family of the great poet Rabindranath Tagore, Devika had not studied in Shantiniketan. She was born in Waltair (present-day Vishakhapatnam) and spent her early years in southern India. Her father, Colonel Manmathanath Choudhuri, was then the surgeon general of Madras Presidency. Her mother, Leela, was one among eight children born to Indumati and Nityaranjan Chattopadhyaya. Her great grandmother was Saudamini Devi, an older sister of Rabindranath Tagore and a gifted writer herself; she was married to Saradprasad Gangopadhyay.

Saudamini, the daughter of Maharishi Devendranath Tagore (the poet's father) was considered well educated for those times, and was one of the first girls to go to Bethune School in Calcutta. Maharishi Devendranath had fifteen children. The family was affluent and anglicised, with deep connections with England. There was a family home in Brighton which the large Tagore household often visited for holidays. Devendranath was the secretary of the British Indian Association when it was set up in 1851.

Devika knew that hers was a high-caste family and was very particular about claiming her legacy (if anyone cared to ask). She said she was a 'Varindra [Brahmin], and my Gotra is Cashyapa on my father's side, my mother's father was a Kulin Brahmin,' in one of her letters.

Devika's father Manmathanath Choudhuri was one among eight siblings. If not as wealthy or illustrious as the Tagore family, the Choudhuris were very well-known in their own right. And their proximity to the Tagores was legendary, strengthened further through marriage.

Manmathanath was the son of Durgadas Choudhuri, a prominent zamindar of Rajshahi, now in Bangladesh. Durgadas had married the very forceful Magnamoyee Devi and had seven sons and one daughter, all of whom did extremely well in life. Five of the sons were barristers and two were doctors. They were Sir Ashutosh Choudhuri, Kumudnath, Jogesh Chandra, Manmathanath, Sruhitnath, Amiyanath, and the most famous of them, the writer Pramathanath, who was also a lawyer. At least four of the brothers married into the Tagore clan. Among them, Pramathanath was very close to Rabindranath. Pramathanath's wife Indira Devi was the daughter of Satyendranath Tagore, the elder brother of Rabindranath. Indira became the vice chancellor of Vishva Bharati in 1956. Pratibha Devi, who married Sir Ashutosh Choudhuri, was the daughter of Hemendranath Tagore, another of Rabindranath's brothers.

Manmathanath's sister, Prasannamoyee Devi, was a well-known writer who published her first book of poems, *Adh Adh Bashini*, at the age of twelve. Her daughter, Priyamveda Devi, also became a celebrated author.

The family connections between the Chaudhuris and the Tagores were thus already very strong, and when the time came for Leela to be married, young Manmathanath, a dashing captain at the time as well as a 'foreign returned' doctor, was found to be a very eligible bachelor indeed.

Since Manmathanath had studied in England, and worked at St Thomas's hospital in London, he was very much at home in Europe. His father, Durgadas, it was said, had once been insulted by an Englishman in India, and that had further spurred his determination to send his children abroad for the best education possible. Manmathanath also ensured that his three children, Nikhil,

Devika and Mahim Choudhuri, studied abroad. Whenever possible, he took them to Europe, where Devika made several friends.

Leela, like her husband, grew up in a large family that was probably even more anglicised than Manmathanath's. Her brothers and sisters were given English names—Noel, Ela, Sudha Stella, Harry. The other four who sounded reasonably Indian were Nisithnath, Rani Matty, Bela and Leela herself. Unlike the rest of the Tagore clan, this branch had southern connections, and it is likely that Leela met Manmathanath when he was posted in Madras Presidency. Later, as the myth around Devika's childhood grew, many interesting facets were added. But she probably did some of her schooling in the south, before she went abroad. There was a private school in England that she wrote about, where she studied, but her memories of it were not very happy. Some reports said she had studied at the exclusive Cheltenham Ladies College but there are no records of her being there. An Indian girl at the school, at the turn of the century, would have been noticed.

Similarly, there are no records of Devika either having received a scholarship or studied at the Royal Academy of Music in London. These were all embellishments that appeared later, and which no one ever denied. One can only speculate that being prodigiously talented, even a short exposure may have been enough for her to learn—and it is possible she had some classes at the Royal Academy of Music.

Devika was an intensely private person, and she deliberately kept it that way. She seldom spoke about her personal life, and this meant that she could invent and reinvent herself as she went along. If there were any mistakes in the reportage which enhanced her profile, they were rarely corrected. Indeed, later press releases reiterated some untruths and half-truths, as they made her out to be even more talented and better educated than she was. All this added to the legend of Devika.

Certainly, she had inherited the gritty determination of the Choudhuris and the Tagores, especially their women. She said that she learnt all about love and strength from her grandmothers. From her paternal grandmother, the tall and imposing Magnamoyee Devi, she learnt to be strong, and from her maternal grandmother, Indumati, she learnt about love. Devika wrote:

> [Indumati taught me] 'Home is love, of a man and woman, and there are many things a man loves, a real man! And a real woman should see he gets <u>all</u> he loves—she should love him with her life.' My Grandmother had 13 or 14 children, some died, but even today she tells us of the great love she & my Grandfather had and in her opinion that is the <u>only</u> thing in life worth having. She was a great woman, one of the finest type. So was my father's mother. I liked my father's mother best. She was really wonderful—tall very beautiful, 8 children alive, others died. She had 14 or 13 of them. But my heavens what a personality. Great learning, <u>great</u> courage—and she ran everyone and everything. Not one of her sons could dare do anything against her wish—and they were outstanding people in their day. Sir Ashutosh Choudhuri the eldest was a remarkable man, in education, in the first Swadeshi movement, in law, he did a lot for culture in general & was very charming. On father's side the women were everything. They had a name and the right ever to run everything and were strong and fearless—[they] would ride in villages—would even <u>kill</u>, everyone feared them and at the same time they were great Hindus—in prayer, meditation. Yes, I think they were greater than the Tagore women who had all, but too much wealth & were spoilt to some extent. I mean they were more undeveloped, but of course some were outstanding and contributed a lot. But those ladies could teach the modern woman a thing or two, couldn't they? They were perhaps placed in better conditions than modern women—we have such a struggle in the world of today. Because values have changed so those truths, those beautiful manners, those sacred considerations are not found in modern life. But I am rather old fashioned. I have ever liked those beauties and charm of those days. People call me old fashioned.

Devika said later that those who knew this side of her laughed at her. But these were influences that she could not reject. Her aunt, the author Prasanmoyee Devi, would demonstrate unusual feistiness when she abandoned her husband's home (he was a rich zamindar) and headed back to live with her parents, along with her young daughter. She pursued her career as an author and remained involved with the freedom movement all her life.

Like her, Devika learnt young to be rebellious and self-reliant. Yet, in her childhood, she had been spoilt and much adored, the only girl among three siblings. She wrote that she had been born 'a very strong baby, 11.5 lbs, ginger hair, grey-blue eyes, very fair and quite a character. I only made a slight noise when mother had to give me milk. We only had hers.' She always maintained that she had been brought up simply, and that is why her mother felt 'she would like to give me a good name—because at least that would help a lot,' and that's why she was named Devika, the little Devi.

The relationships in India would have dimmed in memory, as she was away from the age of eleven till the age of seventeen. During this time, she picked up the clipped British style of speaking, and the aloof, slightly 'formal' exterior. These years abroad without her parents also taught her to value her privacy—a very British trait. She rarely displayed any weaknesses for fear of being laughed at.

An early, positive influence on her was her father. By giving her the gift of independence, reading, travel and adventure, he brought her up as few Indian girls were brought up in those days. They were deeply fond of each other, even while they had their arguments.

> At the age of three-and-a-half, my mother says father got angry with me in a rather loud tone, so I went to my room, tied up my dolls, and my Teddy Bear, and left the house. I went and sat outside near our gate and when the servant asked me, I said, 'Papa bad, Bukka no go to Papa.' Bukka, I called myself. Devika was difficult.

She said she was 'naughty, wilful, really troublesome'. Yet she hero-worshipped her father and identified closely with him, being very much like him in 'face and nature'. His love for the outdoors, for farms and animals and flowers, was something she shared. He would make her read till dinner time and wanted to improve her sense of history.

Himansu's keen interest in making something of her—forcing her literally to take up a career, when she could have just drifted off and become a housewife, reminded her of her father. His confidence that she could make something of her life despite her poor education and lack of knowledge, was probably what she found the most attractive about him. His belief in her made her believe in herself.

Also, one is tempted to think that her attraction to Himansu was partly founded on a desire to replace an indulgent father who supported and looked after her with another father figure. Her own father disappeared from her life by the time she was twenty. He died in 1928—a few months before her marriage to Himansu. This might at least partially explain the strange love she had for Himansu and why she took the abuse and what she would call his 'ugly' behaviour for close to fourteen years. No matter what Himansu did, he continued to fascinate her.

In one of her letters she says:

I had red hair and blue green greyish eyes. A number of people in my family have even violet eyes, red hair, very fair—like Europeans. My mother is of light complexion, I am like my father in face and nature in somethings and colour, & when he went out on Shikar for days, he went dark brown—very dark—and then again it changed. He was crazy about riding, shooting etc., wild outdoors always, he slept outdoors, even in Europe. He had ever cold baths & in snow etc. he would live [outside] practically all day—he could never sit in a drawing room, always on the verandah if guests and then outside. That was his passion, so was gardening and farms and animals & flowers. His pet flower was a rose—he spent lots of money on them & got prizes for roses too. We had a pundit & my father used to sit outside and drink whiskey & get the pundit to read the Gita, after which, my love, I was sent for and had to read Napolean's history till dinner—it was awful! Strange combination he was, but a fine upright man, a real man!

While she was close to her father, she seemed to maintain a distance from her mother. It was only after she left Bombay Talkies and willingly embraced a quieter life with Svetoslav that she was able to understand her mother. Or tried to reach out to her. She was also oddly reticent about her two brothers, one of whom died young.

It appears that the disconnect between mother and daughter was mutual. Leela did not approve of Devika's chosen path. The 'naughty, wilful and troublesome' child had grown into a wilful girl who was quick to rebel if anyone tried to control her. She refused to accept the dreary ordinariness of a woman's life; she yearned for the adventures her father had opened a window to. Perhaps for all these reasons she was fondly called 'junglee' by her Uncle Harry, even when she was in her thirties.

Devika, on her part, said her mother was of 'haughty blood' and 'not very mature', which were odd observations to make, even while she praised Leela's simplicity and austere life. She seemed to prefer the rustic get-up-and-go attitude of the Chaudhuris to the refined decadence of the Tagores.

During her childhood, Rabindranath was in the limelight, having received his Nobel prize, but she was to interact with him only as an adult. Living in the south of India (and later in England), her impressions of the Tagore clan came mostly from her mother and her aunts who were married to the Chaudhuri brothers. To Devika, it appeared that they had been spoiled by their pampered upbringing and the Tagore name. As she explained, 'in the old days, they were well cared for—had everything'. The genteel decline in later years was to take its toll. And Leela was, according to Devika, unable to connect with the changing environment and her own changing circumstances.

Leela would have been around twenty-nine years old when Devika, her second child, was born on 30 March 1908. After her husband's death, she withdrew to a solitary life in Subuthu in the hills of Himachal Pradesh, in northern India. Devika was to describe, in 1945, the transformation in her mother, who had once been 'beautiful':

> Yes, mother was beautiful, but now she is not like those photos, since her several illnesses & is now 67 or so—not old but her asthma & then other illnesses have robbed her of that wonderful beauty. She had to rest & rest & put on weight & her eyes got bad, she wears glasses. Of course she looks very fresh and strong and her nature is cheerful, a lovely example of a simple good clean type of gentle womanliness—a mother, a friend, a <u>real</u> friend and [who] loves a laugh & generally behaves terribly like a child, but a good & great heart, rather human, but not very mature! You see in the old days they were well cared for, had everything. And she is rather of the haughty blood—<u>must</u> have <u>immediately</u> things, but sensitive too & I must say... BRAVE. She has actually cut all her old life & has taken to a simple life & has made it do, so much so that she is very happy in it. There is <u>no</u> such show of <u>any sort</u> which I admire very much in her because I remember... and I like the way she is very much, she is so perfect [now] in her utter simplicity.

One thing that Devika did have in common with her mother was an ability to negotiate all kinds of circumstances. She had access to the top echelons of society when she was growing up, and in her letters to Svetoslav she remembered homes with large grounds, horses and hay barns, as well as butlers and maids. While she chose to strike out on her own on a much more difficult path, the childhood memories did not leave her for the rest of her life.

Referring to her younger self in the third person as 'Bunny', she wrote jokingly:

> She has been told in all the countries that 'young ladies cannot, should not, must not go' to the haystacks but her legs just go

there, & she has been fetched down by butlers, maids, the head farmer, managers, Dukes, the great ladies of the house & all.... [To prevent that] 1) either show Bunny haystack without apples or 2) apples without haystack or there is no prevention to this tragic happening!

After what she describes as a fairly idyllic childhood, apart from the traumatic moments in a private school, Devika went, according to her own account, to a British public school. She spent her summer vacations in London, working on the side and earning enough money to dine out with her friends at Chelsea, occasionally catching an opera. Hers was the life of a happy-go-lucky young woman of independent means, despite all the shortcomings of living in London in the interwar years.

It is evident that the family back home had fallen on hard times while Devika was still barely seventeen years old. In one letter she spoke of her father's desperation to sell a piece of land because he needed the money in retirement. The family made a trip to Lahore to trace the property, but had no luck. 'Luck' was something her father believed in as a positive force in his life, but it appears to have abandoned him towards the end.

Devika wrote in the letter:

We did go to Lahore once and as a girl I was there. My father was then retired and trying to get some land which he bought in Kashmir and which was taken from him after the death of the old Maharajah—no papers could be found and no record!!! Even Sir Albion Banerjee who was then foreign minister couldn't do anything. My father was very upset. He wanted to do a special kind of research there and live there too. That was when I was seventeen or so.

There is some discrepancy here, in dates—or in her memory—for Sir Albion Banerjee was posted in Kashmir between 1927 and 1929, when Devika would have been nineteen or twenty years of age, not seventeen.

In any case, she was back in England by 5 June 1928, congratulating herself on 'news' about the contract she was to formally sign with Himansu. Her father thought this was a stroke of luck, and encouraged her to cultivate her skill in music, reminding her that she sang well. There was no censure in his letter, and he seemed quite relaxed about her joining the film industry.

He wrote:

> Devika my darling
> Many thanks for your letter. I am so glad you have a good house and are very comfy. I am also glad that the overcoat I got for you is useful. Mum says you had it altered at Lahore. I did not see it after it was altered. Probably the Tailor man brought it on the day you were going away. I am so glad you saw Bakore and thought him growing into a nice boy. I know he will do well, his last term's report was not very good. He is still very trying & will get on very well when he is a little older. Yes there's no use forcing him. Let him acquire a little more score. So long as he does his work regularly it is all right. He must not slack in any way. I have given all that I had and shall be glad if he is successful.

He then goes on to speak, rather wistfully, about some Derby tickets he has bought where the prize would be £250,000. As though conscious of his own inability to provide for his family the way he would have liked to, he writes:

> If I am so lucky I shall be able to do you all well and give something away to charity. The unexpected luck you had makes me think that I too am going to have some luck as I had when I got into the service. I was 23rd on the list and there were 21 appointments so when the results were published I was not in but a few days after that it was anticipated that there will be the Boer War and therefore some more vacancies were arranged and I was taken in & therefore I think there is going to be some good luck for me.

Kensington Palace Mansions,
De Vere Gardens, London, W.8.
10th October, 1928.

Miss Devika Chaudhuri,
12, Buckland Crescent,
Swiss Cottage, London.

Dear Miss Chaudhuri:-
    I have much pleasure in confirming the verbal arrangements I have entered into with you securing to myself your exclusive services as a film and stage artiste under my Management and control. under the following terms and conditions.
    (1) As from to-day you bind yourself solely and absolutely to act any female role which I may assign to you in any film or stage play or plays I may produce or any film or stage play or plays which may be produced by other individuals, firms or companies to whom your services may be lent by me.
    (2) In consideration ~~consideration~~ of the above I agree and undertake to pay you a minimum retaining fee of fifteen pounds per month commencing from the 1st of November next and this retaining fee will continue to be paid to you month by month for a period of one year. But this retaining fee will cease to be paid to you under clause 3 and during the period when this clause remains in force you shall have no claim whatsoever on me for the payment of this retaining fee.
    (3) I undertake and agree to pay you or procure for you such salary or emoluments as are generally paid to film or stage artistes according to the importance of the part and to your own capabilities. I, however agree and undertake that your salary or emoluments as an artist when actually working will be ~~at least at the rate of~~ THIRTY pounds pay month. and out of the money or monies you may receive under this clause you shall pay to me a commission of ten per cent and that you shall not receive the fixed retaining fee of fifteen pounds per month as long as this clause enables you to earn THIRTY pounds per month.
    (4) The contract will be for a period of one year for certain but it may be automatically continued for further period of twelve months at my option but I agree that during the second year your fixed retaining fee will be increased to twentytwo pounds per month and this amount will be continued to be paid to you by month month by month until it ceases to be paid under clause 3. It is further agreed that the contract may still be continued for the third year under the same terms and conditions with the exception that your retaining fee when not actually working as an artiste as per clause 3, will be at the rate of thirty pounds per month.
    (5) During the pendancy of this contract you bind yourself not to appear in any film or stage production without my sanction or approval and that you further agree and undertake to remain under my supervision and control until its expiry.
    (6) I further agree and undertake that I shall pay or procure you to be paid all reasonable travelling, hotel and out of pocket expenses whenever you may be required to work outside Calcutta and as you are now in London I agree that your fare to Calcutta will be either paid by me or procured by me through some company or firm to whom your services may be lent by me.
    (7) I also agree that in the event of my deciding to continue this agreement for the second year I shall give you two month's notice in writing prior to its expiry and similiar notice will also be given should I decide to carry on this arrangement for the third year.

                                Yours sincerely,
                                Himansu Rai

Agreed and accepted.
Devika Chaudhuri
  Witness.
    Niranjan Pal

Devika's introduction to Himansu, in 1925, came at just the right time. She was almost eighteen years old, and ready for an anchor and a career. She knew that Niranjan Pal would disapprove of her working in films; he did not think it was a respectable career for girls. He would also want to protect her from Himansu. Perhaps, she thought, she should consider helping with design and art rather than acting. Would that be a better option for someone like her?

She was keen to meet Himansu again and explore the possibilities. She knew intuitively that he had been attracted to her, but he had left for Munich almost immediately after their meeting, to tie up the production details for *The Light of Asia*. And then, when she next enquired, he had left for India with Niranjan.

She had followed the news of the success of *The Light of Asia* and had been very impressed with the reviews. The film had become a hot topic of discussion within the Indian community, about how Himansu had overcome the odds to not only produce the film but also deliver a sensitive portrayal of Buddha. Even Niranjan, usually so critical of Himansu, had nothing but praise for him.

Almost a year after her first meeting with Himansu, Devika was invited for a special screening of *The Light of Asia* at the Philharmonic Hall in London in May 1926. Niranjan and Himansu had managed to raise the money to hire the hall, which in itself was a miracle. She knew it must have been tough, and could not but feel a sense of excitement that she would, at last, meet the man who had been on her mind for so long. Had he changed? Would the past year, with its disasters and successes, have affected him in any apparent way?

Some of the vagaries of the world of cinema had already been explained to her by Niranjan's wife, Lily, who was extremely worried because they had a child to look after, and money was tight. Niranjan was not working in theatre any more, as he was trying to make a career in film production. Everyone knew this was still an unknown area. And who knew what the outcome would be?

After a whole year of waiting, the usually confident Devika felt a little anxious about making a good impression on Himansu. She was to attend the screening as well as the party after that, celebrating one year at the theatre for *The Light of Asia*. She hoped to meet him, but had no idea how keen he was to meet her.

From Niranjan she had learnt that the next film Himansu wanted to produce was tentatively called *Shiraz*, and it was about the making of the Taj Mahal. She told herself that even if he did not give her an assignment, she must make sure she was unforgettable that evening. Niranjan and Lily had already warned her that Himansu was used to idle dalliances and making extravagant promises that he never kept. But Devika knew that once she made up her mind to be charming, it was difficult for anyone to resist her.

To her delight, as she approached the entrance to the hall, she saw he was at the door, in a dark, formal suit. He looked well turned out, hair slicked back, his dark features more attractive than ever. Niranjan, she noted thankfully, was not around.

She greeted him with folded hands, a demure Indian girl, and was thrilled to see the expression of recognition and delight that crossed his face. In his eyes she saw unconcealed desire.

'The little girl has grown up! And looking very lovely!'

Devika was used to compliments and suitors. Even the women whose make-up she did would catch hold of her tiny hands as they fluttered across their faces with powder and rouge and say, 'You must be a princess, with that complexion and those eyes! You must marry a maharaja!'

She had to say something special to Himansu. She had already thought about it and rehearsed the words, which now tripped off her tongue prettily, if a little formally, 'I've come here tonight only for you, to participate in this wonderful success. Congratulations, Mr Rai.'

He nodded his thanks, his voice formal, but he held her hand and raised it to his lips, caressing the soft skin, demonstrating his deepening interest in her.

'I do hope it lives up to your expectations,' he said. He ignored the rest of the guests seeking his attention and solicitously ushered her to a seat next to his own. From across the hall, Niranjan caught her eye and frowned. Unperturbed, she smiled back.

As he helped her into her seat, Himansu whispered in her ear, 'You are easily the most beautiful woman in the theatre tonight.'

He was still holding her hand, but then quickly let it go, in case she misunderstood him or his gallantry seemed overblown. But he had no reason to fear—as was wont to happen frequently in their relationship, Devika understood him only too well. She was reminded in that moment of her father and her uncles, who still possessed a chivalrous streak. But she also noticed that he was beginning to get a little flabby around his midriff and his face. And he smelt of cigarettes.

Devika found the film quite well made and elegant. She had genuine tears in her eyes when it ended on a high note with spontaneous applause from the audience. Turning to Himansu, she put a hand on his arm. His face was full of concern and empathy as she delicately touched her handkerchief to her eyes. The film had moved her, as had Himansu's acting. It also eradicated her doubts about working in films. In fact, a part of her longed for the role that the young Seeta Devi had performed with such aplomb. Always fond of dressing up and wearing jewellery but with few opportunities for either, Devika now burned with envy and desire.

'How beautifully you portrayed India. I am missing it all… Forgive the tears, but you gave us such a powerful message! And the acting—you are a natural, Mr Rai.'

Despite the sixteen years that separated them, Himansu glowed with pleasure at her unstinting praise. Happily, he put an arm around her, ignoring Niranjan's glowering face.

Deftly accepting murmured congratulations from those around him, he guided her into the nearest taxi. And not a moment too soon, for he could see Niranjan walking hurriedly towards them. As soon as the car started, he pressed her hand again and raising it to his lips, kissed it with much more ardour than before, while she blushed.

'I wish other girls had your sensitivity. It is so rare. The last time I met you, you were a sleepy little girl, now you are a woman. A very desirable woman.' Himansu wanted to make sure she knew his intentions before Niranjan could find her and dissuade her.

Even though Devika had been prepared to seduce Himansu into noticing her, she was not ready for this rapid turn of events. Nor for the fact that she actually wanted those lips that had just brushed her hand, to kiss her properly. She had not bargained for the fact that Himansu radiated charisma. She allowed her hand to remain in his for just a little longer.

'We are in the process of producing our next film in India. Why don't you come with us? Or, if not for this one, then maybe the next?' Himansu asked, brushing a stray curl from her face. As she hesitated, thinking of what her answer should be, he leant over and gently brushed his lips over her cheek. Devika wondered if she had made a mistake. Would he misunderstand her eagerness to get into cinema? She wanted desperately to agree, but she was not quite sure what it would entail. 'Only women who are poorly educated, women who are prostitutes, act on screen, at least in India,' she had been told. Without thinking, she spoke her thoughts aloud.

'I am not asking you to be an actress,' he replied. 'To begin with, why don't you help us with the set design? Or with the art direction, or costume design? That will help you make up your mind whether you want to act or do something else.'

They had reached the venue of the party by now. Leaving the thought with her, he went across and held the car door open for her.

Devika and Himansu entered the party arm in arm. She knew she was taking a plunge into a whole new career and wanted to be seen as an intelligent, well-brought-up girl, not someone who was angling for a glamorous role. One must never seem too eager, she cautioned herself.

Himansu offered her a cigarette, and though she had only smoked once or twice before with friends for fun, she took it as though it was her normal practice. She tried not to cough too noticeably, as he watched her with amusement.

'My dear, this is an art I will have to teach you, along with so many other things,' he murmured in her ears.

'Hold the cigarette like this—and do not inhale. That's the trick to begin with. Everything in life is playacting. Do it till it becomes absolutely natural.'

Devika could not help laughing, it was such a simple solution. Hold the cigarette with practised ease and blow smoke rings upwards. She looked at Himansu admiringly. 'There is so much I have to learn from you, Mr Rai.'

'Call me Himansu...'

Behind them, Niranjan walked in with Lily, having come in another taxi, their one extravagance on this celebratory evening. He watched as Devika leaned forward to speak to Himansu. He thought of all the women he had seen him with—English, French, German—but he had never seen that look on his face before. Could the suave Casanova finally have been caught?

But why did it have to be this innocent girl?

Letter from Devika to Svetoslav

Rabindranath Tagore so wanted to teach me...the Poet asked Rai to allow me 3 months every year, he wished so much to teach me, and I could have learnt so well from him. He had dearest a great love for me, you see his own son, his younger relations were a washout more or less—he had no one really of his own blood—there were things which he discussed with me and of which I never have told to anyone, which he wanted to tell to his own. He said so often 'My little flower you shall be the only one, apart from my love, who will see my soul...and let my soul touch you—at least allow it to live in your beautiful mind. Someday it will blossom with you.' Those and many other words he said—he was a lonely man and his one love and only love was never real. It [my visit to Shantiniketan] just could not happen—how will it be without him I don't know but it will be wonderful to go there [to Shantiniketan] just like that.

Bombay, 1945

6

A MONUMENT TO LOVE, 1927–1930s

It was a while before Devika could join Himansu formally to work with him on his new production. Even though they managed to meet a few times before he left for India, the preparations kept him from pursuing her as he would have liked to. *Shiraz* was based on Niranjan's story on the making of the Taj Mahal, but since he had decided not to accompany Himansu to India, there was a great deal to be done, and alone, including the casting and the hunt for locations.

Himansu had heard of a few new actors he could hire, but his director— Franz Osten, once again—and his team would need to meet them before they were finalised. He had already settled on the teenaged Seeta Devi (who had successfully played the role of Gopa in *The Light of Asia*) for one of the lead female roles, and he himself would play Shiraz, the eponymous sculptor who was supposed to have designed the Taj Mahal. This time there were no objections to him playing the lead. The ecstatic reviews in Germany as well as all over Europe were witness to his talent. Somehow, he had, with his usual confidence, successfully played the multiple roles of hero, producer, location scout and fundraiser-in-chief.

Shiraz: A Romance of India also capitalised on the Western fascination with Eastern exotica. It was a completely fictitious account of the making of the Taj Mahal, one which did not feature the reality of Shah Jahan or Mumtaz Mahal. Originally written by Niranjan as a play, it told the story of a slave girl, Selima, who would eventually become the empress for whom the Taj Mahal was designed. The architect, Shiraz, was apparently her childhood soulmate, who could not reveal his identity or his love for her until it was too late. It was an interesting piece of fiction, far from any historical fact. What it did showcase was the exotic marvel that was India—the palaces, the kings and queens, the elephants and tigers—all that might appeal to foreign audiences. It encompassed every prevalent stereotype about India, and in this it closely followed the template set by *The Light of Asia*.

Although Himansu continued to persuade her to come on board, Devika remained unsure. 'There are hardly any educated Indian women in the industry,' she kept pointing out to Himansu. She could not imagine herself in the company of Seeta Devi, although there were a few amateur theatre actors amongst her own family in London.

'In India, I will become a pariah. I have my family's reputation to consider. I am the great-grand-niece of Tagore. What will they think of me if I am on screen with people like... *her* ?' she asked Himansu. The last word was whispered almost viciously. It was loaded with meaning. Himansu immediately realised that behind that soft-spoken and demure exterior, she was fiercely protective of her status and background. She was rebellious enough to join the profession, but was worried about the kind of people associated with it in India.

⁓⁓⁓

They were strolling along the Thames one afternoon in early November. It was 1927. She looked beautiful as always, and even more petite, as she drew her overcoat around her. It had been given to her by her father, and at times like this it gave her the comfort she sought. The darkening sky reflected her own mood. Should she uproot herself and follow her dream? Or would that be too disruptive?

She had, in trying to settle down, found an elegant flat in a double-storey white terrace house at 12 Buckland Crescent, Swiss Cottage.

Even with her earnings from the make-up sessions supplementing the money that her father sent her, she could barely afford the rent, but at least she was independent.

And there were other men wooing her as well. In her coat pocket rustled a carelessly thrust away letter she had received from one of her suitors. None of the men so far had been interesting enough. Devika, by her own admission, had been 'spoilt' by her father. She needed to be with someone she could respect and who could look after her. Even though her father had been struggling for money these past few years, he had always tried to provide well for his family.

'This is not a small-time production, it's an Indo-British-German production,' Himansu replied defensively. 'I think you should come with me. It will be a great learning experience.'

Devika was genuinely torn between the idea of being a part of the film and doing something else that would be considered more respectable, like studying architecture. Her feelings towards Himansu himself were ambivalent. His cousin Pramode, who was also his art director, had told her, as had Niranjan, that Himansu had too many women in his life already. Perhaps Pramode had said it because he was nervous about the growing bond between Himansu and her. He too wanted to marry her, and this was already a problem between him and Himansu.

Devika knew how to keep men interested in her. Usually, it was just by being herself—a sharply intelligent, inquisitive, attractive girl, who was also a good conversationalist. There was also a certain mystique about her that she kept alive by wearing exotic sarees and weaving flowers into her hair. The idea that she came from an elevated lineage helped. In England especially, a well-connected Indian girl who had both British and Indian friends was unique.

If Pramode had not warned her, she would probably have thought of Himansu as an ideal partner for her. They were both ambitious and had a common goal at the time. He was looking for someone like her—beautiful and sophisticated, to rival Western actresses, and she was looking for a career and a mentor. The match was perfect.

In the beginning she had taken Himansu for a wealthy man, till it dawned on her that he had made only a few films, and had to raise the money for each of them. But according to his latest contract for *Shiraz*, he was going to earn around £150 per month, he told her. This was a lot of money for a girl who thought it sufficient to earn £5 for a week's work. Unlike most women from her background, Devika was genuinely interested in money. She kept a strict account of what she received and what she spent. As with everything else in her life, she liked being in control.

She had watched her mother struggling to maintain the standard of living she was accustomed to, and eventually becoming frustrated and unhappy. Devika was clear in her mind. That was not how she wanted to be. She wanted to be comfortably well-off, if not rich. She also wanted to be secure. She wanted a creative and challenging career but filmmaking was a downright risky business in far too many ways.

Another problem, she knew, was that if she agreed to go with the production team to India, it was likely to lead to something more on the personal front. Even the few times they had met, Himansu had made his interest in her quite obvious. Though young, she was sensible. And she wasn't sure he had marriage in mind. Pramode had hinted at the existence of a German woman who claimed to be quite close to Himansu. There was even a rumour about a child. What was she to do?

After initially indulging in a mild flirtation, she decided to keep him at a distance. This was Devika's strength. Her heart rarely ruled her head.

Of course, her puzzling behaviour only made him want her more.

Now, as they walked along the Thames, Himansu paused at a bench and asked her to sit down. From his briefcase he took out a copy of the contract he had signed with British Instructional Films (BIF). The terms were, he explained, were much, much better than any previous contract he had signed, including for *The Light of Asia*, and would ensure a steady income. It was different too from the earlier contract with Universum-Film Atiengesellschaft or UFA, which was only for distributing the film and providing equipment. Here, he had done a three-way deal.

'I have capitalised on the strengths of all the three companies I am working with. I am getting the equipment and technicians from UFA, as before, but I am also getting supporting technicians from BIF. I have signed over my own contract with UFA to the British company, so this time we will also get their support with distribution in both England and India,' he told her.

Shiraz was a true Indo-British-German production. It was directed by Franz Osten, but the assistant director, Victor Peers, was British. The photography was by Henry Harris and Emil Schunemann, while the art direction was by Pramode Nath. Eventually the production credit went to BIF and the distribution credit to UFA. In many ways, it proved to be a good collaboration. It also paved the way for a smooth transition to the next film.

The agreement with BIF (which was then situated at Regent Studio Park Road, Surbiton, in Surrey) had been signed on 9 November 1927 by Himansu, who was at the time staying at 19, De Vere Gardens, in Kensington. It said clearly that from 14 September 1927 to 30 May 1928, Himansu was to work as a business manager at a salary of £25 per week. He would also 'as a further part of the services to be rendered by him to the company' play a 'leading part' in the film. For transferring his own contract with the German studio UFA to the British BIF and thus benefitting them, he would be paid another 'two hundred and fifty pounds by five equal instalments of fifty pounds each'.

The contract also stated that Himansu would 'forthwith proceed to India and will make all arrangements necessary for the photographing of the Film which is to commence not later than the first day of February one thousand nine hundred and twenty eight and is to be completed within a period of nine weeks from the last mentioned date.'

Himansu was also to return to England, if required, to help in editing and assembling the film. Unlike in the past, when he had to use all his charm to raise money for a project and live by his wits, this time his passage both to and from London would be paid, as well as his hotel and travelling expenses during the making of the film. He would get a further five per cent on the final receipts, if the latter exceeded the cost of production. Though an accountant would accompany him to oversee the finances, Himansu could not have asked for a happier situation.

Ultimately, Devika did not participate in the making of *Shiraz*. Intellectually and socially, she still felt superior to the Indian actresses of the time and she did not wish to be associated with them. But she was prepared to help behind the scenes, on equal terms with the other assistants. She also began to think seriously about art direction, following in the footsteps of her friend Pramode. She loved to sketch, and had a natural flair for clothes, make-up and fashion. Her own constrained circumstances had taught her that wearing 'interesting' attire was better than high fashion, which she couldn't afford. She thought she might train with some London designers while Himansu was away.

Meanwhile, Himansu sailed for India, wondering if Devika would join him after all. How could he convince her that she had a career ahead of her in films, and it was not something unsteady and ephemeral? Devika was becoming an obsession for him. The more she resisted, the more desperately he wanted her by his side.

Fortunately, his instinct for the right story worked and *Shiraz*, released in September 1928 and screened in England and Germany and other places in Europe, was even better received than *The Light of Asia*. The quality of the production was recognised as being much higher than anything one might expect from a film made in India. Himansu came in for praise as an actor. But the real coup turned out to be the casting of an educated, upper-class young woman, Enakshi Rama Rao, in the lead role of the empress. This would go a long way in both unsettling Devika as well as convincing her that she should reconsider her hesitation to work in films. She could have been the first educated woman from India to act in an international film. Alas, that accolade now belonged to Enakshi, who she thought was stiff as cardboard. Devika hid her disappointment but was determined not to miss out on the next opportunity that came her way. She must outshine everyone. She had to be the best!

Himansu did his best too, to highlight the fact that Enakshi had earned her place in cinema history. A man in love will try anything.

The *Sunday Express* of 23 September 1928 noticed the attempt:

> Himansu Rai and Seeta Devi, the impressive pair who appeared in the "The Light of Asia" repeat their success in "Shiraz," but the chief interest, for some reason, has been focussed on Enakshi Rama Rau, quaintly described as a bachelor of philosophy who acts well but is not totally at home in the role of Mumtaz.

Enakshi may have been chosen for her 'thoughtful intelligence' and would go on to become a well-known actress, but her awkwardness showed in her film debut.

The *Morning Post*, on 22 September 1928, commented:

> Apart from its scenic beauty and splendour and the vigorous early scenes of the caravan fight and slave raid, and the stamping-to-death ceremony, the memorable thing for English film goers will be the very great charm of Miss Seeta Devi as Dalia, a jealous favourite of Jehan's who figures very largely in the story. Miss Enakshi Rama Rau, the distinguished student-actress who plays Selima herself, suggests a more thoughtful intelligence, as is natural, but the lighter graces are certainly on Miss Seeta Devi's side.

The *Evening News* reporter, A. Jympson Harman, said:

> [When the somewhat 'primitive' film *The Light of Asia*] was being made he [Himansu] told me he had great difficulty in persuading good class, and consequently intelligent, native girls to have anything to do with film acting. Apparently it is not

quite "the thing" in India, any more than going to the pictures was in English social circles a few years ago.

But now, says Mr Rai, very high class Indian girls are eager to act for films. For instance, Enakshi Rama Rau, who in "Shiraz" plays the part of the lady in memory of whom the Agra monument was built, is a beautiful Cashmire girl of a distinguished Brahmin family. She is only 21 and is about to take her degree in philosophy in Madras University.

Another girl in the film, Maya Devi, belongs to a very strict sect of Indians who, I gather, are not too pleased with her for having broken purdah by appearing without a veil on the screen.

There is, says Mr Rai, little ready made acting talent at present in India upon which to draw for film work. All the players in "The Light of Asia" and "Shiraz" with one or two exceptions had to be trained for the work. When one learns that 60,000 people appear in one of the most spectacular scenes in "Shiraz" one feels a little sympathy for Mr Rai.

And, of course, there are no film wardrobes in India. Nearly a hundred tailors worked for three months to make the costumes specially for "Shiraz".

The article was headlined 'High-caste Indian Girls in a Taj Mahal Romance'.

While there was a lot of coverage of the twenty-one-year-old Enakshi Rama Rao, Himanshu got his share of attention, with the *Manchester Evening Chronicle* calling him 'India's Valentino'. It also noted his rueful comment: 'At the moment, one of our greatest difficulties is to get the cultured women in India interested in the cinema.'

Many women were playing important roles in Indian cinema in the late 1920s. But Himansu, riled by Devika's jibes, was on a mission to change the film industry and bring to it more 'cultured' men and women. He said:

A year or two ago there were less than 100 cinemas in all India, now there are 300.

Although 'The Light of Asia' and 'Shiraz' are the first really important productions India has filmed for international exhibition it should not be forgotten that practically every other film shown in India is produced there.

Himansu's approach was probably well ahead of his time. And for the British press to meet an articulate speaker like him from India was unusual. The film correspondent who interviewed him was rather taken with his 'expressively furnished Kensington flat'. He quoted Himansu as saying:

When filming the "The Light of Asia" Mr Himansu Rai announced to a critical European, American and Russian audience that "to exploit the Asiatic field would demand an exceedingly high competitive standard. The propagandist has his own methods of expression, the artist has his, and I regard the cinema as a new and international art, knowing none of the linguistic limitations which hamper other more ancient arts."

There was also a comment on 'domestic estrangement':

For generations my people have been lawyers. My grandfather was a judge in the Indian High Court; my father and uncle are lawyers. I was trained for the Bar and called from the Middle Temple, after studying at London University. When they heard of my intention to become an actor they were bitterly disappointed.

Himansu confided in the interviewer that he had attended classes at Shantiniketan and that he was one among only a dozen students who were personally tended to by the great bard, Rabindranath Tagore.

The interviewer wrote diligently that:

The world famous botanist, Dr Jagadish Chandra Bose, came to the school and regularly Mr Rai accompanied him on plant finding expeditions, "We would find flowers...run with these to the doctor, and returning to the school, he would reveal to us their wonders. They were wonderful days."

Interestingly, many years later, in another media report, this story was passed off as a part of Devika's childhood. A good anecdote for the Western press, correct or incorrect, it was absorbed into the mythology around them.

There were other aspects of Himansu's life which sound plausible but were magnified for emphasis. For instance, instead of launching just one amateur dramatic society, he said he had organised twenty!

> When I left school and went to the University at Calcutta the first thing I did was start an amateur dramatic society.
> Before leaving for London I had organised twenty amateur dramatic societies. When I came to London and passed my law examination, the love of acting was very strong in me.

It was this love of acting that kept him going, he said. The story of his theatrical past was spiced with hyperbole:

> Again I got together a company of Indian actors and we produced plays at the Ambassadors, Aldwych, and Duke of York's.
> Invitations to play in France, Germany and Italy came to us, and it was then that the difficulty of expressing ourselves to foreign audiences presented itself.
> The cinema offered an alternative medium. Determined to cultivate this medium I became a cinema actor.

Unable to resist the opportunity, he narrated the story of *Shiraz* to the spellbound journalist with 'quiet gesture, mellow phrase and passion stirring words,' maintaining that the story was told with the 'strictest truth'. It was, of course, miles from the historical truth, but Himansu had become an excellent communicator, not letting facts get in the way of a good story.

He also spoke of his vision for his films, as the interviewer reported:

"Love will be the keynote of all our pictures," Mr Rai told me. "Going round the world, I am often oppressed by the puerile bitterness and hatred one encounters, but am always made happy with the knowledge that everywhere there exists the love of a mother for a son, the love of a brother for a brother, all knitting humanity together in a great, invisible, perhaps, but very real bondage of love."

It is, too, as a lover that he makes his appearance in this film.

It was almost as though Himansu was addressing Devika's concerns through his interviews. He was assuring her that women from 'good' backgrounds were entering cinema, and that the themes he chose were all close to his heart. His interviews also made it increasingly clear to all those who worked with him that Himansu had a long-term plan.

Just as he had done for *The Light of Asia*, Himansu had planned a grand launch for his new film. According to *Near East and India*, published on 24 September 1928:

> The film had its trade showing on September 21 under the auspices of the Pro Patria Films Ltd, at the London Hippodrome before a large and most enthusiastic audience, which included the Countess of Oxford and a party as well as many well known Anglo-Indian figures. Mr Himansu Rai who supervised the film in India, was in a box, deeply interested in watching himself as the hero Shiraz, Miss Enakshi Rama Rau—a charming film actress of international calibre as Selima, afterwards the Empress Mumtaz Mahal, Miss Seeta Devi as Dalia, the villainess of the plot, and Mr Charu Roy as Shah Jehan. Among the long list of supernumerary characters mention must be made of the dumb actors—birds, snakes, lizards, camels, horses, and the elephants lent by the ruling princes of many of the Indian States.

Another newspaper, *Morning Post,* had claimed on 22 September that the audience that received *Shiraz* with much enthusiasm included, apart from the Countess of Oxford and Asquith and the

Duchess of Atholl, 'the Maharajah of Burdwan, the Maharajah of Jodhpur, Sir Atul Chatterjee (High Commissioner for India), Admiral Campbell, Sir Martin Seton, Sir William Vincent, Sir Muhammad Rafiq, Sir Louis Kershaw, Sir Havelock Hudson, and a host of other well known people.'

The film was expected to be successful, said the paper.

All through from the Western point of view, there was… too much mild love making—not unnatural, perhaps, to the inhabitants of palace gardens. Which are both in fancy and fact, earthly paradises. However, there is quite enough fascinating life and vision about "Shiraz" to make it the world-success which has been heralded, and the applause which greeted Mr Himansu Rai when the limelight was thrown on him in a box at the finish bore its own testimony.

In his usual flamboyant fashion, when the theatre lights shone on him following the screening, Himansu had got up and bowed while the applause rang out. Niranjan Pal, who had written the screenplay, was forgotten, even though he was seated nearby.

In fact, all the announcements made on stage were for Himansu. Even the glittering crowd gathered there was for Himansu, and he had worked hard to ensure they came. He had become the face of the production.

For Devika, the sight of Himansu in the limelight seemed to underscore all that was missing in her life. She was torn by the thought that this could have been her screen debut.

'How could you convince an audience that the emperor chose to build a mausoleum for a girl like that! It doesn't seem credible. No wonder the lovemaking has been called "mild". She has no passion,' she complained to Himansu as he escorted her home, still elated at the success of the film, and truth be told, quite pleased over Devika's reaction. It was one of the few times when he had read her accurately.

'You are the one who should be pleased. You told me that educated women in India shun cinema. Now you can see things are changing—we are creating a revolution. You should be a part of it, not out of it.' He helped her to the door of her Swiss Cottage apartment. After kissing her hand as he usually did, he kissed her on the lips, and she did not turn away.

For a change, breaking her own very strict rule, she allowed him into her apartment.

An hour later, he was lounging on the sofa, his head on her lap. They shared a cigarette, glasses of red wine at hand. There was no doubt that the evening at the Hippodrome had been a resounding success. Himansu was now keen on the final conquest.

'But how could you choose her? That cardboard queen!'

Her curt words about Enakshi stopped him in his tracks.

He knew exactly what was going on in her head as she smoked with a quiet intensity, seemingly too engrossed in her critique to notice his roving fingers that edged closer to the buttons on her blouse, looking for an opening. Her saree was still tightly wrapped around her. Ever since he had completed the final edit of *Shiraz*, he had struggled against the sarees she wore. He knew that this night could turn out to be the perfect occasion to unravel one, but he would have to wait for a few more glasses of wine to do their job. Meanwhile, flattery was the best strategy.

'Don't you think you could have been better than Enakshi? I have asked you so often to shed that old fashioned Bengali reticence and take the plunge,' he said bluntly.

'I've been reading the reviews. Poor thing. Each one of them preferred Seeta. Also, let me tell you, Bengali women are anything but reticent!'

'At least we have broken the barrier.' Himansu sprang to his feet and paced up and down. 'It's her first film, perhaps she was a little stiff... after all, she is a student of philosophy, not cinema.'

He continued, 'Till I met you, I did not realise how important it is to have educated actors. You put the thought in my head, and now we must try to take it forward. Please join me. I need you...'

Himansu tried to make it sound like a matter of life and death as he knelt by her side. 'It is not enough that you are supportive and help me with ideas and suggestions once in a while. I want you with me more permanently.'

It was true that Himansu needed her. Not just professionally, but personally too. He was in love with her—and he also knew that she was an irreplaceable asset.

Devika was thoughtful as she tried not to respond immediately to him, or to the offer. She knew it was only a matter of time before actresses vied with one another to act with Himansu. The reports coming from the London community about the latest film were surprisingly good. The reaction tonight had been an eye-opener.

'Perhaps you are right,' she said coquettishly, flinging her head back and taking a deep drag of the cigarette, then blowing smoke at the ceiling. 'I should consider coming along with you for the next production.'

Himansu quickly sat down next to her and began to discuss the contract they would sign. He knew that Devika would be reluctant to be a part of the team unless she was given a clear role and paid suitably. It was best to keep the personal and the professional separate as he could not afford another scandal on his hands. If Pramode or Niranjan got wind of the fact that he was trying to get her to travel with him, they would not allow it.

As the evening turned to night and then to dawn, the tightly wound saree lay unspooled on the floor.

Their relationship, inevitable after that night, would be sealed with a work contract. Himansu thought it would be best to make Niranjan a witness to its signing. That would neutralise him... and Pramode? After the next production, for which he had already been signed, Pramode would be shown the door.

Himansu was impatient to launch Devika in her first film. He knew that their chemistry on-screen would be dynamite. He had already seen what a great actress she was off-screen. He could just imagine her on screen—with that porcelain skin, those smouldering eyes, that virginal expression. The particular combination of innocence and sophistication she exuded had not been seen before in Indian cinema.

He also knew that despite the difference in years, they could have a great partnership. He had not felt so excited about anything since the success of *The Goddess* almost seven years ago. That seemed like another world now.

A few weeks later, on 10 October 1928, Himansu invited Devika to his place at Kensington Palace Mansions, to sign the contract. He had been speaking to her about it for a few months. But her father's death in June 1928 had finally made her amenable to a signed agreement, as she, more than ever before, needed some financial security.

A very reluctant Niranjan Pal had been asked to witness the signing. Himansu did not want any idle gossip and he wanted Devika to be respected as an artiste in her own right, not perceived as someone who had been brought in because he was in love with her. It was a huge risk he was taking, and he wanted the paperwork to be right. She had to feel secure at all times. Or, he knew, she would leave him.

The contract, signed by Devika Choudhuri in her large sprawling handwriting, said:

> I (Himansu) have much pleasure in confirming the verbal arrangements I have entered into with you securing to myself your exclusive services as a film and stage artiste under my Management and control under the following terms and conditions:
>
> 1. As from today you bind yourself solely and absolutely to act any female role which I may assign you in any film or stage play or plays I may produce or any film or stage play or plays which may be produced by other individuals, firms or companies to whom your services may be lent by me.
> 2. In consideration of the above I agree and undertake to pay you a minimum retaining fee of fifteen pounds per month

commencing from the 1st of November next and this retaining fee will continue to be paid to you month by month for a period of one year. But this retaining fee will cease to be paid under clause 3 and during the period when this clause remains in force you shall have no claim whatsoever on the payment of this retaining fee.

Clause 3 stated that her salary as an artiste would not be less than 'thirty pounds during any month and out of the money or monies you may receive under this clause you shall pay to me a commission of ten per cent...'

Quite unusually for a new artiste, the contract would be renewed at 'my option', and her retaining fee would be increased to twenty-two pounds per month for the second year, and thirty pounds a month for the third year.

Then came the clincher—she would bind herself 'not to appear in any film or stage production without my sanction or approval and that you further undertake to remain under my supervision and control until its expiry.'

And to ensure that she made no plans without telling him, the contract said:

> I further agree and undertake that I shall pay or procure you to be paid all reasonable travelling, hotel and out of pocket expenses whenever you may be required to work outside Calcutta and as you are now in London I agree that your fare to Calcutta will either be paid by me or procured through some company or firm to whom your services may be lent by me.

It was certainly an unusual contract, and one that gave Himansu the upper hand—at a price. Even Devika's choice of Calcutta as the city to travel to did not deter him, although it was the furthest point she could possibly go after landing in Bombay by ship. He was happy to help with any travel she undertook. Already, he was planning a fresh production, *A Throw of Dice*. Calcutta would be on the list of cities to visit, for he hoped to sign on Seeta Devi again, and look for more artistes. Thanks to the success of New Theatres, would-be actors were turning up for auditions at the whiff of a production.

⌒⌒⌒

Now Himansu began 'training' Devika in different aspects of production. He arranged for her to visit studios and familiarise herself with art direction as well as acting. His track record of delivering two very successful films meant that even British studios were happy to open their doors to him. Devika was a quick learner, and charming, so she was always a welcome visitor everywhere.

Harry Bruce Woolfe, the managing director of Pro Patria films, which had distributed *Shiraz,* had also become Himansu's fan. Himansu's indefatigable energy and self-belief as well as his desire to be on an equal footing with British filmmakers was respected by most of his fellow filmmakers and studio owners.

Woolfe now extended an invitation to Devika to visit his studio. She did not respond in the first instance, but by the time he followed up with her, she had realised that it was a rare honour being extended to her; unknown, aspiring art directors and actresses were not usually asked so warmly to visit a well-known studio, to 'learn'.

Apart from politicians, parliamentarians and filmmakers, Himansu had also attracted the attention of the British intelligentsia. And now Devika began to be a part of this charmed inner circle in which she and Himansu were treated as equals. It was a world that she coveted—a heady mix of glamour and intellect. Even the author and playwright John Galsworthy, who was to win the Nobel Prize in 1932, had time for Himansu, especially after having watched *The Light of Asia*. Devika was thrilled when she found a letter from the famous man among Himansu's files.

Himansu was careful about archiving all the letters that reached him, favourable or unfavourable. It was a habit that Devika, with a magpie mind accumulating ideas and habits and histories, was quick to pick up. She now avidly read the letter written by Galsworthy on 15 August 1926, long before she had met Himansu. Galsworthy, in fact, had seen the film on Himansu's invitation. And he was blunt about what he liked and disliked in the production.

He was impressed with the film's 'dignity' and 'beauty', he wrote. He found the 'first two thirds of it entirely satisfying' although the latter part was too 'storified'. The film did not seem to have shaken itself from becoming banal at times, he said. However, he found the acting 'most admirable. The Prince most touching; and your own performance dignified and adequate.' He maintained that even though he was not a lover of the story or of cinema, the film 'almost converted' him. This was high praise coming from such a celebrated author.

There was a lot that Devika did not know about Himansu, though she did her best to keep up with him and had begun to treat him like a guru. Her own scattered education and lack of intellectual knowledge was humbling, and she now read and tried to understand as much as she could.

His passion for cinema fascinated her, and she found herself being swept away by it. She understood that there was a deeply personal reason behind Himansu's planning—not only did he want to bring more professionalism to cinema because he believed that it was the right way forward, he also wanted to make truly path-breaking changes for her sake, to encourage her to become an actress and for her family to accept it. To be made to feel so special by someone who had gained so much respect from the world was overwhelming.

As Devika familiarised herself with Himansu's work at his request, she discovered files pertaining to his fundraising efforts in Europe and India. He wrote relentlessly to the studios, the government, to wealthy individuals...no one was safe from him!

Over time, Himansu had developed a knack for charming money out of unexpected sources. Many of the people he approached for funding had already been in his sights before he met Devika. Now, he hoped that she would bring her own formidable talents into play. He even found support from the Indian Trade Commissioner,

E. Gordon, then based at Grosvenor Gardens in London who, in turn, wrote to potential investors.

In his letter to Sir Maneckji Dadabhoy, a well-known Parsi industrialist with a base in London, Gordon wrote that Himansu was interested in promoting the film industry in India. No doubt prompted by Himansu, he said:

> He (Himansu) has just returned from India after completing a film entitled "Shiraz" under the auspices of British Instructional Films Ltd, who are well-known in the film world in this country. On the last occasion the financing of the production was done by the British Company, and I understand a certain amount of criticism was expressed in India that Indian capital was not used for the venture. British Instructional Films Ltd, are now anxious to undertake a new picture in India, and although I understand they have the means of doing so, they are anxious to meet the aforesaid criticism by raising some of the funds in India.

It was a clever argument. Himansu was adept at finding a reason for why others should support him. Not all, however, were willing to do so, and unsurprisingly, the British government in India was extremely cautious. They were not keen to be seen to be helping him raise money. Harry Haig, the governor of the United Provinces, was quite categorical about this:

> You have received assistance directly or indirectly from the Government of India. The question whether and to what extent the Government of India should assist the cinema industry has been under the careful consideration of the Cinema Committee, and any statement suggesting that the Government of India already had given assistance while it would not in my view be consistent with the facts, would certainly be a source of embarrassment during the consideration of the Cinema Committee's report.

Nonetheless, Himansu was unstoppable. If anything, he became even more determined to achieve his goal. He got busier than ever, commuting frequently between London, Germany and, of course, India. By now he was also now earning enough for Inland Revenue to notice him; he probably had the dubious honour of being the first Indian film actor and producer to be served an income-tax notice.

The tax department, it turned out, had been tracking Himansu for a while before catching up with him in 1930. They wanted to know the details of his income in the past few years and how much time he had been in England. Himansu was quick to point out that he was constantly in and out of the country, often not spending more than one month in London. He gave his address in the south-western locality of Schmargendorf, on Heiligendammer Strasse, in Germany. Since he had signed the contract with Devika on 10 October 1928, he claimed to have left London on that day itself. And there the matter rested for the moment.

Letter from Devika to Svetoslav

I sold all my good things—not <u>one</u> bit is left, silver, gold, jewels, fur coats, even shoes which my father gave me, old jewels pawned in <u>all</u> the pawn shops of London, Berlin, Paris. That's when my husband had <u>no</u> money and we starved for almost 3 years—29, 30, 31. The pawned things I could not recover because I could not afford it. I had a most wonderful ruby & emerald ring and well…what's the use…I really don't ever think or need them & have no regrets <u>whatsoever</u>. My only regret was I could not sell them, I hadn't the face to really [sell these to] people who would appreciate them—one's old heirlooms for hundreds of years. I should have liked decent people to have them, that's all, and so as my life was, I made it a happy thing. I never lived unhappy, even under the most sordid conditions I ever tried to get what I needed for my <u>moral</u> upbringing, that is decent clothes, (a) pair of good shoes like that, so that I always looked neat and clean & and was not shabby & could face the world, if you follow what I mean. In the winter I had only 1 pair of silk stockings, so I went bare feet at home, and kept them for when I went out. I dressed my husband well—I saw to it he had the <u>best</u> always, he dressed very well, he, poor fellow, could not pawn <u>his</u> things, and I dressed in the 'arty' way so people thought it was attractive and smart—they <u>never</u> suspected it was a <u>necessity</u>!

Bombay, 1945

7

TROUBLE IN BERLIN, 1929–1932

A Throw of Dice was a very special film for Himansu. Having mastered the exotic India formula by now, he could travel without worries to his home country with a team that was accustomed to the heat and the dust—along with the woman he loved. But first, he had to negotiate a fresh contract with BIF, and also with the German studio UFA, for a stake in the new film as well as another future film. He was already in the middle of buying the film rights for *Vasantsena*, written by Norbert Falk, who had done the screenplay for some very successful films for UFA, among which were *Carmen* and *Secrets of the Orient*.

Falk, a well-known German screenplay writer, was enamoured of Eastern themes, and was currently working on a new script based on the second-century play, *Mrichchakatika*, or *The Little Clay Cart*, attributed to the ancient Indian playwright, Sudraka. The main protagonist of the play was Vasantsena, a fictional courtesan. Himansu was excited by the thought of making it into a film, and immediately began visualising Devika in it. He decided to cast her along with the popular Seeta Devi, whom he had already signed for two films.

The new terms and conditions he managed to negotiate with both BIF and UFA reflected his growing stature. In his contract with BIF, he referred to the 1927 contract for *Shiraz* and asked for nearly £2,000 to be paid to him for the production of the film. He also insisted that he should be mentioned as the supervisor of the film in India 'on the screen and in advertisements as far as possible'. It is interesting to note how quickly Harry Bruce Woolfe, the managing director of BIF, agreed to his conditions.

On 18 August 1928, Himansu met Woolfe and after a brief discussion handed him a typed letter with a few handwritten changes. On the same day, Woolfe wrote, 'Herewith, we undertake to give you an Agreement as soon as can be prepared, on the terms and conditions as outlined in your letter to us dated 18th August.'

UFA, the other studio he was involved with, also wrote to him confirming that 'We are in possession of your letter dated September 7th, 1928, and in reply we herewith give our consent to all stipulations contained therein.'

It was turning into a dream run. He signed a contract for the production of *Vasantsena* with UFA which said:

> You engage me as a producer for a picture which has the tentative title "Vasantsena". Besides you engage me for this picture in my capacity as an actor. I undertake to carry out the production according to the instructions of your Board of Directors.
>
> The picture is to be photographed in India. I bind myself to begin with the production in India latest on April the 1st, 1929 and to complete the picture in June 1929, will make it possible to complete the production, before the rain interferes the production.

He guaranteed that the picture 'will represent a full evening's entertainment and that it will be at least of the quality of 'Das Grabmal Einer Grossen Liebe'—a reference to *Shiraz*. He stated that he would play the principal part, and the other actors would all be Indians as well. The film would cost 320,000 Reichsmark.

He suggested that the director of the film could be Franz once again. He told UFA that they did not have to pay the cost of the trip to India for either him or Franz or the camera person. But he did request that their return trip be paid by UFA. And for the production of *Vasantsena*, he asked that the cameraman, an assistant director and an art director be paid their fees by UFA. Obviously, the art director was going to be a certain Devika Choudhuri.

Once again, he worked out the terms in a way that he would receive £2,000 from UFA, too.

Himansu had planned the schedule such that they would officially be filming *A Throw of Dice*, but would also do some work on *Vasantsena*. If all went well, he would be richer by £4,000, as both BIF and UFA were committed to paying him £2,000 each.

Keen to ensure that all his expenses were taken care of, he had added in a footnote in the contract that 'it is understood that my costs of living (i.e., boarding, lodging and laundry) are included in the costs of production during the production of the film and the return trip to Europe.'

The correspondence and contracts with the Germans often contained spelling mistakes and grammatical errors, but everyone managed to communicate the essence of what was meant.

Himansu had worked out an elaborate system by which he would also be paid for the 'exploitation' of the film. In the past, he had lost out when the distribution was handed over to another company. This time, he also insisted that his star value be recognised, and that the first credits of the film should be 'UFA presents Himansu Rai' and alongside would be the name of the 'chief actress'.

There was such a good understanding now between Himansu and UFA that it was decided that just in case UFA changed their minds about *Vasantsena*, they could ask him to produce another film, with the same terms and conditions. At present, though, UFA would pay for the manuscript to be purchased from another studio—the Phoebus-Film-Aktiengesellschaft.

It was clear by now that Himansu had moved far beyond the Indian circuit and into a more cosmopolitan universe. What he did not anticipate or notice was the rapid rise of the Third Reich, and the growing use of companies like UFA for Nazi propaganda. It was far more important for him to keep his productions going and he was willing to take on board all those who were willing to help him. Money was being pumped into German studios, and so Germany appeared a much more lucrative place to be. But nothing was what it seemed. Under the new regime at UFA, headed by Dr Alfred Hugenberg and Ludwig Klitzsch, despite an increase in the production budget to 9.5 million Reichsmarks, the number of feature films produced in 1929 declined from 33 to 21, while the number of news reels rose from 100 to 160. Under these circumstances, it was unclear whether the quarter of a million pounds Himansu had proposed for *Vasantsena* would actually be paid. UFA had lost a lot of money recently on *Metropolis*, a film shot on a gigantic scale.

Himansu did not realise at this stage that their screenplay writer Norbert Falk, being a Jew, was in grave danger. In fact, he was soon to end his creative career.

Apart from the political and social changes sweeping the country, the landscape of German cinema was also being transformed. In later years, Devika and Himansu were to speak about their personal interactions with Marlene Dietrich, G.W. Pabst and Ernst Lang, but the truth was that it would have been very difficult for them to connect with the German stars and directors, except perhaps fleetingly.

Marlene's one really big hit with UFA, *The Blue Angel*, was released on 1 April 1930. Her first film had released in October 1929 and she had auditioned for *The Blue Angel* immediately afterwards. Once the film was successful, she left for America and chose not to return to Germany till the mid-1940s. It could be that Himansu arranged for Devika to attend some studio sessions with Marlene, when they returned from India after completing the shooting of *A Throw of Dice*. But for the most part of 1929, both Devika and Himansu were in India, not just shooting but also sorting out their relationship.

In the second half of 1929, Devika may have met Marlene and been inspired to learn the art of skilful screen make-up. The pencil-thin eyebrows, sharply highlighted cheekbones and jawline she flaunted when she began acting were very different from her earlier look—photographs show her to be slightly plump, and darker. In fact, her sleek, international look was very similar to that of Marlene.

Even though both Himansu and Devika were to move between Berlin, London and India, they, like many others, seemed unaware of the implications of the rise of Hitler and the Third Reich. Nor did they speak about the persecution of Jews. This is notable especially because *A Throw of Dice* had an Indo-British-German crew. Emil Schunemann, the cinematographer, was German, and so was Franz. The script was written by W.A. Burton and Max Junck. The story was by Niranjan Pal.

All these hard-won cinematic relationships would be soon dismembered by a wholly unexpected development which stopped everything in its tracks—the success of the talkies in America.

Audiences in America thronged to see *The Jazz Singer*, a 'partial talkie' released in October 1927, in the sense that it was mostly a silent movie, barring the songs. It was not till July 1928 that the first wholly talking picture, *The Lights of New York*, was released, starring Helene Costello, Cullen Landis and Eugene Palette. It was a Warner Bros. six-reeler, made on a small budget, but went on to gross over a million dollars.

Studios all over the world now began to assess the impact of the talkies on their own productions. This new form of filmmaking could make the audiences turn away from silent cinema completely and, as with *The Lights of New York*, more than quadruple the revenue. At the same time, the specificity of the language meant that not all markets could be satisfied with a single film. How could they harness the technology so that it could reach the largest number of people?

As they worked out how to replicate the success of Warner Bros., they also began to rethink their present commitments. On 25 January 1929, UFA wired Himansu, who had reached Bombay with Devika, Franz and Emil Schunemann, to say that they had decided to acquire a licence for 'dice fate' (*A Dice of Fate* or *A Throw of Dice*) on the same conditions as *Shiraz*. They suggested that work on *Vasantsena* should not commence till January 1930. It was a blow to Himansu, but he quickly understood the implications.

In India, the first talkie, *Alam Ara*, would not be produced till 1931, so at this time, Himansu was still on solid ground. But already the tremors caused by the unexpected success of *The Lights of New York* were pushing studios to begin their experimentations with sound. This would drastically change not only audience expectations, but the kind of films that were being made, as well as the choice of actors and story lines. The international character of silent cinema would give way to 'language films' and so Himansu would have to rethink his production mode, and the studios he could work with.

Meanwhile, UFA's support for *A Dice of Fate* (*A Throw of Dice*) was still a comfort, and being Himansu, he did not give up his relentless fundraising. In addition to other things, there were demands from his family in Calcutta for money, as his mother was unwell. They had also heard about his success, and the fact that he was in India.

At the same time, Devika had begun to worry, more than ever, about the perceived ambiguity of her relationship with Himansu. Rumours about the nature of their relationship had already begun to circulate. Aware that her mother would not be pleased to hear about her involvement with a film actor and producer, she did not reach out to her even after arriving in India. Her father, whom she adored, had already passed away towards the end of June 1928.

Then, on 23 March 1929, without informing their families, Himansu and Devika found time to get married the Arya Samaj way, in Madras. Given their desire to project themselves as educated, responsible and respectable filmmakers, this was probably a good move. But even friends and family who were in Madras or close by, knew nothing of the marriage. They (including Devika's mother) stumbled upon it only when the *Hindu* published the news on 26 March 1929.

For a young woman, alone and barely twenty-one, to get married without informing anyone showed remarkable self-belief, considering that she was in India and could have reached out to at least those members of her family who were not estranged. Perhaps this, more than anything else, characterised Devika—once she made up her mind to do something, nothing could stop her. And after making a decision, she did not seek anyone's advice, nor did she allow herself to harbour any doubts.

That her mother disapproved of her actions was obvious. The well-known American philanthropist and sculptor, Winifred Holt, who was in India with her husband, the social worker Rufus Graves Mather, met Devika's mother, Leela Devi Choudhuri, and her grandmother, Indumati Devi Chattopadhyaya, at the Great Eastern Hotel in Calcutta, ostensibly to discuss their work, but really to plead Devika's case.

Winifred wrote in a letter to Devika dated 28 January 1929:

By this time your mother has probably told you that she, your aunt and your grandmother took tea with us, but she has probably not told you that we invited them because we wanted to plead your cause which we feel, in a measure typifies the cause of women in India in whom my husband and I are so deeply interested...

The fact that Devika's mother was reluctant to accept Himansu as a son-in-law and that Devika was equally reluctant to share her plans with her family are also clear from a letter that her uncle Harry wrote to her mother in March 1929:

When I was reading the 'Hindu' of the 26th today I was very surprised to read of Devika's marriage (I have enclosed the cutting).You never mentioned in your letter that Devika was going to be married. I at once tried to find out where Mr Himansu Roy was staying in Madras but I could not get any information. So I wonder if you know anything about it. The other day Major PN Basu...came over one night at 10 o'clock asking for me and wanted to know if I knew anything about a Miss Choudhuri or some such person coming to Madras from Pondicherry. I, of course, professed ignorance as I had no news from you about this. Now I read the news in the Hindu.

It would have been quite a shock for the Choudhuri clan, even with their anglicised upbringing, to discover that Devika was involved with a man who was sixteen or seventeen years older than her, and encouraging her to become a screen actress. They knew that such a life was bound to contain insurmountable challenges. Indeed, apart from her father who had understood her aspirations and had even suggested she explore her musical talents, she probably did not feel she could confide in anyone.

From her family's point-of-view, Himansu would have had few redeeming features. They may have admired him on screen, but they probably asked themselves—What kind of man encourages his wife to do a shabby thing like this? Marry without informing the family, and then not even bothering to inform them afterwards?

They did not know that it had not been an easy time for Devika, either. Hers was as much a marriage of convenience as of passion. She loved and respected Himansu. She enjoyed the adventures of filmmaking and the opportunity to engage with different aspects of it. But there were constraints, especially the shortage of money in a quickly changing scenario.

Although the marriage would only be registered a few years later in London, Himansu and Devika could now travel as a couple. This gave her the recognition and respectability she craved, the latter in particular being out of reach for most women in cinema.

While she was still enamoured of the spotlight that seemed to shine on Himansu, it soon became apparent to Devika that this life of glamour came at a huge price. The pressure was unrelenting. To raise money, to shoot, to design sets, to organise wardrobes, to get scripts ready for the actors—and she, as Himansu's wife, and as the art director (though she would not get any credit for it) had to do all of it. And it was difficult. She was barely twenty-one, while Himansu was a man of the world at thirty-seven. He had lived and loved, and was already a star, while she was struggling to learn. She was still fascinated by the possibilities of her new life, and their common interest in cinema brought them closer together. But her distance from her mother and her family continued to grow, and in many ways, made her more dependent on Himansu.

Dolat Kaka, who was close to the family, wrote from Madras later in the year, on 24 October 1929:

> Shortly after you left Madras we had a letter from your dear mother anxiously inquiring after you. She had read the announcement of your marriage in the '"Hindu" and wrote and asked Mr Kaka if he knew anything about it. I replied and told her this was true and that I had just met you for a few minutes before your train left Madras. Lately your mother wrote to me again, asking if we could manage to put her up for a day with us on her way to Bangalore. I gladly consented but unfortunately she could not come. In that letter too she inquired if we had any news from you but I am sorry to say that in replying I forgot to mention that I had heard from you.
>
> You naughty girl have you at all written to your mother since leaving India? I do hope so. As she is very anxious about you and wishes you will both always be very happy. (These are her own words).

Dolat Kaka enquired after Himansu, and had no problem asking about his cinematic career either:

> How do you like Germany? Do you prefer it to England? What film is Mr Rai producing at present? I wonder how long it will be, before we see the picture in India. I wish you both all success in your work. We saw Mr Rai in "Shiraz " a short time ago. He did his part very well.

It turned out that Dolat Kaka's family had seen *Shiraz* three times!

There was no doubt that Himansu was becoming a household name in India and building a reputation for himself. But he still needed money.

Just before the announcement of their wedding in the *Hindu*, he had written to Munshi Khajulall, who had been very helpful during the shooting of the films in Jaipur, for a loan.

The demands from his family had been growing once they discovered that Himansu was in India. Devika would later confess that these constant demands for money upset 'Golap', as Himansu was affectionately called. The only relative she was to grow very fond of was his mother, whom she found a remarkable lady (she would later stay with Devika and Himansu in Bombay). But Devika had little interest in the rest of his family, and the feeling of distrust would soon become mutual. In the years following their marriage, his father would write sometimes saying that the lack of news from Devika was puzzling. Though Himansu did send money, it was not enough for his parents. His father would write from Bengal on 3 April, 1933, letters similar to those he had written earlier:

> Unless you come, you cannot judge all these difficulties and indignities through which we are passing our days. You sent us a little money (£10) some months ago but even that could not be received due to some defects in directions and probably it has gone back to you. So please send what you can to your bank with instructions to remit the same to me...your mother is in the same condition as before—unable to move even her fingers— far less to write and her existence is a prolonged torture. She is only clinging to life for a sight of you. So if possible, hurry up and come home which may put courage in her failing health.
>
> Ma Devika has not written for a long time. Her letters are eagerly expected by your mother. So tell her to write to your mother. Before closing I would just request you to consider if the business you are doing is likely to be of any use to you or yours. We find that apparently nothing is coming out of it. Last time you were in India for about six months but the exigencies

of your work did not enable you to pay a short visit to your suffering mother. What is the good of such work we fail to understand. It is like a mirage which recedes as we approach it leading to where no one knows

Himansu tried to find other ways to support them. Rather than use the money given to him by BIF or UFA, he came to an agreement with Khajulall, 'to lend me the sum of two hundred pounds in four equal instalments of Fifty Pounds each... the first instalment of fifty pounds care of Messrs Thomas Cook & son, Marseilles, France before the middle of April 1929...'

Khajulall was to further promise to loan him ₹600, to be sent to his brother-in-law, Jagdish Chandra Sen, in three equal instalments on 1 April, 1 May and 1 June 1929. The money would be sent to Jagdish's home at Timarpur in Delhi, and was meant for Himansu's mother, who was unwell. He was to pay back the loan not later than 1 January 1930, along with 9 per cent interest.

Despite the shortage of money, Himansu and Devika were staying at the Hotel Metropole in Mysore at this time, a magnificent guest house built by the Maharaja of Mysore. Much of his correspondence was on letterheads stamped *A Throw of Dice*.

Unfortunately, the loan did not materialise, and the precarious existence that Devika feared most, with constant debts, was to carry on for years—the typical life of freelance producers, living by their wits. As *Vasantsena* was cancelled and *A Throw of Dice* would not do too well, either with the assault of the talkies, much of the £4000 Himansu was expecting would not be paid to him, either.

There were others who were keen to help, at least to send money to Himansu's family, from whom letters continued to come. One was the Delhi-based P.R. Tipnis, a well-known distributor and owner of cinemas. Tipnis, along with N.G. Chitre, the manager of Coronation Cinematography, and R.G. Torney, a Marathi director, were the creators of the first feature film to be made in India. *Pundalik*, released in 1912, was based on the life of a Marathi saint and apparently ran for two weeks. *Raja Harishchandra*, produced by Dadasahib Phalke and generally thought to be the first Indian film, was only produced the following year.

Writing to Himansu on 29 June 1929, Tipnis struck a very cordial and sympathetic note:

> I was really very happy to know that you were able to carry out your programme through your personal influence and the grace of the Almighty.
>
> I am in touch with Mr Khajulal. Also I was able to see your mother in Calcutta on my recent visit. You need not be anxious on her account. We shall manage to send at least ₹100/- per month till you are able to do something substantial for her. I hope Mr Khajulal will be able to remit you the £60/- in time.

Demonstrating the bonhomie that existed between filmmakers and exhibitors during that period, Tipnis added:

> I hope this will find you both in perfect happiness and peace. I await to hear good news. The papers had published the whole account of your marriage.

He added, in acknowledgement of Devika's charm:

> Please pay my respectful regards to your wife. Tell her that I remember [her] always when I see the bottle of Lavender salt left with me.

To stave off the loss of *Vasantsena*, Himansu had to harness all possible sources of revenue. But Devika was left with very bitter memories of the period between 1929 and 1931. By her own account, she had to pawn most of her old jewellery or anything of value to keep the home fires burning. She could not afford to buy anything new, and wore her clothes in an 'artistic' fashion to hide the fact that she possessed just a few. Inside the flat they had rented in Berlin (once they returned from India) she walked around barefoot; the sole pair of silk stockings she owned were worn only when she left the house. Years later, she would remember the feeling of hurt because 'Rai' never bought her anything, not even a saree or a piece of jewellery, or any presents at all. She spent any spare money they had on making sure that Himansu was well dressed for his meetings. Sometimes, when there was no money, they went hungry.

Those days in Germany were probably the most traumatic period of their lives. Hounded by penury, and by the insecurities of an alien land, they had to find the means to complete the editing of *A Throw of Dice*, while also learning how to go about making a talkie themselves. It must have particularly difficult for a young bride who remembered the days when she had been cosseted by her father, especially after she grew up and 'could dress up'. Perhaps there were moments when she felt she had lost everything by marrying a man who had promised her the moon but had given her very little, as yet.

Devika pawned all her jewellery, parting with some prized pieces and family heirlooms like an emerald-and-ruby ring. She was only in her twenties, but her resilience, despite having no one to confide in, was remarkable. Later, she would point to the difficulties of her life and credit them for helping her mature faster and enabling her to face even more grievous problems, using mostly her intellect and without any great display of emotion. She claimed too that she was willing to undergo any trauma, if at the end there was some compensation, some great gift from God.

Certainly, all her suffering at this stage in their lives would eventually lead her to a 'reward', even if it didn't seem possible at that time.

Himansu was still trying to borrow money—or get an advance towards future films. The fortunes of *A Throw of Dice*, though the film was well made, had been severely impacted by the talkies. It did not get the same response as his earlier films, and there was no option now but to explore the new world of 'tone' or 'sound films'. Could *Vasantsena* be converted into a talkie?

He tried knocking on the doors of UFA and BIF, but got almost identical replies which, later in 1930, he tried to turn to his advantage. As UFA was to write about *Shiraz* and *A Throw of Dice*:

> Both films had our approval from the point of view of the manuscript as well as from the technical point of view. The good opinion which we had in this respect as to the two films was also seen with film No. 1 (Shiraz)....We heard only satisfactory news about the business made with this film.
>
> If we did not obtain with film No. 2 the same experience regarding business and had not from abroad as good news as about the first film, we do not trace it back to the manuscript, nor to the technical execution of the shots. We are rather of opinion that the small financial success of the last film can almost only be attributed to the fact that when this film was presented, the interest of the public for silent films had diminished, in a terrifying manner on account of the sound film, so that the artistically and financial qualities, which no doubt are lying in this film, could no more come out in the normal way.

Expectations of a similar 'terrifying' reception at the cinema halls were expressed by BIF. Harry Bruce Woolfe had become a good friend and admired Himansu's spirit, but there was nothing he could do to help at this point. In his opinion, neither *Shiraz* nor *A Throw of Dice* had earned the expected revenue. As Harry pointed out, *Shiraz* had at least done well in the German market, but *A Throw of Dice* had come at a time when the talkies had completely 'spoilt' the market.

In England, according to Woolfe, both the films suffered because of the talkies, even though 'the Press were loud in their praises of both films'.

This sentence was bound to have pleased Himansu. As also the last two paragraphs of the letter:

> When it is possible for talking films to be made in India I shall be very pleased to re-open the question of further production.

Wishing you the best success in your efforts to create a national film industry in India.

Even after all the work had been completed on *A Throw of Dice*, Himansu and Devika continued to stay in Germany. In the UK, the Inland Revenue department had Himansu on their radar. Germany, on the other hand, was still pumping money into cinema, and he had the support of his production mates, Franz and Emile Schunemann. There was another important, and more troubling reason for his inability to leave Germany, but Devika was to discover that only later.

One day, at their hotel in Berlin, among Himansu's papers she found a copy of a letter he had written to a Miss Mary Hainlin. He had probably meant to file the letter away, as was his habit, but had mistakenly left it between the pages of a script that he had wanted Devika to read.

As Devika began to read the letter, she realised with a shock that her husband was addressing a former lover, who seemed to be threatening to take him to the police. And who on earth was Nilima?

Himansu had stepped out for a quick breakfast meeting, or so he had told her. She had seen him writing late into the night, and had even felt sorry for him for the amount of work he had to do. Now she wondered if he was sitting up late to write love letters to another woman. And they had been married less than four months! With trembling hands, she leafed through the correspondence. Her mind, sharp as ever, took over and did not allow the tears to flow. No, not yet.

Himansu had carefully noted on top of the letter:

Written 17th July, Wednesday 1929,...received on Saturday morning 13th July from Miss Mary Hainlin...her letter of 9th July from Munich.

The letter said:

Dear Mary

Your letter came today and I thank you for it. I intended writing to you before I was married, after I came to Berlin. But to write a real letter to you, not just a few lines. The stress and worry made it impossible because as you know the whole world of cinema has turned into a different kind of world and ideas which are at first very difficult to adjust especially to the kind of work I do. The newspaper publicity does not mean that I am doing well financially. On account of the sudden advent of tone films both of our films have no market in England and America, returns from Germany together with other countries will not cover the cost of this. If this were not the case there would not be any money difficulty at all with us. I returned to Europe fully expecting that there would be sufficient funds to make a good present to you & Nilima. To overcome these unexpected conditions it will take about a month or so after which I should be in a position to send you money regularly for Nilima. About doing an insurance for Nilima's future provision I should like to come down to Munich to make arrangements there, this also I cannot do at least before a month & a half. About Nilima of course I have all the dear little photos of her which my wife and I love. If you do not think it would be asking too much we would be happy to have one of her latest photographs—I know the child is with you and always has care—she seems to be growing up so sweetly. My wife and myself will come to Munich—we both want to love and be loved by little Nilima & also have your friendship through life in future. Don't imagine I forget your prayers—they have indeed helped me as they are the prayers of a good woman. Please send away all those worries of yours—I am not really as bad as I must seem to be—when one does not know all the circumstances of another, one is apt to judge a bit harshly for which I of course would not blame you. With kindest remembrances to your dear mother and the sincerest thoughts to you always and much love to Baby from my wife and myself.

Always, yours very sincerely,
HR

The letter fell from Devika's hands. The room seemed to be spinning around her. All the warnings Niranjan had tried to get her to heed, all those innuendoes she had heard Pramode laugh over before the expression on Himansu's face made him stop. The memories came right back. She had been worried, but hadn't realised that it was all true.

What an utter fool she had been. A naive twenty-one-year-old fool, married to a man who was the father of a child by another woman. She looked at the postmark on the envelope to check where the letters had come from. Munich. And he wanted both of them to go to Munich to 'love' the child!

Angry tears streamed down her face. Nilima! Couldn't he have chosen a different name at least? A German name? She was astonished that he did not even try to deny the existence of this child—which meant he had known about her even while they were getting married. No wonder he had begged her to marry him before they came to Germany—so that she did not have a chance to end their relationship when she found out about Mary.

Being Devika, she allowed her usual pragmatic self to take over. Wiping away the tears, she sat down to think. The relationship with Mary could not possibly have evolved in the last few years. He had been far too busy, and not just with work, for he was in London whenever it was possible, to spend time with her. This definitely dated back to before she had met him. Of that she was sure. He was obsessed with her, she knew. From his possessiveness and jealousy, it was evident that he could not live without her. There was no place in his life for another woman.

At least, she thought, as she narrowed her eyes and read through his letter again, he did not sound like he was going to abandon her for Mary and Nilima.

She heard the click of the door-latch being opened, and Himansu entered. He put away his coat and walked towards her, but stopped abruptly when he saw the letter in her hand, the tears still glinting on her cheeks. If it hadn't been so tragic, she would have laughed at his expression. But she had to make sure he was made to feel as humiliated as she was, and frightened enough to never keep anything from her again.

'Where…where did you find this?' He stumbled over his words.

'How could you keep it from me?' Her voice was trembling and he could sense the rage. This was the first big betrayal for her. She had not thought he was capable of hurting her, but this hurt had gone deep. He was sixteen, almost seventeen years older than her. How could he think she was just a puppet? How could he speak on her behalf? It was astounding. Here she had been working day and night, helping with the film, even pawning her jewellery for him, for their dream of making good international cinema.

'And all along, while we are struggling, fighting for our film, you are writing to her…about your child, while we have been trying desperately to make our film a success!'

Himansu tried to put an arm around her, but she pulled away, contempt written large on her face.

'Tell me the truth. Who is Mary, where did you meet her?'

Himansu's face was ashen. He looked much older than his thirty-eight years. Slowly, he began to tell her about how he had first arrived in Germany, with no friends and hardly any money. He had accompanied Niranjan on the trip, to raise funds for *The Light of Asia*. They were desperate, as the only way the film could be made was with European help. The studio that had showed interest was the German Emelka Konzern, and so they came to Munich for the meeting. He had just met Devika and was anxious to return, but Niranjan asked him to stay on till the deal was done.

At the cheap lodgings where he stayed, at Bayerstrasse in Munich, he met Maria Reim and her daughter, Mary Hainlin. Maria was a tailor, and Mary was young, attractive—and intrigued that he was visiting Emelka so often.

'And of course, she was charmed by you,' said Devika, shaking her head. 'When did you know she was going to have a baby?'

'Around the time I was leaving—she wanted money for the childbirth. I gave it to her because she wanted to keep the child.'

Mary's mother wept at her daughter's fate and asked for more money, which he continued to send. But as things became difficult, and a few years passed, he had stopped being regular with the payments. And then, of course, he and Devika were together.

'I didn't want to hurt anyone, so I gave them money whenever I could, thousands of Reichsmarks. But I promise you, I have no interest in the child.'

'Why didn't you tell me?' Devika could not contain her anger. She had no sympathy for his plight—she was only thinking of how she could save her marriage, and their reputation, without this blowing up into a scandal. She had little choice. She had to protect her family, which was now just Himansu and her, and all that they had invested in their career.

'It didn't seem important. She had stopped writing to me, and I thought she must have moved on, as people do—after all, she had no news of me.'

'And now—she read about you in the papers?'

'That's right.'

'And why this nice Indian name? Nilima?'

'It was her idea—you must believe me. For me, it's all just something in the past. I thought you would never get to know. Honestly, I didn't want to tell you.'

'Yes, of course—as we say, it was off-camera. It was never in the script.'

Himansu sat next to Devika and spoke in his most persuasive, softest voice. He knew only too well how to console broken-hearted women. But this time, there was a chance that his own heart would break.

Devika turned away from him and stared fixedly at the wall in front. How many women had he said all this to? Had her mother been right about the men in cinema? And actresses? She felt her face flush with anger. Could she trust him again? Ever?

'Please try to understand. I have to handle her with kid gloves, keep on her right side. I have to show an interest in Nilima, or she might do something foolish...Look at me. Don't I really care for you?' Himansu asked helplessly. He had found the perfect woman, but could his life with her be over already?

He tried again, a little harder. 'I'm in love with you. I want a career in cinema, just like you do. We both share the same goals, we are working hard to learn at UFA, and to make a film, act together, and then head back to India to set up a studio. I finally have you in my life, the kind of a person I always wanted to be with. You must believe me. Why would I want to settle down here in Germany? I love you, only you, Devika...'

She did not take his outstretched hand and, instead, walked over to the window, lighting a cigarette. She shook the match furiously, watching the tiny flame die out.

'And why did Pramode hint that you were already married? And Niranjan too?' she asked.

'Rubbish. Pramode—you know how he is about you. He wanted you to stay away from me. Yes, Mary came to meet me a few times at the studio. They would have seen her. But I can show you her letters. Nowhere does she claim to be my wife. And she knows about you and our marriage. I couldn't be rude to her because she threatened that she would go to the police if I didn't provide child support. I wanted to placate her. I wanted her to know that you know, so that she could not blackmail us. I included your name in the letter for that very reason.'

'You included my name without telling me? And when were you going to tell me, by the way?' Her voice was cold, but not angry anymore.

The fact that Mary had threatened to call the police made Devika realise the gravity of the situation. The consequences could be terrible. Himansu arrested! The headlines would mean the end of their dreams—and their lives. The embarrassment would be worse than anything else. They would have to hush this up together, as a team.

'I was trying to calm her down, tell her to wait till we were able to pay her. Once I had an understanding from her, I would have told you.' Himansu looked at her anxiously, hoping she would believe him.

Devika nodded. She *had* to believe him. He was her husband and she had to stand by him. For better or for worse. She controlled her emotions and thought through her options. She was broken-hearted right now—but she would mend. Walking out would help no one. She had painted herself into a corner with this grand romance, and had to support Himansu in this. She had no choice.

She absorbed the story and got into character. The narrative was an old one—he had been alone and lonely. Along came Mary Hainlin. She offered him comfort. A child was born. What could she, Devika, do but accept the situation?

Himansu lit a cigarette and gazed at her worriedly as she thought it through.

Yes, she told herself, she would stay with Himansu, but on her terms. She would not be able to respect him in the same way as before. The fact that he hadn't told her earlier made her own loyalty redundant. From now on, she could have secrets too. She had always believed in a level playing field.

But right now, she had to stick by his side. She did not want this woman Mary or her daughter Nilima to walk away with whatever money they were going to make or to ruin their careers. Somehow, this had to be made clear. Perhaps she could suggest a settlement, so that they would be free of the child and Mary forever.

She dried her tears and turned to face Himansu again.

'What should we do about it?'

Himansu put his arms around her tentatively and when she didn't move away, hugged her tight.

'Thank you. If we are together in this, it will be easier. And the whole problem can be sorted out. Remember, she is making demands on me as though we had an agreement, but we have no written agreement—we were never ever married!'

Devika shrugged her shoulders impatiently.

'Just good friends, as they say,' she said sarcastically. 'So how do we stop her from making demands?'

'We have to handle her very carefully, we have to come to a settlement. If it won't upset you too much, shall I show you the letter she has just sent me?'

Devika reached out and took the letter from Himansu. It was dated 18 July 1929. Mary had written:

Dear Himansu!

In reply to your letter from Berlin I am sending you a few pictures of Nilima. I wish you would at last now do your duty towards your child. It is a shame that you leave everything to a poor girl. If it is possible for you to go round the world with your wife, it must be possible to pay for your child. I have brought up the child so that it respects you and loves you like a father, even when you never behaved like one. When you were here last time you had Nilima in your arms, I thought you really would do what you promised; not to talk about things you promised me. You have absolutely ruined the happiness in our family and we all will curse you if you don't do your duty. I cannot feed and dress the child with your promises. You have promised ever so much and not done anything. If you can see our lives spoiled as it is, and without money then I wish that all my prayers should not help you and you should never have any success in life. You know I stood by you in your worst times and never made you spend any money, but now I want you to be a father to your child. Poor workmen pay for their children but nobody would expect a man like you would behave as you do. Last year you were here in Berlin and did not even come and see Nilima. I think it would go to anyone's heart to hear her ask and talk about her father. If she sees another child play with a doll or something else she says my daddy brings me the same when he comes. For two years we promised her that you would <u>send her a little piano</u> to play with. It would be easy for you to get one sent direct from the shop. I wonder whether this is asking too much. If you would send at least some money now and then, so we could see the goodwill, but only promises we cannot live on.

Yours,
Very sincerely,
Mary

The letter was followed by a postscript in a straggling handwriting that appeared far too grown-up to be that of little Nilima—'Kisses sends you your little Nilima'.

Devika folded the letter carefully and put it back in its envelope. She was relieved to read that Himansu, just as he had said, had not been to Berlin for almost two years. He was probably telling the truth when he maintained that he had only been there in 1925, when they were setting up the production team for *The Light of Asia*, and again, in 1926, when he had to return to sort out the distribution. He would not have spent much time with Mary in any case, because he was travelling between England, Germany, India, and even America. And Mary seemed to know that he had married Devika.

It was clear to her that Mary had no way of forcing Himansu to do anything. The only thing they had to worry about was the threat that she would go to the police if he did not give her money. In his last letter, Himansu had already clarified that he was going through a tough time and had no money to support Nilima. Devika was concerned that Mary would not be so easily pacified. Himansu was not so pessimistic, but it turned out that he was wrong.

Letter from Devika to Svetoslav

Dearest will you please love me on the ground, in the grass? Won't it be wonderful? We shall play and walk and pick flowers and have a bath or paddle in a stream & when we come to a nice beauty spot we shall put all the flowers round us and sit in the middle and look at the sky!! Won't that be wonderful and you have no idea dearest what it is to sit in the middle of heaps of flowers & look at the sky and around. It's just [that] well—well, you see I'll invite you and you see and tell me then. I've done it alone in many places and I thought that if I loved anyone at anytime really, we both would do it and then I think you would kiss me—or maybe I would and then we may get tired of sitting, and we would rest on the ground, our head on the flowers and—and still we would look at the sky—or would we not?

I don't think for a moment of any "what's" or "hows" as far as our future life is concerned, not at all. I just feel quite natural about it—quite happy & as if I should have been home long ago instead of wandering about here and there. It all seems silly to me, the whole past. Why I can't tell or explain, why I did it & meaningless it was!! Except that as you say it must have been Karma! Anyway now it's finished.

Bombay, 1945

8

KARMA
A Twist of Fate, 1930–1933

Devika was right.

Dealing with Mary Hainlin was not easy. More than Mary, it was her mother, Maria Reim, who decided to make it impossible for Himansu to forget them. They knew this was their last chance. Once he left Germany, it would be over.

Curiously, abortion was not an option Mary had considered. She had decided to keep the child, even as Hitler's theories of racial purity began to get a hearing in Germany. Perhaps the child was fair and her features Caucasian enough to not attract any adverse attention. The 'buxom' Mary, as Niranjan had described her, was determined to keep and raise the child regardless of Himansu's interest, or lack of it. She had appealed to his insecurities as a foreigner to get some monetary support from him, right from the time the child was born. Threats of public exposure had worked too. But now that he was married, Mary knew she would have to change her tactics.

She had been careful to give the child an Indian name. She had kept in touch with and met Himansu and his friends a few times, when he had come to Munich on work. Unfortunately, ever since he began working with UFA, with its offices in Berlin, he had stopped visiting Munich. Or, if he did, she did not know about it. She had not forgotten him though, and possibly followed his career as it developed through photographs and film reviews, most of them ecstatic, in the papers. The irony of it! Now, when it seemed he was making a lot of money, he was increasingly unattainable. If he went away and set up a studio in India, as he had kept saying he would, she would lose any hold on him, since he was clearly no longer interested in her or Nilima. Even in his letters, he was always careful to refer to Nilima as 'Miss Hainlin's daughter'.

And then, as a married man with a young wife, he might have other children. What would happen then? Even though he wrote that he and his wife wanted to love Nilima, he hadn't visited them in the last two years.

In the end, it wasn't all that difficult, really. The flustered letter from Himansu more than made up for her worry that he might not react. She had judged him correctly. Or rather, her mother had. Instead of trying to bluster his way out, he was going to negotiate. He was soft-hearted and could never knowingly hurt anyone. Especially a woman. Even if it did not suit him, he would try to do his best. It was all a part of his charm.

Within a few days, she had registered a case against him for abandoning his child. If anyone at the police station wondered at her child's strange name, she would tell them that Himansu was a rich film producer from India, who could well afford to pay but was trying to escape his responsibilities.

A police notice was promptly sent to Himansu, care of UFA, which he received on 26 July. It came as a shock to him. First the letter from Mary, and now this notice made him realise that he could not stave her off with the occasional sweetly-worded letter.

Devika's reaction surprised him. She was much more stoic than he had expected, while he remained nervous that she might leave him.

'I'll discuss this with Mary,' he promised her. 'I'll try to see that she doesn't ask for much... she'll understand that money is tight right now.'

Devika kept a calm exterior, trying to hide her anger and hurt, because of her fear of what might happen if Himansu was arrested.

There was no point being upset, she told herself. She had to stand by her man.

Settling down for a cup of tea with the now ubiquitous cigarette in her hand, she told him as calmly as she could, 'We have to keep on her right side. You going to jail will mean the end of everything. So let's send her another letter, sound contrite, tell her I look forward to seeing the child...' Devika could not bear the thought of Nilima, but she had little choice.

Himansu looked at her gratefully. At last he had someone by his side who was both empathic and intelligent. Having done everything on his own for so long, he deeply appreciated this partnership.

The difference between Devika and Mary was astonishing. One was the work-hardened daughter of a tailor, the other a beautiful great-grand-niece of a Nobel Laureate. One was accusatory, the other reconciliatory. While Mary wanted him to pay his dues, Devika's pride, he knew, would forbid her from asking him for anything. He sat with her now and composed a letter to Mary, which would hopefully buy him a little more time. He wrote:

> My dear Mary,
> I have just to thank you for your letter & also for the sweet pictures of Nilima. On reading your letter I understood that you quite appreciated my point of view and I was doing my very best to begin to send you payments for Nilima at an early date. But this morning I have received a notice from the Police regarding Nilima. I do not know its contents as I do not understand German & cannot think who to go to for the translation. I can however guess that you have decided & taken some legal steps against me. The purpose for which I am writing to you today is to ask you whether it is not possible even now to come to a friendly agreement between us. If we succeed to come to friendly agreement we will avoid a lot of unnecessary expense. For example court & lawyer expenses. I am today writing to Mr Osten about the matter. Will you kindly see him as soon as you receive this letter?

I am requesting Mr Osten to fix a reasonable sum which I should pay you monthly. If you decide to take the above step kindly at once arrange with the Police that the notice which I have received from them is immediately cancelled so that I do not take the help of lawyers. If you do decide not to come to a friendly agreement please write to me by return and Express Post. Tell Nilima I loved her photos & I shall send her piano very soon.

With best wishes to you,

Yours very sincerely
H. Rai

Himansu knew that, whatever the outcome of this letter, he urgently needed some local help. Someone who understood the language, and could also counter the determined combination of Maria Reim and Mary Hainlin. That was when he thought of Franz, the film director. Franz's brother, Peter Ostermayr, had set up Munchner Lichtspielkunst (MLK), later renamed Emelka. He had bought a plot of land south of Munich, at Grunwald Geiselgasteig, in the early 1900s, and developed the famous production studio in a short time. Both the brothers commanded respect and knew Himansu well, especially Franz, who had been to India and had met Devika, both before and after they were married.

Himansu had already mentioned his troubles with 'Miss Hainlin' to Franz. He wrote to him now, maintaining the friendly formality between them:

Dear Mr Osten

Thank you for your letter of the 22nd instant. Please do not be anxious for The Dice of Fate. The UFA copy was bad. But the Directors had not seen it.

Now I must write to you to do me a favour as my only friend in Germany. I have today received from the Police about Miss Hainlin's daughter's notice. I cannot read German therefore cannot understand what I must do. But I think Miss Hainlin has [taken] legal steps against me. I have today written to Miss Hainlin and asked her to make one agreement—without the police—in a friendly way. I have asked her to see you quickly. Kindly talk with her and arrange that I have to give her for her child a reasonable sum of money every month. I can undertake to pay her fifty marks every month.

To promise to pay her more is not right because I have no money now and never any definite income. If at any time it is possible to give more, I shall be happy—but this cannot be written in the contract. Dear Mr Osten I depend on you to do all you can to arrange this matter in such a way that I must not spend unnecessary money with the Police, Lawyers etc. ...

Even as he composed the letter, Himansu felt overwhelmed by the enormity of what could happen if things didn't work out. It was still early in the morning and Devika was asleep. She had been upset the last few days, wondering what to do in case he was arrested. And the scandal! It was making her unwell. They had been to see a doctor, who had said that it was merely nerves. She was a healthy young woman, he told them, and there was no reason to be upset, was there?

Devika had sat silently, almost in tears, wondering what the doctor would think if he knew that her husband had been accused of fathering another woman's child.

The matter, unfortunately, was to drag on for a few more months. Mary wrote to Himansu to say that she could not get in touch with Franz, as he was travelling. She also wrote that she had no idea what Franz had to do with 'our family affairs'. Perhaps she was a little nervous that people would get to know she had asked for money. What if Himansu backed off, or was able to persuade his friends to support him?

She wrote:

The notice you got from the police does not mean any troubles for you. You must only go there and sign a paper that you agree to pay 60 RM a month for Nilima. That is the sum which the guardianship has said you must pay. I do not think you will not agree with this, because I have some letters, where you say you would send 100 RM a month. If you go there and sign this, it will not cost you any solicitor or anything. If you don't go quick, they will perhaps write to the consulate and you can avoid that.

Once again, she reminded him about Nilima's 'little wish' for a little piano, and signed off with a scrawled sentence at the end of the letter, ostensibly written by the infant Nilima. 'Please send me soon my little piano. Kisses, Nilima.' It was difficult for anyone to believe that a child barely four years old would remember a man who had disappeared from her life more than two years ago or ask him for a piano. But in order to get the money from Himansu, it was important to keep up the emotional pressure. And so she repeated that she would be out of work soon, and that her mother was very angry with him for not fulfilling his duty.

Meanwhile, a sceptical Devika wondered if their relationship would ever recover from this blow. Himansu had shared all the letters exchanged between him and Mary with her. Reassuringly, she found that the letters contained no passion, no love, no reference to times spent together. Himansu never referred to Mary as his 'wife' or recalled a shared past. If ever there had been any emotion, it was buried under the weight of a brief relationship gone sour. The anger Mary displayed was not over him marrying Devika, nor was she asking him to come back. Her only complaint was that after becoming a successful actor and producer, he had not sent any money for childcare. She never even mentioned the word 'marriage'. Devika noted with relief that there was clearly no affection between them.

A few days later, Himansu received a response from Franz in his broken English.

My dear Mr Rai
    I come back today and find your letter. Many thanks for the good news about the picture. Has [it been] seen [by] the directors from the UFA and [do they] like the picture?

Dear Mr Rai please send the paper from the police registered to me. When I have the paper, I go to the police and speak about the matter with the police and Miss Hainlin. When I not have the paper I can not speak anything.

Dear Mr Rai send quick the paper, I am happy when I can do anything for you.

Many kindly regards to your wife and you,

From your
Franz Osten

By this time, Himansu had already received the letter from Mary requesting a monthly payment of 60 RM. Spotting an opportunity, he decided to offer a payment of 40 RM so that it might be possible to compromise at around 50 RM, as he had originally hoped.

He wrote on 31 July 1929:

Dear Mr Osten

Miss Hainlin says in her letter to me which I received yesterday that she will have 60 marks a month from me for Nilima. I wish you can arrange for not more than 40 marks a month. I am sending you an exact copy of the police notice. You will see from it that I am obliged to go to the police at eleven o'clock on 2nd Aug 29—no one at the Police office will understand English so I shall be obliged to take with me one lawyer. This will cost money—I have no money at all now so kindly arrange with the Munich police to send to the Police here & to me Telegrams saying that the matter has been settled & I must not go to the police here. These Telegrams will cost money. Kindly pay it yourself & let me know how much I owe you. I am not sending you the original notice. If the letter is lost somehow through the post and if I am obliged to go to the police at 11 o'clock on the 2nd Aug, I think I must have this paper with me.

Just to be on the safe side, he also gave a letter of authority to Franz so that he could negotiate on his behalf.

> I hereby authorise Mr Franz Osten to fix the amount which I should pay every month to Miss Hainlin for the upkeep of Nilima. I hereby agree that I shall undertake to pay Miss Hainlin accordingly.

When Mary did not respond to Franz, Himansu, encouraged by Devika, decided to get in touch with a lawyer. She felt that that the matter needed closure and it was important to work out a proper agreement, even though they could not really afford it.

Dr Max J. Loewenthal was the lawyer they hired to sort out the issue. He now fixed that they should meet in court on 26 August.

Himansu wrote to Franz once again, on 14 August 1929, and it was apparent from his tone that he was getting increasingly irritated with the whole affair. He referred to Mary as Hainlin, and said that he would 'ask the lawyer to say what you advised me over the Telephone, i.e., 40 marks a month. I shall let you know the result.'

He also informed him that 'it is announced that *The Dice of Fate* will be shown at the Universum, but the date is not yet decided upon. As soon as things are more definite I shall let you know.'

He wrote to Mary on the same day, and while he attempted to sound conciliatory, it was evident that he was upset. He referred to the court case as 'the unpleasant affair'. But he added that as soon as the court business was over, he would send Nilima her toy piano. He did not repeat his offer of a meeting, or express a desire to see the child to whom he sent 'our love and kisses'. He felt no real responsibility towards her. Since he was being pushed to pay, he would, and that was all.

> My dear Mary,
> I have not had an answer from you of my last letter. But Mr Osten telephoned me from Munich and explained nothing

could be done in the matter in Munich. I therefore went on the 2nd August 29 to the court. The court could not accept my undertaking unless I had with me a German Lawyer who knew English. I have to go to the court on or after Aug 24th (of the exact date I will be informed later) with such a lawyer. This will cost me 45 marks at least maybe more ultimately. This money could have been better spent had we been able to come to a friendly arrangement. However, I hope this unpleasant affair will [be] over soon & I shall be able to pay you for Nilima in future after that. As soon as the court business is over I shall try to send dear Nilima her toy piano. Kindly give her our love & kisses.

With best wishes from my wife and me

I am yours very sincerely

H. Rai

This was no fond father longing for his child. And he made sure to refer to his 'wife' so that Mary knew that Devika was aware of the circumstances.

He then requested his lawyer to write to Mary's mother, pointing out that not only had he paid 600 RM at the time of the child's birth, he had also paid many thousands in the intervening months and years. He requested that some sympathy be shown towards him.

Himansu was keen that Devika knew his side of the story. He wasn't a cruel monster who got women pregnant and then ran away. As a matter of fact, he had fulfilled his responsibility towards 'the child'.

And so Max J. Loewenthal wrote to Maria Reim on 31 August 1929:

Respected Frau Reim

I have been appointed as an interpreter to write to you on behalf of Mr Himansu Rai who has been examined in the court for the maintenance for your grandchild. You know that Mr Rai has paid not only for your daughter 600 Reichsmarks after the birth of the child but also a significant sum repeatedly for the maintenance of the child. This amounts to several thousands of Reichsmarks.

You can be assured that he has stopped payment because he himself is without an income in the recent times, and therefore there was no need for an invitation from the court for an explanation. It would have been better if you had believed in him.

Especially the sum of 60 RM per month that you have been demanding for the maintenance of the child is quite high for Berlin, as the court officer also recognised.

Mr Rai has declared during the hearing and I repeat personally in his name that he would be willing to pay an appropriate monthly amount and he will do it for September.

Moreover, he wants to settle this affair through a final settlement with you as the guardian (with the consent of your daughter). Herewith in his name I accept the offer you have made of 2500 RM.

Devika was relieved that a settlement had been reached, but she was also worried about how Himansu would arrange such a large sum of money.

At the UFA studio, meanwhile, Himansu and she were learning different aspects of direction, acting, make-up and so on, given the changing technology, and working out the details of the plot for a new film, tentatively called *Karma*. Himansu was keen that Devika make her screen debut in the film. After that, they had decided they would set up a production house and a fully equipped studio in India, based on what they had seen at UFA.

In the middle of all this, the 'Mary Hainlin affair' was proving to be a huge distraction. 'This is the time for us to be consolidating our knowledge and resources, not trying to pay off someone you had an affair with,' Devika chastised him, as they sat down for a frugal dinner of soup and bread. Fortunately, Himansu seemed quite sanguine, now that their lawyer had worked out a settlement with the mother and daughter.

Around this time, Himansu and Devika moved out of their temporary accommodation in the posh neighbourhood of Charlottenburg, named after Sophia Charlotte of Hanover, the Queen consort of Prussia, whose palace dominated the area. On 20 August 1929, they shifted into a flat they had rented for 200 RM from Ruth Puschel, at No. 17, Berlin Schmargendorf. It was a second-floor apartment, furnished, with a drawing room and a single bedroom for their use, while Ruth stayed in the second bedroom. They shared the kitchen and the bathroom, and the electricity, gas and water were included in the rent. They could use the telephone in their landlady's presence and be billed as per the duration of the phone call. It was clearly a sublet, as the actual landlady lived in Berlin.

To be on the safe side, and worried about an unexpected visit from Mary, they did not reveal their new address to anyone and the legal correspondence continued to be sent to the old address. As they inched towards a settlement, Maria Reim and Mary Hainlin may have panicked because they needed to ensure that Himansu was still in Berlin and would pay them. Armed with the police notice, the mother and daughter approached UFA, and through them, any studio that Himansu worked with, making them out to be legally responsible if Himansu defaulted. The studio managers, in turn, grew concerned because a court case or any monetary indictment could hold up all their work with him.

Other issues began to pile up too. Earlier, Himansu could enter and leave Germany without being noticed, but now, with the press recognising him as the 'Indian Valentino' and covering his films extensively, he could no longer travel incognito. And he had to be doubly careful that more people did not learn about his predicament—it could be the end of his career.

As she continued with her routine at UFA, Devika too had anxieties to deal with. Almost every week, she felt she was learning something new about her husband's colourful past and other matters. But with her usual pragmatism, she looked for solutions, rather than getting tied down by anger and recriminations.

∽∽∽

More trouble awaited Himansu, as he was soon to discover. Some of the women he had known rather well in the past found out that he was in Berlin but had not contacted them. Marie Lolgen, a rich widow who lived in Hanover and who had loaned him large sums of money, was astounded and hurt to learn that Himansu had returned from India a married man. What expectations he had aroused in her can only be understood from the strong words she used in her letters to him, asking for her money to be returned. She said she had generously given money to Himansu, even pawning her diamonds for him. But she had obviously not understood his true feelings and that he planned to marry someone else.

As she wrote to him on 30 July 1929:

Dear Mr Rai

I received your letter and was very astonished you are in Berlin. I don't know what shall I write to you.

But really you have not been like a gentleman to me: last year I have ask you to India for my money... have cried... have had so much trouble through you... must give for security all my diamonds to the bank and till now I have not got returns...

I have always given you my last money. Now I am not a rich widow because I have lost so much last year.

Always you write to me, you cannot pay back but I knew you have made much profit last year and this year you have paid for two persons voyage. I think it is better to pay the debt to a lady.

She ended by saying that she could not help him, and the film studios would be informed if he did not pay.

A few days later, she wrote to say that she had spoken to the director of her bank, who had also been a friend of her husband.

[He is] very angry, and will make absolute trouble for you. Do you know he is really a businessman and does not know in which condition we if [have] been.

I if [have] been always very indulgent and how you wrote generous [letters], but from Jan 29 on you have changed your friendship with me. You have not written, you have not repay and you have not been like a gentleman to me, when you write to me from your <u>big love</u>, affection and gratitude, and return to Germany with a wife. Where are your promises and love to me.

My goodness, you should expect that I have still an amount a [of] feeling for you.

In Germany we have a very bad word about such a man like you but I'll not write. You often has tell me the film actors are bad, yes, <u>now I know</u>! Please send all my letters to me and pictures which I have send you. I don't like it when you keep... yours I have to burn.

God will help me to forget this big insult which you have given to me.

I, the proud German lady which had helped you to roam high. You have forgotten, Taxis, nobody have given you anything, no one gives you ticket to London, nobody hospitality only I have had all this for you. And you write to me from gratitude, you must not to misuse such holy word...

Like Mary Hainlin, she too cursed him and wished to drain away any good fortune that might come his way.

Do you not think that all this matters shall bring you good luck...

We have made a contract, you have written in it, you will repay the loan till 1 of August 1927 at the latest and now it is 1 of Aug 1929.

From her plaintive letters, it is clear that Himansu had taken advantage of her loneliness as a widow and led her to believe there was 'big love' between them.

It was a common modus operandi, perhaps no different from that adopted by other good-looking men of limited means, who were ambitious enough to use any vulnerable acquaintance, only to move on once their purpose had been served. The only difference seemed to be that Himansu, with his unwavering politeness and apparent good manners, presented himself as someone who would look after the interests of those who were close to him. No matter how difficult, he always tried to reach a 'settlement'.

Poor Marie Lolgen, however, unlike Mary Hainlin, could not bring herself to ask for anything more than what he owed her. Luckily, she had had the good sense to get him to sign contracts and so there was a written account of what he owed her, not just their 'big love'. Like Mary, she was worried that Himansu might leave for India at any time, and so she decided to go to court and get an order against him.

The court order would have been difficult for Himansu to avoid, as the message was unequivocal:

Urgent Registered Letter
To the Court Berlin Central
    An urgent application for the grant of arrest from widow Marie Lolgen, Hanover, Hohenzollern Strasse 45
    Jurists Dr Stenman Goldschmidt and Dr Suehr
    Against
    Mr Himansu Rai at present at Berlin NW Jagov Strasse 44 c/o Klitsch
    Through our power of attorney we request that the court order the personal arrest as well as attach the property of the debtor for the payment due of RM 2771.45 as well as the cost of RM700, as he has also cheated the Deutsche Bank Centrale in Berlin and the costs below as well.
    Mrs Lolgen has lent the amount of RM4123.50 and after the interest etc is taken into account, plus the amount returned the still pending amount is RM 2771.45.
    Basically she has brought a court order since the man is an actor and an Indian citizen and travelling abroad constantly, he

is engaged in the production of films. At present he is residing in Germany for a short while. He can travel abroad any time.

As far as the litigant knows the accused has account in the Central branch of the Deutchse Bank in Berlin—or at least had one in Sept 1928 so it is to be assumed that he still has this account today.

So the account should be attached and an order for his arrest issued urgently, because it is not certain the litigant will get her money normally.

A paper for a debt of RM 3600 had been signed on 13th Dec, 1926 and the original has been submitted to the court.

There have been translations of this signed document and one can see from the signatures that the accused lives abroad in Nawagram Dacca in India.

The debt should have been returned in 1 August 1927.

Not surprisingly, this notice, coming at around the same time as the police notice from Mary Hainlin, was shattering for Himansu and Devika. She had stumbled upon the problem of Mary Hainlin by accident, and now she could see, reading between the lines, that Marie Lolgen too had enjoyed a physical relationship with Himansu. She had paid for his lifestyle, his taxi rides, his tickets to London, and given him a generous loan so he could make his film. What kind of exploitative man had she married? Young enough to be heartbroken, she had little choice but to believe that Himansu had not meant to hurt anyone, as he now told her. He had intended to return all the money he had borrowed from Marie Lolgen, he said.

It made her uneasy. Not just emotionally but also financially, as she had always been very careful with her money. She continued to keep detailed accounts and tried to save what she could. She skipped a meal if required, stayed hungry if necessary. This new demand from Marie Lolgen suggested that there could be other claimants as well. How would they manage? Her love for Himansu began to be overshadowed by mistrust. And all along, they had to keep going to the UFA studio where these affairs had to be kept a secret from everyone else. Even as a child, she had been aware that, as an Indian in a foreign land, she had to hold her head high. Now, as a married woman, she had to ensure that their dignity as a couple was intact. Would that be possible?

She tried to be sympathetic because she could see how hard Himansu had to struggle. But she couldn't help the growing nervousness. What if the child were to suddenly show up? How would she deal with her? Or what if she were to appear years later? What if Marie Lolgen came to the studio demanding her money?

Aware of her growing anxiety, and probably heeding the doctor's advice to her to relax, Himansu whisked Devika off to Switzerland on work, combined with a brief holiday. There had been a few requests for her to perform at events, and Himansu thought it would be a good idea to introduce her to a wider audience. He had started his career on stage, and believed that it gave confidence to actors, providing a smooth transition to the screen. His own screen debut had been effortless and he wanted the same for Devika. He was also conscious of the fact that while she may have experienced some difficulties when they were shooting in India and later in Germany—she had never known real despair or deprivation. And here she was, having to deal with his creditors and past lovers.

◈

Tara Ali Baig, the social reformer and writer who was a young girl studying in Switzerland at the time—and would eventually become the president of the International Union of Child Welfare, in Geneva—remembered the first sight of Devika on stage and the excitement of hearing that the 'first Indian film was to be shown in a theatre in Lausanne. It was not a talkie as those were to come later. The producer's beautiful young wife Devika Rani was going to make a personal appearance.' Though she was just a little girl at the time, she was so excited at the prospect of seeing an Indian film that her mother indulged her.

Devika's dance performance after the film, probably *A Throw of Dice*, made the young girl's 'heart race'. Tara was to write later in her memoir:

> I was back in India! It was very possible that her dance was the kind of mixture Anna Pavlova had conceived of in her Indian ballet, more exotic than classical, as this was before Bharat Natyam and other ancient dance forms were revived in India. It was probably nothing more than graceful movements, using some faintly remembered techniques of abhinaya, as well as the language of the hands. To the East at the time and in insular Switzerland, this could well represent the beautiful unknown. In those days a sari was seldom seen in Switzerland.

Tara remembered Devika as 'an other-worldly beauty'. When she appeared on stage in Switzerland, people whispered, '*Mon dieu, quelle est belle*', 'How wonderful to see something like this from mystic India'.

> She had large dark eyes and black hair, a round Bengali face the colour of ivory, and delicately modelled features. People talk about bone structures that retain beauty even after sixty. Devika had that kind of face and a smile that lit up her eyes, so that she almost beamed light at you in a curious way; and you could forget her carefully coiffed hair, the little kiss curls so fashionable then, and the gold jewellery around the neck, all unnecessary ornamentation that never could overshadow her natural beauty.

On this tour through European towns, Devika also featured in a mime show which was a curtain raiser for the film. Himansu had been right—this exposure to an adoring audience was precisely the tonic Devika needed. She was able to showcase her skills and got a glimpse of what it might be like if she were to become an actress.

On their way back, Himansu thought about all that lay ahead of them, and how he could make Devika's dreams come true.

Undoubtedly, there were a few people who hoped that their relationship would be destroyed. He would have to convince her that all his faults lay in the past, that he had changed after meeting her.

Help arrived from unexpected quarters. Even though Marie Lolgen was angry about being let down and insulted by Himansu, she admitted ruefully in a letter dated 4 August 1929:

> I must help you once again, even if I myself does not like it, but I have often helped you without thinking of myself so I will do it once again.

She proceeded to tell him how to respond to the court order. She also explained:

> [In January 1929] I wrote to you to India, you shall repay at least 100 pounds since I must sell my shares which I have to pledge for the money I have given you. You have not written and I would not sell the shares, because it is been a bad time, nobody have had money, so I must give for security our contract and many diamonds of my...

As he had not answered her letter which had been sent to him in India, 'therefore I have had so very much troubled for business and myself', she had no option but to send him the notice for the court order.

It was clear that the notice had been sent after Marie Lolgen had written to him over and over again for her money, which she required especially to retrieve her diamonds from the bank. Since his film, *A Throw of Dice,* was being screened in Germany, he must have the money to pay her back, or so Marie presumed.

On 8 August 1929, he said that he would pay her back by January 1930. It might seem a long time away, but he genuinely hoped that it would happen. He wrote:

> According to my contract with the British Instructional Studio, Welwyn Garden City, in the county of Hertfordshire of England,

I am entitled to receive a sum equivalent to five per cent of the said company's receipts, in respect of the film, 'Shiraz'.

He went on to add:

[I will instruct the Deutsche Bank] to pay to your account in Dresdner Bank at Hanover monies received from the British Instructional Films Ltd in the above manner until my indebtedness to you on account of the loan you had given me is fully cleared.

If there was still anything pending, he assured her, he would pay it out of the £500 he was going to receive from UFA for the production of *Vasantsena*.

She wrote to him on 13 October 1929, pointing out yet again that she did not want to be so tough with him, but her lawyer advised it. It was to Himansu's benefit that even those he let down appeared to want to help him. Devika, by now, was resigned to this reality.

Marie wrote:

Dear friend
    After long time I return home, and till now I have not received the copy of the letter to the English firm which you would send me.
    My lawyer also return to Hanover after his holiday and so I have spoken with him our settlement.
    What can I do he is not satisfied with your letter you have given me, and he will make you more trouble, unless do you not give me another security to the UFA before you leave Britain. So I cannot do anything, you must send me another the next week. The lawyer will wait till the 19 of October but if I [have] not received a letter like this (enclosed) he will again write to the court of Justice and he will prevent that you start for India.
    You need not have sorrow that the UFA think bad about you, you cede money to a lady...
    But now you must give my lawyer the satisfaction in the next days. I am sorry I must again write you such letter.

But despite her slightly contrite tone, she was not above threatening him.

> It is a bad trouble in which you can come, therefore I ask you send immediately the letter which the lawyers wish.
>
> I hope your business is better now. Your film has started and make big success. I send a newspaper enclosed.
>
> I trust you are keeping good health I remain,
>
> your
> Marie L.

Meanwhile, Himansu received the court order asking him to make the payment to Marie. He promptly wrote back on 22 November 1929:

> Dear Madam Lolgen,
>
> I am very much surprised to find on my return from Switzerland, a court order against me to make you certain payments. This is as you know contrary to the undertaking you had given me on 8th August, 1929. Will you kindly write to me and let me know what I have to do under this circumstance? I am on my part making every effort to meet my obligations to you on the appointed day of our last agreement.
>
> With kind regards, I remain,
>
> Yours sincerely
> Himansu Rai

It was in this context that she wrote in another letter in December 1929, as Himansu kept trying to push the date of payment to the following year:

> Last month you have earned a little money and I think you can send to me perhaps 600 or 1000 marks, this is the amount what I need necessary till 1 of Jan.

Himansu was literally fire-fighting. But with his usual chutzpah, he continued to hunt for new pastures where he could find fresh work, as it seemed obvious that UFA would not be able to produce *Vasantsena*. Money had to be generated. He had to swing a deal somehow, somewhere.

Devika too began to look for work, but nothing interesting came her way, apart from the performances in Switzerland. Most people wanted to see her on screen before they would give her a break. But she managed to work for some time on Eric Pommer's film set at UFA, and gained some more valuable experience.

Finally, Himansu's mounting financial troubles were resolved through what appears to have been a stroke of luck, though it may equally have been a complicated deal between UFA and a French company.

A 'wonderful offer' came his way from Paris, from the Alliance Cinematographique Europeenne (ACE) based in Il Bis Rue Volney, to become a producer and principal actor for a film to be made between 15 January 1930 and 30 April 1930. Miraculously, they said they would pay him 'three thousand English pounds' and a part of that amount could be paid immediately.

> On account as a part payment you receive a sum of engl £ 1400 (Fourteen hundred English pounds) today.
>
> You have no right for employment and no rights for claims in case this film should not be produced for any reason whatsoever.
>
> In case we do not call upon you to begin work in connection with this film latest by January 31st, 1930, it should be understood that this film will not be produced; thereupon we will not be under any obligation to pay you more than a total of Engl £1400/- which you have received from us today and we will not be entitled to call upon your services in any way in connection with this agreement afterwards.

Interestingly, when Himansu received the money, he had to almost immediately deposit RM5,000 back with the ACE as a surety against the warrant of distress issued by Nilima Hainlin through her mother Mary Hainlin. And then, on 31 December itself, UFA transferred the liability occurring from the claim of Nilima Hainlin to the Paris-based company.

The fact that all the letters were issued on the same day points to an agreement between the parties that this was a route for Himansu to receive payments outside Germany, so that Mary Hainlin could not lay claim to his earnings. Only a small amount from the total £1,400 to be paid to him was kept as a deposit to settle any further claims. Now that no income was being generated in Germany and UFA had transferred the liability to a foreign entity, it would become far more difficult, and expensive, for Mary Hainlin to approach Himansu with further monetary demands.

The 'miraculous' offer from ACE was clearly just a front; UFA had agreed to bail Himansu out. And the reason they agreed to make this settlement through ACE was not because they suddenly wanted to be nice to him, but because he had taken them to the labour court in Berlin over non-fulfilment of their contract to produce *Vasantsena*. That could have turned into an expensive affair with serious ramifications for the company, so they worked out a financially viable settlement which suited both sides. Himansu got a much needed reprieve and UFA, after having promised to pay £2,000 to Himansu for *Vasantsena*, ended up paying only £1,400. However, after all the trouble and the embarrassment, any plans of them working together in the future would have been completely ruled out. Himansu took a calculated risk as he must have realised that his prospects in Germany were looking increasingly grim, at least for the present.

'Right now, it's only three Marys—Mary Hainlin, Maria Reim and Marie Lolgen, who knows which other Mary will suddenly appear?' Devika said to him bitterly, half joking. She was relieved that they were finally leaving Germany.

Himansu was of the opinion that the rise of Hitler and the changed environment endangered any future prospects of an Indian filmmaker in Germany. It would be easier to take German technicians to India. He wrote to UFA now, to say that he had withdrawn his case in the labour court due to the changed circumstances:

> More especially due to the appearance of the sound film you would not be under obligation to produce the film mentioned in the agreement of September 7th, 1928.

He added:

> In consideration that you fully relieve me of the obligation of carrying out the above contract I herewith relieve you of any claims which may be brought against you by any person or company on the plea that such person or company were engaged by me as artist or for any other service in connection with the production of 'VASANTSENA' which you had intended to make in India under my charge. I guarantee that I have not made contracts in your name.
>
> Any claims the director Franz OSTEN may have are to be settled by you.
>
> I also guarantee that no claim of whatever nature will be brought against you by reason of the attachment and the warrant of distress issued by the Amtsgericht Berlin/Mitte in a suit the infant Nilima Hainlin has brought against me on September 11th, 1929.

UFA similarly issued a letter acknowledging that they were no longer liable for either the film or the warrant of distress, and the amount of 5,000 RM that Himansu was depositing with ACE would be returned to him once the Nilima Hainlin matter was resolved. From the ease of understanding all around, it appears that UFA may have paid Himansu all pending dues through ACE.

Armed with a fresh infusion of funds, Himansu could now easily deal with the two creditors who were knocking on his door. He contacted the German cinematographer Emil Schunemann and requested him to meet both Maria Reim and Marie Lolgen so the payments could be made to them as final settlements.

On 7 January 1930, Marie Lolgen signed the agreement which would free Himansu.

> I declare herewith that I have received from Mr Emil Schunemann for Mr Himansu Rai 3500 RM (three thousand five hundred Reichsmark).
> The borrowed amount along with in the interest and the court costs have been received. I declare that with this all my demands against Mr Himansu Rai have been fulfilled and I do not have any more demands also from Mr Schunemann of any kind. The 5000 RM that I received from Mr Himansu against the British Instructional, London I now return back to him. The payment order of 3rd November 1929 is null and void.
>
> Berlin 7th January 1930
> Signed by Mrs Marie Lolgen

Of course, the 5,000 RM from BIF was only on paper. Finally now, the matter with Marie Lolgen was closed.

Now it was time for the more difficult negotiation with Maria Reim, Mary Hainlin's mother. Fortunately for Himansu, she had finally agreed to a sum of 2,900 Reichsmark after an initial talk of 2,500 Reichsmark. Having consented to proceeding with a settlement at the Munich court on 7 January 1930, Maria Reim now met Emil Schunemann on 9 January and accepted the promised 2,900 RM. The meeting took place at Hotel Hermes, in Berlin, where Maria Reim was staying.

The receipt she signed said:

> I, the guardian of the child Nilima Hainlin, endorse that I have received from Mr Schunemann 2900 RM in the name of Mr Himansu Rai.

This was followed by the signing of a settlement between Himansu and Mary's mother, Maria Reim:

Settlement

Between Mr Himansu Ray in Berlin-Charlottenburg, Windscheidstr 39, and the minor Nilima Hainlin legally represented by Mrs Maria Reim, a woman's tailor in Munich Bayerstrasse 91.

The legal maintenance of Nilima against Himansu Rai and in respect for the past as well as the future, the following contract has been made.

Himansu Rai pays Maria Reim on behalf of Nilima Hainlin in Munich the sum of RM 2900.

The payment has to follow as soon as Mr Himansu Rai gets the order from the guardianship court. The court which appoints the guardians will give him the final decision on the settlement.

Along with the court order Himansu Rai has to give a written declaration to the legal guardian—that he has no claims to the third party mentioned in the arrest order.

An arrest order from Berlin Central court has been delivered on 11th Sept 1929, with the involvement of the third party.

Through this settlement all the claims of the minor Nilima Hainlin against Mr Himansu Rai irrespective of what these claims are or the contents they have now been settled.

This settlement will be in place when the court orders are handed over and not later than 31st January 1930.

Himansu Rai
Maria Reim
Berlin, 9th Jan 1930

They also signed another agreement, which stated that no further claims would be made on Himansu regardless of the court order:

The minor Miss Nilima Hainlin represented by the undersigned guardian Frau Maria Reim has registered a case against Mr Himansu Rai in the court of Berlin Central on 11th September

1929. The claims of the arrest order and the search orders have been settled through this settlement. The undersigned guardian declares herewith against the so called third party in the arrest order, that she gives up her rights that may arise out of this order against this third party.

    Munich 9th January, 1930
    Maria Reim
    Himansu Rai

The settlement amounts were given by Emil Schunemann to Maria Reim on the spot, even though the receipts were dated two days after he handed over the money to her in Berlin.

DR. MAX J. LOEWENTHAL
RECHTSANWALT UND NOTAR
Für den Kammergerichtsbezirk
allgemein vereidigter Dolmetscher
der englischen Sprache

Sprechzeit:
Nachmittags 3.30–5.30
außer Sonnabends.

BERLIN W 50, den November 11th, 192(?)
BUDAPESTER STRASSE 17
TELEFON: B4 BAVARIA 5121

Mr.
    Himansu Rai

               Charlottenburg,
               Windscheidstr. 39.

Dear Mr. Rai!

    Miss Hainlin, during a short stay at Berlin, called on me, and I had a conversation with her regarding the possibility of a compromise, which, I should think, could be favourably brought about. –

    If you want me to do anything in the matter, kindly call some afternoon.

                      Very truly Yours

                      Rechtsanwalt.

Having bought some peace and quiet, Himansu began to start looking for remunerative work. While his court case against UFA had yielded good results, he would need to return to England to produce his next film. He also had to make sure that his young and very beautiful wife was more pleasantly occupied. She was already getting restless, and her anxieties needed to be assuaged.

What he did not know was that the wounds that he had caused Devika would not heal for a very long time. As always, she hid the pain deep within her.

Letter from Devika to Svetoslav

Emotion would not allow me to listen to reason, the pain was so much that even human tears did not relieve—it was a cutting throbbing pain that dulled every other sense which filled [me]—it was like the pain a wild animal feels...to suffer without being able to express. That's why I sat all night—all through sat on the ground straight and after an hour first opened Koran Shareef, then Gita, then the Holy Bible for a message, for a lead to understand my wrong, which had to be righted mentally. Fundamentally—at the root—the structure of me had a foundation, which was lost, which was buried, which I personally took the trouble to hide all these long years—yes hide from eyes who could not see and now when I feel life, when I feel reborn—I myself was hiding it from myself, unknown to me...

Bombay, 1945

9

HIMANSURAI INDO-INTERNATIONAL TALKIES LTD, 1930s

In the summer of 1932, close to two years after their marriage had been solemnised by Arya Samaj rites in India, it was registered at St George's, Hanover Square, an eighteenth-century Anglican church in central London.

Having laid to rest some of the ghosts of the past, it was time for Himansu and Devika to start a fresh production, this time as a team. Devika was no longer 'under training', or working behind the scenes, as in *A Throw of Dice*, their last film with the German studios. Her steadfast support of Himansu during the difficult moments with Mary Hainlin had changed the nature of their relationship. And she was no longer the simple, naïve girl he had married. She had emerged from the crisis as a mature woman who could take her husband's past indiscretions in her stride. Only twenty-three, she had already dealt with betrayal, heartbreak and penury. Now at last, she was looking forward to launching her own career in cinema. Her impeccable training, her ability to sing, her beauty and confidence, all made her a natural in front of the camera. Himanshu and Devika had discovered this during their time in Germany.

They returned to London with the intention of making a talkie starring Devika opposite Himansu. However, all the scripts and ideas they had worked on earlier were with silent cinema in mind.

Having shelved *Vasantsena*, they began scouting for a script that could showcase Devika's talents.

Unlike in the past, production houses appeared excited to see Devika. She was looking beautiful. Her English was excellent and the special singing lessons she had taken had revealed a magnificent voice.

But the issues remained the same. The film had to drip with Orientalism, and had to primarily appeal to the British and the Western world, where Himansu was already known as an actor and producer. This would ensure some funding from the UK as well as India. Himansu began to look for suitable subjects and examined new ideas proposed by Devika and others. Some of the scenarios he tested were fairly elaborate, based on novels such as *The Snake Charmer* by Alfred Schirokauer, a well-known Jewish author and scriptwriter who died young in Amsterdam after escaping from Germany in the early days of the Third Reich.

An extract from the synopsis of *The Snake Charmer*, which had been obtained on 2 September 1930 from 'Miss Woolfe', perhaps a relation of Harry Bruce Woolfe, shows that it was written with Devika in mind:

> Devika Rani the daughter of a Brahmin professor of high standing in Calcutta had sacrificed religion, friends and family for the sake of Ram Das a snake charmer, whose skill and ability had obtained for him a great name throughout in theatrical world of Europe. During their honeymoon journey to Europe, Ram Das inspired by their great happiness composed the most wonderful melody which he dedicated to his young wife. Then the tragedy occurred, Ram Das disappeared.... [She learnt] that her husband had gone on shore [they were on a ship during their honeymoon, en route to Paris] accompanied by one of the passengers, a certain Miss Gates, and that neither had returned.
>
> Devika was in despair. Throughout the whole of that long weary journey she lay in her cabin and prayed and waited for Ram Das in whom she had not lost her trust.

Finally, according to the script, she manages to get into Paris with her basket of snakes and without a passport, thanks to an old sailor who is enchanted with the way she plays her flute at night on the ship. She is smuggled into the city, dressed like a 'lad'. Many more fantastical things happen to her before it is revealed that she is actually a woman, and is reunited with Ram Das.

Fortunately, this film never got made, as was the case with another script, again written with Devika in mind. The story was set in Calcutta under colonial rule. In this, too, Devika Rani was the main protagonist, whose father is accidentally killed during an anti-British protest by the man she loves. It was equally melodramatic and complex.

The film that eventually did get made was based on a treatment written by none other than Devika. It was to be called *The Song of the Serpent* or *Karma*, and strangely, the credit which should have been given to her went to Dewan Sharar, who was helping Himansu with the film production. Perhaps it was thought that she should focus on the acting and leave the storyline to Sharar.

However, unable to hide the reality for too long, an impressed Himansu was to write in a letter on 14 September 1932 to a friend who liked the treatment of *Song of the Serpent*:

> Here is a secret which I am now going to let out—the treatment was done by Devika all on her own in three hours, working at a stretch one evening. None of us believed before she could do it—neither did she herself until it was produced. I find it is perfect and we mean to stick to it.

Devika's contribution as the writer of their breakthrough film would never be publicly revealed, and like many things she did with Himansu for the promotion of cinema, this too would get buried under the weight of patriarchy which persisted at the time. Possibly, had she been asked, she could have written the entire script itself. She had the confidence and the skill. But she was being promoted as an actress, and it was not expected that an actress would write a treatment or a script.

Dewan Sharar (who would later go on to earn fame with films like *Dr Kotnis ki Amar Kahani* in 1946) was at the time a young man, and completely in awe of Himansu. He had gained a reputation in India as a writer and was helping Himansu raise funds in Germany and Britain for his first talkie. Giving Sharar credit for the story may have enabled Himansu to make payments to him for the work he was to do on the production of *Karma*. Initially, the team consisted of just Devika, Himansu and Sharar—they would later be joined by Sir Richard Temple in London and Sir Chimanlal Setalvad in India.

Devika's treatment was an interesting mix of socialist ideology and superstition colliding with the so-called modernity. It was also one of the first films that suggested that wild animals should not be hunted. According to the story, it was only under pressure that the princess of Sitapur agreed to allow a tiger hunt in her kingdom, even though it would upset her people. Ultimately, the punishment for killing a tiger was linked to the near-death of her love, a prince from a neighbouring kingdom, who would be played by Himansu.

Of course, there were differences in Devika's treatment and the screen version. For instance, in the opening scene, as written by her, the Indian princess is playing tennis and receives great applause, while the next scene shows the prince being applauded for scoring a century for Sussex. Then they are both transported (oh, the joys of cinematic treatment!) to an Indian jungle where 'the princess of Sitapur is finishing her song on a beautiful lake'. The prince comments, 'We knew you could play tennis but who can say that the maidens of Sitapur cannot sing? Yes, the sweetest voice I have ever heard!'

In the final cut, instead of tennis and cricket, we have the song on the lake, followed by a romantic interlude with Devika, Himansu and a squirrel, in a jungle near the lake. The real reason for changing the script was that all the outdoor scenes were shot in India and the indoor scenes were re-created once the team returned to England. This led to the final version being rewritten according to the link shots filmed in the British studio.

Nonetheless, some of the scenes written by Devika were incorporated into the final film, such as the one in which Himansu is lying on the ground, ostensibly bitten by a snake, whereupon she kisses him and witnesses his miraculous recovery. The cure and the words of the snake charmer, as written by Devika, remain in the film:

> 'Do not fear great lady, he will recover. I have a cure—the same snake will bite him. I will play my melodies and will attract that very snake. It is an old cure,' the snake charmer tells her.
>
> The snake charmer tries many snakes, and at last gets the right one. It crawls towards the Prince's leg, and to her horror the Princess sees the snake biting the Prince—she screams and the snake charmer gently removes the snake saying, 'Look Great Lady, his eyelids move.'
>
> 'Yes,' says the Princess and without restraint embraces the Prince, uttering at the same time sweet endearments.

It was this scene, in which Himansu lies supine on the ground while Devika 'without restraint' showers kisses upon him, which got written about as 'the longest kiss in Indian cinema'. It was a pretty one-sided kiss, as Himansu lies knocked out by the snake bite, and it lasted all of two minutes. For some reason, most people imagined it was at least five minutes long. Perhaps, to the shocked audience of the time, it seemed fairly lengthy.

Karma brought Devika the fame she had longed for. All the training and observation that she had put herself through while working on *A Throw of Dice*, and later in Germany, created a new star for the screen. There was no doubt that she was a natural, as the accolades pouring in confirmed.

The film credits rolled as 'A Love Drama of an Indian Princess by Dewan Sharar' set in the 'present day'. It was a joint production between Himansurai Indo-International Talkies Ltd, Bombay and the Indian and British Production Ltd, London. Himansurai Indo-International Talkies (with the appropriate acronym 'HIT') was the new production company that Himansu and Devika had launched.

It was their first step towards making films independently and also setting up a studio in India.

They had been careful to get a British director, J.L. Freer Hunt, who also wrote the lyrics, as well as a British dialogue writer, Rupert Downing. The camera work was done jointly by their longtime German associates, Emil Schunemann and Desmond C. Dickinson. Similarly, the production team was British and German—Eric Donaldson and Folke Reich. The original music compositions were by Ernst Broadhurst and Roy Douglas. Fortunately for Himansu, these were the inter-war years when the Germans and the British were still able to work together.

While the exterior shots were all taken in India, the post-production and other recordings were done at Stoll Studios in Cricklewood, London. The Germans were in charge of filming in India, while the British team did the indoor shoots and the post-production work.

As with all of Himansu's previous films, this too was lavishly filmed in India, with the permission of His Highness, the Maharawat of Pratapgarh. There were plenty of tigers, snakes and elephants, and royalty, to create interest in the film, and of course, in the lead were the radiant Devika Rani and the slightly less impressive Himansu Rai.

Himansu had managed to raise money for the film partly through the good offices of the chairman of his newly launched production company, HIT. The brilliant, well known and very wealthy Bombay-based lawyer Sir Chimanlal Setalvad had been persuaded to come aboard by Himansu over several meetings. But the money was mostly raised through Himansu's inexorable energy—and his ability to reach out to prominent members of the Indian and British communities.

Some of them would become ardent admirers of Devika Rani, such as Lt Col Sir Richard Temple. Sir Richard became so closely associated with the couple that he even moved to India to become a director at HIT. He would play a crucial role in the setting up of Bombay Talkies, as well as its survival under Devika a decade later. But his role would go largely unrecognised as he was not a very assertive man. Even his family in England knew little about his involvement with the studio or with Devika and Himansu, and whenever the story of Bombay Talkies is told, there is hardly any reference to him, though he rescued the studio at least twice from serious financial trouble. Not only that, his British connections in India opened many doors for the Rais.

Sir Richard's grandfather had a distinguished career in India, joining the Bengal Civil Service in 1846, and later serving on the Governor General's council. He was the Lieutenant Governor of Bengal from 1874 to 1876 and the Governor of Bombay from 1877 to 1880. The first baronet was also an MP for Evesham and later, Kingston Surrey.

His son, the second baronet, Lt Col Sir Richard Carnac Temple (1850–1931) was a soldier, administrator and scholar who spent time in India and Burma. His first literary effort was *The Andaman Language*, a product of his posting in the Andaman and Nicobar Islands. He also authored a collection of Indian folk tales, *Wide-Awake Stories*, in collaboration with Flora Annie Steel, and the three-volume *Legends of the Punjab*.

Sir Richard was the third baronet in the line. He fought in the Boer War in 1901-02 and won a medal with four clasps, and later received the Croix de Guerre for bravery in war. Though intellectually he was not in the same league as his father and grandfather.

A tall and rather chivalrous man, he had just lost his first wife around the time he met Himansu and Devika. He was introduced to Himansu by Sir Harry Lindsay, who was the trade commissioner for India and the trusting, lonely widower was drawn into a rollercoaster Indian cinematic adventure. In many ways he would become the best investment that the Rais made.

Years later, Sir Richard would claim that he had given two unsecured loans amounting to more than £10,000 to Himansu to establish HIT, and that he had gifted 12 shares in HIT to Devika. Both statements could have been true as he was obviously emotionally attached to the studio as well as to Himansu and Devika—but they would be furiously disputed and would lead to a court case he could not win.

Initial investors were asked to buy shares in HIT. The company had an issued capital of 200 shares at ₹2,500 each, out of which, despite Himansu's best efforts, only 46 shares were purchased. This gave him a working capital of just over ₹1 lakh, and more loans had to be raised from Sir Chimanlal and others.

The plan was that once HIT was set up as a private limited company, Bombay Talkies would be floated as a public limited company with many more shareholders. Himansu, Devika, Sir Chimanlal and Dewan Sharar formed Himansurai Indo-International Talkies Ltd (HIT), in Himansu's words:

> [With] the definite intention that we should do all in our power to make a commercial success of this production (KARMA) so that we may prove that our company has made gains—and then Sir Chimanlal will be able to form with us a bigger company with adequate capital for our own studio in Bombay, our own distribution and exhibition and permanent production.

The managing agents of Bombay Talkies would be HIT, with whom would lie the real power. Setalvad would chair the boards of both the companies. Initially, the fundraising was for HIT, which would produce *Karm*a in collaboration with the British company, Indian and British Production Limited. Once *Karma* was completed, the fundraising for Bombay Talkies could begin. The British company also saw their own contribution as an investment for the future—through which they could use Indian capital to make more films. Sadly, this was not to happen, as *Karma* did not achieve the projected profits.

Himansu, ever the salesman, promised good returns for HIT, saying that, with Setalvad as a director, the company would not lack investment. The tie-up with a British studio to do all the 'indoor shooting' and post-production was a repeat of the successful collaboration in *The Light of Asia*. It brought credibility to the table, and the government was very pleased to see 'cooperation' between British and Indian companies for a change. Using this argument, Himansu was able to access the top echelons of the British government, which in turn appealed to Indian investors. They were thrilled with the idea that the premiere would be held in London and attended by the cream of England, and that in India the film would be screened in the presence of the Viceroy and his wife.

Other connections among the royals and the Parsi community were brought in by Setalvad, who raised close to £7,000 himself. He was also helpful in following up on leads. For instance, in a letter dated 25 December 1931, posted from Berlin, Himansu wrote:

> Dear Sir Chimanlal,
> On our way to Berlin, Dewan Sharar and I broke our journey in Paris and interviewed HH the Yuvraj of Mysore. His Highness entertained us both at a luncheon and discussed with very great interest the prospects of our company.

He then requested Sir Chimanlal to meet the Yuvraj when he passed through Bombay, where he would be staying at the Taj. He added that the Yuvraj had agreed to purchase a few shares personally and to also 'exert his influence on the Maharajah'. This, he said, would be on the same lines as the investment promised by Hyderabad. 'Sir Akbar Hydari has promised us the patronage of the State of Hyderabad. The Yuvraj is keen to see Mysore joining before Hyderabad.'

The idea that the royals of India would contribute towards the setting up of a cinema production house had been floated around the time when *The Light of Asia* was released and Himansu and Niranjan had invited maharajas and members of the nobility to see the film in London. However, nothing had come of it. Now the time was right, and some of the royals may have been flattered at the idea of showcasing their grand lifestyle for the world through cinema.

Meanwhile, the carefully drafted fundraising letters asking for investments in HIT began to be sent out by Setalvad to royalty as well as to the rich businessmen who were establishing themselves all over the country, and especially in Bombay. These letters highlighted the fact that Himansu Rai was the only Indian producer making films that were shown successfully throughout the world, including America. On 3 December 1931, one such letter was sent to Nawab Muhammad Sir Akbar Hydari (who was to become the prime minister of Hyderabad State):

> The Company is proceeding very cautiously and the programme laid down is to prepare one good Indian film to begin with and progress with other films later as the first film gathers success. It is to be a talkie, and from negotiations conducted up till now it has very good prospects both in India, England, America and some Continental countries....
>
> For completing the work we require ₹40,000. We hope to put together about ₹20,000 and request His Exalted Highness's government may be pleased to subscribe ₹10,000 to ₹20,000.

The letter also said that they would like to have on the board of the company any person whom the Hyderabad government nominated. And in the next film, they would like to highlight subjects suggested by the government.

And thus, tapping all avenues available, funds were raised for the film, and for HIT. Even so, tensions remained high as money kept running short. Setalvad was a very careful investor, and while he was impressed with Himansu, he was not going to give him a blank cheque. In a letter written on 2 January 1933, four months before the film was be released, he asked about the 'final completion, publicity and sales'. He also wanted to know about the 'exact financial position till now specially in relation to the British [company]....Our company as you know by this time expended nearly £ 5300.'

He reminded Himansu that through the sale of shares (as a limited company), they had raised £2,500. This included HIT shares bought by Himansu, Devika and some royals. Later, it would turn out that Himansu had borrowed money from Sir Richard Temple, against which Sir Richard was given HIT shares.

Setalvad pointed out that the British production house involved in the co-production, Indian and British Production Limited, was supposed to contribute £4,000 in expenses, towards studio cost, shooting, editing and so on. Either way, he suggested to Himansu that they must recoup their own costs from any money gained from the distribution or exhibition of the film, thus bringing the capital expenditure on par, and then divide the balance of the money between the Indian and British entities. He mentioned the amount of £7,000 he had cabled, and asked for updates on the publicity and the completion of the film. The letter was sent from his home, at 113, Esplanade Road, Fort, Bombay, to Himansu, who was at the time staying at Mayfair Court, Stratton Street, W1.

This was a very fancy London address for a struggling film producer. But Himansu was always careful to preserve his reputation in an industry which was still full of first impressions and get-rich-quick schemes. Indians, in particular, had to be careful to look and appear wealthy, as well as honest, for there were plenty of charlatans on the make in the business—and Himansu's team could not be free of them either. An early learning came when Sharar was trying to do some fundraising in Lahore.

By now, HIT had a very enthusiastic representative there, Rai Bahadur Chuni Lall, who had an accidental meeting with Sharar. Having recently arrived from Iraq, Rai Bahadur Chuni Lall had settled his family in Lahore and was travelling to Bombay to look for work when he encountered Dewan Sharar on the train. According to his daughter, Shanti Mahendroo, Sharar told him about the film and asked him to invest in the new company. An enthused Rai Bahadur went back to Lahore and managed to raise ₹90,000 from a relation.

This was excellent news for the fledgeling company and the Rai Bahadur immediately became a promoter of HIT, and later, the general manager of Bombay Talkies. Now, he was handling the publicity for the forthcoming film, and like everyone else, was worried about the delay. The long-distance coordination between the German and the British teams, with the shoot in India being followed by post-production in England, meant the work was stretched out and the production budget kept ratcheting up.

This led to all kinds of misunderstandings, and while Sharar was in Lahore, Hari Ram Sethi of Punjab Film Company registered a fraudulent criminal case of cheating against him, preventing him from leaving the city and joining Himansu in Europe.

The same Hari Ram Sethi would also file a false case against Niranjan Pal while he was making a film in Lahore. In an attempt at blackmail, he threatened to keep the film's negatives. This was unquestionably a standard modus operandi with desperate men who wanted to become producers overnight, piggybacking on the expertise of others and trying to make a quick buck.

Using the good offices of Sir Chimanlal, Dewan Sharar managed to escape without too much trouble, and in a letter to Himansu on 22 November 1931, he sheepishly apologised for the 'astounding things of this sordid world' and confessed that he would understand if Himansu thought 'very low of the Punjabis'.

But Sharar himself would drag Himansu to court, just after the film was released in May 1933, claiming that he had not been paid any money for his efforts despite having been promised a salary. Himansu was taken aback at this allegation, since everyone knew the multiple problems they were facing. He was to say in his defence in court that 'At the time when the production was begun it was known to all concerned that the production was to be completed within four months.... Dewan Sharar was engaged at 800 rupees a month for the production, i.e. his engagement was to cease with the completion of the film.'

When the work took longer than anticipated, they had all agreed, said Himansu, to not draw any salaries until the film was completed and sold—they would only receive money for their board and lodging. But they would each receive a certain sum when the profits came in.

Sharar had been given his passage to Europe to work on the film as well as a sum of almost £800. Himansu said that he had been asked to write letters regarding payments made to Sharar to reassure his (Sharar's) family in India. These letters were not proof of payments actually made. However, Sharar denied all of this, and was determined to get his money.

Finally, a settlement was reached in the case in August 1933, even as Himansu was trying to organise the screening of *Karma* in India and other countries. The premiere had already been held in London in May 1933.

According to the settlement, Sharar would cut off all connections with the film, and any claims on the company, and in return he would be paid a further amount of £850, with £50 being the signing amount. He would be paid £250 when the court proceedings were stayed, and the last tranche when the receipts from the film began coming in. He would also return the (blank) share certificate of HIT in his possession, as well as resign from his post as a director of the company.

As the court case dragged on in London, Sir Chimanlal became increasingly impatient in India. Unfortunately, Himansu could not, despite all the positive publicity, assure him of an outright sale of the film, or any large-scale distribution either. To complicate matters further, Sir Chimanlal had privately received some feedback on *Karma* which was far from flattering, and which he communicated to Himansu in a letter:

> The film has been very well criticised but general opinion among English & Indian intelligentsia is very poor. I can say that they have seen better films (Talkies) in India recently. The Secretary

of State & Lord Irwin were disappointed though they were very diplomatic in their remarks. This is not real Indian life they are a showing on screen, remarked Sir Mirza Ismail, most ridiculous and very inopportune [to show] a film like this in England.... If the Indian version is not better, the effort is doomed to failure. Personally I think it is most disgusting.

The other blow that Sir Chimanlal delivered was the information that some of the investors were already asking for their money to be returned as the screening in India had been delayed. The delay was exacerbated because two versions of the film had to be prepared, in English and in Hindi.

Himansu understood the situation only too well, as he himself was nothing if not a hustler in a three-piece suit. He knew that he had to deliver a successful film and see that it got wide distribution and had spectacular ticket sales, which meant that he had to ensure it was well publicised.

Once again, remembering that the Royal Command performance at Windsor had given a huge boost to *The Light of Asia*, he decided to write to their Majesties to request them to see *Karma* either at the palace or at the Marble Arch Pavilion where it was to be shown on 15 May. In his letter, he tried to emphasise how this production demonstrated the cordial relationship between Great Britain and India. He said:

> Karma is the first Indian talking film to be presented in London. It was produced partly in India and partly here and is the joint production of an English and an Indian group who are inspired with the ideal of establishing between Great Britain, India and the rest of the Empire yet another link through the medium of the talking film.

Though their Majesties politely regretted the invitation, Himansu went ahead with his plan of organising a special preview on 10 May for the press, and another for the nobility and the elite on 15 May.

After attending the press preview, the *Manchester Guardian* noted that the film would be called *Nagin ki Ragini* in Hindi. The review that followed was all praise for Devika:

> [It had] less spectacle than in other productions of Himansu Rai, but this is atoned for by the performance of the beautiful leading lady Devika Rani.

Otherwise, the reviewer was a little less satisfied:

> [The film] takes up more threads than it can successfully weave; it seems prevented from getting into its stride by a desire to present Indian mentality in Western terms, which is rarely successful. The dialogue though prettily spoken is stilted and throughout seems at variance with the thoughts of the characters.

Similarly, Campbell Dixon, reviewing the film for the *Daily Telegraph*, appeared overjoyed by the 'serene and classic beauty of this dark new star out of the East'. He asked us to imagine a younger Dolores del Rio, 'with a softer accent and singing voice such as is given to few film actresses, and you have Miss Devika Rani'. While scathing about the fact that her acting talents were not given enough opportunity, he added:

> Her beauty and charm are so obvious and her gift for putting across a lyric so rare, she seems to me a potential star of the first magnitude. Given the right stories and expert Hollywood 'grooming' she would be a sensation.

As the excitement built up around the film and most critics gave Devika favourable notices, Himansu seized the moment. He made a list of everyone who mattered in London and ensured that anyone with a title, who was known to him or his well-wishers, was sent an invitation to be present at the Marble Arch Pavilion for a very special screening. Every possible connection was tapped, including the office of the prime minister. Despite their refusal, the rumour was spread that the king and queen would also attend.

This first public screening on 15 May was successful beyond anyone's expectations. And the high-profile premiere meant that the film was covered widely in most newspapers in Britain as well as in India. But Himansu would not rest, and pushed for further recognition. In a letter to the *Times* (London) on 16 May 1933, he tried to get all the names of the people who had attended the Marble Arch Pavilion show just the day earlier, included in the newspaper report. Requesting them to publish the attached list, he added:

> The interesting point in this enterprise is that it consists of a purely British company and purely Indian company acting in complete cooperation on an equal basis. In fact full cooperation in these non cooperative days.

The film, he said, had created somewhat of 'a political moment'.

He held more press previews, seeking publicity and endorsements. This kind of no-holds-barred push had never been tried before for any film made by an Indian. The resulting wall-to-wall coverage was astonishing. And when Devika walked away with the laurels, Himansu was delighted that his instinct about her had been validated. It was evident by now to both of them that she was the real star.

They went to Birmingham next, where the film was screened at the West End cinema on 10 July, and was a huge success. It was followed by a visit to Cadbury's chocolate factory, apparently a highlight of the city. Interestingly, the photograph that appeared a few weeks later in the *Tribune* (published from Lahore on 4 August 1933) showed only Devika biting into a piece of chocolate, surrounded by adoring workers and a noticeably infatuated Sir Richard. There was no sign of Himansu in it, though he was a part of the programme. And it was Devika who made the speech at the theatre.

The entire trip was organised by Sir Richard, who wrote a warm note to the Mayor (and the Lady Mayoress and the citizens of Birmingham) thanking him for the great encouragement he had given to Mr Rai, the producer, in his courageous effort:

Not only to show India in this country but to forge another link in the chain of mutual regard and affection between India and Britain which cannot help but open up new fields for trade to the mutual advantage of both countries.

The letter of thanks, dated 13 July 1933, was sent from Mayfair Court, Stratton Street, an address used by Himansu and Devika as well.

Himansu did not raise any objections to the closeness between Sir Richard and Devika. He had realised by now that she had a devastating effect on most men and this could be a huge help to him, both on and off the screen. The threesome—Devika, Himansu and Sir Richard—made a good team, bringing in different elements and connections. Devika provided the glamour and the 'film star' appeal, Himansu managed the practical aspects of the project, and Sir Richard the connections—especially the British ones.

They had also begun working on how to present Devika on their return to Bombay. Himansu was very careful about how she should be packaged. First, he set about differentiating her from the other actresses. She did not share the same background as the tawaifs and dancing girls or the Anglo-Indians who provided the recruiting pool in the 1920s and 1930s. Rarely did women from 'respectable' families enter cinema. Even if there were a few, none had her beauty, sophistication or charm—or lineage.

Devika Rani, he hoped, would become the catalyst for a huge change in the industry. And it was through this bid for respectability that Himansu wanted to attract more funding. If cinema was full of educated and respectable people, it would become an industry like any other. Listing it on the stock market and getting investors would become far simpler. He made a concerted effort to get this message across in all his interviews. At a time when most of the studios in India were owned by a family or by individuals, he wanted to set up a professional studio, like those he had seen and worked with abroad.

On 5 June 1933, Devika gave an interview to the *Times of India*, dressed in a colourful saree and reclining 'on a divan of a sixth-floor flat in the heart of Mayfair (London)'. She and Himansu had not yet started work on Bombay Talkies, but she spoke about training Indian women for cinema.

> I myself was trained in a Berlin film studio, while my husband was learning talkie technique[s]. There they showed me the necessity for strict rules of life, exercise, early rising and other training which a would-be star must undergo and I imagine many other Indian women, with my training, would give us good acting material. We intend to take to Bombay, European technical experts, photographers, make-up men, but we shall simultaneously employ our own people to learn how these things are done.

Devika never thought of herself as only an actress. Her curious mind led her to explore other areas where the expertise of filmmaking could be put to use. For instance, why not use short commercial films for advertising products in India, instead of posters, as most buyers and sellers could not read?

Exuding enthusiasm and ideas, she told her interviewer that their studio in Bombay would produce at least three international films each year.

> [But the bulk of the output of the films] would be for the Indian market, only. We are hoping to take back with us one or two travelling talkie equipments with which we can take our talkies to faraway villages where they have hitherto never seen any silent films.

Her mindset was undoubtedly modern. She thought of taking the audience from the familiar into unfamiliar territories. She discussed making short films around the Ramayana. She knew these would be loved by the masses, as they would identify with the themes. After they had become acquainted with the medium, rural audiences could be gradually introduced to more modern narratives.

Sudha Rani, who had acted alongside Devika in *Karma*, gave interviews in which she spoke positively about the experience of working with Himansu and Devika. She had played a princess in the film, and was a princess in real life as well. In an interview which appeared in the *Times of India* on 24 September 1933, she said:

> I have come to the conclusion that a great opportunity presents itself to our educated sisters in India. I believe they can create a big and prosperous industry. I believe they can help the industry as well as help themselves.

She added:

> Work on the screen is an opportunity for them to find the economic independence which many of them desire so much. The pioneer work that Mr Himansu Rai and his wife are doing should receive all the encouragement Indian women can give.

Sudha Rani believed that *Karma* would 'not be the only effort in the international market' from Himansu and Devika. Much, much more could be expected.

Sometimes this emphasis on using educated young women as actresses was given an unusual spin. The *Daily Mirror* in London made a special mention of 'high caste girls in a love story' while writing about *Karma*.

> Two Indian girls of high caste appear in the first Indian talking picture.... It is entitled "Karma", which means "fate" and is a charming love story of a young Indian prince and princess.

But, like all the others, it was Devika whom the reviewer called extremely beautiful.

As Himansu and Devika, along with Sir Richard, prepared to leave for India, offers began to come for her to act in British films. The 'Dazzling, Dynamic, Miss Devika Rani', as the headline of *Film World* (Madras, 30 December 1933) put it, was much in demand.

Letter from Devika to Svetoslav

I must confess to you one thing, I am the most painfully shy person you can ever imagine! Of course I overcome it by training and my profession, but by nature I am terribly shy.

Bombay, 1945

10

BOMBAY TALKIES, 1930s

Devika had begun to be recognised, well and truly, as an Indian actress in London. In the months before they left for Bombay to launch *Karma*, she was not just reading scripts to see if there were any roles suitable for her, she was also being offered roles in films, although as an 'exotic heroine'.

Some of the directors who showed an interest in her were internationally renowned, such as Eric Pommer, who had started his career with UFA and moved on after making one of their most expensive films, *Metropolis*. Pommer's contract with UFA was cancelled in 1933 when the Nazis came to power, but his career flourished in France where he was hired by Fox Film Corporation to build Fox Europa as its European arm. It was at this time that Himansu wrote to him and received an enthusiastic response.

In his letter dated 23 October 1933, Pommer wrote, 'I am in receipt of your letter of October 6, contents of which had my full interest.' He wanted photographs of 'Miss Devika Rani' and wanted to know if she spoke French. He said that he would be in London in the coming weeks, and if Himansu could 'spare a minute', they could meet up. Devika later said that she had worked with him at UFA, but he (surprisingly, given her good looks) appeared to have little recollection of her.

Himansu immediately put together photographs of Devika and sent them off on 27 October to Pommer, adding ingenuously, 'Miss

Devika Rani's accent and intonations in French have always been admired even by the French people. I must however, mention that being out of practice her French at the moment is not as fluent as her English.' He also offered to organise a viewing of *Karma* for Pommer as Arley Films in Paris had acquired the rights.

Unfortunately, nothing came of this, or of another exploratory effort with the Gaumont-British Picture Corporation Limited. The company's Lime Grove Studio, where Devika was invited for a meeting, was used two years later for the shooting of Hitchcock's *The 39 Steps* (1935). It was a large studio which employed around 16,000 people and would have added to Devika's stature had the deal gone through.

She was also offered at least one role for the stage, to play the lead in *The Rani of Jhansi* by Philip Cox. He wrote to Devika on 6 October 1933, telling her that the play had received extensive notices in India and Britain and 'people as reputable as G. Bernard Shaw have spoken highly of it'.

But the production that almost did come through involved J.L.F. Hunt, who also directed *Karma*. A film was to be launched that would showcase the might of the British naval fleet, and it was suggested that Devika play the role of Maya, the daughter of a rich merchant living on a fictional island in the Pacific. The storyline was simple—a rebellion is being instigated on the island of Santa Maria, which is loyal to Great Britain. False rumours are being deliberately fed to the population. Maya learns of the rebellion and, risking her life, manages to alert the commander of a fleet, who rescues everyone just in time and brings peace to the island.

Hunt was a Lieutenant Commander in the Royal Navy and was confident that the film would be of the highest standards since the dignity of the navy could not suffer. In a letter addressed to Himansu on 23 June 1933, he expressed interest in casting Devika in *Keepers of the Sea* (or *White Ensign*), opposite Anthony Kimmins, also a Lieutenant Commander in the Royal Navy. This would have been path-breaking had it happened—the first time an Indian actress was cast opposite a White actor—and would have led, undoubtedly, to more offers for Devika.

In an earlier letter, dated 9 June 1933, Hunt had said that the romantic interest would be developed through the person of Maya and the whole story would revolve around her. Tempting words indeed, for someone who had just made her film debut! However, there were pressing reasons why Himansu thought it prudent to shift their interests to India, where their future and their finances appeared to lie, and Devika had to go along.

Despite their best intentions, there were still outstanding dues pending in England. Hunt had written to Himansu from Sound City (a film-producing and recording studio based in Middlesex) warning him of a potential financial crisis. He went so far as to ask whether they should liquidate all their personal liabilities in *Karma*. In a separate handwritten note accompanying the more formal letter, he added that the situation is 'so serious that both you and I are working under the worst possible conditions'.

But it was clear that Hunt was still keen to continue his partnership with HIT. Demonstrating his faith in Himansu, despite all the problems they were facing, he suggested that Sound City Ltd could handle HIT's interest and sales in Great Britain and Europe, especially with regard to *Karma*. He added:

> I am, furthermore, being asked by many people who are interested, financially and personally in the film, how soon it is likely to be ready for the Indian market and I should like very much to have a plan which I could put before them, as this would help me considerably in my negotiations.

In fact, Hunt wanted Himansu to move quickly, before the publicity 'which you have engineered so admirably has time to get stale in India'. He thought it was a sound business opportunity, and imagined that the film would do better in India. Alas, this was not the case.

It was entirely to the credit of Himansu and Devika that *Karma* had raised so much interest in England. The Hindi version would soon be sent for screening to India. Meanwhile, Himansu was busy (long-distance) setting up an Indian team, led by Rai Bahadur Chuni Lall. He was also firefighting, with Dewan Sharar's court case being registered in London, over pending dues. Despite the difficulties, he wanted to organise the film's premier in India with great fanfare, as he had done in England.

Devika, meanwhile, was caught in a dilemma. She could hardly stay behind and pursue a career in England while Himansu left for India to consolidate HIT and organise the launch of *Karma*. She too recognised the need to act speedily, the sense of urgency exacerbated by the fact that money continued to be in short supply.

On 21 June 1933, Rupert Downing, who had been credited with writing the scenes for *Karma*, sent an irate letter to 'H.R.', warning him of legal consequences if he was not immediately paid. He wrote:

> Quite irrespective of the division of the spoils for the Marble Arch performances, a specified sum of money is due to me—whoever has it—and I fail to see any reason why this should [not] be put forward to the persons concerned. If the money is being held by Gaumont British, my friends there would see that I had a square deal.

He threatened to write to Hunt to find out what exactly was going on.

Fortunately, while the crew lined up for payment, Himansu remained buoyed up by the increasing interest from distributors. And Hunt encouraged Himansu to accept offers, such as the one from 'Messrs Fox Films Ltd', to get the requisite number of copies of *Karma* to start operations in India.

Remarkably, the Fox Film Company was also taking a keen interest in Devika's career, and they sent a letter to Eric Maschwitz, the editor of Radio Times, at Broadcasting House in Portland Place, London, promoting Devika. Fox Films wrote that Devika 'would like to know about broadcasting, and perhaps be of some service to the BBC. She is an extremely talented woman.' A short speech which Devika had given at the premiere of *Karma* had already been broadcast by BBC. Fox was also keen to promote this newly found and very unusual talent—just in case they got the contract to distribute *Karma* in India.

This was a time of transition for Himansu into a completely different role—he was going to give up acting, which he loved, and become a full-time producer. He and Devika realised that making cinema in Europe and the US, with the coming of sound, had actually marginalised them as artistes, as they would remain the charming or perhaps 'snake charming' couple who would always be offered Oriental roles. Their repertoire would not expand and certainly, for Himansu as an actor, it was the end of the road. He was older, and his waistline was now even more visibly expanding. With the new tensions he had undertaken—to set up HIT as well as a full-fledged studio in Bombay, it would be increasingly difficult to maintain a strict discipline. He could hardly be cast as a hero anymore.

It was time for them to shift their base to India. It did not make sense for him to raise funds in India, or through Indian maharajas and potentates based abroad, only for them to be utilised by British producers and directors.

Interestingly, while Himansu himself did not approach any studios in Germany for funding, the German government could have been a possible source. A well-wisher sent him this news report:

> The measures promised by Dr Goebbels, the Reich Minister of propaganda to help the German film industry materialised today in the establishment of a film credit bank with a nominal capital of £ 10,000, controlled by the central organisation of the film industry and a number of the big banks.
>
> The object it is stated, is to stimulate the industry through sound credit for the financing of production, while at the same time eliminating unhealthy market conditions.

Himansu had maintained his German connections, especially those he needed for technical support on *Karma*. But he did not apply for any money through this fund. Instead, he targeted Indian entrepreneurs, royalty and rich professionals like Setalvad. The net was spread wide in England and India, and the response had been positive so far.

Himansu had realised that for a steady production assembly, his coffers needed to be full. The ad hoc raising of funds that had seen him through until now had only resulted in people constantly chasing him for money. He wanted stability. With Devika beside him, this was certainly an achievable goal.

Meanwhile, pre-publicity for *Karma* had begun in India, though the film would not reach Indian screens till early February 1934, that is, the following year. Among the many people who praised the film was Sarojini Naidu, the poet, who became a good friend of the Rais. The brochure for the film, dated 27 January 1934, carried a comment by her:

> All real art has a universal significance and speaks a universal tongue. The modern art of the silver screen especially makes a wide…appeal alike to the lettered and unlettered in every land….
>
> A striking example of this is furnished by "Karma" the first Indian talkie to be presented to the West, which has received such generous recognition in many European countries, and most of all in England, where it was first exhibited before a distinguished and highly discriminating audience….

She said she was aware of the immense difficulties and incredible delays involved in the completion of *Karma* and believed it was a brave enterprise and a notable achievement. A tribute both to the 'remarkable courage, vision, patience and resource of Himansu Rai, the producer, and to that lovely and gifted little lady, Devika Rani, the heroine, who blossoms like a magical flower of romance out of the heart of the play.'

Sarojini was also particularly helpful in raising funds for HIT in Hyderabad, where her family lived. It was no coincidence that

FOREWORD

ALL real art has a universal significance and speaks a universal tongue. The modern art of the silver screen especially makes a wide and instant appeal alike to the lettered and unlettered in every land, no matter what the theme or the landscape of the story, provided that it is true to the common experience, emotion and adventure of life, and interpreted with genuine skill, passion, humour, pathos, power. It overcomes all barriers of divergent customs and cultures; it stands, happily, outside the arena of current political controversies and economic feuds. It delivers a single message equally to all races.

A STRIKING example of this is furnished by "Karma" the first Indian talkie to be presented to the West, which has received such generous recognition in many European countries, and most of all in England, where it was first exhibited before a distinguished and highly discriminating audience.

AWARE as I am of the immense difficulties and incredible delays involved in the completion of "Karma", I consider it not only a brave enterprise but a notable achievement. It is, in itself, a tribute both to the remarkable courage, vision, patience and resource of Himansu Rai, the producer, and to that lovely and gifted little lady, Devika Rani the heroine, who blossoms like a magical flower of romance out of the heart of the play.

BOMBAY.
27th. JANUARY, 1934.

Sarojini Naidu

(*Sarojini Naidu*)

by 12 July 1934, Hyderabad State had agreed to take shares worth ₹1,00,000 in the newly set up Bombay Talkies.

Himansu and Devika arrived in India, accompanied by Sir Richard, amid a blaze of publicity. *MV Victoria* anchored at Bombay harbour on 4 December 1933. All the major newspapers, from the *Hindu* to the *Evening News*, covered their arrival. The ecstatic *Tribune* article of 14 December, published from Lahore, noted that Rai Bahadur Chuni Lall, the general manager of Himansurai Indo-International Talkies, was there to receive them, while fans crowded around. It also reported that many radiograms and telegrams were received by them during their voyage, welcoming them back. It all seems to have been carefully choreographed, and everybody who was anybody seems to have been in Bombay at the time. They were welcomed at the Taj Mahal hotel by Sarojini Naidu, they met Rabindranath Tagore, and were received by Sir Chimanlal in his chambers. That was quite a lot to pack into one day.

It was announced that the premiere would take place in Delhi, on 5 February 1934, and would be attended by none other than the Viceroy and Lady Willingdon. They could also claim success with the international release of *Karma*, for the rights had been sold in France, Belgium, Norway, Switzerland, Sweden, Australia, West Indies and Fiji. It was also said that the Hindustani version of *Karma*, shown in Sweden and Norway, had been given a 'very warm reception'.

To drum up even more excitement, it was announced that Devika would be returning to England, where she was committed to being part of two British films. But, of course, the Rais already knew it was futile to try to set up a career in two very different environments. Devika was soon to be recognised as an equal partner in the upcoming studio, besides an actress with an international reputation.

Fortunately, the first step towards setting up the studio had already been taken with Sir Chimanlal's help. The new head office of HIT was at Readymoney Mansion, Churchgate Street, Bombay, while the branch office continued to remain in Lahore, according to *Filmworld* (Madras, 16 December 1933). HIT would play a key role in the film industry throughout the 1930s and till the mid-1940s, as it was the managing agent for Bombay Talkies. This meant that while Bombay Talkies was being set up, HIT was taking all the key decisions, led by Himansu and, of course, Devika.

※

The next thing for Himansu and Devika to do was to recruit staff.

News about the setting up of HIT and the plans for Bombay Talkies had been carried in newspapers and magazines, and requests for jobs began to pour in from many who hoped to be employed by a professionally run film studio. Both Devika and Himansu had been insisting that they wanted educated people to join. This meant that a different class of people began to send in their applications. Sometimes established personalities also suggested names.

For instance, M.R. Jayakar, a well-known lawyer and a leader of the Swaraj Party, who worked closely with the government, suggested that Himansu employ A.G. Bhate, who had studied sound technology in Germany. In his letter dated 2 July 1934, Jayakar suggested that Himansu meet Bhate, who had 'just returned to India after nine years of training in Berlin.... He holds excellent qualifications and testimonials in the department of sound recording and films.' Jayakar added that 'he is accustomed to hard work and will devote his best energies to the business of his employer'.

Similarly, Minoo A. Katrak was introduced to Himansu Rai, on 28 June 1934, as a young man who 'has good sample qualification for the job of assistant Sound Recording Engineer'. Katrak went on to become one of the finest sound engineers in the industry.

Sunalini Devi, Sarojini Naidu's sister and a film actress who largely performed character roles at the time, usually that of a mother, also sent a letter, dated 27 June 1934, to Himansu, addressing him affectionately as 'Golap' and introducing a writer and publicist, probably K.A. Abbas. Congratulating Himansu and Devika on the setting up of the new enterprise, and sending her regards to Sir Richard, she wrote that she wanted to 'bring to your notice a very capable journalist and publicity man. He has had several years of experience as a writer and was doing all the "Ajanta" publicity. He left Mr Bhownani as he did not like the queer methods of work in his studio.'

Incidentally, Sunalini Devi would work with Bombay Talkies even after it changed hands, and in 1952 would still be seen in one of the studio's biggest hits, *Tamasha*, directed by Phani Majumdar and starring Dev Anand, Meena Kumari and Ashok Kumar. By this time, Ashok Kumar had taken over Bombay Talkies.

The studio would come up in Malad by 1934–35 and Abbas would become a key part of it, and become the reason why, even though the films made by Bombay Talkies did not do uniformly well, they all garnered a lot of publicity. He would sell his own first script, called *Naya Sansar*, to Bombay Talkies in 1941.

One of the greatest writers of the time, Munshi Premchand, came to Bombay to write for films around this time, but decided not to take up an offer from Himansu, because, he said, producers were only interested in profit. He had stayed in the city for a year and tried his hand at writing stories for M.D. Bhavnani (who was referred to by Sunalini Devi as Bhownani, in her letter) at Ajanta Cinetone, but found that his very first film, *Mazdoor* (*Mill*) was banned by the censor board because the mill owners feared that it would agitate the workers. It was a while before films with social realism at their heart found an audience. Well before that, in April 1935, a disillusioned Premchand had left Bombay.

Like Premchand, most people who had any connection with the newest studio in Bombay were familiar with Himansu as the face of the company. It was time now for them to be introduced to Devika.

A press release was sent out, with some embellishments that may have surprised even her family:

> Devika Rani is a Bengalee by birth and the only daughter of Late Colonel Chaudhuri and is at present around 23 years old.

This was clearly incorrect because in 1933 she would have been at least twenty-five, if not older, if she was indeed born in 1908. The press release also said:

> When she was young she studied Indian Philosophy and Literature under the guidance of her great uncle Sir Rabinder Nath Tagore and also took part in the plays written by Sir Tagore and performed at his school in Shantiniketan, at Bolepur, outside Calcutta. After her training and studies... she was educated for higher studies in England, at Cheltenham.

It might be noted that references to her training at the Royal Academy of Dramatic Arts and the Royal Music Academy are nowhere to be found in the early press releases. Those particular flourishes were added later.

The attempt was to make Devika's profile as international and as 'respectable' as possible.

After leaving school she travelled extensively with her father all over Europe learning something about the Arts of the other countries and continuing her studies in Singing, Dancing and Painting. In addition to Hindustani, she speaks several European languages and has attracted Europe in a programme of singing and dancing appearing at Zurich, Basel, Lausanne, Stockholm and Oslo.

Getting the chronology a little mixed up for the benefit of the press, it suggested that when Himansu floated HIT, he was looking for:

[A] talented and beautiful female Star who could play the part of a heroine in his first production. After making an exhaustive search his choice fell on Devika Rani who accompanied Mr Himansu Rai...

According to this version of her life, they subsequently shot the film, and she went on to UFA for training. The release mentioned that she had married Himansu around five years back.

Whatever the reality, the legend of Devika Rani acknowledged her as a very accomplished star, who had conquered Europe with her talent and was now set to charm India. It was rare to launch an actress in either India or England with this kind of fanfare.

Meanwhile, preparations for the release of *Karma* had begun and the Viceroy and his wife, Lord and Lady Willingdon, as well as members of the Legislative Assembly attended the Indian premiere at Roxy Theatre on 8 February 1934.

Once again, Devika gave the main speech on the occasion, not Himansu:

A great hour has come, for 'Karma' to be shown in my own country to my own people. I want to thank their Excellencies, the Viceroy and Countess of Wellington for honouring 'Karma' and all it stands for by their gracious presence tonight.

She said she was glad that the all-India premiere would contribute to the relief of the stricken in Bihar, referring to the terrible earthquake which had struck Nepal and Bihar on 15 January 1934, in which more than 10,000 people were reported to have been killed. She also announced that they had written to Gaumont-British, who were releasing the film in Great Britain, to contribute a portion of the proceeds to the state of Bihar.

She added that, tonight, she remembered the welcome London had given to *Karma*, 'India's first talkie on the British screen; the sincerity and enormity of which moved me to unforgettable joy and gratitude.' She hoped the audience would love *Karma* as she had.

It was an accomplished and flawlessly delivered speech, especially for someone in their mid-twenties. No Indian actress had spoken in quite the same way or held centre-stage among such distinguished guests. More than the film, Devika's off-screen presence made her an instant success.

Himansu and Devika were not the only ones to donate generously to those affected by the earthquake. The Lahore branch of New Theatres donated ₹1,500 from the box-office collections, while the staff in Calcutta and Lahore donated another ₹2,000. Before Bombay Talkies arrived on the scene, New Theatres had been at the forefront of Indian cinema and even in the case of the earthquake, they had flown over the affected area and shot a documentary which was now being shown in Lahore, according to *Varieties* magazine (23 February 1934). New Theatres was already well established, but it functioned out of Calcutta, and this was the one advantage that Himansu had. The industry was growing faster in Bombay.

Not one to let the grass grow under his feet, Himansu had already begun to hold regular meetings with the shareholders of HIT. One of the many businessmen who were keen to be part of the board of Bombay Talkies was F.E. Dinshaw, who at one stage owned over 2,000 acres of land in Bombay. He was also a Parsi, and Sir Chimanlal's close friend. A cable had been sent to him while he was at Claridges Hotel, Brooke Street, London, by Sir Chimanlal, which was clear in its intent:

> In view of good support forthcoming now immediate flotation essential of proposed film company which you kindly consented to join as Director with me. Prospectus and other documents ready. Shall be very grateful if you would cable immediately to Dazi or Wadia to sign necessary consent on your behalf to be director stop Have satisfied myself everything in order and you may instruct Dazi to satisfy himself further stop Director's qualification 5000 Rupees shares. Setalvad.

Dinshaw not only agreed to the proposal, he even agreed to lease his two-storied bungalow in Malad to Himansu for approximately one lakh rupees per year.

Himansu liked the bungalow. There were eighteen acres of land around it, enough not just for the separate departments that he and Devika wanted to build, but also for any future expansion. Soon, there would be around forty structures there, which contained the shooting and production spaces, and the sound studio, canteen and smaller bungalows. It was the most professionally equipped and well-designed studio in town. Unfortunately, Dinshaw would not live to see the full potential of the studio; he passed away in 1936.

The main studio was on the ground floor and there was room for people to stay on the first floor. Though it was far from the city, Himansu and Devika began to scout for a home, as well. It would be their first home together, after nearly five years of marriage. It didn't take them long to settle on a bungalow close by, on 57 Dady Seth Road.

Meanwhile, several well-known personalities came on board. These initially included Sir Pheroze Sethna, who had been a member of the Imperial Legislative Council; Sir Cowasji Jehangir, the grand-nephew of Cowasji Jehangir Readymoney (who earned his surname for having very successfully lent money to the British); Sir Chunnilal Mehta, a bullion broker; and Sir Sorabji Pochkhanwala, a Parsi banker who died shortly afterwards, in 1937, and who is remembered for having set up the Central Bank of India.

All these people, predominantly Parsi, had become wealthy through their dealings with the British. They saw Bombay Talkies as an 'establishment' studio, particularly since British officials in England and India were supporting it and recommending its work. Lords and ladies wanted to know more about it, and the success of the core team in raising money abroad was impressive. The presence of Sir Richard Temple, whose grandfather had been the governor of Bombay, and whose father had also lived and worked in India, helped to smooth the path.

And then there was Devika, presented as someone who might—though very unusual for an Indian actress—still make a career in England and who was much appreciated by the press there. Educated, well spoken, beautiful, and a relation of Sir Rabindranath Tagore, she was the unique factor in the Indo-British collaboration.

It would be a decade before the Parsis exited Bombay Talkies. Under Devika, in the mid-1940s, another set of rapidly rising wealth-creators—the Marwaris—would take over the studio. Like the Parsi businessmen, these promoters were also well connected with the government of the time, as India moved away from British colonial rule. It would be a significant shift as undoubtedly the Parsis had been closer to the British than the Marwaris. The Parsi connection was a deliberate strategy adopted by Himansu because he found it easier to deal with cosmopolitan men of the world rather than crass businessmen who had no concept of a larger vision of creating world-class cinema. This was something the anglicised Parsi community understood well.

Regular meetings of HIT began to be held at Readymoney Mansion on Churchgate Street under the chairmanship of Sir Chimanlal, with Rai Bahadur Chuni Lall as the general manager. The agenda of one of the meetings at the end of 1933 stated that all the audited accounts (presumably for *Karma*) would be looked at and that directors would be elected.

After the setting up of Bombay Talkies all had not been going as well as Himansu had hoped. So he plunged headlong into raising its share capital. In March 1934, after the screening of *Karma*, he wrote to a British distributor, Mr Coventry, about the success of the film, saying that it had been screened in Lahore, Madras, Nagpur, Lucknow, Karachi, Bangalore, Secunderabad, Rangoon and Bombay. 'In many places,' he said, 'it has broken box office records.' He urged Coventry to help identify potential financiers for the public issue, in this case, from Gwalior or Indore, where presumably Coventry had good connections.

Once the higher echelons of Bombay's business world had been approached, Himansu wrote to whoever, big or small, it was possible to connect with—for instance, Seth Badridas Daya, at Anand Kutir, Bikaner. Indefatigable and irrepressible, Himansu sent off a letter on 11 May 1934 to him, reiterating that he was setting up a permanent and progressive business.

Similar letters went out to others:

The proposed authorised capital of the company will be ₹25 lakhs, divided into 25000 shares of ₹100 each, of which 10,000 shares would be issued at present.
    The proposed company will not start work until a sufficient amount of the ₹10 lakhs mentioned above has been raised—this is to avoid starting work with insufficient capital, which as you know has often been the cause of failures of many projects.

He took care to point out that the proposed company would always 'retain respectability in their associations and activity so that respectable people like yourself and others can honourably remain interested in the company'.

In the meantime, things were moving rapidly, and the studio's name, Bombay Talkies, was publicly announced in mid-July. It was reported that the directors had themselves acquired shares worth ₹15,00,000, though this figure tended to vary, as positive stories were obviously being carefully planted in the media.

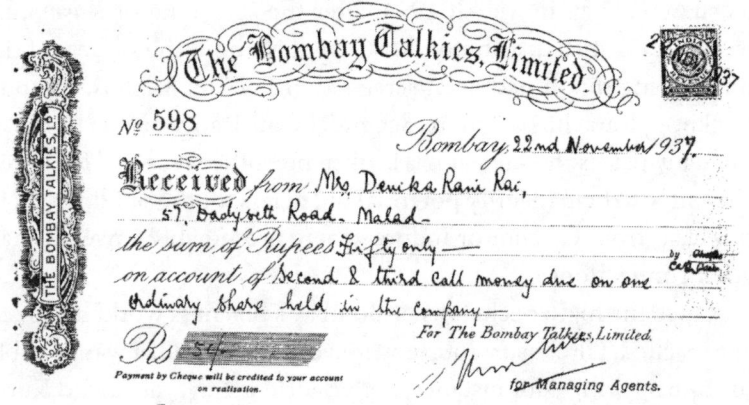

In a letter that he wrote to Lt Col D.M. Field, Agent to the Governor General, Madras States Agency, Trivandrum, on 19 July 1934, Himansu said:

> You will be glad to know that the council of Hyderabad has unanimously accepted our proposal for the State to take up shares of our Company to the value of ₹1,00,000. Our thanks are due to Sir Richard Trench and Sir Akbar Hydari for the support that they gave to the proposal.
>
> We have been definitely assured that the state of Jaipur will also take up shares in the Company.

He did not expect Jaipur's investment to be more than 'one lakh or less than ₹50,000'. He was hoping that there would also be some news from Travancore, and perhaps Cochin. He added:

We have now registered the Company, but are holding back the issue of the prospectus pending the incorporation of the subscriptions of these four states.

There were moments of panic too. On 19 July, the same day that he wrote that he had got the go-ahead from Hyderabad, he also sent an anxious request to his supporter, Sarojini Naidu. They had been under the impression that consent would be given at Hyderabad State's Council meeting on 12 July for the investment in Bombay Talkies 'and the following Sunday it was to be placed before His Exalted Highness for approval'. Himansu had already sent a telegram on 11 July, but wanted Sarojini Naidu to use her good offices and press for the consent from 'His Exalted Highness'.

The intervention worked—and as reported in the August issue of *Silver Screen* magazine, 'The states of Hyderabad and Jaipur supported the studio, with the Nizam of Hyderabad commissioning Bombay Talkies to produce instructional films.' The article went on to say that the company had been floated, as earlier announced, with an authorised capital of ₹25 lakh and an issued capital of ₹10 lakh.

The sums of money invested reportedly ranged from ₹10 to 15 lakh, depending on different media reports. The actual sum was probably closer to an impressive ₹10 lakh, which was more than enough to get started. It is important to remember that all of this—the fundraising and the setting up of the studio, as well as the selection of their first film, was all happening simultaneously. This was also the first known effort to turn the chaotic world of cinema into a professional, well-oiled industry, and the media was vocal in its support. *Silver Screen* said:

> The subscription list is open and will be closed on or before 13 August 1934. The company will be commencing its activities, it is expected, with six films during the first twelve months at an estimated average cost of rupees one lakh per film. A net profit of ₹35,000 per film exploited. The company expects additional income from its production of educational and advertising films.

The arrangement between HIT and Bombay Talkies was clearly demarcated—HIT was appointed the managing agent for Bombay Talkies for twenty years. This was a popular form of managing business at the time; many other companies had managing agents. It was also a clever move as with Himansu practically in charge of HIT, there was a 'creative' head at the top.

If Himansu and Devika ever had any doubts about the wisdom of their audacious enterprise, the fan letters which came in gave them plenty of support. One of these came from an ardent young admirer, K.S. Hira, from 'Love Grove Road, Worli, Bombay'. He wrote to Himansu on 10 February 1934 about how inspired he had been after seeing *Karma* and reading about Himansu's plans. He had come to Bombay from Karachi two years after his graduation and had wanted a career in Indian cinema for a long time, but social norms and his mother's fears had held him back. He said:

> My dreams have been shattered...
>
> It has been my misfortune to be born [in a] 'respectable' Hindoo family. And as such I can't enter [the film world]. Those age-worn traditional orthodox ideas are still there. They are deep rooted in every Hindoo mother. And for a 'respectable' Hindoo child to sacrifice his mother or society to the ideals, it is something!

This stigma attached to cinema would be difficult to overcome, but Himansu and Devika persisted. The real success story of their studio was that many of those who joined them had a formal education, just as they had wanted. Some had even studied abroad, while a few gave up careers in science—such as Gyan Mukerji, who had worked with Dr Meghnad Saha, the famous Indian astrophysicist who developed the Saha ionisation equation, used to describe chemical and physical conditions in stars. Gyan Mukerji would later become a much-feted director and would also direct one of Bombay Talkies biggest hits, *Kismet*.

The excitement around Bombay Talkies was palpable.

Himansu wrote to Niranjan Pal, who had also returned to India by this time, to join him in his endeavour as a scriptwriter for Bombay Talkies. Niranjan was trying, not very successfully, to independently work in the growing film industry in India. Though initially reluctant to team up with the German crew he had fallen out with during the shooting of *The Light of Asia*—especially Franz—he agreed to come on board and would soon become a key member of Bombay Talkies. Almost all the early films were based on his stories.

Meanwhile, the German and British technicians, including Franz, had arrived in India. They were a somewhat motley collection of people who had worked on some of Himansu's earlier films but they provided the desired international flavour. With their help, the best technology was sourced for the studio.

Himansu was careful to pair all the foreign technicians in each department with Indian counterparts so that the junior crew could train under professionals while the films were being made. A lot of thought went into how the studio was organised and how it would function. Since they had committed to their investors that they would make six films a year (later rationalised to three films), there was no time to waste.

⌒⌒⌒

At last, the hard and bumpy road of the past five years—ever since she had married Himansu—was smoothening out for Devika. She had found the home she had sought, and she basked in the recognition showered upon her. Their itinerant existence was coming to an end.

While they completed the move to 57, Dady Seth Road, Devika began to go through the story ideas that were coming in, and the one by Niranjan caught her eye. *Jawani ki Hawa* was a thriller-cum-romance. She could play the leading lady. They would have to find a suitable man for the lead opposite her as Himansu had his hands full and besides, though he was only in his early forties, he looked older than his years. She tried her best to look after him, but they were both far too busy—by now the studio had hired more than four hundred workers!

She had set up her own office, with a 'Do Not Enter' sign outside, like those she had seen in the German and British studios. Why not? This was how the stars were distinguished from the ordinary workers. At home, she got an old family retainer to join, who would take care of all the household chores so that she could work without being disturbed. She had a full-time career now, and she began to spend time with the newly recruited workers, training them with the same assiduousness with which she had been trained in Germany.

Many of the employees, regardless of hierarchy, lived on the premises and ate together at the canteen set up there. All the employees, including the actors, were given monthly salaries, and a legal contract was signed with each. Himansu's training with the German, and later, British studios, ensured that the actors always had signed contracts, and so the artistes felt secure. It was an egalitarian set-up, though there was a clear chain of command. No one doubted Himansu's authority, and many of them all but worshipped him.

However, in that patriarchal atmosphere, and with very few women around, most of the men found it difficult to get close to Devika or to understand her. Always aloof, and extremely protective of her privacy, she chose her confidantes carefully, and this would remain her style of functioning till the end. She had to make an extra effort to be friendly towards those who were important for Bombay Talkies, but she did it as a duty. Having spent most of her formative years abroad, she was always more comfortable with the European crew and, of course, Sir Richard, who was much older but adored her.

There were also deeply personal, and very painful reasons why she could not be completely open about her life—reasons she would keep to herself till she met her second husband, Svetoslav. The one time she had been laughed at in school had taught her a lesson forever. She would not be humiliated in public, and preferred always to appear as the mistress of her own destiny. If this meant she had to distance herself from others, so be it.

She continued, however, to accomplish her work professionally, mentoring those who required it while pushing herself to excel in every field, and this included receiving lessons for improving her own spoken Hindi. She would groom and train actors and dancers, look after the wardrobe, take decisions on the equipment to be bought—but she kept her personal travails to herself, and never once allowed anyone to imagine that the relationship between her and Himansu was anything but cordial—till 1936, a watershed year for them, when she reached the breaking point.

Overall, however, those who worked at Bombay Talkies found that the atmosphere in the studio was very congenial, and very different from elsewhere. Not just those from a 'Hindoo' background, but Muslims, Parsis and Christians too began to feel they could have a career within these secure precincts. At Bombay Talkies, there was idealism as well as a family atmosphere, which made up somewhat for the home life they often had to sacrifice.

Buoyed by the enthusiasm of those around them, Devika and Himansu began shooting for *Jawani ki Hawa*. A festive atmosphere prevailed. Many were to remember this as a happy time, even though the workplace was extremely disciplined, like a well-run school.

Himansu and Devika had, within two years of their arrival, raised money from enthusiastic shareholders, built a world-class studio, and were now working on their new film with a team of international technicians. It was an incredible achievement and would be observed with great envy by outsiders.

Happily, despite all that had happened between them in Germany and later, Devika and Himansu continued to share a few close, though increasingly rare moments, as they built Bombay Talkies from an idea to actuality.

Devika gazed at the grounds of Bombay Talkies from her office one evening, after the workers had left.

Slipping an arm around him, she told Himansu, 'You are the most determined man I know. I remember when we had no money, and you said we would do this. Somehow, I don't know how—we created all this, out of nothing, just a mad dream !'

'It's our baby. I don't know if we will ever have a child, but *this* is our baby!'

A shadow crossed her face. This was not a happy subject.

Himansu took out his tin of 555 cigarettes and lit one for her.

'You and I—we can make magic together.'

She laughed, suddenly a little edgy, and said, 'And we will cast a spell on everyone, won't we?'

'You certainly will! They have never seen anyone like you in Hindi cinema. You will change things forever.'

These words were prophetic. Yes, she would change things. But not in the way that he would have imagined.

Letter from Devika to Svetoslav

I send every month out of my pay, without requesting anything, a little sum of ₹15 for the poor, their bread at St Anthony's shrine in Mangalore—this I have done for many years—any little help is useful for the poor there and they need it badly. This is not a bribe to St Anthony, he takes the money because he has to support so many poor...If we have any special request to our Saint then it is best to write it & put it in a sealed envelope, which should be small, write on the envelope "please keep near St Anthony's relics."

Don't think I am childlike dearest, our Saint is a WONDER. I have been looked after by him from a young girl. He has always protected and blessed me.

Bombay, 1945

11

'A BROKEN, UNWANTED THING', 1934–1939

Initially, everything seemed just fine.

The experience of working at Bombay Talkies offered an opportunity for many among the Indian crew to be trained while being paid a salary. The foreign professionals also made an effort to integrate with the rest of the team. Each department worked hard to come up with new ideas to improve efficiency. It was a very inclusive environment.

While Himansu and Devika stuck to their plan and tried to recruit people for Bombay Talkies who were educated, a few exceptions were sometimes necessary. Many of the technicians who joined at different stages were graduates—Nirmal Sengupta, Savak Vacha and Sashadhar Mukerji, who all joined the sound department; J.K. Roy, who was the art director; and J.K. Nandi and Kumudlal Kanjilal Ganguly, who worked at the processing labs. Among the very few non-graduates to hold a key role was Dattaram Pai, the film editor who used to be a waiter at Majestic Cinema. The foreign technicians included Franz Osten as director, Joseph Wirsching as cameraman, Karl von Spretti as set designer, and Len Hartley as sound recordist.

This early recruitment of professionals was also one of the reasons that Bombay Talkies, though it was set up only in 1934, was already in film production by 1935, and released six films between

1935 and 1936. The production was fairly fast, as they would be shooting one film, while already in pre-production mode for the next one. It was nonstop and relentless hard work. The initial offering was one full-length feature—*Jawani ki Hawa*—and two short films—*Mother* and *Always Tell Your Wife*. In this way they were able to stick to their promise of delivering three films annually. In 1936, despite facing some real difficulties, they produced three full-length features—*Jeevan Naiyya*, *Janma Bhoomi* and the classic, *Achchut Kanya*. While the male leads were changed in a few films, Devika was the heroine in all.

One of the biggest difficulties the studio encountered was finding female actors who were educated and from a middle-class background. Devika Rani was the beautiful, public face of Bombay Talkies, but other educated women who were interested in joining films were few and far between. This would remain a constraint for a long time. But the Rais kept trying, and they were quick to encourage any talented young woman who was willing to become an actress, with or without experience.

Begum Khurshid Mirza was one of the few who bravely stepped forward. In a highly unconventional move, Khurshid wrote to Himansu and expressed a desire to work as an actress. She had done some amateur acting before, was both beautiful and talented, and undaunted by the fact that she was a wife and the mother of three children.

It was not easy for her. Though she acted in a few films at Bombay Talkies under the pseudonym of Renuka Devi, she faced criticism at home. Her parents, Sheikh Abdullah and Waheed Jahan Begum, who were the founders of Aligarh Women's College, had educated all their three daughters. But for them, a career in films was unthinkable. Initially, she had to keep her decision to act a complete secret from her family, though her husband was aware of her plans. Her mother got a shock when she discovered, while watching a film, that the on-screen actress Renuka Devi bore a startling resemblance to her daughter, Khurshid. The mood at home turned very sombre when other people learnt she had become an actress. Undeterred, she finally won her parents over and even after she moved to Pakistan after Partition, she continued to act.

She recollected her initial encounter with cinema as being very pleasant. She, along with her police-officer husband and children, was invited to Bombay Talkies to dine with Devika and Himansu. They were all 'charmed and won over'. Sir Richard also invited them for dinner to the Taj hotel. Khurshid and Devika got along like old friends, and would continue to correspond when Khurshid went back home in Aligarh. Later, when she was to act opposite Jairaj in *Bhabhi* (1938), the film that made her famous, she was told that she would be accorded the same respect as Devika Rani. As a part of her familiarisation, she was 'photographed from every angle while the make-up man was instructed about shading and lighting'. She was also given singing lessons and taken around the studio to observe film production during the three weeks she was there before her own shooting schedule began.

Apart from a safe environment, Bombay Talkies exuded respectability in the manner in which the films were shot, and in the subjects that were taken up. Initially, the films dealt mainly with middle-class or upper-middle-class situations, and the clothes and dialogues were accordingly genteel. It was only after the first few films that the scripts became a little more adventurous, going beyond romance and motherhood to address the caste system, widowhood, tribal oppression and urban crime. But in none of these films was there any overt or covert sexuality. Nor any egregious violence.

This secure and sanctified environment appealed to the women they wanted to attract—as did the monthly salaries, at a time when only a minuscule number of women worked outside their homes. Khurshid herself was offered a generous salary of ₹600 once she had a larger role to play in *Bhabhi*. This was when Himansu earned only around ₹650 per month.

As early as 1937, Khurshid aka Renuka Devi wrote to Devika after she returned home from Bombay Talkies:

Here people were simply brimming with gossip when we arrived [back from Bombay Talkies]. So we have taken the bull by the horns straight off and told them everything. This was the only way to quieten them otherwise they would have been asking and we would have gone on denying. Akbar [her husband] has even written to his people about our adventures and that we have every inclination of repeating it. ...

I saw some stills from "Jeevan Prabhat" in Film India. One of them included myself. I got the thrill of my life. You see I have not got used to playing the part of a film actress yet.

Of course, she was thrilled with the opportunity she had been given. In most studios, women were not treated with so much respect. Even at Bombay Talkies, things would change over time, but in the early years, there was a lot of easy camaraderie, perhaps because some of the women who joined, like Khurshid and later Leela Chitnis, were married and had children. Devika, too, tried to make the newly recruited actresses feel as comfortable as she could.

When Khurshid returned to Bombay Talkies in 1941 to act in *Naya Sansar*, after Himansu's death, she found the atmosphere still very friendly and familial. But she noticed many material changes. The studio had expanded and the large orchards surrounding it had been cut down to make room for small, two-bedroom bungalows. She stayed in one of them with her family, paying a nominal rent. According to her, there was 'no competitiveness and a feeling of goodwill pervaded the production'. Only one film was shot at a time and during the breaks, everyone ate together. The atmosphere was unique, and the studio was run almost like a school. 'The gong was rung at 9 a.m. and everyone arrived on the sets ready with make-up and with rehearsed dialogues.'

The discipline that had been instilled by Himansu and the good practices that had been initiated by the international crew five years earlier, continued after his death. For that, the credit belonged to Devika and to the team members who believed in the values of Bombay Talkies, even though by 1941 the studio was facing some internal factionalism, in which Devika was also embroiled. The two groups, however, worked hard not to let the quality of productions be affected in any way.

At every stage, Khurshid said, she felt well looked after. On the day *Naya Sansar* was released, the studio car took the star and her children to the cinema theatre, where Ashok Kumar, Devika Rani, Rai Bahadur Chuni Lall and Sashadhar Mukerji were already present. There was friendly banter and appreciation as the crowds called out for Renuka Devi.

In her memoirs, she commented that there was a marked difference in the atmosphere at Bombay Talkies as compared to other studios. Though the money offered to her was much higher elsewhere, the other studios did not have the class or the close bonding that she found at Bombay Talkies. She was offered ₹5,000 per month just the following year, for a new film to be shot at Pancholi Studios in Lahore, but once there, she sorely missed the friendliness she had experienced during the shooting of *Naya Sansar*.

This bonhomie was to set Bombay Talkies apart from all the rest. The screenplay writer and satirist Saadat Hasan Manto wrote frankly about his days in the Bombay film world. His experience of most studios was that either the actresses of the period belonged to the class of courtesans and prostitutes, or they were young, ambitious women—who were often exploited. In one of his essays ('Rafiq Ghaznavi: The Ladies' Man' in *Bitter Fruit*, edited and translated by Khalid Hasan) he recorded a meeting with Seth Ardashir Irani at the Imperial Film Company, where he found him pumping the breasts of an aspiring actress as one would 'an old-fashioned car horn'.

When Khurshid changed her Muslim name to a Hindu one for the screen, it was not done just to play to the majority gallery, but to disguise her real identity as well. Men were not exempt from this either, and while Bombay Talkies did not start the fashion of allocating pseudonyms, some other actors also underwent a similar transformation.

When Yusuf Khan joined Bombay Talkies in 1944, his name was changed to Dilip Kumar by Devika Rani. Breaking the news to his father that he had become an actor was almost as difficult for him as it had been for Khurshid. Nothing much had changed in the intervening decade and the actor's profession was still considered disreputable. Apparently, his own father had scoffed at the other family from Peshawar, the Kapoors, when they allowed Prithviraj Kapoor to become an actor. Dilip, therefore, hid the reality from Sarwar Khan, who owned a dry fruits shop in Crawford Market. But the truth was gleefully revealed by Bisheshwar Nath, Prithviraj's father, who pointed out the poster of *Jwar Bhata* (Dilip's first film) to his father. Sarwar Khan, very much like Renuka Devi's mother, was astonished that the hero in the poster, Dilip Kumar, so closely resembled his son, Yusuf. It was a while before he got used to the idea of his son being in the movies.

The selection of new actors, the renaming and grooming, was a continuous process at Bombay Talkies even though the returns were not immediately obvious. Taking risks was wired into the system by Himansu, and Devika gave him her full support. She was a non-conformist, and the years she had spent away from her family, doing things they may not have approved of, kept her independence and rebelliousness alive. The last seven years with Himansu and the personal agony inflicted by him, had given her a gritty courage. She trained herself to understand the importance of position and power, and found that she could be ruthlessly ambitious, just like her husband. But she balanced it with an outward softness that made it all acceptable. Being a woman, no one expected her to be ruthless anyway.

Tara Ali Baig who had already been very impressed with Devika in Switzerland in 1929, visited the studio with her husband, Rashid, more than a decade later. Sir Richard drove them to Malad. As she was to write in her memoirs, *Portraits of an Era*, she noticed that 'Devika had such a soft and cultured way of speaking, and with her feminine charm and laughing eyes, always gave the impression of being extremely gentle and delicate.' Yet she found a tough side to her as well. Devika told her how she got a script out of an elusive writer by locking him into a room at the Taj Mahal hotel with lots of pen and paper—and staying away till he had done the script. Tara felt that she had a 'rare understanding of a very complex business world'. After Himansu's death, Tara maintained that Devika 'held the company together, made bigger and better films, increased the company's assets enormously, and in the process launched such famous names as, among others, Dilip Kumar, Madhubala...'

In its quest for educated artistes, especially women from good families, the studio sometimes ended up facing the wrath of a whole community. The Parsi music composer, Saraswati Devi, whose real name was Khursheed Manchershah Minocha-Homji, was introduced to Himansu by Sarojini Naidu's brother, Harindranath Chattopadhyaya. While her sister, Manek (renamed Chandra Prabha) did a spot of acting, Khursheed alias Saraswati Devi was to compose the music for two hundred songs or so, first at Bombay Talkies and later as a freelance music director.

Saraswati Devi's entry as a composer was resisted by the Parsi community and they held protests outside Bombay Talkies. To make matters worse, her sister Manek also joined Bombay Talkies. The sloganeering and press reports against the studio intensified. But Himansu stuck to his guns, and his publicist K.A. Abbas, who felt that all controversies were free publicity, invited the press to cover the daily demonstrations which took place outside the studio gates. Everyone thus heard about the studio's first film, *Jawani ki Hawa*, long before it was released!

In fact, Baburao Patel, the much-feared editor of *Filmindia* frankly admitted in September-October 1935, that he watched the film only to get a glimpse of the Parsi girls. He said, 'I had gone there thinking probably that there was something to look at, but when I saw them— by God. I won't tell you what I said. It is not worth expressing in good company.' It was a rude remark, typical of Baburao, but clearly the Parsi protest had worked in creating an audience for the film which, according to him, required 'drastic editing'.

But he did add, 'Devika Rani is easily the best artist in the picture. She is sweet and sympathetic and gives a bright promise of a great future. We wish her every success! The other girls are apologies and poor ones too. The Parsi girls, God bless them.'

In the January 1936 issue of the magazine he again wondered how *Jawani ki Hawa* was allowed to be released for public exhibition. 'Is it because the Parsi community happens to be smallest in numbers and as such incapable of disturbing the equilibrium of the Government?'

Saraswati Devi turned out to be an inspired choice. Her knowledge of traditional ragas gave her music a classical tonality, including marching songs such as '*Chal chal re naujawan*' (sung by the actor Ashok Kumar) from the film *Bandhan*. Her biggest challenge was that she had to compose for and train actors who knew little about singing. It was to her credit that she often managed to extract talent where none was apparent.

She composed at least two iconic songs for Bombay Talkies— '*Koi humdum na raha*' for the film *Jeevan Naiyya* and '*Ik chatur naar badi hoshiyaar*' for the film *Jhoola*. Both songs were sung by Ashok Kumar and much later, by his younger brother, Kishore Kumar. In the later versions, some variations were introduced in the lyrics. '*Koi humdum na raha*', originally written by J.S. Casshyap was re-written by Majrooh Sultanpuri for *Jhumroo*. But the basic tune set in raag Jhinjhoti was retained. Similarly, the lyrics of '*Ik chatur naar*', first written by Pradeep, were extended by the lyricist Pradeep Kishen for *Padosan*.

To give Himansu his due, he was always good at spotting talent. According to an article in *Parsi Khabar*, written by Sharad Dutt (posted online on 16 April 2018), Saraswati Devi and her younger sister Manek had been trained by Pandit Vishnu Narayan Bhatkhande in Lucknow. They had even formed an orchestra, with Manek playing the sitar, dilruba and mandolin while Saraswati Devi

played the organ. In later years, after Bombay Talkies closed down, she composed music for playback singers such as Lata Mangeshkar. Tragically, she died alone and in penury after fracturing a leg when she fell from a bus in Bombay. None of her erstwhile colleagues from Bombay Talkies, some of whom were very big stars by then, came to her rescue. The only help she received was from her neighbours and a few friends. Today, she is recognised as one of the first women composers of Indian cinema, along with Jaddanbai. She was a music teacher towards the end of her life, and died at the age of sixty-eight.

It was these kinds of discoveries, and nurturing of new talent, on and off the screen, which made Bombay Talkies special. There was also an easy fluidity of professional interaction between the acting, cinematography and lighting teams, which meant that every evening, after the shoot was over, everyone would sit around and interact with Himansu, Sashadhar Mukerji (from the sound department, who was very close to Himansu) and other technicians to analyse the day's proceedings and discuss the next day's shoot.

Occasionally, Devika would join them, but she also had the responsibility of getting the costumes ready for the next day's shoots; there could be up to three sets of each costume, in case anything got spoilt. If she was acting in the film, she had her own lines and songs to rehearse. She was also working across departments, and training fresh actors to emote and dance. As a result, she had less time and fewer opportunities to bond with the others after work.

As the writer Manto would point out in his essays on cinema, the training at Bombay Talkies allowed any intelligent and interested technician or actor to pick up a working knowledge of filmmaking. This close, collective effort also meant that sometimes credit was given to a person for work done entirely by someone else. In his essay on Paro Devi, Manto points out that Gyan Mukerji received the credit for films directed by Sashadhar Mukerji, even when he had not directed a single foot of those films. But there was no resentment, and the camaraderie, at least in the early years, seemed genuine.

The continuing interest and support from the powers-that-be meant that a few visits by the governor of Bombay, Lord Brabourne, and his wife were to be expected. According to Niranjan, Brabourne had a soft spot for Devika Rani and would often visit her surreptitiously. But there were also well publicised visits—including when he and his wife came by in May 1939 to see the technologically advanced and well-equipped studio.

The visit got excellent coverage in the *Times of India*, which reported on 17 May 1939:

> The Governor of Bombay and Lady Brabourne... were received by Sir Chimanlal Setalvad, Sir Pheroze Sethna, Directors of the Company, Mr Himanshu Rai and Sir Richard Temple and shown over the most up-to-date cinematograph studios in India.

The article stressed the 'delightful' surroundings and the 'magnificent' studio. It added that Lord and Lady Brabourne were able to watch Devika Rani while she was shooting a scene.

Totally impressed, the reporter talked about the projection theatre where 'scenes are shown to the executives' shortly after having been shot. There was a mix of homegrown and imported technology in the studio, especially the laboratory, including a system of filtering out the omnipresent dust. The Bombay Talkies studio may not be extravagant, concluded the reporter, but it is efficient. This was this kind of reputation that the studio enjoyed, which meant that visitors and investors were equally impressed.

Fortunately, the Indian and foreign crews continued to be well integrated. Though tensions were rising in Europe, on the campus an amiable atmosphere existed between the British and the Germans. But the presence of the latter would not have been missed by Lord Brabourne or those who succeed him, such as Governor Lumley.

Despite all the state-of-the-art equipment and the technical skill of the international crew, the first few Bombay Talkies films did not do as well as expected. This was surprising because *Jawani ki Hawa*, released in 1935, was a fast-paced murder mystery, shot entirely on a train which had an engine and four bogeys and was specially kept running to Lonavla and back during the shoot.

The hero was a tall and extremely good-looking actor, Najam ul Hussain. (Interestingly, his name was not changed for the screen.) Devika Rani, for her part, looked, spoke and sang with an innocence rarely seen on screen at the time.

Najam and Devika were depicted as the young lovers Ratanlal and Kamala, who run away to escape the wrath of her father, Maganlal. On the train, they are chased by the irate father. During this chaos, a murder takes place. The rest of the film is a whodunit, as Kamala offers herself as the murderer, but since this is palpably untrue, a hunt begins for the real killer.

The other two films which came out in the same year were short features—*Mother* and the rather presciently named *Always Tell Your Wife*. They were experiments, and possibly also made to fulfil the promise of three films made to investors. None of them led to any explosion at the box office either. Devika played the lead in the two shorts, and the actor opposite her was seemingly irrelevant because J.S. Casshyap, a diminutive and highly forgettable actor, is remembered more for the crisp dialogues he wrote for most of the Bombay Talkies films rather than his acting. He also wrote some songs.

Could he have been chosen because Devika was seen to be getting a little too close to Najam?

A subtle shift was taking place in the studio, which Himansu did not grasp at the time, caught up as he was in ensuring the smooth functioning of the operations as well as keeping the company afloat. The partnership that he and Devika had built up over the last decade was beginning to fray in the harsh, competitive environment in which they now found themselves, surrounded by people who were hungry to succeed. Devika too was under a lot of pressure to perform, and as the glamorous face of the studio, she had to ensure that each film was a success.

They worked hard, grooming and training the vast majority of employees, for many of whom this was their first regular job. The foreign crew also needed looking after, with the Germans in particular struggling to communicate with their Indian counterparts, at least initially. Sir Richard Temple required some amount of hand-holding and then, of course, there were demands from the board members of both HIT and Bombay Talkies. There was not a moment to relax, for either Himansu or Devika.

With hundreds of employees or 'workers' as they were called, many of whom also lived on the premises, there were scores of interpersonal issues creating ripples under the surface. It was only natural that some of the tensions should spill over into the personal lives of Devika and Himansu, who were now spending a lot of time apart, often with new-found 'work' friends, who could see that the couple, individually, needed support. What many of them did not know was that there was a much darker aspect to this distancing between Himansu and Devika, which neither of them spoke about. It was something that almost broke Devika, but she would only reveal this ten years later. For now, Devika desperately needed some solace, and as it happened, it was close at hand.

Thanks to the film they had recently shot together, Najam, her very handsome co-star, became Devika's confidante. They were practically the same age, and while rehearsing in private, and later while performing in front of the camera, they discovered a kindred spirit in each other. The sheer physicality of filmmaking, of being in 'love' for the camera, ignited a passion that refused to die after the cameras stopped rolling.

So far, Devika had only been close to one man—Himansu. He had romanced her in real life and on screen. For her, a light flirtation was acceptable with people who mattered. But to be drawn towards a mere co-worker was completely out of character, especially since she considered herself to be very different from other actresses. But this time, she was propelled by ominous circumstances.

The studio in Malad was far away from Bombay, in the suburbs, and there were very few people Devika could meet or even spend time with as friends. Whenever she went to town it was only to attend board meetings or meet common friends, and so Himansu or Sir Richard always accompanied her. She was, in any case, hesitant about discussing her problems with anyone, for fear that they would blow up and affect the studio.

It was different for Himansu. He would routinely linger over drinks and cigarettes after the daily shoot, with team members such as Sashadhar Mukerji and Niranjan Pal. This meant that he had little time for Devika, and added to their troubles as a couple.

On the other hand, Najam, though also a married man, appeared to have all the time for her. He was very different in every way from Himansu. To begin with, he was tall and athletic. He was also younger (by now, Himansu was forty-four) and very well spoken. It was flattering for Devika to have his undivided attention in the midst of the daily struggle at work at the studio. As for Najam, it may have begun as sheer courtesy towards the beautiful wife of the boss, but as they rehearsed and worked together, the attraction became real.

According to the publicity booklet of *Jawani ki Hawa*, Najam, even if you discount the hyperbole, came from a distinguished background:

> Sheikh Najam-ul-Hussain had been selected out of 2,000 young men to play opposite Devika Rani. [He] is endowed with a gorgeous voice for the microphone, powerful eyes and a face which photographs well. Hails from Hoshiarpur—a scion of a noble and ancient family which once ruled over Kashmir and Doab. A distinguished graduate of the Punjab University, an all-round athlete and sportsman. Studied music under famous singers. Both the songs sung by him in *Jawani-ki-Hawa* are his own composition.

About Devika, despite all her achievements so far, the booklet revealed little that was not already known, except adding that her 'pet aversion' was 'To see herself as others see her, and nothing can persuade her to see herself on screen.' This humility was probably meant to make her seem more human to the less privileged members of the viewing public.

Jawani ki Hawa had a lot riding on it, as the studio's first film. Besides, the cast was huge. Apart from the crowds, which included wedding guests, musicians, dancers, railway passengers and so on, according to the brochure, the film had thirty-six named characters. It was directed by Franz Osten, written by Niranjan Pal and produced by Himansu Rai, but among the actors, only Devika got star billing.

Niranjan's own foreword in the booklet made it appear as though the film dripped with romance—'Love's way is as the wind':

> The heartstring of the heroine... [was] attuned to the melody of love. She idealised love. Here is a rare attitude of mind in these days when the carnal aspect of passion has found nauseating expression everywhere, when in the cause of realism, so called, we seemed to have lost all reticence and reverence. A character who thus equipped travels into the province of love, is ready for a great adventure and a great fulfilment.

Did Devika get carried away with all that talk about love? Did she feel something was missing from her life? As Niranjan wrote almost prophetically in the booklet:

> [*Jawani ki Hawa*] is the story of a girl who placed love above all else; it shows how the shadow of love cast on the pathway of life can divert the footsteps of the young and initiate [them] into unexpected channels.

In 1935, Devika was almost twenty-eight years old. She was no longer a young, innocent woman; she was cosmopolitan and sophisticated. She was already being feted as the most beautiful woman on the Indian screen, even before the film was released. So why did she allow herself to be attracted to a married man who lacked many, or perhaps all, of Himansu's persuasive skills? The answer probably lay in Najam's youth—and the sympathy he offered her. His naivety may have even reminded her of herself before Himansu arrived in her life. All the men she had met so far, including Himansu, were much older or had to be cultivated and flirted with for business. She was not exactly surrounded by specimens of masculine charm, as Bombay Talkies was also finding it difficult to get educated and good-looking male actors.

Najam was sensitive to her needs and happy to risk everything for a few hours with her, as indeed, the consequences would have been terrible were they to be caught together. Like all clandestine affairs, the excitement possibly made their relationship more fun than it might have been otherwise.

For Devika, the affair was a complete anomaly. She was rebellious, but a 'good' girl for whom 'honour' meant a great deal. This 'affair' was completely out of character unless, as we now know, there was a trigger that pushed her over the edge. It was also precisely the kind of behaviour she looked down upon, as she had made evident with her attitude towards those actresses who were once courtesans or dancing girls.

The pressure continued to build, both on the personal and professional fronts. Bombay Talkies, the studio which would be described by the *Motion Picture Magazine* in October 1937 as having 'revolutionised the Indian Motion picture world' needed a row of successes. After all, it was 'a huge studio erected and fitted up on the latest lines to make what is today one of the finest production units in the world and certainly the best outside of Europe and America'.

While they could continue to make films, at some stage, questions would increasingly be asked about profitability. In the past, Himansu could settle debts with some dexterous juggling of assets and accounts, not to mention loans from girlfriends and other gullible individuals, including Devika and Sir Richard. But now, he had to report to a watchful board of directors, led by Sir Chimanlal who was wont to ask uncomfortable questions, while professing full faith in Himansu and Devika.

Himansu's public facade of an affectionate and caring man began to disappear in private into a dark, suspicious and angry person, who could resort to violence. Initially, only Devika was subjected to this side of him. Unable to cope with the 'ugly' happenings at home, she began to confide a little in her mother. She also began to rely increasingly on Najam. As the abuse continued, as she wrote later to Svetoslav, she began to think of herself as 'a broken, unwanted thing'. But she had to draw a veil over all that was happening with her, as her pragmatic self realised that if the truth were to come out, the studio would collapse.

One wonders now whether Himansu's abusive behaviour was an early sign of the nervous breakdown which would overwhelm him some years later. Or was this decline triggered by insecurity when he saw his wife with Najam? Undoubtedly, the two of them made a stunning pair.

Clearly, Devika felt isolated and alone, yet she did not reveal that behind the scenes was a painful story of domestic violence. From what she would say later of those traumatic years, despite everything, she still respected Himansu as a professional and wanted to maintain that image.

When Devika first met Himansu, she was not yet twenty. It was only after they were married that she realised that he walked on a very thin edge. A workaholic and a high achiever, he had enormous expectations from those around him. If she upset him, he would not just criticise her, he would give her the 'usual thrashing', as she put it.

She would write later of her 'scars...which human beings have inflicted on me in all their vile ugliness and horror...those things that happened had really taught me how to take punishment bodily, mentally, and at the same time, grow within and try to better myself.' In her 'childlike misery' she began to think of this violence as part of her training to remain humble—and yet hopeful of a better future.

Nothing in her sheltered life had prepared her for this. The only time her father had scolded her, she had run away—at the age of three-and-a-half. Now, twenty-five years later, she began to realise that she might have to walk away again, from all that she held so dear, and had worked so hard for. How else was it possible to survive—

how long could she keep up this dual existence of acting for the camera, and then acting in real life? How long could she continue to pretend that she was not bruised and beaten?

The affair with Najam gave her the warmth and attention she craved—quite apart from escaping the machinelike life she now led. She never spoke about the affair and its aftermath, or defended her actions—and her rectitude for most of her life was often mistaken for arrogance. It was only in a letter written on 26 June 1945 to Svetoslav that she admitted that Himansu did not hesitate to abuse her physically, sometimes leaving her bloodied and unconscious on the floor. But she added proudly that she took his physical and verbal abuse with courage so that no one would know what she had gone through. She did not want to be an object of pity. Nor did she want Himansu to feel he had power over her. She kept the pain to herself and drowned herself in work.

By 1945, when she wrote the letter to Svetoslav giving all the facts, she was already acclaimed as the industry's top star, and was the head of Bombay Talkies. With the memory of the abuse always fresh in her mind, she was almost dismissive of her own achievements, saying she was not a 'great artist'. Her insecurity could also have been due to the violence she had endured. She had worked in around fourteen films (till 1945) but only a few of them were outstanding, she said—which was far from truth. Perhaps Himansu had destroyed her confidence with his frequent criticism of her poor acting skills. Somehow, even though she won accolades and glowed on screen, she accepted his punishment and humiliation without a murmur. She believed him when he said she was not good enough.

Till she met Najam, she did not think she had a chance to get away from the prison where she worked like a 'slave' and was frequently beaten. Najam offered her release—a new beginning. He also offered her love—a simple love, not the complex and hurtful offering from Himansu.

The pressure of making at least three films each year also brought her close to breaking point. Just as the first three films ended, another film on young love almost thwarted, *Jeevan Naiyya*, had gone on the floor. Though she was exhausted, she could not stop working. And there was no escaping Himansu, who had to be faced in the office and at home.

Things began to spiral out of control when Devika and Najam began shooting together for *Jeevan Naiyya*, their next film. This was in 1936, an eventful year.

By now, whenever Devika looked at Himansu's face, she was frightened, for he was angry all the time. And if an artist is scared, she wrote in her letter to Svetoslav, 'nothing comes, no inspiration comes, nothing'. She was scared that he would accuse her of poor acting or some other slip-up, and she would be beaten. The new fear was that this fear would begin to show on camera as well.

She said in her letter that she would work hard on each picture, three per year, with each one taking up to two or three months. Her resentment is apparent. She no longer spoke about Himansu as her husband, but as a dictator who cared for nothing but work. He would not even let her rest when she had malaria and was running a temperature of 102 or 103 degrees. It must have been dreadful to be under the hot lights in that state. But she not only played her own role, she would also dress the other artistes and the dancers. Even when she showed her work to him, 'he never said a nice thing, we were satisfied if he passed it'.

In another letter, she recalled that once, when her period was very heavy, she was given no respite and had to dance on the set. She fell unconscious when she reached home.

But the worst was when he came into her dressing room before she went on the set and berated her, picking up the thick script and hitting her with it on her face. He was 'shouting, "What do you think you are paid for? What the hell do you mean by giving such a rotten close up? What do you think you are paid for?" and he went on and on till I dropped and fainted.'

She was proud that she did not fall till she had lost consciousness. That must have annoyed Himansu, that she was not scared. She took all the beatings without flinching, and always looked him straight in the eye. 'Not a sound, not a cry, and a still face, straight on.'

One person who definitely knew about the beatings was the old family retainer who worked in the house. After these episodes, he would help her get up, wipe away the blood, and give her some brandy and ice. Once, he even attacked Himansu with a stick to stop him from hitting her. But Himansu could not dismiss him as he would have told her mother everything, and then there would have been a scandal. Ultimately, the old retainer's presence may have saved her sanity.

Devika would be reminded of her 'suffering and misery' each time she saw old photographs or films. She said she did not regret that it had happened to her and she was not 'sorry in the least and I am glad in a way that I was able to stand it and I am not bitter'. It was her way of building her resistance and her ability to take any kind of physical or verbal abuse. It helped her through difficult moments even at Bombay Talkies. Whenever she faced Himansu's anger, she trained herself to show that she was not frightened of him and 'behaved quite gay'. Some support was shown by the German team members, especially Franz, who was one of the few people who knew that she was keeping up a pretence.

It was this refusal on her part to show her fear—and being carefree on the surface—that gave everyone the impression that she was responsible for creating the crisis at Bombay Talkies. In that male-dominated world, Devika was definitely the less popular of the two. But as the pressure of making films grew and the violence at home increased, she became worried that Himansu could harm her in more ways than she could bear. It speaks volumes about her loyalty to Himansu and the studio that she never spoke about this darkness in her life to anyone at all.

Rather than let people know of her suffering and humiliation, she decided to leave with Najam while *Jeevan Naiyya* was still being filmed. One must assume that she had reached some sort of breaking point because she was not the sort to abandon a film halfway, especially knowing that she could become the butt of lurid gossip. Devika was not a quitter—and this was apparent from the way she handled the situation, as it developed.

Najam and she left at night for Calcutta, where they took a room at the Grand Hotel. They were planning to join New Theatres, which was in hot competition with Bombay Talkies then.

Did Najam know about the abuse? Possibly. The circumstances would have had to be very compelling for an up-and-coming actor to run away with his boss's wife in the middle of a high-profile project. It is also likely that they had been seen together and may have wanted to escape before things became ugly. Some of Himansu's impotent anger and abuse may well have stemmed from his discovery of their affair. Bombay Talkies had been their dream project, and it meant nothing if Devika was not by his side. Her threat of joining New Theatres would have been a serious blow, since Bombay Talkies was built around her persona and there was no one to match her—there was no comparable actresses at the studio or in Bombay.

Himansu was in a fix. What would the board and the shareholders say? They had managed to keep the incident out of the press—but a solution had to be found, and quickly. Like other misogynistic men who abuse their wives, he probably did not blame himself. So long as Devika was silent about it, he could carry on.

Her departure, quick and overnight, made him understand that she was not going to beg him to stop. But without that assurance, she would not return. In that sense, even if she was not in love with Najam, Calcutta represented safe harbour. There might be a scandal, but at least she would be alive, and not bait for all and sundry without a man by her side. It was a city where she would not be a stranger. Her flight sent Himansu a clear message—that she did not need him anymore.

A clandestine affair would have been ruinous for Devika personally. But she could not live with any more secrets. Why suffer on a daily basis—it was better to escape and live with a man with whom she had a good mental and physical rapport. Besides, she had too much pride to explain anything to anyone. It was more in her character to take the blows and move on. In this way, she would survive and so would the studio. There would be a temporary storm, and then everything would calm down (as it had happened when she married Himansu).

Perhaps the escape from Himansu made Devika realise that he no longer had any power over her—she was free, and she had survived. But the reasons for her elopement would only be known to Himansu, Devika, and perhaps Najam. Even the conjectures of insiders like Sa'adat Hassan Manto were way off target.

According to Manto:

> When Najam-ul-Hussain ran off with Devika Rani, all of Bombay Talkies was in turmoil. The film they were making had gone onto the floor and some scenes had already been shot. However, Najam-ul-Hussain had decided to pull the leading lady out of the celluloid world into the real one. The worst affected and the most worried man at Bombay Talkies was Himansu Rai, Devika Rani's husband, and the heart and soul of the company.

Was this, then, another reason for the distance between Himansu and Devika? According to all those who were at Bombay Talkies, Himansu Rai was the bedrock of the company. In which case, what was Devika? Had she not been an equal partner and struggled alongside him from the beginning? She had sold her jewellery, lived in near penury, stood by him even though he had betrayed her, helped pay off his debts, raised funds through her personal contacts, shared his dreams, abandoned her family to marry him, worked day and night for the films at Bombay Talkies. Yet, in the eyes of most people, he was the one who was being exploited by her.

Had the dominant patriarchy cut her out completely? At what point did Devika begin to realise that people saw Himansu as the worker and she as the usurper? That people sympathised with him, and saw her as just another actress on the make?

As Manto says, 'Himansu Rai was a very hard working man, a filmmaker totally absorbed in his craft, and basically a loner.' What he did not know was that before Bombay Talkies was founded, Himansu had not been a loner. For at least eight years, he had his muse, Devika, with whom he shared everything. Now his ideas were shared with Niranjan or Sashadhar. And then, when he came home, it was Devika who got the brunt of his frustration.

The popular image of Devika, at least among the men who claimed to know her, is reflected in a short story written by Manto called 'A Woman for All Seasons'. In this thinly veiled satire based on the happenings at Bombay Talkies around the time Devika left with Najam, all of Manto's latent bias is revealed—Devika is exploitative while Himansu is 'hard working' and nice. What he does not seem to understand is that Devika, like Himansu, had to constantly cultivate those who were likely to support the studio—she had to be every bit as clever as Himansu was. But what was acceptable in Himansu's case became flirtatious and adulterous behaviour in hers.

Manto calls her Lateeka Rani, and introduces a few changes in the narrative so that it is not obvious who he is talking about. His Lateeka is cold and imperial, she does not make a single move without calculating the impact it could have. Right from watering the plants in the Englishman's garden (to gain his sympathy, and get him to invest in Bombay Talkies) to running away with her lover, the actress plans it all. Even before her husband dies, she has already designed the clothes that she will wear at the funeral. There is no empathy at all in the writer for Devika–Lateeka.

One of the characters in the short story, a rejected leading man, says:

> She is a woman utterly devoid of the capacity to love. She has not eloped with her new leading man because she loves him but because it is a move to revive her sagging career. She has gone on her own and taken him along as one takes a domestic. Had she asked me to play this role, she would have been disappointed

because I would have refused to play her game. She is now ready to return because, according to her calculations, her return is several days overdue.

Did Manto think that Devika–Lateeka would run away with a lover in order to grab attention? Or did he mean this would ensure that Bombay Talkies would value her more? That may have been closer to the truth.

What Manto did not know was that Himansu did ask her to return. Evidently, he was the only one who really knew why she had left. He did his best to persuade her and agreed that she would retain her prime position in the studio. According to his family, which was never very fond of Devika, he threatened to sue Najam for adultery and divorce Devika. But because she came back stronger than she had left, it soon became apparent that she had the upper hand. He was simply unable to carry on without her.

Devika returned, not as a scarlet woman but as a victor. Even though Himansu's psychological issues were never resolved and he would still be occasionally overwhelmed with rage, the couple were back together. But the main difference was that now that his mental issues began to be more apparent, she was quietly recognised in her role as his primary caregiver. The power equation shifted as he became more and more dependent on her. Behind their pact was the obvious understanding that the studio would collapse if either of them left.

***

And what became of Najam, the man who had sacrificed his career, his marriage and his life? Tragically, Najam became the scapegoat and a laughing stock when Devika went back to Bombay Talkies and Himansu, leaving him alone in Calcutta. The loss for him was far greater, because after he an Devika broke up, he more or less lost any relevance in Indian cinema. To his credit, he did not speak about his humiliation and went ahead and joined New Theatres.

New Theatres had been set up in 1931 by Birendranath Sircar (or B.N. Sircar, as he was known). In 1936, they were ready to make a foray into Hindi cinema. Had Najam and Devika come as a package deal, it would have been the perfect launch for the company.

Najam, unfortunately, soon lost his top billing as a hero. For a few years he played second fiddle to other actors such as Prithviraj Kapoor in *Anath Ashram* (1937) and K.L. Saigal in *Dushman* (1938). Despite being overshadowed, he did act in one major hit called *Nartaki*, which was directed by Debaki Bose and starred Leela Desai. Leela played a courtesan who falls in love with a priest's son, Satyasundar (Najam). They are forced to leave the temple, but undergo a spiritual transformation and finally Satyasundar returns to the temple. The story was fairly close to the bone and, as had already happened in real life, the lovers are separated in the end.

Najam retained his phenomenal good looks and while still in Calcutta, there were rumours of an affair with another leading lady, Jahan Ara Kajjan, who was by all accounts, far more flamboyant than Devika. She was a singer and theatre actor who worked for Madan Theatres, and was extremely successful. She died before the age of thirty and did not transition to Bombay.

After acting in one last film in 1942, *Meenakshi*, Najam left for Pakistan in the post-Partition days. He remained on the sidelines there, in films such as *Ashiana* (1964) and *Heer Ranjha* (1970), in which he played Heer's father. On hindsight, his leaving Bombay Talkies was a major indiscretion from which he never really recovered. After their brief time together in Calcutta, he did not meet Devika again. He died in 1980.

Manto's short story 'A Woman for All Seasons' may have contained a grain of truth in its depiction of the characters of Prafula Roy and Lateeka Rani. In the story, after Lateeka returns to the studio:

Household servants told everyone that Prafula had become extremely ill tempered and always looked angry. Sometimes he would abuse Lateeka in the most vile language but she never reacted. He could not sleep well at night and often Lateeka could be seen massaging his head or pressing his feet.

According to his fictionalised narrative, people in the studio began calling her a witch and wondered if Prafula Roy would smash her head and his own.

There was little doubt that her return to Bombay Talkies was traumatic for both Devika and Himansu. As the gossip about them spread, he was seen as the cuckolded husband who had begged her to come back and she was the adulterous wife, on the lookout for another escapade. It was now well known that they had separate bedrooms, though he would often request her to sleep in his room at night. But now, he needed her more than she needed him. She had proved that there were other men out there, younger and better looking than him, whom she could have if she wanted. He became more insecure, and her dominance was resented by many of the men in the studio, who saw in her the power to destroy what they had created. In their eyes, Himansu was the real architect of the studio and Devika the negative force which needed to be controlled. In that setup, where all the wives sat at home, this very public denigration of a respectable man by a mere wife, even if she was Devika Rani, was unacceptable.

For the studio, the biggest problem was, who would play the lead opposite Devika? There was a film on the floor, *Jeevan Naiyya*, which had to be completed. The portions which had already been shot with Najam would have to be scrapped. It was at this point that Sashadhar Mukherjee, the formidable problem-solver, came up with an answer that changed the course of cinema once again.

Himansu trusted Sashadhar implicitly, and he had never let him down so far. Sashadhar was one of four brothers—Ravindramohan, Subodh and Prabodh Mukherjee were the other three—who all contributed to Indian cinema and left remarkable individual legacies. Their children and grandchildren would end up becoming stars and directors. Sashadhar began his career as a sound recordist at Bombay Talkies and later some of his relatives such as Gyan Mukerji and Kumud Kanjilal Ganguly would also join the studio.

Sashadhar now suggested that his brother-in-law, Kumud Kanjilal Ganguly, who was working in the laboratory as an assistant, could be a possible replacement for Najam. There was a dire need to get someone who was pleasant-looking but who would not be attracted to Devika. Kumud, as it happened, was petrified of her—in short, he was Devika-proof.

Kumud had been studying law in Calcutta after earning a degree in science. As Kishore Valicha tells us in his biography on Ashok Kumar, *Dadamoni*, he wanted to work in films behind the scenes and had gladly accepted Sashadhar's employment offer in the Bombay Talkies laboratory. At the time he joined, the tall, thin young man had been asked to give a screen test and to sing, but the audition, to his great relief, was a 'miserable failure'. He had no intention of becoming an actor. Despite this, he was coerced into doing one short, highly forgettable scene in *Jawani ki Hawa*. He had to catch a train (which was the setting for the entire film) just as it left the platform.

When Sashadhar asked Kumud if he would act opposite Devika Rani, he refused outright. He was simply not interested. But he was marched off to meet Himansu in his frayed gaberdine trousers, which cost all of five rupees. To Himansu he blurted that 'acting is for call girls and pimps'. Taken aback, Himansu asked him if he had forgotten that Devika, his wife, was also an actress.

Like other educated, 'respectable' people working in cinema, Kumud was more worried about what his father would say. And indeed, when he learnt about this latest demand on his son, his father turned up in Malad with two job offers—one from the postal department and the other from the income-tax department. Either job would help rescue his son from the humiliation of becoming an actor. Himansu met him and explained that he had no doubt that Kumud would 'rise to eminence'. As usual, he carried the day, and Kumud's father relented. That may have sealed the discussion, but not before Kumud tried, over and over again, to wriggle out of the commitment, including pretending to fall sick and threatening to chop off his hair.

He also kept trying to dodge Devika, even cycling away in the opposite direction if he spotted her car. To her credit, when Devika saw him sneaking in one day from the back entrance, she offered him lunch. Finally, all his protests were set aside, his name was changed to Ashok Kumar, and he was committed to act in at least one film.

In a short while, Kumud's salary was increased to an astounding ₹150. He would worry about the money constantly, hiding it in his pillow and eventually sending it home by money-order. He needed little for his own expenses as he had shifted to Malad, since Himansu preferred all the workers to be on the premises so that they could 'function like a large family within a common township'.

Finally, the shoot for *Jeevan Naiyya* started again, with a very nervous new hero and with Devika Rani playing her part with surprising élan, considering that everyone in the studio would have known about her escapade. The best way was to hold her head high and to sail forth with confidence. The past years with Himansu had trained her well to hide her real feelings, and that came in handy now. It helped enormously that she was cast opposite a complete novice. Although the shooting was difficult for her, it was a thousand times worse for him.

Devika assured Ashok that she would not allow him to be completely overwhelmed. But despite grooming, and the presence of well-wishers such as Sashadhar and Himansu, Ashok was completely uncertain of what he was doing. There was an endearing clumsiness about him, coupled with an extreme nervousness whenever Devika was around. His diction was sing-song, while Devika remained natural and relaxed.

His awkwardness meant that even a simple scene could become a nightmare. Ashok Kumar would later recollect for an article in *Filmfare* that his first shot for *Jeevan Naiyya* did not go very well. He had to jump in through a window to rescue the heroine from the clutches of the villain. He dived in through the window as instructed, only to land on Devika and the villain, who broke a leg. As he said in the article, 'Devika Rani goes flying in one direction and falls to the ground, bruised all over.' An ambulance was summoned and the villain was taken to hospital, while Devika received first aid. Shooting was suspended for four months. Himansu could not help laughing and asked Ashok, 'Don't you think you rather overdid it?'

Another time, he had to do a 'love scene'. But he just could not manage it. All he had to do was to place a necklace around Devika's neck and say '*Main tum se muhabbat karta hoon.*' (I love you). But he was so nervous that he requested everyone to leave the set and was adamant on shooting at night so there would be fewer people. Even the sound recordist, in this case Sashadhar Mukerji, had to leave!

As he put the necklace around Devika's neck, Ashok recalled in the article:

> Everything is going right, and the necklace is being lowered, when suddenly it won't go down any further.
>
> As I struggle to push it down I break out in a sweat. I push harder and the heroine's carefully done hair comes streaming down over her shoulders.
>
> The necklace had got stuck in her bun.

Surprisingly, the film did quite well, running at Roxy theatre for eight weeks, though it had tough competition from *Street Singer*, made by New Theatres with the phenomenal K.L. Saigal and Kanan Devi in the lead roles.

The success of the film motivated Ashok to continue with acting, even though the lipstick and make-up still 'upset' him. He enjoyed participating in different aspects of filmmaking, now that he had conquered his demons. He was often involved with the script, as well as editing and sound, and even if it took him some time to hone his performance as an actor, these other skills would win him immediate accolades.

An accidental actor, Ashok worked hard to make a name for himself over the next few years. His sincerity, combined with the faith Himansu seemed to have in him, served him well. His next film with Devika, *Achchut Kanya*, written by Niranjan, would turn out to be a real game-changer.

Jeevan Naiyya and *Achchut Kanya* were poles apart. The first was a middle-class melodrama in which the heroine, Lata, is the daughter of a prostitute and is worried that her husband-to-be, Ranjit, will not stand by her when he finds out the truth about her. An attempt is made to blackmail and kidnap her, and Ranjit goes blind. She reappears to look after him devotedly—while Ranjit does not have any idea that the nurse is Lata. They are reunited when Ranjit gets his vision back. This scripting device would become a hit and other Hindi filmmakers would copy it. It was a convenient way for estranged lovers to be together and renew their love if one had gone blind and so was unaware of the identity of the other.

Achchut Kanya was much more layered. The story dealt with a rarely discussed subject—the caste system. And though it is not reformist cinema—the lower-caste Kasturi (Devika Rani) dies at the end—the issue was at least brought forth and highlighted.

Even the hyper-critical Manto was to say in his essay, 'Ashok Kumar: The Evergreen Hero' (*Bitter Fruit*):

> Most of their movies were hits. The doll-like Devika Rani and the young and innocent Ashok Kumar looked just right together on the screen. Her artless gestures and girlish ways won the hearts of film goers who had until then been fed on love's 'heavier', more aggressive screen version. These two almost fragile young lovers became the toast of India.

Ashok's popularity just grew and grew with every passing day, and Manto noted that on sighting him, 'traffic would come to a stop and often the police would have to use lathis to disperse his fans'.

Devika's fan club was also quite large, but she had no time to enjoy it. Unlike Ashok, she shared the responsibility with Himansu of keeping all aspects of the studio going smoothly, as well as preparing herself for the next film.

The problems with Himansu continued, and she had to struggle hard to keep things on an even keel. Angry or calm, erratic or sane, he had earned a lot of respect for himself in the industry by creating and sustaining the impossible—a well-functioning studio. She knew she had to be by his side and regain the respect she had lost with her Calcutta fling. However, unaware of Himansu's prior mental condition, there were many who, when noticing his lapses, decided that she alone was responsible for his nervous breakdown.

Typically stoic, she did not speak about it as she took him for regular mental and physical check-ups. She told no one—and even their colleagues at HIT or Bombay Talkies only came to know when she was asked to submit the bills for his treatment, at the time of his death. Prior to that, she took him to a discreet clinic at the other end of town, near Colaba, so that no one would find out. The psychiatrist treating him, Dr 'Cracky' Masani (called thus to distinguish him from his brother, who was a GP) became a friend over the years, and kept their secret. As did the other doctors treating Himansu.

There were rumours that Devika attempted to have an affair with Ashok around this time. This seems unlikely, but it is entirely possible that she would have wanted to extend the hand of friendship towards him as they had become a very popular on-screen couple. She certainly needed a few supporters by her side in these difficult times. During the next few years, she remained friendly with all the men who worked with her, even though they usually came from sharply different backgrounds. She believed that if they got to know her better, they would understand her deep commitment to the studio—and that she was not the superficial flirt she was made out to be.

Ashok Kumar was not so careful with other women, confessing later in life that he had multiple affairs because women were attracted to him. There was then, as now, a completely different value system for men as compared to women.

Achchut Kanya became a huge hit. And Devika's elopement became a thing of the past, as Bombay Talkies chugged along. Though Devika had risked everything, it had made Himansu realise her importance. People's memories were short. Outside the studio, most did not know about her elopement and especially after *Achchut Kanya*, people interacted with her as a talented, respected actress and an equal partner to Himansu.

The *Times of India* of 4 September 1936 carried a review of *Achchut Kanya*, stating it was drawing a full house at Roxy Theatre:

> [It was] assured of a run that should set up yet another record and an all-India one at that. Beyond question, no better production has ever come [out of] any studio in this country... *Achhut Kanya* places [Bombay Talkies] at the head of India's picture making units; and all connected with it, producer, director, stars, cast, technicians and the story writer may congratulate themselves on having turned out a masterpiece.

It even compared Devika to Garbo and said her singing was 'marvellous'. At the time, in Calcutta the film was already in its thirty-fourth week.

Ashok would recollect that even Jawaharlal Nehru, accompanied by his daughter Indira and Sarojini Naidu, came to see *Achchut Kanya*. During the screening, slogans such as 'Jawaharlal Nehru zindabad' were shouted by supporters in the audience. Seated next to Nehru was Devika Rani, who had become a friend of the charismatic politician. Apparently, Sarojini Naidu nodded off to sleep while watching the film, but woke up when she heard Ashok's on-screen singing, and was surprised to learn it was the young man next to her who had such a melodious voice.

It was exactly this kind of support and patronage that Himansu and Devika had enjoyed in England from politicians and statesmen, and it was a unique feature of their lives that they remained well-connected to the elite in India as well. This was partly due to the time and care they took over relationships, especially with the British, for which much of the credit must go to Himansu and the years he had spent working in Europe—and of course, Devika's personal rapport with Sir Richard.

The Rais had proved they had an outstanding ability to present themselves as a part of the ruling establishment—'respectable' people who brought respectability to a much-maligned art form. And since the Indian elite were closely linked to one another, they were able to connect with all the important politicians and power brokers of the time. Within the studio too, people like Franz Osten, K.A. Abbas, Saraswati Devi, Sashadhar Mukerji, Niranjan Pal and now Ashok Kumar gave them the required support to make the cinema that they wanted.

Within the roller-coaster world of Bombay Talkies, things began to look up and the films started to do well. But even as their dreams were realised and the studio began to stabilise, Himansu's inexplicable outbursts of rage continued. Devika remained his sole support. She redoubled her efforts to keep the state of his health and their visits to psychiatrists and physicians as private as possible. And she continued to work from 8 a.m. every morning—as an actress, designer, mentor, fundraiser, and so on—till late into the night.

There was no time to rest or to take comfort in anything. And there was no one to comfort her either. Though surrounded by hundreds of people, she was completely on her own.

Letter from Devika to Svetoslav

Please get me a teddy bear, I had one for years & then he wore out. He was medium sized, but lovely. I had several wooden dolls too, beautiful but a real nice teddy is a fine fellow to look at. I'll keep him on my divan. I like those fluffy dogs too, with long ears and sad eyes, white or black, black better—& French dolls too. Didn't you see in my office 2 dolls, they are the remnants of all my collection. I never lost those two somehow. Those French dolls with still mask like painted faces—so lovely. I love looking at such things. I like elephants too, cloth with small beady eyes and flappy ears—fat medium size & Indian marwari dolls, Radha and Krishna. I'll keep them all on my Diwan. I love sitting among them, but they must be nicely made, its horrid when the stuffing comes out... But a real Teddy is hard to beat—they are most fascinating.

Bombay, 1945

12

THE WAR WITHIN, 1930s

As the clouds of war began to gather over Europe, their impact was felt in Bombay Talkies as well. Even though there was an effort to stay away from the overtly political—as films could be censored or banned—messages about social reform, nationhood and service to the nation, without mentioning the freedom struggle, were often slipped in.

This restraint in keeping out overt political messages was remarkable, especially as Niranjan Pal was the writer of most of these films from 1935 to 1938. He would have found it difficult to keep his own revolutionary thoughts at bay. After all, he was the son of the legendary Bipin Chandra Pal.

Niranjan was often provoked into remarking that the British, who were extremely friendly and egalitarian in England, became racist when they were in India. That, and the many social problems he observed in India gave a reformist edge to the stories he wrote, even though the films usually ended on a note that allowed the status quo to be maintained. But he did try and highlight the major issues of the time.

Films like *Janma Bhoomi* (made in 1936 after her elopement and return, in which Devika felt she had not acted well—and indeed, she does appear stiff and disinterested in the film) dealt with city dwellers giving up their comfortable lives to go back to their villages, the real India, their janma bhoomi. There is a Gandhian, utopian vision of the village, where people are innocent but constantly exploited by the moneylenders and priests and so on and have to be rescued by the noble and high-minded Ajoy (played by Ashok Kumar), a doctor. Ajoy's fiancee, Protima (Devika Rani) follows him to the village. After many misunderstandings and complications, they finally win the trust of the villagers. In the end, the entire countryside is uplifted with 'the voices of men, women, and children [raised in] praise of their Janma Bhoomi,' according to the brochure of the film.

This theme of the 'real India' residing in the villages has never really gone out of fashion and has been utilised socially and politically for years. There has always been the (somewhat misguided) belief that the organic growth of villages—the mud huts, the flourishing crops and animals—were somehow more natural and unspoilt while the city, or urban life, was unnatural. The rural values of innocence were closer to the 'janma bhoomi' and had to be preserved. This belief may have born of Gandhi's oft expressed desire to take India back to a pre-mechanised era.

However, carefully woven into *Janma Bhoomi* was transformational propaganda, such as teaching villagers to take medicines only from qualified doctors rather than village quacks. This could have been a way to please the British as well—to demonstrate the usefulness of 'educational' cinema and emphasise that films were not just meant for crass commerce. This was also one of the original agendas of Bombay Talkies, something that Devika was keen on and Himansu had also proposed when they had set up the company.

Having made their peace, at least outwardly, after the embarrassment of the failed elopement, Himansu and Devika continued to work together on their common goals. Himansu's friends, and those around him, were unable to prise him away from her, despite all their efforts. In fact, she seemed to have consolidated her position even more firmly. Perhaps now, more than ever, he realised that the studio might collapse if she were to leave. She was his muse, the rationale for the studio, the face he had to showcase. Regardless of whether a film did badly or well, Devika remained the prime reason for the survival of Bombay Talkies. To Himansu, this was obvious from the reviews that came in, and the response of the viewers.

It was true even for a film like *Achchut Kanya*, which attracted attention for its treatment of the Indian caste system. While *The Times of India* of 4 September 1936 carried an ecstatic review of the film, the magazine *Filmindia* concluded:

> Once again Devika Rani comes to the rescue of the producers and saves the picture from failing utterly. This brave woman who started her screen career with numerous handicaps has shown rapid improvement and in this picture she puts over a bit of singing which is quite good considering her natural difficulties. Her acting, though not so convincing as an untouchable is still quite good and best among the whole lot. Her make-up was not at all appropriate for the role. Her ultra modern pencilled eyebrows made her more an unapproachable than an untouchable. She acted well, but she did not live her part in the picture. Critics therefore remained unconvinced.

In his own guarded way, the powerful editor of *Filmindia*, Baburao Patel, managed to indicate that Devika was indispensable, despite her plucked eyebrows.

However, he was not so cautious where Niranjan was concerned, stating:

> The story has numerous defects, indeed too numerous to mention them all here. Throughout, the story betrays a weak development lacking in imagination and melodrama.

He did not have much sympathy for Franz either:

> The direction is insipid and inefficient. The foreigner who lacks an intimate knowledge of this extremely difficult social problem, lacks also the genius to identify himself with the spirit

of the story. The scenes have therefore turned out to be flat and unconvincing.

He was not able to find a single 'vividly portrayed' scene in the film ('Round the Town', *Filmindia*, August 1936).

Baburao Patel was feared in Bombay for his caustic tongue, but Bombay Talkies carried on making its own brand of cinema and Devika retained her pencil-thin eyebrows. There were enough other troubles to deal with, not just for Bombay Talkies, but for filmmakers everywhere.

When the second All India Motion Picture Convention was held on 26 December 1936, Chimanlal B. Desai, who was presiding, spoke about the twenty-three years of filmmaking in the country and the problems that continued to plague it. Desai, who began as a distributor of films and then became the proprietor of Sagar Film Company, knew the business well. In his speech, which was faithfully reported in *Filmindia* (December 1936), he brought out all the struggles that beset the studio system at the time. The lack of steady financial support was right on top of his list, and he blamed the government for not providing any finances, through loans or otherwise. On the contrary, he pointed out, the government was 'the mother that is supposed to feed the child, and instead is throttling it...gradually.'

This was not an easy time, especially as taxes were high and the colonial powers preferred that their own, imported cinema do better than the local product. Desai said that the raw films and studio material were inappropriately taxed. He said, 'Every year we buy raw films to the extent of approximately 22 lakhs of rupees and pay to the government about seven lakhs of rupees, for allowing us to buy that film.' Even on the ₹35 lakhs which the industry spent on machinery and chemicals, they had to pay tax.

Censorship was another big problem, according to Desai, as there was no industry representative on the censor board:

[The censor board] keeps the industry in a state of panic, and the producer, left to fight his own battle, against a danger which is always unknown, naturally adopts the line of least resistance. The result is that he cannot undertake the production of any historical or political subject as he is almost sure to have it banned. He cannot even attempt a subject affecting our social life, which he thinks the censors might object to, as unfit, immoral or communal. The producer has therefore to seek insipid subjects, and give them conventional treatment. He cannot afford to have a single picture banned, as the loss would be too great for them to bear.

He also pointed out that censors did not seem to mind the 'lusty legs and flying kisses' which were part-and-parcel of 'foreign films', but dances and 'ultra modern scenes' were often banned in Indian films 'on the grounds of public morals'. He said bluntly that while over 300 films were produced annually in India, barely half a dozen scored an all-India success. On the other hand, out of the 300 Hollywood films being shown in India, at least one hundred did very well. He rued the fact that there were just 650 theatres in the country (while Russia had ten thousand and Britain had half that number). Russia, he noted, had one theatre for 16,000 people; in India, the ratio was one theatre for six lakh people.

Himansu could not have agreed more with Desai. Some of the films made by Bombay Talkies may have made profits, but the pressure remained on the producers, in this case Himansu, who needed to cover the salaries and overhead costs of 400-odd employees. There was little doubt that this created a lot of stress, especially because Sir Chimanlal and his board were keen on a robust bottom line. There had to be a continuous production line, and when work started on a production, everything had to be in place to make sure that the film did well. The ambition and intricacy of these productions can be seen in the very first film, *Jawani ki Hawa*. Niranjan Pal, who had written the story as well as some of the songs, was more familiar with English, so the lyrics were written in English and then translated into Hindi. You could tell the writer had a sense of humour—more appropriate for the British stage, perhaps—and there were many clever lines.

For instance, in the song 'It's dangerous—most dangerous to die', Tarachand, the lunatic says:

> I would like to make it clear
> I have one decided fear
> My antipathy deep-rooted is to die.
> So, do all I can, I strive
> To keep myself alive
> And you know you can't succeed unless you try.
> For it's dangerous—most dangerous—to die.
> It's essentially dangerous say I.
>
> My friends call me ridiculous
> They say I am meticulous
> And never happy 'less I make a fuss
> For I never, never ride
> Either outside or inside
> On a motor bus,
> It's dangerous say I
> And it's certainly most dangerous to die.
>
> I eschew the aeroplane
> Nor will I go by train
> Whether overground or subterraneous
> For the accidents you read
> From accelerated speed
> Are dangerous—most dangerous—say I
> Yes, it's absolutely dangerous to die.

All the songs in the film were translated by J.S. Casshyap, the dialogue writer credited for the simplicity of the language used in all the Bombay Talkies productions. But not many knew that the lyrics were an adaptation of a song that had been written for *Blue Bottle*, a play that Niranjan had scripted while in England.

Jawani ki Hawa may not have done as well as expected, but its technical excellence was appreciated. The *Motion Picture Magazine* (published in October 1937, more than a year after the film came out) commented:

> A society picture of the lighter sort, was nevertheless characterised by an intense emotional appeal which proved an excellent vehicle for the histrionic talent of Devika Rani. The high technical standard of this film in respect of photography, sound recording and processing came as a revelation to Indian film audiences.

The next two films (*Mamta* and *Always Tell Your Wife*) also received excellent reviews, with the *Motion Picture Magazine* (October 1937) stating:

> Instead of one long feature, they presented two pictures (double bill), a short but powerfully moving drama titled *Mother*, and a sprightly comedy *Always Tell Your Wife*. The latter was the first complete pure comedy ever made in this country and as such a noteworthy production, though its box office success was not remarkable.

Casshyap played a starring role in both these films. No one could accuse him of possessing good looks, which may have led to their debacle at the box office. Even the presence of Devika Rani and Najam ul Hussain could not save the two films.

Then came *Jeevan Naiyya*, with its attendant scandals. Up to this point, Devika had been the undisputed queen of Bombay Talkies. But now, there were enough people trying to explain to Himansu that she was bad news. That, like they had replaced Najam, they had to find other actresses as well.

But this did not mean Devika stopped making an effort to turn defeat into victory. She had learnt to do this intuitively—by making her enemies and friends dependent on her, by disarming them and going out of her way to do things for them that they found surprising and touching. Ultimately, they would either be shamed into admiration for her, or would withdraw, wounded.

Not even thirty years old, Devika already had a formidable array of very ambitious enemies lining up against her, anxious to prevent Himansu from falling under her spell again. Some of them had an inkling of his illness and wanted to prevent her from stepping into his shoes, if ever he took a turn for the worse. For it was clear by now that he was no longer the old Himansu, in control of himself and every last detail of the studio.

Over the next few years, Devika quietly accompanied Himansu on his regular visits to doctors and psychiatrists. It was a secret she would assiduously keep till his death. Despite their differences, she wanted him to retain the respect he had always commanded. It was therefore essential that she present a strong public persona. Fortunately, she had support from old friends like Sir Richard, who, though very close to Himansu, had some sense of the troubles she had to deal with. Franz was another friend, also much older, who knew something of why she had chosen to run away. He went out of his way to be kind to her on the set on particularly bad days.

∽∾∾

But loyalties in Bombay Talkies were beginning to change. Those who disliked her did not bother to hide their feelings. One former friend who was visibly upset at Devika's return was Niranjan. This was despite the fact that he had introduced her to Himansu in the first place. In those days he had disapproved of Himansu. Now he did not hide his disdain for Devika. He, too, tried to dissuade Himansu from retaining her as the lead actress. Sashadhar did the same.

This split Bombay Talkies into opposing camps. Niranjan and Sashadhar could not accept the fact that this adulterous woman was back to rule over them—and she was determined not to allow her position to be affected. The war within Bombay Talkies was to rage for a few years more.

⌘

Meanwhile, Ashok Kumar's fledgling career as an actor began to take off. Soon after Devika's return, he was cast in *Janma Bhoomi* (1936), *Achchut Kanya* (1936) and *Izzat* (1937) opposite her. *Janma Bhoomi* and *Achchut Kanya* were written by Niranjan, and he wrote the screenplay for *Izzat*.

Moving away from middle-class romance, Bombay Talkies began to be known for its reformist cinema. There was a conscious effort to highlight issues pertaining to caste, gender, and the exploitation of rural and tribal communities. India was fighting for independence, and a subtle dual narrative was adopted to allay the suspicions of the colonial masters.

None of the films offered any solutions to the social problems, though. Both *Achchut Kanya* and *Janma Bhoomi* examined life in rural India, and the former created an interesting narrative of a thwarted romance between a lower-caste girl, Kasturi (Devika Rani, playing a teenager at twenty-eight) and the upper-caste Pratap (Ashok Kumar, at twenty-two). Devika played the young teenager in a ghaghra-choli with as much enthusiasm as she could muster. And no one would have guessed she had problems dealing with the man who had written the story. Some of her most memorable songs, such as '*Main ban ki chidiya*', a duet with Ashok Kumar, were recorded for this film.

Janma Bhoomi told a more idealistic story about a young city-based doctor who goes to work in a village. Devika plays the sophisticated, saree-clad socialite whose heart is in the right place. In the late 1930s in India, there were many such urbane, idealistic women, led by the likes of Rajkumari Amrit Kaur, Sarojini Naidu and Vijay Lakshmi Pandit, who were active in the freedom struggle. They were familiar to the cinema-going audience and so, the image of a sophisticated Devika teaching villagers to resist superstition was quite on target. The relevance of such a representation in relation to the freedom struggle would not have been noticed by the British censors as there was no explicit call for a revolution, though there were plenty of visual references.

For instance, there are scenes in the film of large congregations of people singing songs dedicated to the 'motherland', as a part of the ongoing freedom movement. As obvious anti-British propaganda was not allowed, it was only possible to embed coded messages in the songs, which often escaped the censor's attention.

Both the Indians and the German crew understood the implications of such transgressions, but they could be attempted because Sir Richard Temple, who was still on the board, would have been able to stave off any uncomfortable inquiries. Songs like '*Jai, jai janani janam bhoomi*', written by J.S. Casshyap, composed in raag Bhopali by Saraswati Devi, and sung by Ashok Kumar and a chorus, had obvious nationalistic overtones and yet escaped scrutiny.

> *Gayee raat, aya prabhat, hum nidra sey jaage,*
> *Jai jai janini janam bhoomi, hum balak hain terey...*
> *Saath saath, hum grammat ki seva mein lag jaayen,*
> *Kamar kaskey, kamar kaskey, kamar kaskey,*
> *Ham nidra sey jaggen,*
> *Jai jai janini janam bhoomi, hum balak hain terre.*

> The long night is over, the day has dawned, and we have woken from our sleep
> Praise be to the motherland, the land of our birth, whose children we are...
> Together we should start working for the villages,
> Tighten our resolve, tighten our resolve, tighten our resolve,
> Let's wake up from our sleep,
> Praise be to the motherland, the land of our birth, whose children we are.

Devika looked beautiful in *Jeevan Naiyya*, but in *Jeevan Prabhat* (1937) she really hit her stride. As *Filmindia* said:

> *Jeevan Prabhat* that excellent social picture starring Devika Rani is still running in the 16th week at the Minerva Talkies, Bombay. The picture is reported to have been received wonderfully well at all centres throughout India.

Niranjan was the writer and the theme was infertility and the caste system. As in *Achchut Kanya*, the focus was on the treatment of women in India—the restrictions placed upon them and expectations from them. Devika played Uma, a Brahmin girl who is reprimanded by her parents for being friendly with a group of potters who are Harijans, or lower-caste. She is married off to a Brahmin, Nandlal (Mumtaz Ali). But in a melodramatic twist, since she is unable to have a child, she finds another bride for her husband and goes home to her parents. Once there, she discovers that she is pregnant. As she is still friendly with the potters, especially a young man called Rammu (Kishore Sahu), Nandlal suspects that Uma has been unfaithful. Finally, the truth is revealed, and Nandlal is united with Uma.

The film did well, mainly because Devika was able to carry it on her slight shoulders, alone. But it seemed as though the ghost of Najam, who was struggling to carve out a career in Calcutta, hung over the production. A deliberate decision appears to have been taken to choose spectacularly underwhelming men as heroes, and Mumtaz Ali was among them. He rose from being a dancer and small-time stage performer to a hero (*Jeevan Prabhat*). He was an orphan who had been looked after by B.G. Horniman, the well-known editor of *Deccan Chronicle* in Bombay. Horniman introduced him to Himansu Rai in 1933. Like many others in Bombay Talkies, Mumtaz Ali would also leave a legacy—in the form of his son, Mehmood, who became one of cinema's most popular comedians.

Mumtaz Ali may not have been the sophisticated actor she wanted to romance on screen, but Devika was no longer in a position to object. Films had to be made with whatever talent was available. Being 'educated' was less and less the definitive criteria.

Critics like Baburao Patel were to remark:

> I cannot approve of the poor taste shown by the producers in choosing the men to work with Devika. Kishore Sahu (in *Jeevan Prabhat*) is another 'misfire' as an actor. What a pity that one of the sweetest girls of the screen should not get a suitable hero.

For Devika, playing opposite men like this on screen couldn't have been easy, but she did it with the same determination with which she led her life—unwavering on the path she had set out on.

Touching thirty by now, she had begun to consider her role off-screen as more important than the role of an 'actress'. But she also needed to make sure she was financially secure. For she still had no income of her own. Her salary went to Himansu, and he would give her some money, with which she had to run the house and manage expenses. She did not have any stake in the studio either. Having pawned most of her jewellery in the early days, she owned nothing of value apart from one share in HIT, and a few in Bombay Talkies. Between her and Himansu, they had barely any savings, because he always gave the studio priority over their needs and, as always too proud to ask, she kept quiet.

Instead, as a thorough professional, she decided that she needed to prove her value to the studio both on and off screen, and then perhaps make a bid to be paid directly. In an unsettled world, if she was in demand, her valuation would go up. She needed to stay in the limelight. Another cause for worry was that at forty-seven, Himansu's health was not any better. She could no longer rely on his support.

People around her, especially the international crew, appreciated her presence. They knew it would not have been possible to complete the films so quickly—*Achchut Kanya* was made in just six weeks and *Jeevan Prabhat* in eight. With her at the helm, the studio could produce three or four films in a year, and keep the costs low.

Her screen presence remained as natural and innocent as in *Jawani ki Hawa*. And if the studio's requirements meant that she had to act opposite those who were not her social equals, so be it.

Like Himansu, she learnt to compromise. But unlike her, Himansu was not able to withstand the blows which came rapidly in the next few years. Sadly, at a time when he was most vulnerable, the people he depended on would desert him.

The first salvo came from a very annoyed Niranjan, who decided to quit after writing the screenplay for *Izzat* (1938). His anger with Devika had not yet subsided when he had a spat with Himansu over some articles he had written, in which he expressed his disillusionment with the sort of films that were being made in India. He refused to retract his views.

Niranjan had always been iconoclastic and idealistic, which is how he managed to create such a large body of memorable and path-breaking work. He never ran short of ideas and he matched Himansu with his own kind of bravado and passion for cinema. They made a great team, working to their individual strengths and overlooking each other's shortcomings. Except this time.

Niranjan's views in the articles were not new, and he had not forgotten the altercation with Franz when they were shooting *The Light of Asia*, more than a decade ago. To Himansu's embarrassment, he had written:

> I place no faith in the ability of foreign experts and technicians to make Indian films. No foreigner... can correctly interpret the intricacies and subtleties of our culture in a manner which will be easily intelligible to the average film goer.

Niranjan was worried that with the audiences being easily satisfied, studio owners had no motivation to bring in better artistes or raise the standards of work because, naturally, these options would be expensive. To air such views while working in a studio with a British and German cast and crew was clearly problematic. But perhaps the most compelling reason for his exit remained Devika.

Niranjan was to say in his autobiography, *Such Is Life,* that he was often asked why he broke away from Himansu and Bombay Talkies.

> Some suspect I had a serious quarrel with him, but I left to make it easier for Himansu to serve two masters at the one time. At a critical juncture, I had strongly advised him to dismiss Devika from Bombay Talkies for her indiscipline. The advice had fallen on deaf ears.... Having come to know that advice I had given her husband I became Devika's sworn enemy and she was just biding her time to have her revenge. Whether Himansu tolerated Devika, being very much in love with her, or he knew her value which he could exploit, is an unanswered question.

His departure was a blow for Himansu. And his dramatic and public reaction to it pointed to his own fragile state. After Niranjan gave him his resignation letter, he was followed to the car by a 'ranting Himansu. He screamed he would not let me go and tore the resignation to bits.' He almost wrenched the steering wheel off. This open and disproportionate display of anger and frustration was what Devika had dreaded most. It contradicted the image they were trying to build for Bombay Talkies. It also revealed the fact that Himansu's illness was worse than she had projected.

But Niranjan's departure also meant that at last, a space had opened up for new writers, and some from within Bombay Talkies, like Abbas and Manto, would emerge from the wings. Although Niranjan had often maintained that he would be happy if there were more screenwriters, he had remained the only writer who received a fixed salary, whether he wrote or not. Before he left, he had finished the screenplay for *Savitri* (1937), which would feature Devika and Ashok.

By the time the mythological was made, Ashok was considered a real money-spinner. The nervous young man had stuck it out and made it good. To be fair, despite his reservations about Devika, Ashok worked very hard on his performances. Initially he gained from her popularity because she already had a large fan following, which meant that people would watch the film, whether he was good or not. He really came into his own when Leela Chitnis replaced Devika as the leading lady, in 1940. It may have been that he felt more comfortable acting with an equal (and not the studio boss) for the first time—and she was a good actress. Even when he had starred opposite Maya Devi in *Prem Kahani*, in 1937, he had been nervous and a little hesitant.

Prem Kahani was proof that the non-stop production of films could affect quality. After five films in less than a year and a half, shot in the heat and humidity of Bombay, and the trauma of the real-life elopement in between, Devika took a break. But Maya Devi was a poor replacement. Neither was the film comparable to the quality and scale of *Achchut Kanya*, or even *Jawani ki Hawa*. The problem was again the script, where Niranjan, for once, seemed to have lost the thread. Or more likely, he had lost interest, and had also begun to repeat himself with certain tropes and characters being over utilised. Though he built narratives around his female characters, these women were not strong or even rebellious, but mostly victims of circumstances.

Savitri, which was based on the Mahabharata, was perhaps the only film that Niranjan wrote where the woman was empowered to trump her destiny and decide her own fate. Savitri (Devika) was a princess, 'a maiden of exceeding beauty and withal, a maiden, rich in maidenly virtues, rich in holy lore', a 'divinity in mortal guise', according to the film's brochure. As a result, all the men in her life were intimidated and her father, King Aswapati, sent her out to seek her own husband. She met and fell in love with Satyavan, whose death within a year had been foretold by a sage. He was the son of an impoverished king, Dyumutsena, but Savitri married him, and then pleaded and argued with Yama, the God of Death, till he consented to give him his life back. It was a costume drama with elaborate headgear and outfits, and Devika came into her own in the role.

Another costume drama was *Izzat*, which was based on a true story by the late Dr G. Nundy and examined the 'self-respect' of the

Bhil tribals as they stood up to the power of the Marathas. Kanhaiya (Ashok Kumar) resents his humiliation at the hands of the Marathas and decides to regain Bhil honour and land. During this struggle, Radha (Devika Rani) gets killed. The film then moves quite rapidly towards its tragic end. Niranjan wrote the screenplay for the film, and while Ashok had the dominant role, decked out rather bravely in necklaces and earrings as befitting an Indian-film version of a tribal, Devika in her skirt and cropped top covered with beads was a cross between a girl from Hawaii and one from the hills of northern India. The cast and crew expended more energy spinning up and down the hills than on the actual script, but it was unusual to construct a film around the honour of a tribe.

Filmindia thought that the outdoor scenes were 'beautifully taken'. The *Motion Picture Magazine* (October 1937) said '*Izzat* brought to the screen the chivalry and primitive culture of the Bhils, a picturesque and gallant aboriginal tribe of India.'

While things were coming to a head at the studio, Niranjan's departure left a gap which Himansu found difficult to fill, at the personal even more than the professional level. As for Niranjan, he lost a steady job but also a good friend in Himansu, who had given him the freedom to exercise his creativity; none of his attempts at filmmaking before or after worked as well.

Himansu had relied heavily on Niranjan and Devika, and now both had betrayed him. His inability to cope with an increasingly insecure environment became more evident and he became precariously short-tempered. But this did not deter his loyalists—from Sashadhar to the board of directors led by Sir Chimanlal Setalvad—from continuing to believe in his genius, and his goodness.

Niranjan's departure also meant that Himansu was, more than ever, dependent on Devika. Despite his declining physical and mental condition he held on to his dream that someday, Indian cinema would reach screens worldwide, with a breakthrough international film from Bombay Talkies. He had a very talented team, but the cosmopolitan environment and the intellectual stimulation of the early years were not available to him anymore. Was Bombay Talkies becoming a machine that mechanically brought out film after film? Everyone, including the German and the British crews, were doing their jobs, in a very competent but routine manner. Where were the big ideas?

Only Devika understood this and remembered their grand ambition. The inability to reach those heights was a constant regret they shared, even though there was a growing chasm between Himansu and her. He was no longer sure of her affections, and she was always doubtful of his. But they had a child between them—Bombay Talkies—which kept them from breaking up and or even moving too far away from each other.

In the meantime, Devika had the rumours to deal with. She was dismayed at the young actresses who were coming in now for auditions and jobs, ever eager to please and ready to do anything. She kept her views to herself, but she may have suspected, as did Ashok and a few others, that Himansu had contacted syphilis. All she could do was to ensure that he had regular sessions with the doctor. Until now, she had been more worried about his mental health, but now it became important to understand if it was linked to his physical state. And, like everything to do with Himansu in the last years of his life, she confided in no one. Despite his unreasonable rages, and his inability to be coherent at times, she wanted everyone to respect him as of old. She also stopped fighting against the visible changes taking place in the studio and began to accept that some of their dreams were now unattainable. If she became too rigid about things, production would grind to a halt.

The influx of women who sought work at the studio, often pushed into it by their husbands and families, was a very visible sign that they had not been able to effect the one crucial change they had wanted. These were not the highly educated women that Himansu and she had hoped to bring into cinema. There were a few exceptions, like Renuka Devi and Leela Chitnis. Both were mothers of three children each, and while the latter had to work in order to support her family, Begum Khurshid (or Renuka) was passionate about acting.

There were others, though, like Hansa Wadkar—just sixteen years of age, but looked much older when she had make-up on. She made Devika uneasy. 'Please don't bring in the daughters of courtesans and Devadasis,' she had said to Himansu a long time back. Hansa's lineage could be traced back to both. She was a spunky girl who had to work to support her husband, ten years older than her. At sixteen, she had already been in four films when she met Himansu. He offered her a six-year contract. This was a long period of commitment to offer someone who had little experience in Hindi cinema and naturally, most people wondered why.

For Devika, this was a difficult moment, but she let it pass. There were already far too many girls working at Bombay Talkies who came from dubious backgrounds from her point of view, including one with the interesting name of 'Gulbadan', meaning a body made of flowers. Perhaps she wanted to withdraw, worried that she would be trapped into acting with girls like Hansa. But she had no means of escape. She needed the position, she needed the money. Besides, where could she go, at the age of thirty-one, and with a sick husband?

Ironically, at least with Himansu by her side, she could still mingle with the best of Bombay. No one knew how sick he was, so long as he took his medication. They would meet the governor one day, and the next they would be dining at the Taj with Sarojini Naidu, who had an almost permanent suite there. Or they would dine with Sachin and Hiten Choudhuri, two brothers who reminded her and Himansu of the world of intellect that lay beyond Bombay Talkies.

Devika hoped to persuade Hiten, who was half in love with her, to join them at Bombay Talkies—perhaps this would change the kind of cinema they were making now? Himansu's illness had made Devika look around for people who could support her at the studio in case anything happened to him. Sachin and Hiten Choudhuri were on top of her list.

The extremely intelligent and well-connected Sachin threw the most exciting and eclectic parties at his flat in Churchill Chambers, Colaba. It was possible to run into famous lawyers, economists, poets, and a whole host of interesting people there. Best of all, he was unemployed. It wasn't long before Devika began wondering if he could take up a management role at Bombay Talkies. He even lived right next door to the registered office. What could be better?

Sachin would, indeed, join Bombay Talkies, but he became better known as the founder of the *Economic Weekly*, which morphed eventually into the *Economic and Political Weekly*. His younger brother, meanwhile, successfully handled a variety of businesses for different companies.

The studio held no enchantment for Devika anymore and she longed for another life, rather than sweating it out in front of the workers, who probably gossiped about her all the time. One day, lost in her thoughts as she made her way to Himansu's office, she saw a man with some young girls, probably his daughters, standing outside the door. They stared at her with wonder—was this really Devika Rani, looking like an angel in a crisp cotton saree, with her porcelain skin glowing? She smiled at them, hiding her annoyance, and carefully closed the door behind her so no one could hear what she had to say.

Himansu was working at his desk, correcting a script. He got up courteously as he always did, and drew up a chair for her.

'I don't think we should carry on hiring these young girls, uneducated and pushed forward by their families,' she snapped at him. 'Please don't expect me to work with them.'

He raised his eyebrows and lit a cigarette, slowly. His hands were shaking. She was surprised at how tired he looked.

'I know, my dear, but it is difficult for you to be in every film and we need to have a spread of at least four or five actresses before we can start making more films.'

'And you signed a six-year contract with Hansa Wadkar? Do you know what they say about her background?'

'Backgrounds are not everything, Devika. You, of all people, must know that. Yes, I agree we must get better people, and we have got Leela Chitnis, haven't we?'

She knew it was a futile argument.

'I notice you've forgotten to take your medicine again,' she said. He looked around, found the pill on a plate in front of him, and swallowed it with a glass of water. She shook her head, irritated.

'And which script are you working on?'

'*Narayani*,' he replied, holding up the sheet. As she leaned over to see, her heart sank. There were all kinds of illegible marks everywhere on the paper. She had better take him to see Dr Masani again.

She couldn't understand what was wrong. He looked so normal, in his fresh white shirt and the suit which she insisted he wore. How could she bring the old Himansu back?

She had requested him not to attend the shoots and spend more time in his office. That way, there was no risk of a public breakdown. He needed rest—no trauma of any kind, the doctors had said. How could he rest, though, how could any producer rest, when films had to be churned out?

'Are you... are you feeling okay?'

He gave her his trademark smile, heartbreaking in its beauty, and nodded cheerfully, a can of 555 cigarettes as always in his hand like a trophy. His apparent resilience amazed her.

'Completely fine, my dear.'

She knew she couldn't argue with him anymore. But she had to hold on to their authority in Bombay Talkies. She had to work harder than before, for both of them. She knew that both Sashadhar and Rai Bahadur Chuni Lall were getting increasingly involved in managing Bombay Talkies and HIT, and she couldn't cede any more space to them.

As though proving her apprehensions right, in the next film, *Durga*, Devika found herself as the lead, with Hansa Wadkar playing her best friend. Worse, she was once again the village girl, with a cute little ribbon on her head, playing a fourteen-year-old adolescent. She was aware that her age and the excess weight were beginning to show. Yet, she was brilliant. Her dialogue delivery was childlike, and she made the character entirely believable through the intensity in her eyes and the liveliness with which she played her part. The heartbroken audience only knew her as a lost orphan who would soon be married to a much older man, a widower.

Despite her reluctance to share the screen with Hansa Wadkar, she couldn't refuse the role, because after Niranjan's departure, a new writer had been recruited. This was the famous Saradindu Banerjee, whose book had already been adapted to make the strikingly memorable film, *Bhabhi*, for Bombay Talkies.

Saradindu had created one of Bengal's most popular detectives, Byomkesh Bakshi, and was now with Bombay Talkies. As an experienced storyteller, he brought a different sensibility to the studio. His films, *Navjeevan*, *Durga* and *Kangan* (all written and produced in 1939) were romantic and appealing and gave all the three heroines of Bombay Talkies at the time—Devika, Leela and Hansa—a chance to blossom and be appreciated. Once again, Bombay Talkies shifted focus, this time from 'reformist' cinema to gentle romances with women-centric roles. If the stories brought attention to any social evils, it was incidental—such as child marriage in *Durga*. But overall, Saradindu's women were more free and liberated, more assertive than any seen thus far. It was a welcome change.

The classic Saradindu film, though, was the first one that he wrote for Bombay Talkies. *Bhabhi* (1938) was based on his book, *Bisher Dhuan*. It was a romance, and because it was based on a book, it had a clear narrative. The characters were well delineated, the dialogue was humorous, and both Renuka Devi and Jairaj played their roles well. The film was also extremely well shot, especially the street scenes and the city scape. And so, Niranjan's departure unintentionally ended up bringing fresh zeal to the filmmaking and the actors also demonstrated fresh energy. Perhaps the tension between Niranjan and Franz had made the productions much more stilted earlier. From now on, work flowed smoothly. Even reviewers noticed the change.

Filmindia (January 1939) loved *Bhabhi*:

> Beautiful in conception and neat in execution the story is a masterly blending of soothing pathos and elevating romance...

And then Saradindu gave Devika one of her most striking roles, in *Durga*. Apart from Hansa Wadkar, it had Rama Shukul, who played Jawahar, the young doctor who is in love with Durga.

To be on par with Hansa was galling for Devika, but ever the consummate actress, she never objected in public. However, she declined the next Bombay Talkies film, *Navjeevan*. It was her way of protesting.

Devika's absence in *Navjeevan* was noticed by many—just as she had desired. Baburao Patel wrote, tongue-in-cheek:

> Bombay Talkies has given a beautiful story as usual... and once again we don't find Devika Rani in the cast. This time, however, a new girl has been introduced in Hansa Wadkar, new in the sense that this is the first time she has been allowed to shoulder the heroine's role.

This was clearly a jibe aimed at Hansa, for almost everyone knew who she was. She had just acted in a film alongside Devika. She was not 'new' to the show business, and anyone who followed Marathi theatre and film would have heard of her.

Hansa's life was a series of unfortunate scandals which were constantly unfolding in public. But she remembered her days at Bombay Talkies fondly, thanks to Himansu. In her biography, *You Ask, I Tell*, Hansa said that Himansu 'was very close to me'. She said he treated her like a daughter and gave her good advice. She recalled that she was on a contract to work with Bombay Talkies and her monthly salary was fixed at ₹350. The studio also made arrangements for food and for passes for her to commute to the studio and back. But her personal life remained far from happy. Once, when she came home after a shoot, her suspicious husband, Bandarkar, whipped her cruelly with a belt. She bought some port wine and got drunk the next day—she was only sixteen then. It was her way of fighting back. Her troubled marriage would continue to torment her for the rest of her life.

At home, she had to support her husband, her mother-in-law, brother-in-law and other relatives, and so she found peace and quiet at Bombay Talkies, where everything was well organised. She remembered that the clothes required for a scene were kept in big boxes in sets of three, with each box carrying the scene number. The sites for the outdoor shoots were identified in advance, and the artistes just had to go onto the set and start working. She was particularly happy that the women were well looked after. For a troubled young woman, Bombay Talkies offered safe harbour. She says:

> Everybody in the studio adored Himansu Rai. Even the pet birds and the animals. He would sound the horn on reaching the gate. All the peacocks and birds in the studio recognised the sound and would start shrieking. Horses would start neighing, almost as if to announce his arrival. As soon as he reached the studio, the first thing he would do was to go to the birds and animals, feed them and then turn to his work.

The fact that he allowed her paid leave while she was pregnant, and that the leave was extended for three months while she recovered from a terrible miscarriage, was something she appreciated.

Navjeevan was the first film in which Hansa acted for Bombay Talkies as a heroine. She remembered the German crew, whose techniques she observed, sometimes with amusement. She noticed that when the camera started rolling, Franz Osten would close his eyes. She found it strange that he did not watch the shot. When asked about it, he replied that he wanted to check her articulation, and anyway, the camera work was being done by someone else and the action had already been explained to her. It was a strange answer, for neither Osten nor the rest of the German crew understood either Marathi or Hindi!

Whatever the system, it appeared to work, and in the end Hansa's hard work paid off. *Durga* and *Navjeevan* turned out to be pivotal films for the studio.

After *Durga*, Devika reduced her screen appearances. She cut back on her roles, as Himansu's behaviour grew more and more erratic. Her own nerves were on edge all the time and she stayed away from the media, in particular. But worse was in store for the team at Bombay Talkies.

World War II had broken out and the British Government was on the lookout for any German sympathisers. Bombay Talkies, with its very prominent German crew, naturally came under scrutiny. The shoot for *Kangan* (1939) starring Ashok Kumar and Leela Chitnis was underway when British officers arrived to arrest the Germans. Himansu tried to resist, but was unsuccessful.

It was to later emerge that Franz Osten had actually enrolled himself in the Nazi Party, but was possibly not a full member. Did anyone at Bombay Talkies know? Was Osten at the studio only as a director, or was he representing or working for the German government in any way? Or had he come to India to get away from Hitler and the policies of the Nationalist Socialist Party, which had already announced restrictions on the creative industry?

All the film studios in Germany were eventually brought under the umbrella organisation, Universim Film Aktiengesellschaft (UFA), which was already working with, or increasingly influenced by, the Nazis in 1933. Osten, whose brother had set up the Emelka studio, had to sign up with UFA, as did all the other filmmakers. In his book *Age of Entanglement: German and Indian Intellectuals Across Empire*, Kris Manjapra confirms that Osten joined the Nazi party in 1934. This was around the time when Himansu and Devika were setting up Bombay Talkies and asked Osten, the cameraman Josef Wirsching, and others to come to Bombay.

Manjapra says that Osten was, in fact, not keen to join UFA, and submitted incomplete papers about his pure Aryan origin:

> [He was] informed in a letter of June 1934 that his company, Ideal Film, would not be allowed to operate because the required paperwork proving Osten's 'Aryan roots' had not been submitted. Osten stalled in providing his information to the Nazi government's Reichsfachschaft Film (the Reich's film department). He eventually joined the Nazi Party in 1934, but had subsequently sought to create increasing distance from the German film market.... Osten began an effort to Indianize his films and to shed the trademark Indic Orientalism that marked his Weimar work.

For him, as for the other Germans who joined Bombay Talkies, Himansu's offer might well have come as a welcome way out of a difficult situation.

It is interesting to note that the actor Marlene Dietrich, having spotted the signs of change early, had already joined Hollywood by 1930 (which is why it is likely that Devika may have had just a fleeting meeting with her; after *The Blue Angel*, Marlene had joined Paramount and made six films with them). Goebbels attempted to bring Marlene back in 1936, but he failed. She worked with the Allies, even entertained the Allied troops, and eventually became an American citizen.

But Goebbels was determined to beat Hollywood at its own game. He was fascinated with American cinema and wanted to emulate their set-up, in the Nazi style of course. Soon, it became difficult for films to be imported to Germany. And once Hitler came to power, he announced that everyone who was working in any industry had to join the umbrella organisation meant for their profession, and all filmmakers had to join the Film Chamber of the Reich. The Reich Ministry of Public Enlightenment and Propaganda had set up the Reichsfilmkammer in 1933. The main task of the body was to prevent Jews and foreigners from having any participation in the German film industry. The freedom that the industry had enjoyed under the Weimar Republic now eroded rapidly. By 1939, when World War II began, a whole new regime was in place and the Nuremberg Laws had already been passed. Jews were kept out of making films, just as they were excluded from all other areas of work in Germany.

The Germans at Bombay Talkies would have known about the changes taking place—and about the exodus of the Jews working in cinema. For instance, they would have known of Fritz Lang, who was forced to leave Germany after he made *The Testament of Dr Mabuse*, which was banned by the Nazis in March 1933. Lang left for Hollywood, as did many other German filmmakers, including Billy Wilder.

For the British, the fact that the Germans at Bombay Talkies had been making Indian films (and not Nazi propaganda) did not matter, as they were all enemies of the State. Thus, at seventy, Franz, along with the other team members such as cameraman Josef Wirsching and set designer Karl von Spreti, was taken away to be interned at Deolali, at a camp for 'anti nationals'.

Possibly because of his age, or more likely his connections, Franz was released earlier than the others and sent back to Germany. By then, thanks to the rise of Hitler, many of those who would have known him had either fled abroad, or had got absorbed in the task of surviving under the new regime.

Franz had been away from his homeland, off and on, for almost two decades. When he reached Germany, his well-wishers found him some work. To begin with, he set up the archive at Bavaria Films. Later, at the age of seventy-five, he became the manager of a Bavarian spa. It was a sad end to an exciting career. He made other films—around thirty-three silent and ten 'sound' films—but it is his legacy of sixteen films for Bombay Talkies for which he is most remembered.

Josef remained in the internment camp and was released after the war. In between, he was moved to Dehradun and Sitara, but he continued to correspond with Devika, as did others at the camp.

In 1947, he rejoined Bombay Talkies and continued to work as a cinematographer. His last film was *Pakeezah*. He died in 1967 from a cardiac arrest before completing it.

Without doubt, the arrest of his key German technicians in the middle of a shoot was a huge blow for Himansu. Not only that, his insecurities grew—Devika and he had nurtured excellent connections with Lord Brabourne and the governors who succeed him, including the present one, Lawrence Roger Lumley, the 11th Earl of Scarborough. They had maintained close connections with all the Viceroys, including Lord Linlithgow, in anticipation of precisely such a time. But now, when they needed them to somehow convince the authorities that these particular Germans were friends and not foes, no one was willing to listen. It was a time when even Sir Richard, an army man himself, could not help.

Indeed, the British were in no mood to be considerate. The war had already taken a huge toll on the Empire, and the non-cooperation movement led by the Congress Party was adding to their woes. They were determined to lock up any troublemakers, and soon the Congress leaders would also be interned for opposing the war. It was dangerous to have Germans in India making films that could possibly instigate a restless population against the British. The Germans and the Japanese were already coming together and the Bengali leader Netaji Subhash Chandra Bose had indicated his intent to raise an army against the colonisers. The British authorities were thus inclined to be extra cautious, and thought it best to keep all the likely troublemakers behind bars.

But for an increasingly unwell Himansu, this was almost the last straw. From now on, Devika would have to rely on her supporters within the board, and a few within the production team, to ensure that she and Himansu retained their position and power. As Himansu became more fragile, mentally and physically, she would have to make sure that she was seen as his natural successor and remained Bombay Talkies' lead actress. Ever pragmatic, she knew it was a question of survival. And some more compromises would have to be made along the way.

Letter from Devika to Svetoslav

I am built by nature [to be] a very independent type. So far I have not really ever asked a favour, and have never let anyone outside do [anything in] my life for me—of course my career...was different, one has to in business adapt to circumstances, but my honour I have kept like a jewel & it is untarnished—that is dearest a pride to me! It was not very easy!! It is a great pride to myself...a wealth if I may say it, that at the end of 15 years of a career life, a career woman, I can without hesitation say, my honour is untarnished!! Yes, God I thank for that and I pray that God will bless me and give me further strength to ever keep my honour, to ever feel clean and to help me become what you wish me to be, and help me make you happy.

Bombay, 1945

13

LIFE WITHOUT HIMANSU, 1940s

Bombay Talkies was nothing if not professional.

Luckily for everyone, Himansu and Devika had always placed the Indian crew alongside the Germans and encouraged them to pick up their techniques. And so, even after the arrest of the Germans, the shoot for *Kangan* did not pause.

Kangan was another sweet romance written by Saradindu Banerjee, who was good at working in all the twists and turns that could keep an audience in thrall. Based on Gajendra Kumar Mitra's *Rajnigandha*, it had the limpid-eyed Leela Chitnis playing Radha, a village girl who falls in love with an aspiring poet, Kamal (Ashok Kumar). When he leaves for the city to become a 'noted novelist and playwright', Radha has a terrible time in the village, rejected by Kamal's father. Ultimately, the two lovers are reunited and Kamal clasps a kangan (bangle, signifying marriage) around Radha's wrist, while his father has a change of heart.

Reviewers noted that the story was again a deviation from the reformist cinema of Niranjan Pal, and there was no sign of Devika Rani in the film. But the filmmaking had improved.

Filmindia (November 1939) said:

> The departure of the German technicians has been marked by not the slightest fall in the technique. On the other hand the young associate directors N.R. Acharya and S. Najmul Hasan

Naqvi have to some extent, improved upon Franz Osten's rather wooden and stereotyped direction. *Kangan* ushers in a new era—an era we hope of artistic progress in the career of the Bombay Talkies.

It was pointed out that '[The usual standards] of photography, sound recording and processing are uniformly maintained—which is an unqualified tribute to the young Indians who recently took over charge from the veteran German technicians.... Leela Chitnis has jumped to unique stardom this year.'

Over all, it seemed that the transition from the Germans to the Indians was a seamless affair, and the studio came up with one of its biggest hits, much to the chagrin of those who expected it to suffer a setback.

The transition was a great tribute to the Rais, of course, who had hoped that one day the Indian technicians would be on par with the Europeans and the training they imparted would bear fruit. It is notable that, not surprisingly, Himansu was given most of the credit for this, and Devika's contribution was barely acknowledged, although it had been part of a joint plan.

Navjeevan (1939), which was released after *Kangan*, was less successful. It featured the lively Hansa Wadkar and Rama Shukul, but the efforts of the studio team did not come together as well as they had for *Kangan*. Rama Shukul was usually a very bankable star and everyone had thought this would be another hit.

Meanwhile, behind the scenes, there was trouble brewing. Himansu's mood swings were becoming less controllable. During one shoot, he slapped Savak Vacha, the sound recordist, so hard that he lost his hearing in one ear. It was a difficult and embarrassing time for Devika, but it also enabled her to gain some sympathy from those who despised her, as well as from some of the younger and more ambitious crew, who felt she should take charge instead.

Her importance grew in proportion to Himansu's deterioration, which was now difficult to conceal. The genius who had sown the seeds for professionalism in cinema and opened the door for national and international filmmakers, was becoming increasingly incoherent. Naturally, Devika became the link between him and the rest of the studio.

The physical and verbal abuse continued, as she mentioned in her letters to Svetolsav. And she continued to draw a veil over this part of their lives. She was also spending more time on his treatment, and that meant acting in a film became nearly impossible, for her. The beginning of 1940 was particularly stressful, and while work continued on various productions, she recused herself to focus on bringing Himansu back to the real world.

By now, the board of Bombay Talkies was becoming anxious about the situation. Devika struggled against the inevitable, but she could no longer cope alone. Finally Himansu had to be admitted into a clinic on 1 May 1940. On 19 May, the world was informed of his death.

The exact reasons behind his death at Belle Vue Nursing Home, 'La Citadelle', at Queen's Road, Marine Lines, in Bombay were never made public. This discreet clinic, run by Dr A.P. Bacha, was a long way from the Rais' residence at 57, Dady Seth Road, Malad. The distance and the lack of public transport meant that very few from Bombay Talkies visited him. Devika alone remained by his side. Many doctors visited him at the clinic, although he was primarily being treated by Dr 'Cracky' Masani.

No one from Himansu's own family was with him in these last days. His mother had passed away. Lilu, the sister who had stayed with Himansu and Devika, had left for Calcutta to be with one of her sisters, Mrs S.N. Das Gupta, in Ballygunge. Of the other sisters, Mrs Chinmayee Ray was at Hazra Road in Calcutta, Mrs Hemanta Choudhuri was at Mymensingh, while Mrs J.C. Sen was at Maharaja Ranjit Singh Road, New Delhi. His father was alive, but usually stayed with one of the sisters.

None of them, it later emerged, had known the extent of his illness. This led to the rumour mills working overtime. Devika never spoke about it, but the parade of doctors—specialists, psychiatrists and GPs—who attended on Himansu also added to the mystery surrounding his death.

From the time he had been admitted to the clinic, Devika had ensured that he had nurses watching over him round the clock. But oddly enough, there was no nurse in attendance on 19 May, the official date of his death. There were two nurses who attended to him day and night, at the princely sum of ₹12 for the day nurse and ₹15 for the night nurse. He was admitted on 1 May, and the night nurse was appointed the same day. The bills showed that the nurses were paid up to 18 May. Perhaps, in his last moments, only Devika was with him? Or was the date incorrect, and he had actually died the day before?

Everyone's sympathies were with the young widow, though it was obvious that many wondered at the circumstances of death. Especially because the nursing home was known more for its handling of gynaecological and abortion cases (even though illegal) than for straightforward medical treatment of seriously ill patients.

The doctor who turned in the largest bill—of ₹670—was Dr K.R. 'Cracky' Masani, the psychiatrist. A general practitioner, Dr C.R. Pereira, had also apparently been treating Himansu from January 1938 to March 1940. The nature of the treatment was never revealed.

Devika had her wits about her even when Himansu was close to death. She knew that they had barely any savings and the medical expenses had been enormous. This meant she needed to urgently renew his life insurance policy, which had lapsed, and in which she was not a nominee. Fortunately, Sir Chimanlal helped out in time, and Himansu's insurance policy was renewed just a few days before his death. Dr Lalkaka from the insurance company visited the clinic in those last crucial days for a check-up. No one seemed to have noticed that Himansu was dying, nor is there any mention of the maladies that ailed him.

Himansu was not yet fifty when he died. What did he die of? Was it syphilis, as Ashok Kumar thought? Was it a mental breakdown which led to other complications? Was it a combination of alcohol, cigarettes and stress? Or was it simply Devika—or someone else—who ensured that he would not live, as her worst detractors suggested?

The band of doctors who attended on Himansu would have us believe there was a variety of causes. He must have suffered severe psychological and physical issues as he had both psychiatrists and general practitioners attending on him, and blood tests were also conducted.

Himansu's family in Calcutta heard many disturbing rumours. Most of these were about Devika's behaviour towards Himansu. The family got in touch with her on 22 December 1940, nearly six months after Himansu's death. All this time, Devika had been requesting Himansu's father to sign a form that would enable her to claim the full amount due against the life insurance policy, of ₹9,658.

The insurance money was crucial to her as Himansu's closing bank balance was merely ₹654, despite the fact he had been working in cinema for close to seventeen years and had built a very successful studio. Out of this, ₹500 had been deposited in the bank by Franz Osten. Since Franz had been sent to a detention camp, the money had to be paid to the custodian of enemy properties. In effect, only ₹154 remained in the bank.

Mrs S.N. Das Gupta, Himansu's sister, did not mince words when writing to Devika. The family was very upset about the allegations against Devika, which had been conveyed to them, and also desired that some part of the insurance money be given to Lilu, Himansu's youngest and unmarried sister. Devika was reluctant to do so because, as she explained, Himansu's debts and the expenses for his medication and funeral had been quite high, and were to be settled with this money.

Mrs Das Gupta wrote on 22 December 1940, from the home of Dr S.N. Das Gupta, 48-8, Mancharpukar Road, PO Ballygunge, Calcutta:

> It is a pity that the shadow of a great calamity has stood between us like a cloud which has made our vision blurred. Many gossips and rumours have floated from Calcutta to Bombay and from Bombay to Calcutta and have darkened the correct comprehension of the situation.

She added:

> How glad I would have been if we two could have met once and I could have seen your face in the bright sunshine, touched you and felt you in my embrace that you are the same, loving, kind and pure sister that you were ever with us and the calamitous circumstances have left no dark shades on your beaming angelic face. The world around is so naughty, that after every tremendous shock it becomes necessary for us that we are the same as we were in our eyes and in the eyes of God.

Obviously, the family felt the need to stress that they had been somewhat disturbed by what they had heard from the 'naughty' world. Possibly, there were also rumours about her 'purity'.

Devika told them that her salary had, in the past, been given to Himansu to dispense with as he thought fit, and they had no savings. However, she could, out of her own future salary, give some money every month to Lilu, if that would help. She must have been aware that such dependency would be anathema to Lilu and others in the family. They preferred that an amount of at least ₹5,000 (from the insurance money) be given to Lilu, which could go towards her marriage expenses or any other expenses she may incur.

Mrs Das Gupta replied:

> It is indeed very kind of you to have proposed to make monthly financial arrangements for Lilu, but you will realise that from

our point of view it does not appear fair that you should by your own efforts continue to support Lilu for life. Moreover as she is with me and as father is with my other sister, none of them now is in any actual necessity of any monthly allowance. But it would have been well if a few thousands of rupees could be kept for Lilu in the bank as something on which she may fall back.

Mrs Das Gupta pointed out that Lilu was more needy as all of her ornaments had been stolen, and from her tone there appears to be a suggestion that this may have happened while Lilu and her mother were in Bombay.

Devika replied, attaching the relevant bills, as instructed by Rai Bahadur Chuni Lall—who, like everyone else at Bombay Talkies, was very sympathetic to her plight—that around ₹7,000 had already been spent on Himansu's medical and other expenses, and only ₹2,813 was left. She also explained that she could not send the money unless Himansu's father signed a document, in the presence of a magistrate, stating that he had surrendered all his interests in the estate of his late son. Only then could she approach the high court for sanction to pay the remaining amount of ₹2,813 to Lilu.

However, Himansu's family was reluctant to get their father to sign the document as Himansu's death had not yet been 'disclosed to him'. They told her that they hoped to get his signature 'soon'.

In the event, Devika managed to retrieve some of her reputation by being open to supporting those who (because she was now a widow) should have been supporting her. Her spontaneous gesture in offering to give a small sum from her salary to Lilu, each month, would also not have gone unnoticed by those who had accused her of avarice. Far from being rich, it appeared that she did not have very much at all, even after having worked non-stop for over ten years with Himansu!

Though her financial situation would improve after Himansu's death as she would receive her full salary as well as the fees due to her as a managing agent at HIT, Devika would continue to receive occasional letters from Himansu's family, requesting her to pay some debt or the other. She wrote to the Bombay Talkies manager (by that time her friend, Sachin Chaudhuri had replaced Rai Bahadur Chuni Lall) a few years later, when a bank tried to involve her in the repayment of a loan her father-in-law had taken:

> I understand that these people want some debt of my father-in-law to be paid.... During (Himansu's) life he was very much against these sort of things, he used to send his father money for his expenses but never encouraged them to ask for money which they spent on what he used to term useless things. After his death, I offered to send my father-in-law a little money from my pay, but was refused by his daughter—Himansu's insurance was Rs ten thousand and his illness cost nearly that. I had put in a claim as a succession certificate was granted after 9-10 months after his death, he did not sign his insurance in my name so Sir Chimanlal told me to do this. I would be glad if you consulted some good lawyer and gave them a strong reply—I do not owe anyone anything and have not any wish to get entangled in these people's affairs—one man on my father-in-law's behalf once wrote and asked me for some money, he said I had nothing to do with it, only if I wished he could arrange a small sum etc. I did not reply, [and] I want to finish off altogether with them, they never helped [Himansu], were always a burden on him and I don't think were even grateful, except my mother-in-law, who in my opinion was the most wonderful woman I have ever met. I don't wish to have anything to do with their debts, they have their own zamindar sister's husband and own people. The little money that remained out of the Rs ten thousand is money which I can invest, and after my death it goes somewhere. Of course I have not touched it, I paid up every penny [Himansu] owed out of my own earning, and am glad to say I have no debts now. God has helped me and I am grateful for his infinite goodness. [Himansu] also owed them <u>nothing at all</u>...he was cursing these people when he replied [to them].

She did not repay the loan and asked Sachin to send a stiff reply.

～～～

But all that lay in the future. For now, the news of Himansu's death had reached the rest of Bombay and the cremation was as well attended as any film premiere. Himansu, who loved a good production, whether an event or a film, would have been very pleased.

According to Manto, Devika had got a new set of clothes made for the occasion. He may have got that detail right, because among the bills submitted by Devika to Bombay Talkies was one for a saree, 'with a border', which had been bought on 22 March 1940, two months before Himansu died. The bill stated that the saree was bought by Himansu. Could it be that he wanted his wife to appear as glamorous as she always did, in the last event in which they would star together—his funeral? Even this bizarre gesture was possible because their love, which made them hate each other at times, also bound them together, and he had always been proud of her, and she of him.

The funeral was very high profile, and the arrangements were very well made. The body was kept for some time at the studio for people to pay their respects. There are reports that only sandalwood was used for the funeral pyre, but the documents and payments have no record of that, though ₹250 was spent on the funeral.

The Film Journalists Association of India issued a joint statement on 20 May enumerating Himansu's numerous contributions:

> [He] introduced for the first time Indian films to the international market, and his work as founder and producer of the Bombay Talkies...contributed a progressive trend in Indian films and secured the cooperation of educated...persons as artistes and technicians.

It was rare for a cinema producer who had not been seen on screen for the past seven years, to receive such tributes and accolades. But then, there was also an urgency, both to reinforce his legacy as well as lay claim to it. The successful contender would receive substantial benefits. And the Bombay Talkies shares could not be allowed to fall.

Baburao Patel would later tell Devika about the hypocrites he had spotted crying at Himansu's funeral while plotting at the same time to oust her.

It was at this time that Devika realised how endangered her position was because the rival group, led by Sashadhar, were in line to present themselves as the successors to Himansu. If they had their way, the young widow would soon be sidelined. Rumours were already swirling around regarding her 'various affairs'. People were becoming aware that she may not have been as shattered by Himansu's death as she should have been.

Sixteen-year-old Hansa Wadkar was an eyewitness to some events during this time which made her uneasy about Devika. But then, as she herself admitted, she had a special fondness for Himansu. She says in her biography, *You Ask, I Tell*:

> Himansu fell sick. It was May 1939. His condition worsened day by day. One day I got a phone call, 'Himansu Rai has passed away.' For a moment I was in a state of shock. He was like a father to me and a great support. His death was a big loss.

Hansa recollected:

> The funeral was the next day. Though I had been advised rest, I went to the studio. Many people were there. His body was kept there for final respects. I touched his feet and paid my homage...
>
> I came out after paying homage and stood with other girls in the verandah. Devika Rani, gently wiping her eyes, came close to the dead body a couple of times and later went to her room. I wanted to meet her. There was a board outside her room which said 'Do Not Enter'.
>
> But I was the heroine of Bombay Talkies. Who would stop me? So I pushed the door open. Devika Rani was inside with two or three men laughing and chatting with them. I looked at

her for a moment. The two men got up and left. Devika Rani came to me. We hugged each other and cried bitterly.

After this, she says she no longer felt 'comfortable' in the studio. A week later, she asked Devika to release her from her contract as she did not want to work in films, anymore. The contract was valid for three years more, but Devika tore it up, and Hansa was free.

Hansa's last film with Bombay Talkies was *Azad*—another winner from Saradindu Banerjee—and possibly the last film in which Himansu was involved. Once again, it was directed by N.R. Acharya, and was a further departure from the early cinema of Bombay Talkies. A somewhat liberal, romantic film, it brought forth the importance of love in a relationship and cemented the reputation of the on-screen duo of Leela Chitnis and Ashok Kumar. It also broke some rules by showing an unmarried woman, with an unknown past, staying with an unmarried man. This unusual live-in relationship had been explored by Saradindu in another successful film, *Bhabhi*, in which a young sister-in-law lives with her brother-in-law, but in that case it was a completely asexual relationship. Later, another Bombay Talkies film, *Kismet*, in which an unmarried couple live in the same house (where Ashok Kumar is a tenant) was made by Gyan and Sashadhar Mukerji.

Just after Himansu's death, Amiya Chakrabarty, a handsome young man whom Devika was very fond of, got his chance to become part of a Bombay Talkies production. *Bandhan*, starring Ashok Kumar and Leela Chitnis, was the first time Amiya got an on screen credit, for the screenplay, along with Gyan Mukerji. The Mukerji brothers had begun to spread their wings now that Himansu was no more. The producer of *Bandhan* was no longer Himansu, but Sashadhar. The credits in the accompanying brochure put it even more starkly—'The Bombay Talkies Ltd, Founded by Himansu Rai'. The on-screen logo now bore his black-and-white photograph. There was no mention of Devika in the credits.

But Devika had already made her overtures to the board, and found that everyone was sympathetic towards her. She had managed to get her protégé, Amiya, into a production, and had also begun speaking to her friends, Sachin and Hiten Choudhuri, about the possibility of working at Bombay Talkies. She had started building up a possible team.

On 26 September 1940, as decided in a previous meeting on 30 August, 1939, a resolution was passed to write off the money owed by Himansu to HIT. The resolution read:

> Sir Chimanlal H Setalvad proposed and Lt Col Sir Richard Temple seconded that the sum of Rs 14890/ due to the company from Mr Himansu Rai be written off.

Despite the growing animosity within the two groups in Bombay Talkies, the board of directors of Bombay Talkies and HIT continued to repose their faith in Devika. Undoubtedly, she continued to work hard—and they could also see that she had plunged into the making of *Anjan*, the first film she would produce and act in after Himansu died. On 22 September 1941, she was to write a very grateful letter to Sir Chimanlal Setalvad, as the board had passed a resolution on 1 September 1941 offering her a contract for a further period of five years and an increment of a hundred rupees per month. She said:

> I cannot express to you how deeply touched I was to hear of this resolution. Encouragement and sympathy from people, I do not come in contact with, gives me so much courage.

She did not meet Sir Chimanlal so often anymore because she was completely absorbed with her work at the studio. She took care to mention how much replenishment the technical aspect of the studio required—and equipment needed to be replaced. She also mentioned that a new Mitchell camera had been bought, which had improved the quality of the cinematography.

'I have not seen you for such a long time and do hope you are quite well,' she added, not knowing that the distance between her and the board was growing, and the group led by Sashadhar was making inroads into the very special relationship Himansu and she had once shared with Sir Chimanlal.

'My picture *Anjan* will be released on the 27th, please give it your blessing,' she said, signing off with 'deep respect and love'.

It would be one of the last times when she could cordially address the chairperson of Bombay Talkies. Very soon the relationship would be vitiated by the politics in the studio.

It had not helped that she had been on leave for a fortnight from 16 August to the end of the month. She resumed as the controller of production department from 1 September 1941. In her absence, Sashadhar had been holding that position. Her return and elevation did not bode well for her rivals, who now began what seemed like a campaign to vilify her and her work, including trying to pull her film off from the theatres, and replace it with their own.

Ironically, because of the ongoing issues which would emerge towards the end of 1941 and early 1942, Devika would not receive the promised ₹100 increment in her salary. It was not till 1 October 1943 that Keshavlal Mody, who was to emerge as a powerful figure in HIT, (thanks to her support) was to write:

> I have the pleasure to inform you that...orders were passed today increasing your present honorarium by Rs 100/- per month, thereby raising it to Rs 1500.

But even as Devika geared up to roll out her productions, Sashadhar seemed to be in the controlling seat. Devika felt this was a position she—or someone of her choice—should have occupied. After all, she was the co-founder of Bombay Talkies.

But her position as the lead actress was no longer unassailable, with newer and younger claimants such as Mumtaz Shanti and Hansa Wadkar appearing on the scene. Leela Chitnis was the same age as her and already acclaimed as a very competent and sophisticated actress. And all of them all seemed to be delivering bigger hits than her.

She now began to think about how she could get into the lead again. Himansu's death had bought her about six months in which she could consolidate her position, making use of the sympathy extended to her. Everyone was respectful of her apparent grief, even though her ability to deal with everything systematically and stoically, despite having no man by her side, or anyone else close to her, may well have puzzled them. What they did not know was that living with an increasingly unstable husband had taught her to be even more fiercely independent. She needed to make her own decisions. The abuse from Himansu meant that she trusted no one. As she said later, the thrashing toughened her.

In the past seven years at Bombay Talkies, Devika had managed to remain enigmatic, and a little distant—except when she had production matters at hand or was acting in a film. Intuitively, she knew that sometimes the boldness of her approach helped defuse certain situations. But in other cases, she had to play the matriarch, appear much older than her age, and be the universal mother to all those who flocked to the studio, seeking roles, work or publicity. All this meant that she was wiser and more mature than most thirty-two-year-olds. Her only Achilles heel was her good looks, which made people think she was far too innocent and vulnerable. And so, her position was weakened by the main problem which had begun to surface even before Himansu died—men!

Himansu would have already known about the rumours concerning her and Amiya. It was an open secret that they were very close and that Amiya would visit her in her 'private chambers'. While Himansu was alive, this would not have been an issue, as they were all professionals working together. Himansu and Devika were living separately anyway, and everyone was aware of this. But after his death, these things would not be so well understood. Indeed, Amiya began to assert himself, and soon there would be a tussle between him and Sashadhar over who would direct the next film—which only ignited more gossip. In the beginning, though, Amiya seemed happy to be credited with the screenplay of *Bandhan*. And Sashadhar, for the first time, was acknowledged as the producer, which too was a big step forward. Both the rival sides appeared satisfied.

Devika would have been relieved as she was also busy trying to get Himansu's shares in HIT transferred to her, aside from dealing with the problem of the life insurance money that was due to her. She also wanted to make sure that the board did not treat her simply as a fading actress, and that they realised that she was actually working hard at the studio.

The twelve shares of HIT which had belonged to Himansu had to be transferred to Devika as his wife and heir. Once she had all thirteen shares in her possession (including the one share already in her name), she would wield real power in HIT and also own a valuable asset for the first time in her life. But the transfer of these shares to her became a bone of contention and a controversy, just like so many other aspects of her life. Had the twelve shares really belonged to Himansu? Or had they been given to his old friend Sir Richard Temple as collateral against a loan of £3,000, as claimed by Sir Richard? Was this yet another case of Himansu having borrowed money and not repaid it—as he was often accused of doing? In which case, how could Devika claim the shares?

Or did Sir Richard have them all along—and Devika talked Sir Richard into giving her a valuable gift of the twelve shares, following Himansu's death? In fact, this was the claim made by Sir Richard, to everyone's surprise. He claimed that Himansu had given the shares to him and he had handed them to her as a gift, not asking for anything in return. This seemed odd, but not if one remembered that they were supposed to share a special relationship.

Rumours made the air heavy as Sir Richard was taken to court for bankruptcy, and the shares were a part of the claim against him. But Devika stuck to her story that the shares belonged to Himansu, and now to her. She made a 'verbal' and later written appeal to the board to transfer the shares to her, and it was done. She denied that Sir Richard had given them to her.

She would have heaved a sigh of relief then, as these shares made her position as a director on the board of HIT stronger. All these years, Himansu had been a director and no one had questioned his position. But she knew that people were asking questions about her—and she was keen to put an end to them. She was now on par with the other directors. Her real target, though, was Sir Chimanlal —the old friend who was now showing an interest in the rival group led by Sashadhar. The extra shares gave heft to her position.

HIT, being the managing agent of Bombay Talkies, was important for her as it controlled and ran the studio. What she didn't know was that there were several people plotting to dislodge her and the problem of the shares would come up again very soon. Just as one problem seemed to be sorted, she would be faced with another. This was a period of a struggle far more intense than any she had faced so far.

She knew that she urgently needed to handle the Mukerjis, Gyan and Sashadhar, who were making her natural ascension to the top of Bombay Talkies difficult. As Valicha said in his book on Ashok Kumar:

> With [Himansu] Rai around, Sashadhar Mukerjee's position had been dominant. It had enabled him to have a say in the running of the studio. He sat in on the story sessions, the recordings, the editing and even on the scripts. He was in fact involved in the execution of each film that was made at Bombay Talkies.

Now, Devika wanted a say in all the films being made—through her close associate and loyal confidante, Amiya.

Meanwhile, Sashadhar's film *Bandhan* had become a big hit. The songs also became very popular—such as 'Chana jor garam' and 'Chal, chal re naujawan'. This was not to say that Bombay Talkies was not already doing well. The ship had been steady for some time, despite the various storms that had broken out recently. This was partly due to the fact that the quiet and affable Ashok Kumar had been working hard at improving his acting abilities. No one had anticipated what a potent pair he and the gentle Leela Chitnis would make. The viewers sensed a chemistry between them, which was translated onto the screen.

Ashok and Leela themselves realised their popularity only when they went by train on a promotional tour to Lahore, along with Rai Bahadur Chuni Lall, and were mobbed at every station where the train stopped. At Lahore station, there was a virtual stampede and they could only alight at Moghulpura, the next station. The kind of adulation that they received grew exponentially with every film, beginning with *Kangan*. *Bandhan* established them as a star couple—good-looking and urbane. Leela became known as the only 'graduate' lady to act in Indian cinema, and Ashok's salary went up to ₹500 per month.

Their second film together, *Jhoola*, was also produced by Sashadhar. This time, the direction was by Gyan Mukerji, while the dialogue writers included Shahid Latif. Sashadhar was definitely becoming a money spinner for the studio and the board was beginning to recognise his contribution. But Devika, despite being recently widowed, was determined not to be left behind.

The two rival groups—one led by Devika and the other by Sashadhar—were now bringing in new people so that they could increase their hold on the studio and consolidate their position. To stop being steamrollered by Sashadhar, who knew a great deal more about both the running of Bombay Talkies and filmmaking, Devika decided to hit back by going to the board and getting an understanding that the two teams could take turns producing films, alternately.

Following the success of *Bandhan*, it was now Devika's turn to throw her hat in the ring. Fortunately for her, Ashok did not want to get embroiled in the conflict between her and Sashadhar and was happy to participate in Amiya's debut film, *Anjan*. Devika would play the lead. It was a little risky, going by the rave reviews the new educated lady on the block, Leela Chitnis, had received. It might have been simpler to allow Leela to play the lead once more, but

Devika needed to establish the 'extra' contribution she made to the studio—she could act, sing, train others, and produce films as well. Her competition with Sashadhar was out in the open.

Anjan was a typical Bombay Talkies melodrama and did not get the same reception as *Bandhan* or even *Kangan* had, though it did not go unnoticed. In the film, Indira (Devika Rani) is a nanny in a feudal household, where both the good family doctor Ajit (Ashok Kumar) and the villainous estate manager are in love with her. When the old dowager who owns the estate dies, Ajit is accused by the manager of having killed her. Of course, it is all resolved at the end. The truly outstanding aspect of the film was the music by the well-known flautist, Pannalal Ghosh.

Devika knew that she would have to do more to win the battle. The other camp seemed to better qualified as of now, as all the tried-and-tested talent was with them, while Devika was struggling to put together candidates in key positions. She wanted loyalists who would support her. She was also hunting for new actors and trying to see how she could combat the charisma of Ashok Kumar.

Another blow for her was the provocative new film *Naya Sansar* (1941), which was written by Khwaja Ahmed Abbas and starred Renuka Devi and Ashok Kumar. It did extremely well and managed to bring in ₹27,000 in the first two weeks after release. It was a crisply told tale, with dialogues by Shahid Latif and J.S. Casshyap, while the lyrics were by Pradeep and the music was composed by Saraswati Devi and Ramchandra Pal. The story was about a dedicated journalist, Puran, played by Ashok Kumar, who is concerned about the corruption of his ideals. He starts his own newspaper, *Naya Sansar*, quitting the one he had previously worked for. The love interest was played by Renuka Devi, who was shown as a journalist. The cinematography was by R.D. Pareenja. The film went on to win the Bengal Film Journalists' Association award for best story and screenplay.

It was a frustrating time for Devika—and also humiliating to see that the studio she had set up with her own sweat and tears was now being taken over by these upstarts, who had all been trained under her husband and her. But, always a fighter, she was preparing her strategy to regain lost ground.

Once again, she turned to Amiya for support. He wrote a lively story and screenplay, *Basant* (1942), another complicated romantic melodrama. As the brochure put it, 'This is the story of a kitchen maid who became a matinee idol; of a despised orphan who became a loyal wife and an exemplary mother.' It was a tale of how misunderstandings were likely to push women into the arena of suspicion (a theme which would have appealed to Devika). But the question was, would the production have the finesse of the previous Bombay Talkies films? This time, the story, screenplay and direction were all by Amiya Chakrabarty—something that would not have gone down well with the Mukerjis or Ashok Kumar, as he was not one of the lead actors.

Mumtaz Shanti and Ullhas were in the lead. The dialogues were written, as always, by J.S. Casshyap. *Basant* was Mumtaz's debut film, and she gave a wonderful performance. She went on to act in over twenty-two films, but it was *Kismet*, the Bombay Talkies film she acted in with Ashok Kumar, which changed her fortunes. Unfortunately for Devika, that film was produced by Sashadhar.

The screenplay and direction of *Kismet* was by Gyan Mukerji, while the scenario and dialogues were by Santoshi and Shahid Latif. The music, which was to become a big hit, especially the patriotic song 'Door hato ai duniyawalon, Hindustan hamara hai', was scored by the young Anil Biswas.

Basant and *Kismet* had similar stories, and the central character in each was a stage artiste. It could have been a mere coincidence that the story line and characters in competing films had common elements without either side realising it, or it could have been deliberate. *Kismet*, however, became a noir film with Ashok Kumar at the heart of it, playing a controversial anti-hero.

The plot of *Basant*, Amiya's directorial debut, featured misunderstandings galore, but it had a certain insouciance and liveliness which ensured that the film went on to run for fifty weeks in many theatres. Finally, to her immense relief, Devika also had a hit!

To make her proprietorship apparent, the opening credits which acknowledged Himansu Rai as the founder of Bombay Talkies also stated that *Basant* was a Devika Rani presentation. This kind of acknowledgment, especially for a woman, was rare and possibly not seen for decades afterwards, but it showed Devika's determination to ensure that she received due credit for her hard work. When she had worked behind the scenes while Himansu was alive, credit had never been an issue. But now, she felt she could not take anything for granted. She was fighting every step of the way. She realised that unless some things were made apparent and obvious, the control of the studio was likely to slip out of her hands.

But it was a tough battle. Sashadhar and Gyan, and even Ashok, had an advantage over her—they had actually learnt all aspects of production under Himansu's guidance, for years. They were a cohesive group and were used to working together seamlessly.

However, barring the early years, when she helped in the production of *A Throw of Dice* and later, *Karma*, and in the setting up of Bombay Talkies, once she became an actress and a mentor to other actors, Devika had not been involved in production. Instead, in the little spare time she had, she became a key member of the fundraising unit with Himansu. She had the responsibility of mingling in high society and with government officials, which none of the others had.

It was a difficult time, and she felt lonelier than ever. Her days were long and tiring, and with little appreciation from anyone— except Amiya, and she could not openly seek his company too often. She began to feel unwell and exhausted.

She would be ready to get to the studio every day by 8 a.m., and often ended up driving all the way to town, in the heat and dust, if there were meetings to attend at the registered office of Bombay Talkies, or with Sir Chimanlal. She carried on with her acting, as well as training others when required. Yet, she felt she that few noticed her hard work. The present factionalism in the studio was all blamed on her by those who did not know she could not destroy the studio she had worked so hard to set up and sacrificed so much for. Being Devika, she shrugged off the accusations. She never allowed gossip or other people's opinions to disturb her. But in the eyes of old timers at Bombay Talkies such as the Mukerjis, she had demonstrated her real character years ago when she had run away with Najam.

Devika knew the struggle over production had to be sorted out. She also knew about Sashadhar's briefings to Sir Chimanlal and Rai Bahadur Chuni Lall against her. She had thought that he, and the others, would respect the effort she had put into the studio but it was becoming increasingly clear to her that this group she had battling since Himansu's death would, within a couple of years, try to wreck their joint legacy by ousting her. But now, with some unexpected help, she started weaving a plan which would make it impossible for Sashadhar and his group to stay on. It would be a coup, and as the plan unfolded, so did the realisation become obvious that only one among the two warring sides could continue to work in Bombay Talkies.

Kismet, though a success, saw the animosity come out in the open against each other. Ashok Kumar was the lead actor in the film, and he had been careful to stay on the right side of Devika all these years. He had even continued to work in the laboratory while *Kismet* was being shot. Valicha tells us in *Dadamoni*:

> He [Ashok Kumar] had a pair of scissors in his hands when he realised he would have to leave Bombay Talkies. Tears welled up in his eyes. In frustration he fisted the thin wooden partition wall, causing a hole in it. The hole stayed there for a long time. When Ashok Kumar got back years later to take over Bombay Talkies, he saw it and remembered.

But what was the reason for Sashadhar's unhappiness with Devika? Was it Amiya's arrogance? Or Devika's dismissive attitude towards him? Or her so-called ineptitude? Or because she brought in new people (as she had always done) without consulting Sashadhar? Or was it just the patriarchal attitudes that prevailed at the time—a woman at the top was unheard of and difficult to tolerate? Whatever the final trigger, it seems clear now that many things were not as straightforward as those chronicling the history of Bombay Talkies—mostly men—would have us believe.

When, ultimately, Devika too plotted and planned and won a 'signal victory' after a hard struggle, the father of someone close to the scene of the battle wrote to her on 10 February 1943:

> Dear Madam,
> I am Dikshit's father writing to you. My son has recently written to me about your signal victory—after a very trying and tiring struggle—against an overwhelming opposition and asked my blessings for you.
> Reading between the lines of his overflowing letter, madam, I have been able to form some general acquaintance with you. And old as I am—a relic of an age fast disappearing—it has given me genuine satisfaction to note that placed as you are, and even in this age of general disbelief and despairing ideals, you still keep faith in some of the old decencies of life—blessings, for an example.
> Well, blessings are sooner given than asked and believe me, you have my heartful of blessings because you have been brave. But I shall tell you the secret of blessings. Be good to men and faithful to God, and you shall not lack my blessings, or of anyone either. Blessings will flow to you spontaneously, as rivers flow to the sea. That is all.

Letter from Devika to Svetoslav

My dear friend

To sit in an office and deal with finance and get things going is not my real self. But I am grateful to God in one way that I have not to beg or be supported by anyone. It's a blessing to earn one's living, and the people are most kind to me. I have no money of my own. My husband earned just enough to keep us respectable. He was an idealist & said that money would come later....So we started life on nothing and have known starvation, and wealth in all parts of the world, trying to form a Film Industry here. Since then he has gone, & I just carry on but with no inspiration. People with real minds & vision don't happen here much. To build on sound and progressive lines and do good with it on the whole, is not usual and Government has restricted us to 3 films a year, and now only 2 from next year, out of which one has to be an Instructional film....

Forgive me...I am a rather lonely person in my mind and so when things come out I say too much—it's a bad thing and I know you so little. I'm depressed with our outlook, our silly false life. You say something is bound to happen, but I don't see where? There is no reality at all & we just live a sham life, kidding ourselves, and rotting—which is mental death, and one sees how awful conditions are...no one does anything, we are so hopelessly depraved that we haven't the guts to say a word—just like trapped rats in a cage, eating whatever is given to us, and what is worse being content to go on like this. It's our fault—no one else's—that's what depressing. I'm going now or I'll never stop.

Bombay, 1944

14

DEVIKA'S REVENGE, 1940s

The problem that had been simmering for a long time came to a head after Himansu's death.

Devika was struggling to consolidate their joint legacy—and she felt she was being thwarted at every step. It became obvious to her that Sashadhar had to go. Not just Sashadhar, but perhaps all those working closely with him—Gyan, Ashok, Savak. They were hostile to her very *presence*—whenever she suggested a new project or brought in fresh talent, they objected. They resented having a woman in charge and made it clear that they did not trust her.

Himansu had been too unwell to publicly appoint her as his successor. This was something she would have to do herself. She had no other identity—she had lost touch with her family but for the occasional letter, and she had no close friends outside the studio—and no savings and no income, except what she earned from Bombay Talkies. Yes, she knew a lot of rich and powerful people, but Devika's own dignity would not allow her to ask for help from anyone. She had to work this out herself. For the outside world and the media, she remained as serene and charming as ever.

The worst thing was that the 'rival camp' would not even allow her films to run at cinema halls without disruptions. After all the opportunities she had given them, how could they do this to her?

A year after Himansu's death and the release of her film *Anjan* (1941), starring Devika and Ashok and directed by

Amiya Chakrabarty, she wrote an emotional letter to Sir Chimanlal Setalvad:

> It is long since I wrote to you. I understand from Rai Bahadur Chunilal that you and he have agreed and decided to take my picture, Anjan off and put on Jhoola on or about the 20th, the reason being that Anjan is not making enough money etc. Since you are satisfied with such arrangements I have nothing to say.
>
> It pains me to think that the work which we all loved in my first picture was not a success. I am not at all happy in the present form of work, we all work like slaves, dully and I feel it is time we made some sort of arrangement by which the workers have a plan as to how we all stand which will cause more satisfaction and result in better work.
>
> Now just alternate productions continue, some take more time, some less and the result is two productions a year.
>
> I cannot have any interest to work in this manner, to tell you the truth I wish I had not any work at all as I am rather disheartened and tired. I shall within sometime think out a way of getting the right type of interest in the work and let you know as things can't continue as they are.
>
> With respect,
>
> Yours affly,
> Devika

Anjan was the 'first film' she made under the new arrangement of the two camps producing films alternately. Clearly, the system wasn't working very well as they were being valued differently. *Jhoola*, which starred Leela Chitnis and Ashok Kumar, directed by Gyan Mukerji and produced by Sashadhar, was considered a better film, and so the film starring her and Ashok Kumar and directed by Amiya was denied a longer run. Was this done deliberately to undermine her or was this a genuine issue? She knew that her relationship with Sir Chimanlal had deteriorated of late and he was openly siding with Sashadhar, but she had not imagined he would endorse an action that would deepen the rift at Bombay Talkies. Surely, more than her, the company would suffer if only Sashadhar's films were promoted and distributed properly?

Her letter was enough to set the alarm bells ringing. The board had been helpful to her, but they obviously did not feel she was competent to run the studio or make films. Without Himansu, she had to prove herself all over again. Devika suspected that Sir Chimanlal and Rai Bahadur Chuni Lall were no longer as friendly towards her as they had been. Perhaps they had held a grudge ever since her 'Calcutta fling', as she now thought about it. It had happened close to six years ago, but with Himansu's death, the old memories seemed to have come back. She thought Sir Chimanlal had allowed himself to become more prejudiced towards her, and now even Rai Bahadur Chuni Lall, who used to stand in the corridor and offer her a rose every morning, was turning against her. There was a time when he would specially order 'chaplis' or sandals for her from Lahore!

Devika was made increasingly aware that she needed to assert herself. Being the only woman in a men's club meant that she could be easily undermined. To prevent that, she required a strategy to become the boss—and if he refused to give her the support she needed, she required a means to remove Sashadhar. She knew that her own regard for Sir Chimanlal had undergone a sea change. Well, she was going to fight him, in the boardroom, as well as in the studio. He had only seen her as the sweet, hardworking wife of Himansu Rai, till she had run away. Now she was the poor little widow. Once again, she would shock him with her ambition.

All her life, whenever Devika reached a point of no return, she used the one weapon that always worked—the threat of walking away, which was imbedded in the letter she had written to Sir Chimanlal regarding her film, *Anjan*. It had worked in her childhood, and it had worked when she had run away to Calcutta with Najam. Sir Chimanlal, the chairman of Bombay Talkies and HIT, had no choice but to give in, yet again. None of the shareholders would disagree—Devika was their lucky charm, and they were receiving healthy dividends. She was also the one person on the HIT board who understood cinema, and in the end, Sir Chimanlal was far too decent a man and did not want to be seen as 'harassing' the widow of an old colleague.

A meeting of the board of directors of HIT was held on Monday, 20 July 1942, at 5 p.m., at the office of the chairman, at 113, Esplanade Road, Fort, Bombay. The minutes said it all:

The following Directors were present:

1. Sir Chimanlal H. Setalvad, KCIE, LLD, JP
2. Shrimati Devika Rani Rai
3. Rai Bahadur Chuni Lall
4. Keshavlal D. Mody, Esq.
5. V. C. Setalvad, Esq.

The minutes of the meeting of the Board held on the 15th June 1942 were confirmed.

The Chairman brought to the notice of the Board that the existing arrangements of the Production Department of the Bombay Talkies, Ltd. of pictures being produced turn by turn by Mrs Devika Rani Rai and Mr S. Mukerji was not working well and party and group feelings [were] growing in the Studio in the two different units. This was not in the interest of the Company, [and so] he recommended that Mrs Rai should function as the Controller of Production for all the pictures in the Company and whenever necessary or desirable act as an artiste while Mr S. Mukerji be the Producer for all the pictures in the Company.

Though the matter was to be discussed further after a few days, it became obvious to all that in her position as a director on the HIT board, which was the managing agent for Bombay Talkies, Devika was able to assert her superiority. Instead of being on par with Sashadhar Mukerji, she would now be the controller of production, a position Himansu had held. She would oversee all the productions and possibly even suggest changes to the crew and technicians.

This unnerved the Mukerji camp. It was a calculated blow, and they would have to do more than just produce good cinema if they were to preempt constant intervention in their work.

The rift was reinforced. Sashadhar and Amiya faced each other across a widening divide, and rumours flew thick and fast. Devika had to ensure that all the films did well, but reports continued to come in that the films produced by her team, or those in which she had acted, were being run down. She received letters stating suspicions that her films were not distributed properly. Could this be mere paranoia or was there any truth in it? And could it be that she was now past her prime and was better off not appearing in films anymore?

Even at thirty-four, Devika was being feted as the most beautiful actress. Just the previous year, the *Mirror* (20 April 1941) had said that the vote for the most beautiful woman on the Indian screen went to the 'demure' Devika Rani, who was 'glowingly sweet rather than tantalising' and for many the 'sweetest looking girl'. Compared to others, such as Kananbala, Leela Desai, Naseem, Shanta Apte, Khurshid and Leela Chitnis, 'She has a plastic and malleable softness, a natural grace and poise which simply appeals to the sensitive frame of mind, and charms without exciting you.' The article observed that other actresses such as Leela Desai were too dumb, while still others, who were beautiful, such as Naseem, were learning to come out of their 'dumb, doll-like beauty'.

Such outrageous flattery did not stop Devika from trying to see how she could make herself more attractive on the screen. After the setback over *Anjan*, she was keen to improve her appearance. She had not liked her look in *Durga* either. She knew that her child-like appeal brought out a streak of chivalry in most—except those who wanted to take Bombay Talkies away from her. She wanted to look younger and thinner on screen so that she could compete with the newer actresses. She decided to fall back for advice on their German cinematographer, Josef 'Teddy' Wirsching, who was interned at the time at Deolali and would be there through the duration of World

War II. She sent him photographs from three different films to ask about her 'look'—to remove the wrinkles through lighting and make-up and also deal with the problem of her deep-set eyes.

It clearly did not strike her as an odd thing to do, to ask for make-up tips from someone who was incarcerated as an enemy. But Josef was a professional. Regardless of the fact that he was in jail on suspicion of being a Nazi, he wrote back in detail, highlighting the changes and the look most suitable for her:

1. The picture of 'Mamta' there is nothing to improve—if you get the effect as it is it will be alright. [*Mamta* was an earlier film, made in 1935, in which Josef had done the lighting and the shoot.]
2. The picture of 'Durga'—I had never liked it—the expression of the face and the eyes is a result of the hairdresser i.e. ears free and hair brushed straight back, this kind of hairdress makes the face old and hard.
3. Photos of Narayani No 157 and 120.

No 157—a good picture, it should have more sidelight. Make-up: If you can shade the eyes as roughly indicated on the photo it would be better i.e. a light line above the eyelids and then gradually shading up to the eyebrows and if possible drawing the eyebrows a bit lower on the outside.

As to the rest of the pictures the same as said above [applies] to them too.

He described the kind of make-up she should use, shading up from the cheekbones to the ears, as her face looked a bit too full. He also suggested where the spotlight may be positioned for her and hoped that his 'suggestions will prove helpful to reach the satisfaction you are out for'.

Ever the perfectionist, Devika had also asked for details of how she had been filmed when the Germans were in charge of production. 'Teddy' replied:

There was no special lighting for your face except 'your spot'... this light is a spot-light, very diffused (milk or matt glass) as near to the camera as possible and in about the same height as your eyes. This spot is to avoid lines, wrinkles and deep eyes (all the things you complain about). In addition there is one or two side-lights a bit higher up.

He answered all her queries, including about her make-up being chalky, and even sketched out how her eyes and eyebrows should be shaded.

There was nothing in the letter which made it particularly personal, but Devika would keep in touch with 'Teddy' Wirsching and his wife, and the other Germans who had been interned. When, in 1945, the Wirschings were in Camp Sitara, one of the fourteen camps set up by the British for the POWs, and families were finally allowed to join the internees, Devika sent a hamper with cheese and cake, and later, tins of sardines—and received a grateful letter from Charlotte Wirsching. The cake, incidentally, was a gift from Amiya. As a part of the camp activities, 'Teddy' had taken up carving and reciprocated with a toy bullock cart specially made for Devika, which she expressed great appreciation for.

Even though she was now the controller of production, the strain of working in a hostile environment was beginning to take its toll on her. On 27 July 1942, she got a medical certificate from Dr C.R. Pereira with which she hoped to justify a short vacation, with Amiya Chakrabarty if possible. After Himansu's death, she hadn't had a chance to take a break, as she had been caught up with sorting out paperwork and shooting for *Anjan*.

Dr Periera wrote on the medical certificate:

> This is to certify that Mrs Devika Rai is under my treatment for neuratheria and that I have advised her to have as much rest as possible to prevent a nervous breakdown.

The reference to a nervous breakdown made it seem as though the problems at the studio were pushing her over the edge, something the board of HIT would have done anything to avoid. But though she was on leave, she had to remain in town as there was another attempt to destabilise her, and this time, it was much more serious.

Thus far, the board had accepted her claim that she was entitled to the 12 shares of HIT that had once belonged to Himansu. But Sir Richard had also claimed that he had gifted these to her. Sir Richard had been declared insolvent in 1940 and in the resulting court case there was a danger that these shares would be handed over to those he owed money to. A letter now arrived for Devika from the solicitors in the 'Jamnadas Kherajbhai vs Sir Richard Temple' case.

The legal tone sent chills down her spine. Shah and Company, Solicitors, Yusuf Building, 3rd Floor, Esplanade Road, Fort, wrote to request her response on the claims made in the case and, of course, everyone in HIT would have also known about it. In any case, she needed support from HIT to prove that the shares belonged to her. Jamnadas Kherajbhai, a Bombay businessman who had brought the case against Sir Richard, was a shareholder in Bombay Talkies, and possibly saw this as a means of getting some shares in HIT as well. He knew that HIT was the real power, as it managed the studio.

Kherajbhai was trying to establish that these shares had been 'gifted' to Devika without relevant paperwork, and should therefore be given to him (Janmadas). It was an interesting coincidence that the old case was dredged up just when Devika was fighting for her survival at the top of Bombay Talkies. Perhaps, by discrediting her, a vacancy could be created on the board of HIT?

Rumours regarding the once-upon-a-time closeness between Sir Richard and Devika began to do the rounds again—about how the two had met in London and how Sir Richard had gone out of his way to fix events and invitations for Devika and Himansu. In his thinly veiled portrait of Devika, 'A Woman for All Seasons', Manto described his protagonist, Sir Howard Pascal—he was sixty-ish, had a slight stammer, was a bit down at heel, but knew a lot of people. Manto wrote:

> The far sighted Lateeka [i.e., Devika Rani] saw in him [i.e., Sir Richard] someone who could be of great use. She decided to cultivate him, paying the sort of attention a nurse pays to a patient. In a few days, over dinner, things worked out in accordance with Lateeka's plans. A film company would be formed....
>
> Sir Howard Pascal had been given an apartment on the top floor of the studio. Lateeka would arrive early, and spend a little time with Sir Howard who was a keen gardener.

Manto was obviously reporting studio gossip and probably did a fairly accurate job of it. In his story, Lateeka is with Sir Howard Pascal when she hears the news that Prafula Roy (Himansu) is dying. Had the real life Devika visited Sir Richard when Himansu was dying so he would give the shares to her? After all, there was very little reason for Sir Richard to make up a story like that.

But the gossip about Devika and Sir Richard, especially in 1939, could be dismissed as on 31 August the same year he had married the tall and graceful Marie Wanda Henderson, an art teacher at the Sir JJ School of Art in Bombay, a few months after Himansu's death. This was his second marriage, as his first wife had died in 1932. This detail escaped the rumour mongers, but even more surprising was the fact that though Sir Richard was still associated with Bombay Talkies, no one from the studio was present at his wedding. It was attended by the bride's mother and one Miss R. Milner. Shortly after this, Sir Richard would leave his apartment at Bombay Talkies. This was also the time, from 1939 to 1941, that Devika was fighting for her survival. During this period, Sir Richard was no longer a director at HIT, as he had sold his fourteen shares to Keshavlal Mody. Thus it is quite likely that the two old friends, Devika and Sir Richard, could no longer meet as frequently as they had before.

Thankfully for Devika, there was no proof that the twelve shares which she had inherited had ever been with him. And as he himself admitted, there were no documents to prove any exchange either between him and Himansu or between him and Devika. Finally the matter went to the high court where Devika maintained that the allegations against her were not correct. She pointed out that after the death of her husband on 19 May 1940, she had immediately, on 25 May, asked for the twelve shares to be transferred to her as Himansu's heir.

It was interesting that she thought of the shares within six days of her husband's death. Most widows would have taken a little longer over the mourning period, but Devika was always level-headed, and besides, she now had to look out for herself. Twelve shares, worth at least ₹9,000 each, were not to be sniffed at.

The letter she had sent to the board of HIT was attached to her reply to the court. This letter was also mentioned the minutes of the meeting which took place on 27 May 1940, in which the directors present were Sir Chimanlal H. Setalvad, KCIE; Lt Col Sir Richard Temple, Bart, DSO; and Mrs Devika Rani Rai. Clearly, Sir Richard was present when her application to transfer the shares was approved, and it could not have gone through without his concurrence. According to the certified true copy of the minutes provided to the court:

> The Board considered the application of Mrs Devika Rani Rai that the 12 shares in the company held by the late Mr Himansu Rai be transferred to her name. The Board resolved that this be done.
>
> (Mrs Devika Rani Rai did not take part or vote in the passing of this resolution).

Soon after this evidence had been produced in court, Janmadas Kherajbhai, who had taken Sir Richard to court in the first place, reached out to her, complimenting her on her work. He kept in touch, would invite her for dinner and on 7 October 1943, he wrote to her:

I send you hereby my hearty congratulations for finishing the work of "Hamari Baat" [her new film] at such a high speed and quality. Of course, I will be able to say more when I actually see the same.

He was careful to send his regards to Amiya who, he said, 'cannot be forgotten'.

The story of the shares was a curious one and certainly led to speculation that Sir Richard was being used as a pawn by someone. If he was speaking the truth, why would he, on the brink of insolvency, *give away* the shares with which he could have made some money? Did he do it because Devika was the widow of a friend? Did he think they would be taken away anyway? Or did he want her to give him money in exchange, since he was bankrupt?

After Himansu's death, and even earlier, things had not been going well for Lt Col Sir Richard Temple, who had once been crucial for fundraising and for bringing many of the early supporters of Bombay Talkies, especially the British, on board. Though he was the grandson of a former governor of Bombay, Sir Richard had become rather more enamoured of the film world, and quite enchanted with Himansu and Devika. He became a director of Bombay Talkies as well as HIT. And that's when the trouble started.

According to his statement given in the court:

> In about 1932/33, I advanced a loan of about 10000 pounds to Himansu Rai Indo International Talkies Ltd. The monies belonged to me and my family. The loan was secured by an agreement signed by Mr Himansu Rai as the Managing Director of Himansu Rai Indo International Talkies Ltd, and also in his capacity as a constituted attorney of Sir Chimanlal, Chairman of Himansu Rai Indo International Talkies Ltd. This agreement was repudiated by Sir Chimanlal. The repudiation involved me into trouble with my trustees and eventually the responsibility of the loan fell on me.

However, since Himansu was a close friend, Sir Richard (who appears to have been a thorough gentleman and a somewhat simple person) neither took any security, nor pressed Himansu for damages, as the latter did not have any money anyway.

He said that in return for the £10,000 which he had loaned Himansu, he had received 14 of the 46 HIT shares which were issued, at a face value of ₹2,500 each. Now came the twist—he said the shares were eventually transferred to Keshavlal D. Mody, a businessman, for a cash consideration of ₹28,000 and for absolving him of his liability (in the insolvency case) of ₹30,000. Thus, eventually, the shares brought him around ₹58,000, though the face value was only ₹35,000.

Interestingly this was the second time Sir Richard had been sued over money. The first time had been in 1911, when he was taken to court by a moneylender Hirachand Punamchand. The latter had asked Sir Richard to contact his father to repay the debts. Sir Richard's father then paid ₹1,500 by cheque which was only a part of the debt to the moneylender. Having encashed the cheque, Hirachand now wanted the rest of the money. It became a famous case—because the court decided that since the moneylender had accepted part payment from a third person as a settlement of the debt, the matter had been resolved. This case would be often quoted in courts in matters of indebtedness.

But regarding the shares, curiously, both Keshavlal and Devika appear to have benefited from them. Not only would the shares have been seized otherwise by the court, they would have catapulted Kherajbhai into a very powerful position at HIT. But now Devika's position was strengthened on the HIT board, while Keshavlal Mody would eventually chair HIT, on the basis of his fourteen shares.

It is possible that Devika and Keshavlal had agreed to help Sir Richard by bailing him out in the insolvency case in exchange for the shares. At the same time, Devika had thought ahead and put Keshavlal in a stronger position so that he could be by her side at

HIT. She was also better off with thirteen shares of her own (including the one she already had) and the support of Keshavlal, with his fourteen shares.

∽∼∽

Now that both Devika and Keshavlal were on the HIT board, they could make the next move. She had been hearing reports that the rival camp was gathering its forces together. Rather than work under her, the group was planning to walk out en masse and had even found land for a studio in Goregaon. The studio would be called Filmistan. She had learnt that many of the key people at Bombay Talkies, including Sir Chimanlal and Rai Bahadur Chuni Lall, not just Sashadhar and Ashok, were planning to leave. But before they quit, she decided to turn the tables on them.

A meeting of the directors of HIT was arranged on 13 August 1942. This was Devika's revenge, as between Keshavlal Mody and her, they had 27, a clear majority, of the 46 shares of HIT. At the meeting, the following resolutions were passed:

1. The Company hereby cancels the appointment (made by the directors of this Company) of C. Setalvad as Ex-Officio Director of the Bombay Talkies Ltd, and hereby nominates and appoints Mr Keshavlal D. Mody to be the Ex-Officio Director of the Bombay Talkies in his place.
2. As regards the Distribution of the pictures of the Bombay Talkies Ltd, it is resolved that Directors shall not renew Contracts with Distributors henceforth but they shall distribute all pictures for exhibition through Managing Agency Office.

Devika was still seething from the humiliation she had suffered at the hands of Sir Chimanlal, even though she had always tried to maintain good terms with him. Now it became obvious that she would further publicly call for the cancellation of his appointment as ex-officio director in Bombay Talkies along with that of his acolyte V.C. Setalvad, ensuring that he would lose interest in staying on at

HIT. He was informed that he could not enter into a contract with any star, technician or any member of the staff.

While Keshavlal Mody took over the day-to-day business, a special resolution was proposed recognising Devika's contribution to the studio:

> Mrs Devika Rani on account of her international reputation and acknowledged merits as a producer and financial stake the company is hereby appointed the 'Controller of Production' and 'Sole Manager' of the Studio and the production department of the Bombay Talkies and all present arrangements existing at present on that behalf contrary to the above are hereby cancelled.

The directors further asked that these resolutions be communicated to the Bombay Talkies board and a copy placed in the studio of Bombay Talkies. Nothing could be clearer—the rival group were getting their marching orders.

All through this, Devika's way of dealing with the rivalry was to treat the men orchestrating it as a bit of a joke, and thus keep her spirits up. It should be remembered that she was only in her mid-thirties when these power games were going on. As she was to describe in a letter, her mind, too, often played games as a coping strategy, and she, child-like, would rebel at any form of repression. She chose a very amusing visualisation exercise to deal with Sir Chimanlal and others when they did not agree with her during a meeting. In a letter to Svetoslav on 17 June 1945 she wrote:

> I may be anywhere, it happens without control, because I like it and it just happens. For instance once at a board meeting when Sir Chimanlal and others were trying to harass me, I made up my mind not to listen so that I didn't lose my temper and believe it or not... I happily thought what would these people look like if they had each other's noses. I fixed the noses in my mind on each face and pictured them talking like that. It amused me so much that I forgot all. This kept me busy for 2 hours! When

they asked me what I was smiling at and I told them the truth they were so angry and horrified—specially old Chimanlal. Another thing is I am impatient. I like quick intelligence, quick understanding, slow people kill me. Of course I've trained myself but I am very impatient.

Sir Chimanlal would have been infuriated that she was having a laugh at his expense—he happened to have a particularly large and striking nose. Her forthrightness in speaking about the game she played in the boardroom may have been immature and disrespectful, but it also showed her self-confidence.

In a letter on 11 September, she wrote to Rai Bahadur Chuni Lall, who was still the general manager of the studio, telling him that she was going on a month's leave.

When you said the other day that I was not looking well I did not realise how tired I was till I reached Dr Pereira who again told me that it was most necessary that I had complete rest. I suppose that this is the outcome of the strenuous time we have [had] after the hard work of our picture *Basant*.

In her previous letter requesting leave, she had mentioned 'neuratheria' as a cause. Given what had happened to Himansu, she knew she needed a break. And she must have hoped that alluding to the 'strenuous time' post the making of *Basant* would make Rai Bahadur Chuni Lall a little more sympathetic. In any case, as the controller of production, the sole manager, and a director at HIT, she could now do what she wanted.

On 16 September 1942, an 'Extraordinary Meeting' of the shareholders of HIT was held at the registered office of the company to endorse the earlier resolutions of the board. It was attended by Keshavlal Mody, Devika and Rai Bahadur Chuni Lall.

By a resolution, V.C. Setalvad, who was sympathetic to Sir Chimanlal, was removed as an ex-officio director of Bombay Talkies. It was obvious that there was going to be a coup against the chairman. That's when Rai Bahadur Chuni Lall decided to take the matter to court, to prevent Sir Chimanlal from being replaced.

On 29 September 1942, at a meeting at the office of the chairman, at 113, Esplanade Road, Fort, Bombay, all these matters were discussed once again. Present at the meeting were Sir Chimanlal, Rai Bahadur Chuni Lall, Devika, Keshavlal and V.C. Setalvad. Everyone could see that Devika had the courage to walk into the lion's den and ask for the resignation of the chairman in his own office. However, even though the directors supporting the resolution were in the majority, the move to oust Sir Chimanlal was delayed and put under consideration.

Also on the agenda that day was a discussion about the top stars, Ashok Kumar, Mumtaz Shanti and Shah Nawaz, all artistes of the company, who had asked for leave of absence without salary for four, three and four months respectively. This was undoubtedly intended to disrupt work at the studio, but Devika did not back down. They were granted leave.

Devika had distanced herself from those who had supported Himansu but who, unfortunately, were not prepared to support her. She did what she had to legally, through the board—as she had learnt from Himansu. All the paperwork was complete and all the meetings were well documented so that no questions could be asked later.

Even as she fought them alone, supported mainly by Keshavlal Mody, it saddened her that the other directors did not give her any credit for her hard work, although the films she had worked on, such as *Basant*, were headed for a golden jubilee in Karachi and Bombay, and she was quite sure a diamond jubilee was in the offing. This record had been held by *Sant Tukaram* and now it was felt that *Basant* would surpass it. *Kismet* was also doing well (even if it had been produced by Sashadhar, it was still the studio's film) and the new productions were progressing well 'in spite of the inclement weather and great hardship in getting raw film', as the confidential note from the managing agents to the newly appointed board of Bombay Talkies said on 16 June 1943.

It had become obvious by December 1942 that there could be no reconciliation between the warring camps. It was also obvious that the company had hardly any funds left despite the 'able' management of the people in charge. In an earlier board meeting, it had been admitted that there were not enough reserves to pay the income tax of ₹30,066, and Rai Bahadur Chuni Lall had made some alternate arrangements for the payment. It is hard to understand how this could have happened while successful films like *Basant* and *Kismet* were being made.

Whatever the reason, Bombay Talkies was in turmoil. Sashadhar had decided he would not continue under Devika, who was now practically running the show. On 21 December 1942, another meeting of the board of directors was held at Setalvad's office at Fort, Bombay, where the five directors, including Devika, were present.

At the meeting, a proposal for the en masse resignation of many crucial members of Bombay Talkies, from the acting, scriptwriting and technical departments, was tabled and accepted. Among the names mentioned were Sashadhar Mukerji, Ashok Kumar, Gyan Mukerji, Savak Vacha, as well as V.H. Desai, D.N. Pai, Pyarelal S. Santoshi, R.C. Pradeep, Shahid Latif and Harbans Singh. Their last working day would be 1 February 1943.

On that day, Devika lost many of the people she and Himansu had trained and invested in for eight long years. Their key actors, directors, editors, writers, and so many others would now set up a rival company and compete with Bombay Talkies.

Rai Bahadur Chuni Lall also put in his papers. And it wasn't long before Sir Chimanlal left. But to Devika's credit, she took all this in her stride. For the first time, perhaps, people realised that under the diminutive, petite figure was a very strong fighting spirit, a 'Bengal tiger', as she often referred to herself.

Although she had to deal with directors on the board who were basically businessmen, Devika had among them, at last, a friend who would support her. Throughout the crisis, Keshavlal Mody was beside her, stepping forward when required, to help her take over the complete management of Bombay Talkies, and put her own candidates in important posts.

From this point onwards, Bombay Talkies would pass into the hands of Marwari businessmen. The era of Parsi and English domination was over. Creative domination also began to decline at HIT. Over the next few years, only Devika would provide the creative inputs, as all the experienced hands, such as Sashadhar and Chuni Lall, who used to interact with the board, had left the studio.

After the wholesale resignations, Devika quickly gathered her resources and began exploring the subject of her next film. She also began scouting for a general manager to replace Rai Bahadur Chuni Lall. For the time being, Keshavlal Mody took over that role, while she approached Sachin Choudhuri to see if he might be interested.

Before Sir Chimanlal Setalvad, V.C. Setalvad and Rai Bahadur Chuni Lall resigned, they had sought a buyer for their HIT shares. Zakaria Wally Mohamed had offered to buy 15 shares at ₹9,500 each and 4 shares at ₹7,000 each. The condition was that the purchase would entitle him to appoint two directors to the HIT board, and at least one ex-officio director at Bombay Talkies. The catch was that the share transfer had to be approved by both Keshavlal and Devika, so it was unlikely to go through.

This agreement was followed by another, at a board meeting of HIT on 11 January 1943, at the office of Sir Chimanlal H. Setalvad. At this point, Sir Chimanlal was paid ₹1,53,017 for 17 shares in the company and both Rai Bahadur Chuni Lall and V.C. Setalvad received ₹9,001 for one share each—which were bought by Ambalal C. Shah. Devika had found this investor with Keshavlal's help.

This was the last point of severance with the old board. Sir Chimanlal, V.C. Setalvad, as well as Rai Bahadur Chuni Lall, resigned from HIT and Bombay Talkies. A formal resolution by the board of directors placed 'its appreciation of the great services rendered' by the three, especially Sir Chimanlal, who 'was the founder of Bombay Talkies'.

As always, Devika had planned well, and used her formidable charm to keep all the difficult meetings and exchanges going smoothly, while also bringing on board rich traders and businessmen who were interested in cinema. Or, at least, keen to make money from it.

At last, the power struggle, the worst Bombay Talkies had seen since its inception, was coming to an end. The key players, especially the studio's leading star, Ashok Kumar, had quit and a hostile takeover had been prevented. But it was exhausting work, as she also had to oversee the productions, and almost every day, she had to undertake the long drive from Malad to Esplanade. No one knew the stress she was under as she fought to save the studio—and herself. The factionalism had taken its toll and at this point, the company was burdened by a debt of ₹1,33,000.

Apart from the public departure of Sir Chimanlal and Chuni Lall, it was formally announced on 11 January 1943 that Keshavlal D. Mody had taken over the general management of Bombay Talkies Ltd after Rai Bahadur Chuni Lall's resignation. The very next day, Devika again drove to the registered office of the company at Readymoney Mansion to attend the first board meeting in the absence of Sir Chimanlal, with the new members. It must have felt very pleasant to finally experience victory, almost two years after Himansu died. She had managed to wrest back control of the studio they had started together.

At the meeting, it was decided that Keshavlal would take over as the chairman for one year. Now that her two main enemies, Sir Chimanlal and Chuni Lall, were out of the way, she called another meeting on 17 February 1943 at the registered office of the company. The attendees were Keshavlal, Devika and Ambalal C. Shah. A surprise on the agenda was Sir Richard Temple.

For those who had guessed at the possible truth of how Devika had got her twelve shares, this may not have come as much of a surprise. A true friend, indeed! All that time she had spent with him had been worthwhile after all. With his unacknowledged help, she had managed to retain HIT, and hence Bombay Talkies.

Now she repaid the debt she owed him, with a tidy sum. The apparent reason to reward him was his help in negotiating the sale of the shares held by 'HEH The Nizam's Government'. The formal resolution passed by the HIT board also mentioned that Sir Richard Temple 'was to be paid a sum of ₹9,000 as an absolute gift for the purpose of enabling him to pilot his financial crisis which is pending'. This money, and whatever he had earlier received from Keshavlal for the fourteen shares, helped Sir Richard with his bankruptcy proceedings. Devika was careful to ensure that the company's legal advisor, Haridas Prabhudas Parekh, was present during the proceedings.

At a subsequent meeting on 13 May, Keshavlal was made the managing director, a post that had been held by Himansu. There was also a proposal to motivate the workers at the studio through cash incentives. By June, a decision was taken to give two months' salary to the staff, as a bonus. Bombay Talkies had been steadied, and with its films doing well, there was money in the coffers once more.

Then came the not-so-welcome news that work at Filmistan was progressing rapidly. Devika received an invitation from Rai Bahadur Chuni Lall, on behalf of the board of directors of Filmistan Limited, for a function on 29 of May 1943.

> Sir Chimanlal H Setalvad, KCIE, LL D,
> Chairman
> and the Board of Directors of
> Filmistan Limited
> requests the pleasure of
>
> Mrs Devika Rani Rai's company
>
> at the Inauguration Ceremony of the Studio
> at Ghodbunder Road, Goregaon, on Saturday, the
> 29th May at 6.30 pm
> Sir Homi Mody KBE has Kindly Consented to Preside.

Devika had just turned thirty-five in March, but unlike in earlier years, there were no bouquets or celebrations. Instead, the same people who used to fete and flatter her had now sent her this hurtful invitation!

Fortunately, all those years with Himansu, when they had nothing and had to rely on the kindness of strangers as well as their own wits to survive, had left her with few expectations from others. She only had to look around the sprawling Bombay Talkies to know that no matter who tried to destroy her, she would always find a solution. Ultimately, it was they who were forced to leave and she stayed on.

Wiping away her tears of anger, Devika pledged that she would show them she was still the queen of the silver screen. Using her trademark red pencil, she wrote out a reply for Swami, her secretary, to type and post on her behalf. There was not a word out of place and no one could fault her manners:

> Mrs Himansu Rai thanks Sir Chimanlal H Setalvad, KCIE, LL.D, and the Board of Directors of Filmistan Ltd for their kind invitation at the inauguration of their studio at Goregaon but regrets her inability to come due to work in Production. She wishes the directors every success in their new venture.

This also sent the message to those at Filmistan that, at Bombay Talkies, no matter who left, the work never stopped.

In this ongoing war, she would get sweet revenge very soon. Filmistan, launched with such fanfare, struggled right from its inception. The group led by Sashadhar and Ashok soon realised that it had only been the genius of Himansu and Devika, working day and night, which ensured the emergence of Bombay Talkies. It was an idea that would have died without their personal connections, hard work and goodwill.

The original team behind Filmistan lasted less than half a decade. A few, including Ashok Kumar, returned to Bombay Talkies (though Devika had left by then). The studio itself would continue to exist, changing hands in the late 1950s.

Meanwhile, in August 1943, a young businessman who would become a key player at Bombay Talkies and also a close friend of Devika, Seth Prahladrai Brijlal, was introduced to the directors of HIT with a request from Seth Govindram Gordhandas Seksaria (a textile magnate who held a substantial number of HIT shares, bought from Ambalal C. Shah) to take him on as his representative on the HIT board of directors. It was obvious to everyone now that to have real control over Bombay Talkies, it was essential to possess shares in HIT. Prahladrai was formally appointed on 15 October 1943, on the resignation of Ambalal C. Shah as a director.

One of the conditions of appointment to the board of HIT was that any new director should be known to the other directors, which Prahladrai was. Perhaps thinking that at last they had like-minded people on the board, Devika proposed that they limit the number of directors to three. This was accepted by Prahladrai as well as Keshavlal. And so it was settled that the three directors on the HIT board, the managing agents of Bombay Talkies, would be Devika, Prahladrai and Keshavlal.

Neither of the two men was a particularly sophisticated intellectual or film- maker. But Devika's only goal now was to keep the studio going, and these two men had the two most important things she was looking for—money and connections to people who had money.

Notably, Devika was the only actress in the industry who was the production controller, sole manager and a director of the company. She sometimes also presided as the chair of the board of directors at Bombay Talkies. It was unprecedented, and possibly unlikely to happen again, in cinema or elsewhere.

Moreover, she was a brilliant actress.

Word had already got around about the new film she had decided to make. *Hamari Baat* was directed by M.I. Dharamsey, who had earlier been a sound recordist, and the story was written by Amiya. The roster of actors included P. Jairaj, David and Suraiya. Even though there were attempts to run it down, the film did well.

Was the title *Hamari Baat* a tongue-in-cheek reference to real-life events? In one scene, in a fit of jealousy, the hero strikes Devika so hard that she becomes unconscious and is hospitalised. Was this quietly indicative of the violence she had endured in the years with Himansu?

Compliments came from friends like Betty Hutheesingh, Jawaharlal Nehru's sister, who said, 'Your picture was grand and you look lovelier than ever.' Touchingly, she was keen to invite Devika over, even though her husband was out on parole and very unwell. He had been jailed with Nehru and other Congress leaders for opposing the use of Indian troops in the British war effort.

Betty wrote in her letter to Devika on 25 October 1943 that her sons were very enamoured of her, even more so when she told them that Devika was an old friend of their father, Raja Hutheesingh. 'With sparkling eyes they asked me if you were his girlfriend in those days!' She added that Raja had sent his love to Devika the last time Betty had met him in the central prison, Poona. She explained:

> Raja was arrested along with my brother [Jawaharlal Nehru] on 7 August 1942. For over a month I had no news of him—then letters were allowed, but sight denied. Last month I saw Raja after 13 long and lonesome months. It has been a terrible year of heartache and suffering.

Strangely, Devika did not even remember Betty's surname and had to be reminded of it by Swami.

The challenges at the studio remained, but Devika was learning to deal with them. She wanted to ensure she knew everything about every part of the business and that there was a clear path to profitability. If this was a competition, she wanted to win, to show the world that she was a true professional. But somehow, no matter how much effort she put in, the challenges remained—not just for her, but for other production houses as well. The war had resulted in many restrictions on raw stock and other materials, and even cinema houses were cutting down on screenings.

When distributors from Jagat Talkies reached Lahore for the release of *Hamari Baat*, they found that the cinemas had been closed since 7 December due to a shortage of coal. The cinemas would open from 14 December, but screen only one show daily. However, the distributors (who also represented New Theatres Ltd and Shree Ranjit Movietone Co.) said that they hoped to tie up to screen two shows 'daily next week, only then we shall release *Hamari Baat* at Lahore most probably from 24 December. The picture has already been released on Idd at Rawalpindi, Sialkot and Lyallpur with success.' There were also plans for a Delhi release, and Devika and Amiya were expected to be present. But for the shortage of coal and other such problems, the enthusiastic distributors were convinced that the film would have 'created history'.

With such a positive response from her fans and distributors, Devika was upset at the persistent rumours and chatter in the industry that her films were not doing well. She suspected that her rivals at Filmistan were determined not to allow Bombay Talkies to succeed.

In any case, she now saw herself more and more in the role of a studio head. She was no longer interested in acting herself, and desperately needed people to replace the stars who had left, especially Ashok Kumar. The net was spread wide. She asked the board to extend the contractual agreements with Amiya, as well as Anil Biswas, the talented music composer. She also requested help from exhibitors to meet new artistes in Lahore and other cities. She even had Anil Biswas advertise for artistes.

One of the aspirants Biswas met in Lahore was Munawar Sultana. A beautiful woman and an aspiring actress, she presented two of her photographs to him, to 'send to Mrs Rai … regarding pay though she was asking for 2000/- per month'. But it was hoped that she would settle for ₹1,600 or 1,700.

Though Munawar did not end up working with Devika, she did become one of the busiest actresses of the 1940s and 1950s, moving from Lahore to Bombay on a salary of ₹4,000 per month. She was persuaded by the charismatic actor-turned-director Mazhar Khan, in 1945, to act in *Pehli Nazar*. In 1948, she acted in a Bombay Talkies film, *Majboor*, but this was after Devika had left and Ashok Kumar had taken over.

Meanwhile, *Hamari Baat* got good reviews and kept Bombay Talkies in good cheer for most of 1943. Soon, work would begin on its twenty-fifth feature film, an instructional film made for the government.

Then came the big disappointment. Keshavlal Mody told Devika that he would like to move on. Though he had been a pillar of strength for her and she was loath to see him go, she honoured his wish and his resignation was accepted on 8 January 1944.

This meant she had to find replacements for his multiple roles, most urgently. Prahladrai could take over as the chairman of HIT, but she needed a manager for the studio. Realising that she also needed some creative energy, not just money-making skills, she turned to the two Choudhuri brothers, Sachin and Hiten, whom she had always admired. To her great relief, Sachin succumbed to her persuasion. Without wasting any time, on 12 February 1944, he was appointed as the manager of Bombay Talkies.

Devika was also able to get a third director to fill the vacancy caused by the departure of Keshavlal. Seth Maneklal Chunilal Shah, another textile magnate, was invited to join the board of HIT in mid-March. Keshavlal sold him all fourteen of his shares. Thus she managed to provide a steadying hand, by getting quick replacements when anyone quit and the studio remained under her control.

Things were on an even keel—under the circumstances. Given that the studio's films had been profitable, it was resolved that the workers would once again get an equivalent of two months' pay as bonus. This was an extravagant move, but Devika wanted to ward off any poachers who were thinking of intruding into her territory. The high salaries would begin to impact the cost of production very soon, but as of now, whatever Devika asked for, she got.

Both Prahladrai and Seth Maneklal Chunilal Shah were clearly overawed by Devika. Neither of them had met a glamorous and determined woman like her before. Besides, if she ever felt that either of them was having a problem, particularly Prahladrai, she would spend hours with him, sorting it out. This could even be an issue unrelated to Bombay Talkies—perhaps about his boss Seksaria, or the stock market, or something personal. Over time, Prahladrai became a devoted fan, even perhaps a little in love with her.

But for Devika, it was her relationship with Amiya that provided the psychological support she needed at this time. He respected her unquestioningly, and their mutual affection was now becoming apparent to all. At the same time, he began to be recognised in his own right as a very competent screenplay writer, director and producer.

But could the relationship work? People's eyebrows rose because Amiya had once worked in the canteen and it was Devika who had groomed him into a scriptwriter. Amiya was actually not an uneducated man, and it was said that he had spent a few years in underground activities against the British before he came to Bombay Talkies.

It was certainly true that Devika surrounded herself with young and very devoted men, which was precisely what Himansu had also done. Only, in her case, it would be misinterpreted and given sexual overtones. While she may have had a deep and very romantic relationship with Amiya, there was a very good reason why she would have hesitated before allowing him into her bed. She was very worried about his tuberculosis, as he had been unwell for some time.

Having spent a few years looking after Himansu, she was understandably reluctant to get involved in another relationship with foreseeably tragic consequences. The only way was to find a cure for Amiya. She began personally supervising his treatment, trying to ensure, as discreetly as possible, that he got the best possible advice. She began sending him for check-ups without anyone finding out the reason for his absences. After all, she was the boss.

She arranged for his treatment at the Bel Air Sanatorium, which sprawled over 44 acres in Dalkeith, Panchgani. This meant that both of them visited Panchgani very often, and in 1943, she thought of buying a cottage there. Her trips were frequent enough for her to have made friends in Panchgani, and for once, she felt like any other woman, not a film star. Mrs Parsons, who had a cottage there, and with whom she and Amiya sometimes stayed, had children who had never seen an Indian film. They would play pranks on Amiya, bringing some fun and laughter into her life. She was blossoming and coming into her own after Himansu's death, and the settlement at Bombay Talkies had left her free to make her own decisions. It was not a perfect life, but she felt she was getting there. Perhaps she was even making plans for the future—Mrs Parsons, it appears, began knitting a 'baby coat' for her.

On 19 November 1943, Devika wrote to Dr da Cunha, who had been looking after Amiya at Bel Air.

> I wish to thank you and Mrs Da'Cunha for your kindness to me during my stay in Panchgani. On the way back to Bombay my car failed in the ghats but eventually a military lorry took my driver back to Panchgani and I got another car.
>
> I also want to mention that we had to recall Mr Chakrabarty urgently and I could not write to you in time. It was in connection with a propaganda film we have to make for the Government of India, the subject of which had to be settled almost immediately. His being away in Panchgani did not enable him to have the peace of mind regarding the story as we could not consult the Government people from there....
>
> I hope you will not forget my request for a house which I can buy in Panchgani. I had seen the empty house nearest to the Prospect hotel going from Mrs Parson's bungalow, the name is a mohamedan one which I have forgotten. It seems to have a very good position. I think you had told me about that house. When looking for one kindly do not mention I am interested in it as the price is sure to go up. In having a place far away I should not like to spend too much money for it. Hoping you are well. Kindly give my regards to Mrs Da'Cunha.

The house would be useful because of their frequent trips to the sanatorium. Devika found that these drives and holidays created a pleasant escape for both of them, and Amiya felt much better in the hills. However, she was still not sure where this relationship would take her.

She had already arranged for Amiya to be examined at the Madras Anti Tuberculosis Clinic and Anti-Diabetic Clinic, and Dr V.C. Gupta wrote to her from there, at the beginning of 1943:

> I am glad to hear that you found Mr Chakrabarty in good health and spirits. I hope he is following our usual sanatorium regime such as rest, good food, fresh air and so on. I am glad to note that you are personally going to see that he does not do any exertion etc. I hope that he will be alright in your kind hands. The important thing is (1) weight, he should not lose weight (2) temperature, if there is any rise, he should be kept in bed (3) if he feels tired he should rest at once.
>
> I know that he is a very nice patient. He never complained or grumbled.... So when he comes in summer for a change, then he will thrill all of us, as he thrilled all of you.

Thrilled or not, it was obvious that Devika was taking a keen interest in Amiya's welfare. She continued to correspond with the doctors, who hoped that he had become, in her care, 'very fat, hale and quite hearty'. She told them he was 'quite well with all [the] food'. She, too, was putting on weight—for the first time in seventeen years, she did not worry about it. It was a time for making some very tentative personal plans, based on the hope that Amiya would recover.

Simultaneously, she had to ensure that the films were being churned out as per schedule, at least two if not three each year, as in the past. She now had a greater responsibility, as she was in charge of all the productions. Amiya was a key factor in her success. He was steady, reliable, talented and loyal—but even in his absence, production had to carry on. It was also necessary to pay for all the expenses. Fortunately, Sachin was with her from 1944 onwards, and Hiten had also been helping her out after Himansu's death. At least she had these two very intelligent and capable men by her side in Amiya's absence.

The propaganda film which she and Amiya would produce next was called *Char Ankhen*. It was about the contribution of nurses to the war. This was not exactly what either Devika or Amiya wanted to do, but it was a requirement of the British government. Possibly due to Amiya's fragile state of health, Sushil Majumdar directed the film. It starred Leela Chitnis and P. Jairaj, while the music was by Anil Biswas. Needless to say, it did not exactly set the cash registers ringing.

But this was the happiest Devika had been in a long time. While she missed Himansu, she had successfully emerged from his shadow. She had won against her enemies, and she had a man in her life who was gentler than anyone she had ever known. It was like a balm to her soul.

Then why did she continue to feel as though something was still missing in her life?

Letter from Devika to Svetoslav

Sometimes I have a thrilling day, spend a few hours in front of the mirror, and try all sorts of hair styles, make-up. I use pale shades and vermillion lipstick, darken my eyes, and then pale shades and pale lipstick, lighten my eyes, and [use a] deeper shade, darken my eyes and dark lipstick and enjoy it very much. In a month I've regularly done this at least 3 times. It gives me a thrill & keeps me happy. Silly I know, but I can't live without it—it makes me feel good you follow what I mean. Not that it makes me look any better—it never has done, only mentally playing with nice things and colour. I enjoy it and feel happy. So your little wife is a handful, really. You don't know the impossible person she is, such things interest her, and actually give her a thrill—make-up is of great interest to me always. I feel undressed if I don't use lipstick—can't do without it! I've told you all this because you should be warned of my mad ways. This is only one of them and do what you will, I can't help it—if you even lock up everything you'll find it will break out somehow. Bunny wife of yours is really a big handful for you—the real trouble is she's got so many sides of her nature, she herself doesn't know them. Of course if you really don't like it she won't do it, but she will want to, it's in her blood, this cosmetic business.

Bombay, 1945

15

DAZZLING DEVIKA! 1944–45

Devika was now the acknowledged boss of Bombay Talkies. The years of suffering and abuse were behind her. At last she was being valued for her own hard work as the head of the studio—not because she was Himansu's wife. Along with her acting skills, her management skills also came to the fore.

When questions were raised by shareholders of Bombay Talkies as to why the resignations of so many of their leading artistes (including Ashok Kumar) and technicians had been promptly accepted by HIT, a carefully drafted note was submitted on 27 January 1943 addressed to the chairman of Bombay Talkies, by HIT, the managing agents.

The letter pointed that there had been certain disputes between the previous directors of Bombay Talkies, who were also on the Board of HIT—Sir Chimanlal H. Setalvad, V.C. Setalvad and Rai Bahadur Chuni Lall—and the present directors—Devika Rani Rai and Keshavlal D. Mody. But these 'disputes were happily ended and an agreement was arrived at on 21st December, 1942, whereby the said members went out'. The letter added that on the advice of Sir Chimanlal it was determined that HIT was 'competent' to accept the resignations of the artistes and others, according to the agreement between Bombay Talkies and HIT:

The said agreement inter alia contains that they shall have the sole and complete [authority for the] general conduct, management and execution of the business affairs and undertakings of the Company and to make all such arrangements and do all such acts and things on behalf of the Company as may be necessary or expedient for the general management and conduct of the business of the company.

To emphasise the matter further, the managing agents began to submit reports of how smoothly the studio was now functioning.

For instance, the report on 13 May 1943 from HIT was very upbeat. In this Devika conveyed her sincere thanks to the board of directors for their 'kindly fixing' an entertainment allowance for her. The workers thanked the board for the bonus they had received, and for the increase in their war allowance. The report added:

> The Board will also be glad to learn that the shooting work of the new picture is going on in full swing. An impressive cast has been assembled for the picture [Hamari Baat] headed by Mrs Devika Rani, Mr P. Jairaj, Miss Suraiya, Mr Shah Nawaz and others. In this connection, we are glad to inform the Board that we have secured the services of Mr Jairaj and Miss Suraiya on yearly contract basis. Jairaj is already a well known figure in the Indian film world, while Suraiya is a young budding artiste gifted with remarkable histrionic talents who if properly groomed, is sure to become a front ranker. For writing lyrics we have secured the services of Mr Nagendra Sharma, one of the best known Hindi poets of today.

The previous lyricist C.S. Casshyap had already resigned.

The good news for Devika was that from 1943 onwards her salary and bonuses were regularly increased. On 29 December 1943 she received a New Year gift of a bonus of ₹20,000, from the board of directors of Bombay Talkies, 'as a token of the Company's appreciation of the meritorious services rendered by you to the Company'. After years of struggling to make herself financially independent, Devika at last felt her true worth was being recognised.

On 29 December 1943, the ever-obliging Keshavlal increased her salary from ₹1,600 to ₹2,750 per month with an entertainment allowance of ₹300 per month.

With a new confidence, she started reaching out to the media and to other people, this time in her own right. She wanted to establish the fact that the films she produced were doing well. For, whether it was true or not, she continued to hear that Filmistan, the rival studio, had a huge propaganda machine working against her. They were both competing for the same space in the popular imagination.

Over the years, this harangue against her had remained high-pitched and shrill—she was a demon, an adulteress, a flirt, a man-eater. And now, an over-the-hill actress and a terrible producer. Ironically, many of those who had betrayed her were still reaching out to her for work. In some cases, their children were, too. To most of them, she remained inaccessible. Yet, a few, like Madan Mohan, Rai Bahadur Chuni Lall's son, kept writing letters, hoping for a response.

Madan, who would go on to become one of the leading music composers in Hindi cinema, was looking for a break with 'Aunty' Devika Rani. He and his siblings, Shanti and Prakash, had grown up at Bombay Talkies, when their father had been the general manager. But Devika was not prepared to encourage or give a chance to those who she felt could be disloyal. What if they were trying to gain entry in order to destroy Bombay Talkies? How could she forget that Rai Bahadur Chuni Lall had abandoned Bombay Talkies and joined the rival studio, Filmistan? It was very odd that his son should write to her and not to his father. She did not know that the Rai Bahadur had severely discouraged his children from joining any part of the film industry.

Madan persisted. He wrote from Bangalore on 10 May 1944, where he was a young recruit in the army. He was hurt that she had not replied to his previous letters and wondered what the reason could be. He clearly imagined she would feel kindly towards him, regardless of what his father may have done. He noted that *Chaar Ankhen* was being released at Imperial and wondered about her future plans, and whether she was hiring some 'fresh people'.

> No answer at the moment
> DKR
>
> No. 3229, C.C.63, Pre-O.T.
> O.T.S., BANGALORE
> 10th May 44.
>
> My Dear Aunty,
>
> I wrote you a letter from here, but have not yet been favoured with a reply. I don't know what the reason can be. May be you have not recieved my letter, as I do not expect delay from you. I was down with fever for about a week, and am allright now. How are you keeping? I read the advertisment of "CHAR ANKHEN" in the papers & note that you are releasing it at Imperial this week. I wish it a great Success. What is your future programme? I heard that you have engaged some fresh people. Are you making the next picture with them? Please reply soon, & tell me, if I can be of any service to you. More when I hear from you
>
> With my very best wishes,
> Yours Affectionately,
> Madan.

Devika wrote 'No answer at the moment' in her red pencil on each of these letters, even when Madan asked in desperation if she hated him or had any reason to detest him. 'Write to me so that I know what you feel about me,' he begged over and over again, refusing to give up.

When he joined All India Radio (AIR) in Lucknow after quitting the army, he wrote to her again:

> My Dear Aunty,
> I don't know the reason but you did not reply my letters which I wrote to you quite a time back and I am sure you received them. I can't guess the reason, won't you tell me? It is my affection that makes me write to you again. I wish you knew how much affection I have for you. I wish I did not have to say it. Why didn't you write to me? Shanti and Prakash are at Bombay. Have they met you?
> Probably you would like to know what I am doing these days. I am the feature and Musical features incharge here. I am doing very good work and [this] is a good preparation for the Film industry. I have become quite a musician and a singer. I compose a lot of music and believe me it is music.

Madan, who later composed some iconic tunes, many of them sung by Lata Mangeshkar, was mostly self-taught, and very confident. While at Lucknow AIR, he became well known for his compositions. He knew, and had worked with many of the established classical musicians and singers of the time, such as Ustad Akbar Ali Khan and Begum Akhtar.

This was in the early 1940s, and he was only in his mid-twenties. His family had interacted frequently with Devika when they were at Bombay Talkies and from the tone of his letter, it was clear that they had shared an informal relationship with her. And why not? Rai Bahadur Chuni Lall was one of the first people to join Bombay Talkies, and was the general manager for about a decade before he left with Sashadhar.

Devika was in no mood to relent, but realising that Madan was not giving up and might even turn up one day, looking for a break as a music composer, she finally wrote back, thanking him for his sweet letters:

> No, I am in no way angry with you. I have not written because I was very busy. It is most wonderful my dear to know you are doing good work. Yes work hard, don't care for anything but honest, sincere, hard good work and you will be rewarded. God sees to the rewards.
>
> Your aunty,
> Devika Rai

She was only twelve years older than him, but the chasm between them was enormous. Her letter did not contain an invitation to come and work at Bombay Talkies, which was what Madan was angling for. Indeed, with Anil Biswas creating some memorable melodies, she did not really require another music composer.

But to journalists, whom she had ignored all these years, she now opened her doors. She began to hold press conferences and private meetings. After such a long silence, the press was surprised and pleased—even the powerful Baburao Patel of *Filmindia*. She wrote to invite him to visit Bombay Talkies and he sent a very cordial reply. This was indeed a coup, as Baburao could make or break careers and had an acid pen.

In his warm response to her, he confessed he was a fan and that his daughter kept a photograph of Devika on her desk, which he would glance at affectionately every morning. He too had heard about the recently ended war within Bombay Talkies and minced no words while referring to her former employees and colleagues. His letter brought great comfort to her, especially as she was still troubled by the ceaseless gossip and innuendo.

Baburao said that he respected her natural charm and intellect, and that he still remembered the hypocritical scenes several years back at Himansu's funeral:

> [I saw] several professional weepers at Mr Rai's funeral and many of them gave an almost realistic performance. With my

tired eyes which have travelled round the world seeing numerous things and, holding them in mind, even then I saw through the rivers of tears for what they were worth.

Some had tears of joy, some had those of opportunity while others had those of escape. It is strange how one man's death affects so many people and so differently....

I felt an overwhelming sadness clutching at my heart at the loss of a great artist who put his ideals on a high pedestal and died worshipping them.

I couldn't even approach you to console you as mere words could not have conveyed any consolation to you under those circumstances. Yours was the loss and yours was the supreme grief.

Many of those professional weepers have now gone away taking with them their unholy load of hypocrisy and insincerity. You are thankfully rid of them and you are now alone.

He encouraged her, saying:

I am sure you are not the one to be daunted. Mr Rai had given you a splendid schooling to face the music of life, your own traditions lend to you the moral courage to go through it. You have many silent friends who do not bother about giving you mere lip service.

Baburao had often maintained that Devika was the best part of any Bombay Talkies film, and that he missed her presence when she was replaced by other actresses. Now he asked her to be wary and not trust anyone till they provided a test on the 'touchstone of sincerity'.

Meanwhile, Devika had to deal with some other ghosts from the past. She had a visit from Harkishan Rai Bhalla, the owner of the Lahore-based Sitara Films Limited. He wrote to her afterwards, on 24 July 1943:

One thing that particularly struck me and made an indelible impression on my mind was the way in which you treasure

THE MOTION PICTURE MAGAZINE FOR MODERN PEOPLE
~~104, APOLLO STREET, FORT~~   55 Sir Pherozeshah Mehta Road,
BOMBAY   Fort.

21st April '43

<u>Personal</u>

My dear Mrs. Rai,

 Your sweet letter came like a bolt from the blue as I have never before had the pleasure of receiving a letter from you.

 I welcome the psychological transformation in you and I already trace in it an unmistakeable evidence of greater success and glory for you in the future.

 You have kept yourself away from all of us too long, and the loss has been ours. Your present gesture therefore rekindles in me old feelings of respect for your natural charm and intellect.

 I still remember several professional weepers at Mr. Rai's funeral and many of them gave an almost realistic performance. With my tired eyes which have travelled round the world seeing numerous things and, holding them in mind, even then I saw through the rivers of tears for what they were worth.

 Some had tears of joy, some had those of opportunity while others had those of escape. It is strange how one man's death affects so many people and so differently.

 I had no tears as I have always considered them to be an exclusive privilege of women, but I felt an overwhelming sadness clutching at my heart at the loss of a great artist who put his ideals on a high pedestal and died worshipping them.

 I couldn't even approach you to console you as mere words could not have conveyed any consolation to you under those circumstances. Yours was the loss and yours the supreme grief. To attempt to console you would have been an effort to insult you.

 Many of those professional weepers have now gone away taking with them their unholy load of hypocrisy and insincerity. You are thankfully rid of them and you are now alone.

 I am sure that you are not the one to be daunted. Mr. Rai had given you a splendid schooling to face the music of life, your own traditions lend to you the moral courage to go through it. You have many silent friends who do not bother about giving you mere lip-service. Their prayers will always make your progress less difficult. To recognise such persons you must develop a vision of your own, till then I would advise you to go warily and not trust every one till th person provides a test on the touch-stone of sincerity.

I couldn't come the other day for two reasons: I was ill and had an inconvenient stomach pain which took the colour away from my face too often; secondly, I fight shy of a crowd, particularly of my so-called brother journalists with whom I have nothing in common.

I am always at your service whenever you want me so long as you do not summon me to Malad. The reason is petrol shortage. I hate to walk and I have no patience for trains. These slow-moving conveyances create an inferiority-complex in me, more so when I am keeping our most charming lady of the screen waiting for me at the end of my destination.

And yet I may risk meeting you once more if you promise to be natural and not polite and graceful like a queen. That will give me another pain in the stomach from which I'll take a longer time to recover.

'Filmindia' will always back up Devika through thick and thin. But don't make the thin end very thin by giving us another 'Kismet' glorifying a criminal.

Money-making is no doubt an essential purpose of motion picture production, but greater minds like yours should also use the opportunity for some greater purpose such as awakening the social conscience of our people and by helping to correct the maladjustments of our current social values.

What more beyond assuring you that as a lay film-goer I am your devoted fan and whether you appear on the screen or not I shall always pay my silent homage to you, atleast, by an affectionate glance every morning at your autographed photo which graces my little daughter's desk in our home.

Wishing you all luck and glory,

Yours sincerely,

(Baburao Patel)

To
Mrs. Devika Rai,
Bombay Talkies Ltd.,
M a l a d.

pkk.

the hallowed memory of your late lamented husband. When I entered your Office and saw the table and the chair which were once occupied by the late Mr Himansu Rai and behind which was placed his photograph duly garlanded and his two pairs of sandals lying in front of the photograph, this sight touched the tender chords of my heart and I felt how symbolic all this was of the high character and refined culture of a good Hindu Lady. Though Mr Himansu Rai was no more there in his physical form, yet I felt his presence everywhere in the studio.

This, of course, was part of Devika's plan to publicly claim the legacy of Himansu. Years later, after Devika had sold her shares in Bombay Talkies, Ashok Kumar found a large marble bust of Himansu Rai lying on the floor of the studio, dusty and covered with bird droppings. He would clean it up and take it home. Obviously, once Devika left, these niceties had also stopped.

Harkishan, who claimed to be a close friend of Rabindranath Tagore, told Devika that the poet had visited him in Lahore:

Your uncle, Gurudeva of revered memory when leaving us after a fortnight's stay…touchingly remarked that he then had two homes, one in Bengal and the other in Lahore.

Devika must have made an unforgettable impression on Harkishan at their meeting, though as a distributor, exhibitor and producer, he had been corresponding with her for a while. He invited her to her 'home' in Lahore and added:

The fame of your charming and graceful manners and genial temperaments has already spread in the four corners of the country and on actually meeting you I found you even better than what I had heard about you.

Keshavlal Mody, who was at the time the chairman of the HIT board, had taken Harkishan around. Recollecting the visit, Harkishan said:

[Keshavlal told me that Devika] personally looked to each and every detail and that the main working hand in all the productions of Bombay Talkies was yours. No wonder, therefore, that the Bombay Talkies enjoys an enviable position in the world of pictures.

Devika replied to him on 4 August 1943:

I am so glad you met Mr Mody. He was indeed very happy to meet you and told me such nice things about you. It is a matter of great relief that I have with me a man of his business capacity and understanding who not only will carry on the traditions of a great company like ours but to go forward improving the business at every step.

Her only regret, she said, was that her husband was no longer alive:

I am sure if you had met him you would have gone away far happier as perhaps his presence would have given you an insight as to how and by whom this organisation has been built. We are just his orphans trying to carry on in a very materialistic world. We keep his table intact and shoes because it reminds us of all he stood for.

Despite Devika's apparent fondness for her team at Bombay Talkies, she was quick to turn down invitations which reminded her too much of those who had left her and gone away to form Filmistan. When the managers of Chitramandir, a theatre in Nasik, wrote to her on 10 August 1943, inviting her for the proposed silver jubilee celebration of *Kismet* later in the month, she politely declined their very flowery invitation which requested her 'graceful attendance'. Though it was a record-breaking film from Bombay Talkies, it reminded her of the dreadful split that came immediately afterwards. Ever polite, on 16 August 1943, she wrote back to say that as she was just completing *Hamari Baat*, she could not find the time.

Unfortunately, she also had to skip the silver jubilee of another film, even though it was closer to her heart. The management of Krishna Cinema, Ahmedabad, had written to her to say that they wanted to plan a celebration on 17 July 1943, as *Basant* 'had smashed all previous records... both in collection and in the length of the run'.

Incidentally, this was the film in which the actress who would charm the world and be known as 'Madhubala' made her debut as Baby Mumtaz. People actually came back to see the film again and again because of her. The actress Nimmi who was also a little girl at the time remembered that Baby Mumtaz sang a song at the end of the film, '*Mere chotey se man mein*'. When the song finished, Baby Mumtaz told her audience—come again tomorrow and 'I will sing for you once more'. According to the book, *I Want to Live: The Story of Madhubala* by Khatija Akbar, it lured naive viewers back. Nimmi, went to see the film many times, 'protesting each time "but she has asked us to come again"'.

Devika was quick to write back to the organisers of the silver jubilee at Krishna Cinema:

> Your kind wishes and sincere felicitations came as a pleasant surprise. I have given your messages to everyone concerned with the production including Mr Amiya Chakrabarty, whose screenplay and direction made *Basant* what it is.

But her problem remained that she was working 'full speed' on her new film and had to be on the sets. She was not only acting in the film, she was also taking her role as the controller of production very seriously, and personally replying to every request and letter.

Old enemies were reaching out to her as well, including Niranjan. He wrote (unaware that the 'two Mukherjees', Gyan and Sashadhar Mukerji, had left):

> When you are being inundated with congratulations on the unique record of a double jubilee celebrations, as one who has

always cherished a fond affection for Bombay Talkies may I not offer my congratulations also?

I have always believed in giving youth a chance and you deserve the gratitude of the Indian Film Industry for bringing into the forefront a group of brilliant young men since you undertook to shoulder the responsibility of a producer. The two Mukherjees... Acharya and Amiya Chakrabarty... what a record for any producer! I sincerely pray that your latest selection Dharmsey, too, will fully justify your choice.

He suggested:

Side by side with the production of entertainment pictures you may see your way to give a lead to the industry by taking up the production of shorts and documentary films which is now a commercial proposition.

Every exhibitor had to compulsorily include 2,000 feet of shorts during any film screening, and so Niranjan was referring to a good opportunity for business. But Devika chose not to reply. When he wrote later, to suggest that some of his stories could be made into films, she politely turned them down. She had not forgotten how shabbily he had treated her when she had returned from Calcutta. She had been disturbed and unhappy, and had expected some sympathy from him. After all, he had known her longer than anyone else at Bombay Talkies. She also knew that he had overlooked all of Himansu's past dalliances and continued to work with him. But in her case, one indiscretion had been enough for him to decide that he wanted her out of Bombay Talkies. What really hurt was that he did not even try to find out why she had felt the need to take such a drastic step. No, she could not help him now.

But she did not want any more acrimony around her. The years immediately before and after Himansu's death had been difficult enough. She wanted to celebrate her own success and that of her films, rather than wallowing in past misery. She would rather rejoice in sentiments such as those expressed by a friend, J. Lall, from HMV, who wrote to her in July 1943 about 'divine' justice:

> So it is the 50th week for 'Basant'!
>
> My heartiest congratulations. It is a case of hopes (and may I add) and wishes come true. I often think there was divine backing to it.
>
> We should celebrate it. Can't you please come for lunch? If you tell me which day will suit you? I will phone Chakrabarty and Mr Mody too.
>
> The next picture will have to run for hundred weeks—so you better make sure that it does do that.

It would have given her even greater satisfaction that the first film launched by Filmistan was a failure. *Chal Chal re Naujawan* was directed by Gyan Mukerji and starred Ashok Kumar and Naseem, and it sank without a trace.

The studio that was meant to give stiff competition to Bombay Talkies did have some spectacular hits, though it would soon lose the star that had brought it into the limelight. Ashok Kumar quit after a falling out with Rai Bahadur Chuni Lall over a few scenes he wanted to improve and reshoot in *Eight Days*, a film written by Saadat Hasan Manto. The film had been practically directed by Ashok Kumar, though he placed Dattaram Pai's name in the credits.

When he found that the Rai Bahadur was reluctant to change the scenes because of the added expense, an enraged Ashok walked out. He was no longer the mild, malleable young man who had been picked to play opposite Devika. He was now a top star, earning in lakhs.

After starting Filmistan, he had soon discovered that while it had been easy to criticise Devika, making films and running a studio were far more difficult than he had imagined. To add to Filmistan's woes, a few years later, Gyan Mukerji, who had once given Amiya Chakrabarty competition, would suffer a nervous breakdown. His wife had left him, and the depression he fell into made it difficult for him to carry on working. He became increasingly incoherent, and finally, to help him out, Ashok began to try to interpret his instructions to the actors. Eventually, Gyan left for Calcutta and died there, a broken man. The film he had been working on, *Sitaron se Aagey*, was completed by Satyen Bose.

The stress and strain of filmmaking would take many minds and lives. Himansu was only the first, very public figure whose professional and personal life were clearly destroyed by the circumstances in which the early filmmakers had to survive. And there were many before him, whose names had vanished already from public memory. For those who were sensitive or unable to handle its vicissitudes, the film industry would become a circus where thousands of dreams swung on a trapeze between high hope and relentless heartbreak. There would be many who followed Himansu on the road to that particular hell—among them, a young and very talented Guru Dutt. But not before he, ironically, made *Kaagaz ke Phool*, a film on the rise and fall of Gyan Mukerji.

―⁂―

It was not all smooth sailing for Devika, too. She kept getting anonymous letters and information that her rivals were still working against her. Well-wishers at theatres spotted attempts to sabotage the screening of *Hamari Baat*, even though the audiences were appreciative and greeted the film with 'wild applause'.

One letter from a Miss Sophia (obviously a pseudonym) spoke about the mystery behind shifting *Hamari Baat* from Imperial cinema to Majestic cinema in Bombay. The undated letter addressed to various media houses said:

> As a matter of fact, this was a very very clever and wise move of Mrs Devika Rani Rai, the owner of Bombay Talkies, as I had the following unfortunate experience at the Imperial Cinema on more than two or three occasions. Myself and some friends of mine tried to purchase tickets for the higher class, but we were refused as every time the house was 'said to be full'.

When they went into the theatre, she said, they found two-thirds of the theatre vacant. This made her think it was a 'dirty trick' by someone not on good terms with Bombay Talkies, who wished to show that the film was a failure. Miss Sophia suspected it could be the handiwork of some wealthy man who was buying up all the tickets. She said that this production of Bombay Talkies was a jewel, and that the miscreant 'need not waste his time and money in hampering the success of one of the Indian producers'.

Miss Sophia asked plaintively whether no organisation or association of exhibitors existed which could investigate the way in which these 'criminals' were trying to skew the opinion of the viewing public in a particular direction.

Devika took these anonymous letters seriously enough to send them to the press, to see if they knew anything. As more letters arrived, Amiya and Sachin too may have begun to suspect a conspiracy to drag them down. Or, as one of the letters suggested, was someone trying to widen the rift between Bombay Talkies and Filmistan to prevent those who had quit from rejoining Bombay Talkies, given that Filmistan was not doing as well as it should have?

It turned out that, despite so many of the Bombay Talkies stars having walked away, none of them could really cut the umbilical cord. Those who left remained nostalgic about the way the studio had been run, the way the artistes and technicians (including all of them) had been groomed, and the collegial atmosphere that made the production of films so smooth.

Their romantic attachment towards the studio was as obvious as the resentment they felt towards Devika. Over the years many press interviews were given stating that it would have been simple for them to take over the studio if she had not set herself up as the successor to Himansu. The narrative would be, 'She destroyed the studio! Devika produced films which did not run!' It was repeated so often that Devika did not bother to deny it.

This was also touted as the main reason for the eventual dissolution of the studio and the demise of Bombay Talkies. The truth was that the studio made a profit of ₹1,46,761 in 1944, just before Devika's departure in 1945—and they were able to pay a dividend, as well as a bonus of around ₹35,000 to the workers. By mid-1945, there would be a severe cash crunch, but a plan had been put in place to refinance the studio, by Devika, before she left. However, the uncertainty over the partition of India and the departure of some its stars meant that a slow downfall began after it changed hands in 1946–47. And no matter how much money was injected into it later by Ashok Kumar and others, the studio would continue to bleed.

In fact, if anyone had bothered to go through the documents she kept so meticulously, they would have realised that there were problems in Bombay Talkies long before Himansu's death. But being Devika, she did what she had to—and refused to talk about it. She felt the evidence was there for everyone to see. She never confirmed or denied anything, just carried on working as she always had. She tried to do what she thought was the right thing, and if it did not suit anyone else, it was their problem, not hers.

Another anonymous letter, again hinting at underhand dealings, was sent to 'Mother Devikarani Rai Esq' on 7 April 1944 by 'her affectionate son, X, Y, Z'. The sender wrote that his real name was Sunitichandra. That Sunitichandra was a fan was more than obvious because he claimed to have seen *Hamari Baat* eleven times. He thought it was the best film in the market, but warned her that Sashadhar might come back and try to take over the studio again. Devika did not throw these letters into the rubbish heap but carefully preserved them, even sharing them with close members of her team.

She had high hopes from 1944 onwards and was beginning to feel happy again. She could not be completely disheartened as her distributors were sending her very good news. On 31 January 1944, she heard from Jagat Talkies Distributors:

> We have the pleasure to inform you that the picture 'Hamari Baat' is released at Nishat Talkies, Amritsar. From 28th instant, with great ovation and it has grossed Rs 3567/- in the first three

days, in spite of two shows daily which are restricted all over the Punjab.

The film was well received, partly because Devika was appearing on screen after a hiatus of two years. Her last film, *Anjan*, was released in 1941. From Delhi and Peshawar, distributors sent her telegrams:

> Amidst Tremendous Applause Unprecedented Rush Surpassing All Records Stop Your Appearance Hailed With Wild Clapping And Performance Profoundly Appreciated Stop Entertainment In Every Inch Acclaimed Bombay Talkies

But letters warning her of sabotage continued to come in, including one from another besotted fan, Gool Homi Bana, who, having seen her at the theatre, compared her to an angel and said she was the 'Public-Heart-Winner No 1'. In a letter dated 31 October 1943, Gool said:

> Mahatma Gandhi or any another blessed person of the world cannot compete with you in attracting people. I also herewith most heartily congratulate Mr Amiya Chakrabarti for releasing out so rapidly and screening HB [*Hamari Baat*] so soon with your two still going strong other films.

Gool pointed out that 'evil-minded and envious persons' were trying to 'do mischief' and that a 'strong propaganda had been made against your HB'.

> [I spotted] some persons near the Booking Office and inside the Theatre spreading out false rumours deprecating your very nice picture. Not only that but bad reports of your HB have been spread at other places also that your HB was a failure!

Gool claimed that these negative reports had spread all the way up to Surat, and urged Devika to ensure proper publicity was done.

Devika responded to the information by personally writing to distributors and others who may have also received similar reports.

For instance, even before this warning from Gool, she had written on 30 October 1943 to Jagat Talkies Distributors:

> In our humble way we have tried to do what my husband would have expected us to do, that is, make a first class motion picture with entertainment and with a little message to people who need something to think about in these days of stress and strain. With the reaction of the public and the thousands of telegrams I have received, I am glad that our work however simple has been liked and appreciated. Mr Lall of the HMV who has seen *Hamari Baat* feels that the songs will be very much appreciated up North and has written [to] me to that effect.

Lall had written to her earlier, on 28 October:

> I saw 'Hamari Baat' and I felt proud that you and your boys had produced such a polished picture. It compares with the best from America. And, as a duty to the country, you should start a school for teaching other producers etc the art of dressing and making up their artistes. What you did to Suraiya was a near miracle. There is not the slightest doubt that it will run and run long. All of you deserved this reward and it is yours.

He wished Amiya and her team the best of luck and wanted to know when he could expect to meet the two of them in Bombay.

It must be said that throughout this period, in late 1943 and early 1944, Amiya was by her side, supportive of her work and enjoying her success. She did not seem to mind if many thought they were a couple, as his presence made the mundane issues easier to deal with.

◦≈◦

One of the biggest problems Devika faced at this time had to do with the restrictions imposed on raw footage by the government. She wrote to officials at the Department of Information and Broadcasting in New Delhi to argue her case that the department should make a distinction between studios like Bombay Talkies, which produced their own films, and others who bought licenses and hired studios. As there were many who produced films in 30,000–35,000 feet, she suggested, more stock could be given to Bombay Talkies, which produced more films. She sent a telegram on 8 March 1944 to Mahamadi, an ICS officer who was the deputy secretary in the department, about a further increase from the proposed 50,000 feet for positive/negative rushes to at least 75,000 feet for positive rushes. She kept requesting for as much as she could get. Her training with Himansu meant she could confidently enter into a discussion on the technical aspects of production.

In 1945, she shared some of her concerns with an old friend, Commander Arthur Jarrat, who had been with Gaumant British in the early 1930s and had helped Himansu and her during their time in London, when they were trying to find the means to set up a studio. She complained that the addition of songs in Indian cinema made the limitation on raw stock even more unjust.

> No matter how good a story, acting, technique, a film will definitely be a 'flop' if it has not at least 3 good songs. Distributors if asked what a film is like, either reply 'you know the songs are not good', or 'the songs are good' which is killing for a producer. Anyway knowing the market we push in songs, nine [songs] in an eleven thousand feet film—you can imagine when stories have to change, in subject matter, musical comedy is not possible always and the public wants drama...in one film one has to create romance, drama, excitement, a happy ending—it is a formula and we give different versions of the same thing.

As much as she valued creativity, Devika was also obsessed with making profits so that the workers (including her) could be well paid and get a bonus. Every minute expense had to be monitored. Among the first things she did when she took over the studio was to check the supplies at the stores. When she was informed that there was often a mismatch between the bills and the inventories, she began an investigation.

The discrepancy had plainly been overlooked for some time. But Devika had always kept careful accounts of everything she bought, which would then be cleared as expenses by the accounts department. She even included small expenses like cosmetics and sanitary pads—every rupee was precious, because for many years she had so little. She now went through the store expenses forensically. The manager in charge, Kantilal M. Shah, wrote to her that he had been under the impression that all the cash memos and bills had been delivered simultaneously to the central stores, along with the merchandise. But after her letter reached him, he had (suddenly) realised that all the goods which had been ordered had not reached as the respective bills had not been raised, even though payments had been made against the cash memos. Though the answer was reasonable, it was obvious that money was being spent on non-existent inventory.

Devika continued checking the prices and this obviously led to some restructuring. Kantilal M. Shah was one of the persons who left in the aftermath of this stringent scrutiny.

Even M. Khajulall, a 'beautiful tie-and-dye silk specialist' based in Jaipur, who had worked with Himansu from the early days of silent cinema, met with rejection by Devika. He had been asked to send some silver ornaments and georgette silk sarees for the studio. To his surprise, after years of supplying goods without a single question being asked, almost everything he had sent was returned.

Devika was firm. She wrote to him in April 1943 that while most of the silver ornaments were nice, they were too heavy. She said she was returning almost all the sarees, as the 'prices of bandhani sarees in Bombay are much cheaper than the bandhani sarees you sent me from Jaipur'. She said most of these sarees would have cost half or less than half in Bombay. She later returned the only saree she had kept, because it wasn't long enough. The georgette silk sarees in question were priced at around ₹60, and the cotton sarees at ₹11 or ₹13. Devika thought even these were too expensive.

She also tried to get a good deal on some urgently required film cameras from New Theatres. Representing her, Mansata Film Distributors in Calcutta spoke to B.N. Sircar to find out if he would sell one of his cameras. But it seemed he was using all three, and the one spare was meant for emergencies. Devika did not give up the search and eventually persuaded Josef Wirsching, who was still interned, to sell his cameras to Bombay Talkies. When other cameras became available, they were also tracked down and acquired.

⌘

While she enjoyed the challenge of streamlining work at the studio, bitterness frequently arose over the betrayals she had faced and also when she observed the kind of people who had recently entered the film industry. In a letter to Commander Jarrat she wrote:

> I want to run away from here. Especially these days this industry has become a complete "racket". Black market money all over, as most of the people interested are not pure film people. They are speculators and businessmen, who know this is a medium for quick return on any money invested. The exhibitors are worse [and] with all your experience, you'd be surprised to see the way they do it here. Luckily for us, my husband formed the company on very sound lines. It is a public limited company and is small but well run. We have not, unfortunately, our own distribution, which would have been wonderful but have distributors who pay us a minimum guarantee.
>
> We produce 3 pictures a year, even that is difficult, no stars, have to build up new ones and get poets, writers, all trained [by us]. When they are good they go or give trouble because other companies will pay anything just to take a man out.

But she was confident, she said, that her present team would stay with her, because Bombay Talkies, though not very large and with only one sound stage, was still considered the best in India for presentation, technique and production. Her confidence was further boosted by the letters of support she received from those who had worked with her when Himansu was alive and believed that she had been betrayed after his death.

S.V. Kriparam, who had worked in Bombay Talkies' first film, *Jawani ki Hawa*, and had left to join the army, wrote to her on 17 August 1944 that 'much water had flown under Malad Bridge'. He said that he had sympathetically noted the 'drift of old friends. And betrayal of once loyal and faithful dogs'. He observed that she had suffered both as a wife and an artiste after Himansu's death:

> Division of B.T.'s staff, and creation of a rival—nay hostile group was a forgone conclusion, for those who could read the faces behind the masks, and could fathom motives. It all needed time and turn in circumstances. I had predicted that years before.

Like so many others, he too was 'glad to learn that you are managing it so very efficiently'.

Four years after Himansu's death, and one year following the departure of her rivals in early 1943, Bombay Talkies was still going strong. From the press to the politicians to the industry itself—everyone was surprised that this petite and seemingly fragile woman had managed to hang in there with her sheer tenacity and grit. They had known her as an actress and appreciated her professionalism. Now they saw her as a shrewd and canny manager.

Devika began to be recognised as an iconic survivor.

Letter from Devika to Svetoslav

My dear friend,

How very kind of you to have written! I was really surprised and happy to know that you really liked being here—our life is so very different and cut off from the world in general. We can't imagine other people being interested except that they have the same sort of feeling going to the zoo, or some place that "must be seen".

People coming here have so often asked "Are you really Devika Rani?" I've always laughed but never had the courage to ask "Why do you ask that?"

You know we loved having you—everyone talked about you after you left, so many of my "babas" wanted to talk to you. They didn't say so when you were here, I would have let them cluster around to get a breath of the fresh and hopeful atmosphere which surrounds you.

If ever you feel like coming, do—only given me notice as I can arrange that we have a few hours off.

It's 8.15 a.m. now and I must say au revoir—my usual machine life starts.

Bombay, 1944

16

BREAKING FREE, 1944–45

On 24 January 1944, a letter arrived from Bharati Sarabhai, Kashmir House, 94, Napean Sea Road. Bharati was very interested in theatre, having written a play, *The Well of the People*, which was published in 1943. She was the daughter of Ambalal Sarabhai, the well-known industrialist, and the sister of the pioneering scientist, Vikram Sarabhai.

The fact that someone from a well-established family, with a deep interest in arts and culture, was writing to Devika indicates that she had crossed the barrier that most Indian actresses faced. More and more now, she was working on projecting herself, not as an actress, but in the context of her lineage and intellectual interests. Since she no longer had to act in every single Bombay Talkies production, she had the time to develop connections, and build a network of friends and admirers. Though she rarely went out, she was able to meet the people who mattered, mostly at Sachin's well-attended soirees at his home. Both the Choudhuri brothers were very fond of her and went out of their way to support her, and she too tried to help them build their careers. It helped that she was Tagore's great-grand-niece—a fact that Himansu had taken care to project to the world. Her background as the daughter of a doctor who had lived and practised in India and abroad was also a factor in the appreciation she received.

Devika had socialised with the more powerful and distinguished British and Indian families when Himansu was alive, and these relationships remained in place even after his death. The new emerging elite of the time, especially in Bombay, were fairly Westernised. Many of them had studied and lived abroad. The women of this elite group usually came from wealthy families and were quite independent. Some of them were much more progressive than the others because of their political connections and because the men in their families were in and out of jail. World War II would soon come to an end, and it was hoped that the British would leave India shortly afterwards. A new regime would be taking over. New ideas were being explored.

In this time of churn, women were becoming more visible. They were speaking up for themselves and exploring new identities—in the freedom struggle, in literature, science, and art and culture. Bharati Sarabhai's sister-in-law, Mrinalini, for instance, was an accomplished Bharatanatyam dancer. Just a few decades earlier, dancing in public had been considered degenerate.

Bombay offered a cosmopolitan and inclusive space, buoyed by its roots in Marathi, Parsi and other cultures. With their individual backgrounds in cinema and theatre, Devika and Bharati Sarabhai would have a lot to discuss. Bharati, and others like her, respected the fact that, though a young and beautiful widow, Devika continued to act and work in different aspects of filmmaking, not to mention running a studio with hundreds of employees. Her position and reputation gave her entry into a new social hierarchy which wanted to see more independent women in the public space. Through Sarojini Naidu, Betty Hutheesingh, Kamaladevi Chattopadhyay and the board of Bombay Talkies, as well as other friends, she had already met the liberal and intellectual (and soon to be) prime minister, Jawaharlal Nehru, and many among the Indian political elite, including Dhirubhai Desai and Minoo Masani.

Bharati wrote:

> I hope you will not mind my writing to you without an introduction? Our common friend Tara Ali Baig has been trying

to get in touch with you but with no success, and has asked me to write to you directly.

I am deeply interested in the People's Theatre Movement and for a long time hoped to find some opportunity of meeting and discussing some aspects of this movement with you.

Bharati invited Devika for a meal with her and her sister Mridulaben, and added:

My sister-in-law Mrinalini, too, is interested in this scheme. You have so much experience that a talk with you is sure to be extremely stimulating. But that is if you want to!

Tara who had by now become Devika's close friend had always maintained that she was responsible for setting the norms and standards for the film industry which have 'brought wealth and fame to India.' High praise indeed.

While Tara would visit another day, Devika now invited Bharati to the studio for lunch, instead of meeting at the Sarabhai home. Bharati wrote back:

I can come on Friday, with my other sister Gita, at 11.30 and stay for lunch. I met Mr Svetoslav Roerich yesterday, after your letter had come, and mentioned that we would be motoring to Malad to see your work and discuss aspects of other work—for love of our work is common to both of us, I presume. He wondered if he could join me in my visit. He paints himself, and is also interested in all this work. May I bring him, or would you rather see him some other time?

Devika's meeting with the three of them went very well and Svetoslav Roerich, a tall and elegant Russian emigre, wrote to her within a day, on 28 January 1944:

Dear Mrs Rai
Please accept my very warm thanks for the lovely day we spent with you and your co-workers.

For some time past, I wanted to meet you and all I expected of this meeting was more than fulfilled.

My very best wishes to you and all your co-workers for the combined success of the work you so splendidly guide.

The meeting left them very impressed with each other, and it's easy to see why they would get along. They were both attractive, hardworking and talented—and mavericks, each in their own way. It would have been very unusual to find someone like Devika in any of the studios of Bombay.

Most of these studios were funded by businessmen, who were more interested in making a profit than anything else. Devika, though in a minority on the board of HIT, was attempting to bring new talent into the industry while limited by the frustrating government guidelines, which were even more restrictive due to the war. Even in these difficult times, she was intent on creating worthwhile cinema. This was her tribute to the early days of Bombay Talkies, which she missed very much.

The tight war economy had slowed down production. While many tried to dodge the taxes imposed by the government, Devika found she could not join the black-marketers. Her idealism may have been misplaced—and frustrating for those who thought that Bombay Talkies would become profitable, if only they could bend the rules a little.

It was obvious to her visitors that it took some ingenuity to keep the studio going the way she did. But by February, Devika was working on a new film, *Jwar Bhata*, with a newly discovered actor, the tall and good-looking Yusuf Khan, who she hoped would make up for the loss of Ashok Kumar. She had chosen Shamim Bano and Mridula Rani for the female leads and Amiya was the director.

Yusuf had come to them through Dr 'Cracky' Masani, the psychiatrist who had looked after Himansu during his final years. Masani called Devika and sent a letter of introduction on 15 February 1944:

He [Yusuf Khan] is a very keen and intelligent young man and has always wanted to be a film artist. From my knowledge of Mr Yusuf Khan, his desire is a sincere and earnest one, and I shall be grateful if you will help him in any way you can.

Devika scribbled a note on the letter for Amiya Chakrabarty, affectionately addressed as 'Chakram', with her trademark red pencil:

Dr Masani has sent this young man and by his letter he wishes that the boy gets something. He comes from a respectable [family].

Yusuf's name was changed to Dilip Kumar, he was given some training, and presented as the next rising star.

※

But even while instructing the newcomers, as she often did, Devika could not stop thinking of the tall, bearded man she had met recently. She wrote to him somewhat passionately, partly impulsively and partly with a kind of genuine warmth she rarely felt for anyone these days. Her letters, over the months, praised Svetoslav extravagantly, especially his saint-like appearance and his softly expressed but deeply moving ideas, and her reaction may have led a lesser mortal to misunderstand her intentions.

But Svetoslav was no ordinary man. He had grown up with a very intelligent and dominant mother, a uniquely talented father, and a brother who many considered a genius. He was surrounded by extraordinary people and was himself capable of great artistic work. Praise was something he took in his stride. What fascinated him was beauty and intelligence, and Devika had both. And yet she seemed deeply unhappy, lost and searching for a goal or an anchor, which she had not yet found. That intrigued him.

He allowed himself the freedom to explore his thoughts about her from the safe distance of Naggar, in Kulu, where he had been living with his family for the past decade or so. They began to correspond. What began with a few formal letters would grow into a deluge. It was as if they could not stop writing to each other. Soon, telegrams and twenty-page letters were going up and down, between Bombay and Naggar, on a daily basis.

It was as though, until they met, neither had anyone in their life who really understood them. They wrote to each other about how lonely they were—Devika in the middle of a crowded studio, surrounded by four hundred people, and he, up in the mountains, living with his immediate family and a few others.

She would write to him with great empathy, as they came closer and formed a deeper bond. She also tried to understand his psychology and what he was looking for. This was Devika at her best. Just as she could, as an actress, get under the skin of a character, she could come really close to a person by figuring out what they needed—and also what they wanted to hear.

Once they had got to know each other better, she would write, more freely:

> You and I, we do deserve a little happiness. I wonder how you were all these years with your temperament, alone, how you must have <u>suffered</u>, you above <u>all</u> people need love so much… you are made for marriage, for home, for love, for a woman's company, you are really dearest a man who can't be really happy without a woman to love you—it somehow belongs to you—your whole personality as if it were meant to have a wife, to protect, to care for, to love, to make a home for.

She was pained to think of his 'utter loneliness', and went on to say:

> It is different, beloved, for one who does not feel, but you, <u>you</u> feel with every fibre of you, and to think of all that wealth of yours, the wealth of your knowledge, life—all your keen love, perception, everything just to have it, and have no one you love by [your side]—dearest it must have been <u>dreadful</u> at times for you.

The timing of their first meeting had been just right. Both Devika and Svetoslav had given up on ever finding the sort of intellectual and physical companionship that meant so much to them. Fortunately, they were able to recognise that maybe, just maybe, they had got lucky.

Devika had found the elusive, all-encompassing happiness she wished for, which she had with Himansu in the early years, and now in a limited way with Amiya. But in Svetoslav she discovered a deeper kinship—she had found a fellow traveller. In the first meeting itself, something happened to her, something that she said she was fearful to even contemplate.

A restlessness came over her as she began dreaming of the place where he lived, a mountain abode that spelt the perfect retreat. It seemed to be the sort of pure, untrammelled space that could offer peace. And Svetoslav Roerich, with his elegant good looks—the long, flowing beard and gentle demeanour—was like a breath of fresh air, releasing her from the suffocation of Bombay Talkies.

As the head of the studio, there was always a deliberate barrier between her and the others. She was on a pedestal and they were down below. Most were in awe of her, and few felt they could match her luminescence and quick wit. Even with Amiya, there was a distance—and there were many days when they could not meet because of production deadlines and the meetings she constantly had to attend, or the social engagements she had, though she tried to take him with her whenever possible.

She had been working at a crazy pace since the age of eighteen—first looking after Himansu, then his productions, the films, and now the studio… could she break away from all this? Was there someone out there who would look after her, for a change? Someone she could learn from and lean on? Could she slow down? Could she break away? Could she reach into that absolutely wonderful stillness radiating from Svetoslav?

But right now, in Bombay Talkies, her main job was to teach Sachin the ropes, besides balancing the account books, training the newcomers, holding Prahladrai's hand…

Work went on all day. Even though she had just completed a film, the next production was already upon her. And then there were marketing and advertising plans to look after, board meetings to attend, and egos to be massaged.

But when she sat down to write to Svetoslav, she forgot why she had been so troubled. She would write the letters lying in bed at night, flat on her stomach, legs in the air, the writing pad in front of her, her scrawl spreading all over the page as she wrote without deleting a single word—as did he. They seemed very clear about what they had to say to each other.

Her mind raced with possibilities as she looked at the photographs that had been taken during Svetoslav's visit to the studio. Perhaps through him she could be released from this constant need for money and success—his life seemed so simple, serene. It seemed to open up a whole new space, spiritual at its heart. In a strange way, it was exciting. She was done with this brutal way of living, of the cycle of success and failure, money and penury. She was ready for a new experience, a new life, where none of this mattered.

But was he ready for it? Their lives were so different, they could have been living on two different planets. Would he find her too crude, she wondered, too earthy, too poorly educated?

Svetoslav belonged to an aristocratic Russian family, with parents who were unconventional and spiritually adventurous. He was four years older than Devika and extremely talented, educated at the best institutes—he had studied architecture in London, at the Royal Academy of Arts in 1919. Then he moved to Columbia University and finally, Harvard. The Massachusetts University Sculpture Department was where he engaged further in art.

Apart from his early years, he had never lived in Russia. His family was already in Finland when the Russian Revolution began in 1917 and they had been living in exile ever since. There was no place for the erstwhile aristocracy in communist Russia.

His parents, Nicholas and Helena Roerich, took advantage of this time to travel the Western world. They also explored the different religions and cultures of Central Asia with a rare exuberance. Nicholas soon earned a reputation as a great and prolific artist. Helena wrote books on 'living ethics' in collaboration with mahatmas and rishis, all of whom remained anonymous, and visible only to her and a few others like her. This was the era of Theosophy, and like Madam Blavatsky and her followers, Helena delved deep into mysticism.

Thus Nicholas and Helena, with their two sons, George and Svetoslav, became cultural nomads for a while, creating and assimilating as they travelled between England, America and India. Both the boys were child prodigies, going by their list of achievements and linguistic skills, and so it was only natural they would become a formidable foursome.

The Roerichs were wealthy, and with some support, they set up an art and museum centre in New York. But they were off soon, on an expedition that would last three years. Svetoslav stayed back and looked after the centre, while his parents and brother trekked across the Himalayas from 1925 to 1928, collecting information on the flora, fauna, monuments, religions and cultures of Central Asia.

In 1931, Svetoslav joined his family in India and they made the rugged mountains of Naggar, in Kulu, their home. Svetoslav had by now developed into a full-fledged artist, specialising in portraiture. He believed that 'art strives for higher levels of perfection' and along the way he also propagated the Roerich Pact—something his father had initiated, under which art would be identified and preserved all over the world. The pact had been signed at the White House in the US, and then placed at the Hague. It could be considered a precursor to UNESCO's agenda.

Undoubtedly, this was a unique family of thinkers. In July 1928, Nicholas launched another ambitious venture, Urusvati (which translates from Sanskrit as 'The light of the morning star'), also known as the Institute of Himalayan Studies. Many of the ideas that the Roerich family worked on were prescient and showed them to be far ahead of the times they lived in.

Their house, a wooden Himalayan cottage which had once belonged to a local raja—as well as Urusvati, the Himalayan studies centre—was spectacularly located with a clear view of the Western Himalayas and a rather precarious road that led up to its gates. It became the main home of the Roerichs, where they lived with some Russian and a few local helpers. It was definitely a reclusive existence, snowbound in winter, and the road was often swept away during the monsoon. Its remoteness allowed the family to further explore their theories on spirituality, beauty, art and life, and to write, paint and reflect.

As much as money mattered in Bombay Talkies (and money was fast becoming the focal point of all existence), in this remote Himalayan home, it mattered not at all. There was always enough local produce to live on, especially from the apple and cherry orchards, as well as the livestock. And there were, of course, the Swiss bank accounts and the inherited family wealth that the Roerichs could fall back on. Exhibitions and orders for paintings by Nicholas and Svetoslav brought in some additional income. But much of what the Roerichs did was for spiritual or scientific advancement, and they somehow managed to keep commerce out of it. The main philosophy at the core of their lives was to evolve spiritually, spread awareness and to educate.

When Svetoslav met Devika, he was an established artist and keen to explore the visual medium a little more, perhaps on celluloid. The invitation to meet Devika, extended to him by Bharati Sarabhai, came as a welcome opening into the possibility of making documentary films.

Before they met, Devika had imagined that the rich Russian could bring in some much needed business to Bombay Talkies. Perhaps she could charm him into producing some films based on his ideas. Or he could help Bombay Talkies get contracts for film production from the Russian government. Maybe some kind of exchange programme could be set up.

But once they met, work became secondary. Svetoslav would later say that it felt as though he had always known her, even when they met for the first time. And they both felt the need to get to know each other on a personal level. Nonetheless, he introduced her to a few Russian officials who were interested in using the technology available at Bombay Talkies. Contracts were signed, and Bombay Talkies did earn some income from the project.

Besides these work meetings, each time Svetoslav came to Bombay in 1944 and 1945, he and Devika met as kindred spirits, finding so much more in common—even friends. It was surprising that they had not met before.

Only someone fully attuned to Devika, like Amiya, may have noticed the immediate rapport between the two at the first meeting itself. After all, Devika was the host and she also needed to focus on her other guest, Bharati Sarabhai. But again and again, she had looked at Svetoslav, almost wanting to reach out and touch him. Or make him notice her in some way.

He was a foreigner, but he did not feel alien to her. He was very different from the Germans and the British whom she worked with at Bombay Talkies. In any case, her relationship with them was entirely professional and formal. Sir Richard and Franz Osten, to some extent, were the only two non-Indians she felt close to, but both were much older than her. At this point, Sir Richard had got remarried and Franz had returned to Germany. Her interaction with them now was almost negligible.

Svetoslav was not just closer to her in years, but with his elegant demeanour and courteous ways, he reminded Devika of all that she had lost in the last eighteen years. Suddenly, she found herself thinking that while she may have her roots in India, it was her time in Europe that had shaped her and given her the confidence to work and support herself. Chatting with Svetoslav, she was reminded of the days when she travelled with her father—the sophisticated parties, the banter, the landscapes covered with snow, the music. None of those memories were tainted by the rough life she had seen at Bombay Talkies, and were free of any of the ugliness she had experienced with Himansu. Overcome with nostalgia, she wished she were a young woman again, pure and 'clean'—a word she often used these days. She wished she could scrub away the past.

When they met at the studio for the first time, she had felt 'very lonely'. She wrote to him about this more than a year later, on 8 July 1945:

I thought so much of you after you left with Bharati, and I thought I should not meet him often, he is just somehow so near to me and I dismissed that thought I had. If I now think, that feeling that I should not come so near, because <u>if</u> I <u>did</u> I would fall in love terribly with you because when I just looked at you the 1st time I felt you knew me so well, and there was a sort of immediate contact and understanding!

When he described where he lived, in Kulu, she fell in love with the images he drew of greenery, peace, fresh air.

I love quiet surrounded by nature—I could never wish for anything better. You see when we were small, up to the age of 10, we lived an absolute country life, peace and really happiness, we never had electric light, and all my life I was always attracted to the country. In the Tyrole...it was ideal, in Switzerland, in the lakes of Italy, in the Riviera, in England Devon, and the other country places—simply beautiful.

As she drew closer to him, she wondered what would happen to Amiya. She did not want to be unfair to him. He had supported her all through the last few years with Himansu, and later, when she was fighting to retain control over Bombay Talkies. She had been close to breaking point, and he had steadied her. How would he react to her falling in love with someone else? So far, they had been discreet. What if Amiya got upset and went public? Devika thought of all those who knew them as a couple—and those who didn't. What would they say? She went through the files of letters and invitations sent to her recently, stopping occasionally to read.

Krishna (Betty) Hutheesingh had written to her from Shahibagh, Ahmedabad, on 4 March 1944:

My dear Devika

I thought you would ring me up after your ten days vacation but you never did. Then Amiya da told me he had been to Malad.

> When are you going to pay us a visit? You know Raja is on parole and will soon have to return to his prison... I would like you to come over before he goes back. Could you manage to come and dine with us on the 13th or if dinner is difficult to manage come to lunch any day that you are free.
>
> We came here for a week and will be back in Bombay on Tuesday morning so please ring me up and let me know when you will be able to come.
>
> I am so glad your picture is doing so well. My boys have seen it twice.
>
> Love from us both

Betty would soon return to 20, Carmichael Road in Bombay, where she planned to meet Devika. Incidentally, this was the house where a future prime minister, Rajiv Gandhi, was to be born a few months later, in August 1944. And of course, Indira, Betty's niece, knew Svetoslav and his family quite well.

As she went through some more letters, she realised that many of her well-wishers, who had nothing to do with cinema, knew about her closeness to Amiya. How could she keep this a secret from Svetoslav? Perhaps it was better to tell him?

Mrinalini Sarabhai had written:

> Vikram and I passed through Bombay on our way to and from Kashmir, but though I wanted him to meet you, we could not get to Malad as we were in Bombay only for a day, both the times. I wish you were nearer.
>
> I am waiting to see your new picture and am so glad you are once more taking part in the films. Amiya Chakrabarty seems to be getting on very well. Please remember me to him.

Mrinalini and Vikram would definitely know Svetoslav too. If Svetoslav came to Bombay, could she go out with him and ensure that no one mentioned Amiya? Perhaps she should seek out those acquaintances who did not know her too well. Maybe someone like Rattan Chand Rawlley, who wrote on 6 April 1944:

> I don't know why I was suddenly reminded of you on Sunday last when Sarojini Naidu came along to wish Zarina many happy returns of the day. I suppose it was in connection with your birthday which falls on or about the 20th of March. If so, here are my good wishes etc.

He also told her about a political novel he had written, *Mr John Bull Speaks Out*, which he wanted her to read. Sarojini had recommended it as brutal but good reading.

Actually, Devika's birthday fell on 30 March and her new friend remembered the precise date. A telegram arrived promptly from Naggar on 30 March 1944:

> Best wishes and greetings [for] your birthday. Roerich

She replied, obviously very happy:

> Many thanks stop Deeply appreciate kind thought stop How did you remember stop Deep regards Devika Rani

She followed this up with a letter, once again showing her appreciation and interest in Svetoslav, who, ensconced far up in the hills, would have received few letters of this kind.

Not surprisingly, the person most affected by this new friendship was Amiya. He had known Devika very closely for the past six years. Now, as she became more and more interested in her new Russian acquaintance, he was pushed to the sidelines. He wasn't surprised by what happened next—the more she was drawn to Svetoslav, the kinder she was towards him, Amiya. That was just how she was. Behind the tough exterior was a woman who had learnt to manage all sorts of people, in a professional and personal capacity. From Himansu she had learnt that even when you have to hurt someone, you must be gentle about it. She remembered how he had done his best to accommodate the demands of Mary Hainlin (this of course was before his illness had set in). She herself had kept her real feelings towards many people at Bombay Talkies a secret for years.

Till it had reached breaking point and she could no longer maintain the charade, she had tried to get them to like her. Even her worst enemies must adore her, eventually. It was almost like a mantra. As for her lovers and failed admirers—well, she would go out of her way to ensure that each one of them felt comfortable, so that when she abandoned them, they would not complain and would remember her kindly, if not with fondness.

It was a paradox, and he had seen it during Himansu's last days—the more she was attracted towards Amiya, the kinder and gentler she was towards Himansu, accepting all his abuse and tantrums. She knew she could rest a while in Amiya's arms and cry on his shoulder. He was aware that the years since Himansu's death had been rough on her. Could Svetoslav make her forget how much she had given up for the studio?

Quietly, carrying on with his work, Amiya observed her dilemma. In any case, he could do little, and so he said nothing. They had an understanding, but ultimately she held all the cards. For most of these past few months, she had hardly come to the studio, saying she was ill and housebound. The invitations to visit her had stopped. The portents were clear.

Svetoslav wrote to Devika affectionately on 13 April 1944, following up on the first few interactions with her:

> My Dear Friend,
>   Many thanks for your sweet letter which I found on my return to our Mountain Retreat, redirected from Bombay.
>   I cut my stay in the plains short and returned here to complete some work.
>   Yes, I did enjoy very much meeting you and I am looking forward to our next meeting. In the meantime I have your picture before me on my desk as I can look at it while I work. I think I met someone I really liked.
>
>   With kindest greetings
>   S.N. Roerich

There was an underlying sweetness and honesty in these early letters. The fact that he called her a friend, and told her that he liked her meant a lot to her, caged as she was within the usual stressful atmosphere of the studio. For the time being, even having him as a friend felt good, and it helped her to cope with the day-to-day tensions. But she wanted more.

A few years earlier, she had started sending a small donation of ₹10 or ₹15 to Reverend Father D.S.F. Coelho at St Anthony's Charity Institutions in Mangalore, requesting him to place a petition on her behalf near the relic of the saint, at the shrine's altar. The amount was mentioned in her official monthly account statements; it was meant to feed the poor. This time, too, the Reverend promised to pray earnestly to ensure that her wishes were granted. Just over a month later, she received a letter from him, saying:

Please accept our hearty congratulations.
Newspapers announce wonderful success of your picture shows—crowded houses—repeated shows.

What he may not have known was that Devika was praying for a variety of things. She had just survived another crisis with the departure of Keshavlal Mody by appointing Sachin Choudhuri as general manager of Bombay Talkies. She had also just met an interesting Russian whose twinkling grey-blue eyes had enthralled her, and whom she was keen to meet again. And yes, she wanted the films she produced to sweep the box office. At least two of her three wishes had come true! It was a good omen.

In 1944, Devika produced *Char Aankhen*, *Jwar Bhata* and *Hamari Baat*. The films did medium to good business. *Hamari Baat*, especially, was well received at the box office. Bombay Talkies was now back to optimising its resources and making three films in a year. But for Devika, the biggest challenge was to find a way of communicating her interest in Svetoslav to the man himself.

For most of 1944, they had a fairly formal relationship, but in the beginning of 1945, things began to change. The last time Svetoslav was in Bombay, they had managed to spend a lot of time together. It was very helpful that she had a car and they could drive out to the beach. Sometimes they would just sit and talk in the car—or make love.

In a letter written on 13 May 1945, she looked back to those days.

> I used to be full of misery at this awful, lonely thought—when I wrote to you I honestly felt dearest that of all people you would really understand my unhappy thoughts. I can't explain why I thought so, but I did so admire you, I thought of you like a Saint, a man like Christ on earth who was so compassionate, who knew, who would receive my thoughts with all the tender understanding.

For the first time in her life, Devika also opened up about the abuse inflicted upon her. Slowly she revealed to him that the perfection he saw in her as an actress hid a darker reality.

> [She] is so scarred, been beaten, been starved, been made to work and work without consideration, been crushed mentally, but God has saved [me] from being broken… [I] said to God, I will do everything to the best of my ability, and I will do so cheerfully so that may prove to you I am living my life as a religion, but you must some time, give me happiness, real true happiness.

She felt her reward was her meeting with Svetoslav.

Fortunately, he too believed that their relationship was unique and spiritual, and they had been through many incarnations together. At the same time, the physical passion they shared was like nothing she had known before. She wrote to him:

> I find you terribly attractive. In fact, I can hardly take my eyes away from you. Every movement of yours is terribly fascinating to me—your reactions, your voice, your manner of talking, the way you stand and walk, that natural grace and poise which of course comes from blood & birth of centuries of breeding,

the way you laugh, the way you sit, the way your hands react, the little flicker of amusement in your very naughty eyes, the grave look you have when you are worried, your perfect hands, your lips, the lovely way you drink a glass of wine or water, your perfect manners, your wonderful insight, your general charm and dynamic personality, absolute wonder of your eyes...

It was unusual for a woman to wax eloquent over a man in such terms—but this was Devika. Once she committed herself, there were no half measures.

She wrote pages and pages of overwhelmingly flattering love letters to him every day for several months. For Svetoslav, who had been living a lonely life in the mountains for close to sixteen years, this came as an explosion of sentiment and unabashed love from a woman who he knew other men would give anything to attract. They began to refer to each other as husband and wife. He could not live without her now.

He said, as she noted on 2 May 1945, that he had 'reverted to [his] earlier stages in life'. She felt he had returned to his childhood, because he needed her all the time. In the letter, she called him a baby:

> Why not admit that that really you are as simple and childlike as a baby, sometimes like a very naughty one, insisting without reason, being upset without reason, feeling hurt without reason, always wanting to be loved at odd times & places, getting up in the middle of dinners etc. But love... that is certainly not like any Baby—it completely takes your wife's breath away and how she loves it—that mad rushing love of yours, wanting everything completely, immediately, madly, not a moment without those hot impatient kisses... I love you passionately, I fall in love with you, I flirt with you every day...

Svetoslav could not hide his impatience, even in public, to hold her in his arms. He began spending more time in Bombay while Devika continued to execute her duties at Bombay Talkies. She had told him of her commitment to her work, and he respected it.

This was to set the tone of their relationship. She was the strong, independent woman, and he was the one who needed her.

Having faced every sort of problem without flinching, she understood she had to do the really difficult thing now—she told Svetoslav that she had to tell Amiya about them. While they continued to work together in the studio, Amiya had not said anything to her yet. But she could not leave him just like that, in silence. Once upon a time, they had a pact, an understanding that one day they would be together. There was an expectation of marriage, even if it had never been verbalised.

In the last few months, she had tried to avoid being alone with him. She carried on as normal, even arranged for his treatment. A few times, she saw him looking at her quizzically, and with sadness. Luckily, the production of the new film had kept him busy.

But they were uneasy with each other. She knew he had heard the rumours about Svetoslav. Her life was hardly a secret. There was always someone watching her, ready to critique 'the dynamic, dazzling Devika Rani'.

No one valued her privacy or thought she was entitled to a life of her own. Swami had started maintaining a fresh file of the anonymous letters coming in, denouncing her for her affair with a 'Russian Roast'. Some of these letters were threatening in nature and she kept them to show Svetoslav, so that he was aware of what she was going through.

Until now, she had not confided in Amiya because she was not sure her relationship with Svetoslav had a future. Then, on a very eventful day in March 1945, when they made love and Svetoslav proposed to her, 'her whole life changed'. Being cautious, she still said, 'let us see'. They had known each other for a whole year by then.

She told Svetoslav:

> You said you trusted me. Apart from everything else I respect you, and I shall not betray that trust. Having lived I have come to know to some extent the value of things and have learnt to respect them.

I did not tell you but I have only one thing to do. It is not difficult but it deals with a friend. I think he may have a feeling that one day he may marry me. I say I think because he has never said so—I shall tell you about it. I am sure you will all understand, and help me too. I will not tell him about us, but I will have to tell him something which makes it clear and easy. I had not told him anything because he had TB and I thought it unnecessary to hurt or harm his progress by any hard word. This is my obligation to make it clear. You must believe me and you must leave it to me to do in my own way.

Ever careful, she added:

The people around one... and ties of different sorts, they have to be managed and arranged so that one can at any time with honour, leave them if one wishes. It may be years, but I feel it is good to arrange things from now. Even before you spoke to me, I had thought of this 3 or 4 months ago.

Apart from speaking to Amiya, Devika had a few other boxes to tick, all very important tasks that she had to complete before her departure, if she were to marry Svetoslav.

First, the accounts for the last year, that is, 1944 had to be passed while she was still at Bombay Talkies, and she knew it had been a profitable year. Second, she wanted to sell her shares in HIT to a buyer who had been located by Prahladrai—this person would replace her on the board and she could make some money from the sale of the shares. This would ensure a smooth transition. And third, she wanted to quit HIT and Bombay Talkies, but with full respect and honour. She hoped they would let her go, though there were still a few years left in her contract.

Not just the sweetness of her flattery or her sheer beauty, but her managerial skills and her honesty also impressed Svetoslav. He felt that she must complete all the unfinished agenda at work before they got married, so that she was ready for a new life, just as he was preparing for a new life with her—with a renewed focus on his own career. Motivated by the ever-sensible Devika, he had come to the realisation that he needed to create his own identity, away from the overwhelming shadow of his very talented family.

He began thinking about an exhibition, something Devika was very keen on. She encouraged him to hold a series of exhibitions in Moscow, as the Russian press was taking a greater interest in his work. For the reticent artist, this was a new experience. He was still an outsider, and had lived as a recluse for many years, so recognition from his own country was welcome.

By mid-1945, he was also getting commissions which she felt would keep him from worrying about their relationship as and when they got married. She wanted him to be as busy as she was, and earn a 'little money' as well. An independent income was important as they planned a future together. Since he lived with his family, the expenses so far had been borne by his parents; now, the newly wedded couple would also contribute.

But she was firm that she was not going to act again, though Svetoslav suggested that she should not give it up. She said they were not going to get involved in 'all sorts of undertakings'. And if he was keen on exhibitions in Russia and other places, they needed to have 'peace of mind' to protect 'our painting'. She wanted to give her 'experience of life to her love, her own husband, than [to] all [other] people; by serving her husband well, she will be doing the most powerful thing a woman can do and the only thing God perhaps wanted woman to do, that is, love her own husband, in every way.'

Devika was clearly anxious to make her feelings very clear on the subject. In order to do this, she came up with arguments which were surprising for a woman who could be called 'liberated' in many ways. But so anxious was she to leave the world of cinema, which she found bereft of ideas and of great men and women that she was prepared to sacrifice her hard-won independence, her recognition in the film world, to become a 'wife' supporting her husband.

On 8 May, when Svetoslav said he had spoken to a few people about her going back to work, she asked:

> Is it to help them or to find something for Bunny [Devika] to play about with so she does not miss her career? Well let us see dearest—you have taken some trouble and time on all this with these people. I will certainly uphold your prestige, but I do feel it most important that you and I thrash this...subject out—and your ideas too, which I quite understand must be the most "fertile" and really interesting. In the meantime, I am keen on only one thing—to get "free" from BT [Bombay Talkies], and to be free to go to you.

Her annoyance and disdain for her present life were quite apparent as she insisted she did not want to have anything more to do with Bombay Talkies, and hoped that Svetoslav would not bind her into commitments. In the meantime, she had also fallen sick again, which may have been partly due to the stress.

Devika was also worried that his family, far more educated and learned than her, would not accept a mere actress as his wife. To her great relief and happiness, as soon as he reached Kulu, he sent a telegram which reached her on 14 May 1945, stating that he had told his family about her:

> Hope You Are Better Dearest Stop Have Completed My Mission Most Successfully Stop Everyone Most Happy Sending You Their Fondest Love Stop Kulu Is Cold And I Already Have A Cold Stop Feel Extremely Happy Stop All My Love More Always.

At last! She had been 'accepted' by his family—his father, mother, brother. This marriage was going to be very different from her first one, and she wanted it to be traditional, spiritual, elevating.

She told Svetoslav:

> Their Blessing meant so very much to me. Our Parents' blessing is everything for us because you see we are part of them and

if they feel happy we start life together with their love, good wishes, there is nothing greater.

She received blessings from Svetoslav's parents even before meeting them or going to Kulu. His mother wrote her a 'beautiful letter'. She said, 'Love him, trust him, my little Devika. He is worthy of a great love.'

'Dearest,' wrote Devika to Svetoslav, 'it shall be my religion, that line. I shall look upon it as the greatest message and sacred duty of my life.' She placed the letter in her copy of the Gita, near her Lakshmi and St Anthony. 'Tell her, her letter to me was actually as if the Gita became alive to me.'

Devika began planning her life in Kulu—which included learning Sanskrit from his brother, George. 'It is strange though as he says, a Russian teaching an Indian Sanskrit.' Calling his parents and the whole family 'saints', with biblical fervour she wrote:

> All these years of suffering, all the pain, the scars, everything today, has, as it were, been healed, I feel reborn—I feel so completely as if my search has ended, and God in his infinite mercy has said "Get up and walk".

During this period, Devika continued to focus on bringing in more income for Bombay Talkies, as the films were not doing as well as they should have, and the salaries of the workers had been raised once more. When Commander Arthur Jarrat, the chief film-buyer for Gaumont British, was asked by Lord Louis Mountbatten to organise propaganda films for the army and the navy, he visited Bombay Talkies in May 1945.

According to Devika, who knew Jarrat from her time in London, told Svetoslav that he was 'surprised' and 'astounded that our place was so well run, and that from the pieces of films I showed him, he felt we had gone far ahead than most British Productions technically, and ours was managed most efficiently.' Jarrat apparently said that if he were to begin to praise her, he would not know where to stop.

Devika wrote that 'he has made lots of money, buys for Eng [England] 5 million pounds of pictures a year from America—and has a circuit of 400 cinemas in [England].' He was 'very fond' of her and just the same as he used to be. Even though he was interested mostly in making money for the British Empire, which did not make her very happy, she found him to be a 'good' man.

She thought he could be very useful for the future of the business. And she was tempted by his suggestion that they either buy or take over a 'sick' printing press. But she was even more thrilled because 'he was very excited to see me, he could not believe it was me, he said I looked so young, so fresh, he was astounded.'

She was also happy because he congratulated her on her reputation as a professional and said that India House in London had spoken very highly of Bombay Talkies.

> This is the thing which is now...complete...I had worked on it, it meant a lot to me to hear that my work was good, I felt very happy dearest I have completed one thing. It is not the best I could have done, no, but when I am leaving my profession for good, I am so happy to hear that the work we all had done was appreciated by a man who really knows—and a man who knew me at the start, who wished me "luck" 11 years ago, he now stands on the ground of that work and says "My God, it is really wonderful." So satisfied that the thing I did after Rai died was liked by a man who "knows" in my profession. God has given me that great satisfaction!!

It appears that Jarrat had questioned her and found that she had done some splendid work, possibly the best in Bombay—and in some respects, better than in England. If she had the money, her studio would not be in any way inferior to even the American studios, he told her. Because he was a technical man with international exposure, he appreciated all the adaptations that had been done at Bombay Talkies. Devika felt as though a professor had given her a certificate with 100 per cent marks for her work and good conduct, so she could leave school for the 'university of life, love, and divine spiritual betterment'. She tried to persuade Jarrat as well as Groves, the official who had come with him, that they should consider making short films on India in which Svetoslav could be involved, and fixed to meet them again in Delhi.

Unfortunately for her, the contract did not fructify, and paranoia set in again. Were her enemies trying to stop the growth of Bombay Talkies? Her anxiety was genuine because every move she made seemed to take a long time to show results. This was frustrating for both her and Svetoslav as they were keen to complete her tasks at Bombay Talkies at the earliest. Svetoslav, in particular, alone in Kulu and having got the house organised for her arrival, had begun to find the separation painful. Especially when he could sense that obstacles were being put her in her path.

She would bitterly acknowledge that her ascension at work had been made more difficult by men who wished to demonstrate their fondness for her in ways she did not like. She did not consider them more than 'tables and chairs' but they would become emotional, including, as she told Svetoslav, one 'business partner who is very fond of me, the man I told you who cried...' when he learnt that she was leaving.

This would have been Prahladrai, who was just twenty-nine at the time, but according to her looked like a much older man. She had to keep all her 'partners' charmed so that they would be on her side when she needed them. In this she was a practical businesswoman, but she did not always succeed in keeping them at arm's length. Some of the men misunderstood her intentions if she invited them over for dinner or spent extra time with them.

The need for discretion meant that her plans for departure kept getting delayed. Some of these men would not take her involvement with Svetoslav kindly, and there would also be unrest in Bombay Talkies if people knew she was leaving. She knew that every step she took was observed keenly, not just by the hovering media, but also by her rivals at Filmistan. She had to leave with grace and dignity, without the studio falling into any kind of disarray.

A few of the men who claimed a special informality with her struck her as being more vicious than the others. She was careful to use pseudonyms for them, even in her letters. Svetoslav had already cautioned her that their letters could be read and scrutinised by the British government because he was a Russian. It was important no one should know the darker side of the world she lived in, especially at this sensitive moment when she wanted to leave.

The latest attack on her concerned an erstwhile supporter from the studio, whom she called 'Baby'. The man loved her and had not taken the news of her romance or departure very well. She had to 'manage' him and ensure he came out of his heartbreak without damaging her, the studio or himself. Any scandal had to be avoided. She had told him about Svetoslav and he reacted very badly. He sought a face-to-face meeting, some kind of closure. He needed to know why she was actually leaving. He wanted to have a confrontation with Svetoslav, the man who was taking her away from him.

On 27 April 1945, when she was sitting down for dinner with Sachin at home, this man came over, as she wrote to Svetoslav.

> Baby rang the bell and came in. Sachin talked & told him he was busy but he pushed his way in. I suppose he expected to see both of us, but his face fell when he saw me alone [without Svetoslav], and then he said he wanted to eat dinner, but Sachin did not invite him. He was very troublesome in a quiet way & I also was quite composed but when he said I was causing a bad feeling between Sachin and him I told him he could dine, [though] I had already had dinner! But eventually Sachin got rid of him in a nice way, it was 10 mins to 10... and I was happy to think that he did not have the pleasure of seeing us together.
>
> Anyway next morning Friday he came and swore at me for bad manners, & he said I would starve & his curse is sure to come true. He said I was looking beautiful, like a beautiful Devil

& he was sure I was leading a bad life & if I thought I could find any happiness he would see I didn't & he would smash my face and disfigure it & then let us see who would take notice of my big business ideas.

'Baby' was visibly disturbed that after being so close to him, she was barely coming to the office now and had proclaimed that she was in love with someone else. But the more he abused her and shouted, the calmer Devika became.

She had spent many years listening to all kinds of rants. They no longer affected her. Instead, the angrier he got, the more resigned she became to the fact that he was not going to leave till he had finished screaming at her. She knew it was pointless to argue—better to let him vent his feelings. She was not scared. At the most, he would hit her—that had happened so often in the past with Himansu, and she had survived. She had the scars to show for it.

He told her that he was her best friend.

And specially he had given me this (friendship) because Rai had told him I was bad & he felt sorry (Fancy Rai, he never could have!) & now these businessmen would also ruin me etc. etc., and it was only my face, which although looked so simple was a Devil's...

I thanked him and told him that although I was grateful for his offer of friendship I cannot accept it as was decided & at the same time I felt that since I am a bad person, I should be obliged if he left off his idea of reform as I was too far gone at this age, and the question of disfiguring my face I left entirely at the hands of God—as none can foresee destiny & if it was my lot, well I should see about it. And in any case he should, being such a good man not have any worry about me. It was unpleasant really.

From the description and the time, it would appear that 'Baby' could have been Amiya or even Sir Richard, though such behaviour would have been completely out of character, especially for the latter. It had to be someone who had known Himansu, and there were very few of the pre-1940 group left in the studio. To Devika's credit, she never named the person for the attack or unpleasantness and continued to work with him.

Since she had been ill for the past few months and alone at home, she had been looking for someone to stay with her. Initially she had been suffering from nerves, but after her meeting with Svetoslav, she suspected that their very active sexual encounters had led to the nagging pain in her abdomen.

She had gone to a German male gynaecologist, Dr Kahn, for a check-up. She was shy about telling Svetoslav the details but felt he had to know.

> He examined the womb [and] I asked him whether it was displaced as I had led a very strenuous life of working, dancing, riding and had several falls. He became quite alert at once and said why do you ask that particularly? Then I told him that I was getting married and although I told him so he must keep it to himself entirely. He was very nice and laughed and said that if he revealed any of the secrets he knew there would not be any practice for him anymore. So he said "Well, tell me, do you want any children", and remembering dearest that you don't want me to have any I said "no we don't"—so he said "Well your uterus is very slightly turned very slightly to the right, it is turned in slightly and in my opinion it is perfectly all right as it is and it won't any way interfere with your marriage in any way to hurt you, or be bad at all—it is so slight that the position to the right is not noticeable. But if you want children then I will have to know and we shall have to train it up. If you don't, this slight thing will help really not to conceive quickly if you douche yourself immediately.

He told her not to worry, and she was relieved that she had gone to the right place. She told Svetoslav that she was so worried when she went to the clinic that she took his letters with her, tucked into her blouse like a talisman to ward off bad news. It worked!

The pain in her abdomen was followed by a bout of pneumonia and very high fever, but she had not as yet found anyone to stay with her, though Svetoslav had wanted her to hire a nurse. But now with this very physical threat from 'Baby', it was obvious that she could no longer stay alone. Apart from security issues, she had to keep any ugliness from blowing up before the general body meeting took place, where the accounts would be passed.

To keep an eye on her, Sachin found a friend—the tall and elegant Mia Marcia, an academic who was half French and half Dutch. She would move in with Devika to 'protect' her.

Among the few men who refrained from exploiting her were the two Choudhuri brothers in whom Devika had reposed her faith. They retained their innate goodness and chivalry. Their father had practised as a lawyer in the Dacca High Court, and the family boasted many prominent members. Sankho Choudhuri, the famous sculptor, was another brother. Their niece was the writer Mahashweta Devi and the filmmaker Ritwik Ghatak was a brother-in-law. Those who remembered Sachin from the time that he was the general manager at Bombay Talkies found that the only change he made later (when he founded his weekly journal) was trading in his khadi kurta-pyjama and shawl for a silk shirt and tie.

There were many who wondered whether there was more than what met the eye between Devika and Sachin or Hiten, his younger brother, who was 'exceedingly good looking', as one admirer remembered him, 'with dreamy eyes, a soft voice and captivatingly impeccable manners'. But their friendship would continue even after Sachin left Bombay Talkies and launched the *Economic Weekly*, which would eventually become the *Economic and Political Weekly*. By then, his stint at Bombay Talkies would have taught him everything he needed to know about production and money management. Incidentally, it was the family of Gobindram Seksaria, whom Devika had brought into Bombay Talkies as shareholders, who would support the *Economic Weekly*.

After the events of 27 April, Sachin also spoke to 'Baby', as he was worried about the threat to disfigure Devika's face. He apparently 'settled' him, and 'Baby' claimed he was only interested in seeing that 'good' came to her. The situation was managed tactfully, but it was obvious that Devika was unsafe. She had to leave before these underlying tensions broke into the open and before something untoward happened to her or to the many men who loved her.

Though he did not have to, Amiya left shortly after Devika's departure, having completed his last film at Bombay Talkies. He continued to direct films for other production studios and died at the age of forty-four. Despite all of Devika's efforts, she was unable to save him from tuberculosis, or heartbreak. She had been his mentor, his boss, his best friend—and the woman he had hoped to marry.

For Devika, however, like Najam, Amiya had already receded into the past. The next part of her life would only be about Svetoslav. In her letter of 22 May 1945, she wrote:

> I even feel that surging love of both simply consumes us to oneness as it were, our souls, united, our whole selves. It is then to me as if our very heart was one—blood, everything, throbbing with creation, with all that is Godly—the most sacred, the most intimate, grand, beautiful!!!

She added for good measure:

> I worship you completely, I wish I could kiss your beloved feet right now, and every minute of my life I want to only make you happy.

They were separated for nearly four-and-a-half months, from March 1945 to August 1945, as Devika tried to achieve her three goals before she left. They missed each other desperately and in her letters, she recalled the beach where they had spent so much time together, away from the crowds.

> That was our real home during all these months, my love. What perfect happy days we spent, how much we were with each

other, and how much we longed to be alone again. I have never even been near our beach. I couldn't without you—I simply couldn't bear it....

[I hope] my friend has listened to my instructions to him on the "Beach". I remember he was most attentive as he was being made love to and being kissed too! How is he and all the things I adore? Have they forgotten their love? The Brown fellow is a bit weak but from what I gather it has not the slightest objection and in fact is longing to be really cared for and petted. This brown fellow of yours has been completely spoilt by you and listens only to you—you should give it some strict instructions to follow.

While Svetoslav was impatient to be with her, she used the fact that she had fallen ill after he left to gain some time and sympathy, but stubbornly insisted that she needed to sort out things so that there were no future regrets or recriminations. She had already linked her illness to the fact that they had been on a rather 'knockabout' time and subsequently her periods had given her a lot of trouble too. Menstrual cycles were something few men could argue with, least of all someone as sensitive as Svetoslav. If she needed rest, she had to be allowed it.

Writing to him on 4 May, she said she could not stand the heat and dust, yet had to travel 25 miles to Colaba, usually in the late afternoon, 'the hottest time...every day for a month'. But then she added, 'Don't worry, all is well. My flu may really save me the complete unpleasantness of having to go to work, at least a few days peace.'

She had been taking Metatone and barley water to get rid of the congestion in her lungs, but she said her 'suffering' was because, while she was used to 'very hard work', she also took 'certain amount of care in time, food etc—both you and I left everything to the wind, as we had to, there was no way out'. But whatever it was, she said she 'was the happiest person' and that 'all other things faded before this love of ours'.

She told him that a priest had come to visit her and she had given him her wedding bracelet to throw away, as she was now 'married' to Svetoslav. She used every means to reassure him of her unwavering love, so he would not be upset over her refusal to get married immediately. He worried, and even cried, because she did not want him around, even during her illness or hospital visits, as she wanted their romance to remain a secret. She told him how much she admired his photograph all the time, falling in love with him every day. She also had a shirt of his, which she kept on the bed next to her; it was 'well petted'.

The shirt turned out to very useful. When he called her on 7 May, she was ecstatic and wrote in her letter:

> I want to dream of you, to picture you, to feel you. I'm going to lie down with your shirt and kiss it (I won't put it on)...I'm very, very happy, you gave me new life by phoning me...I take you in my arms, and draw you close to me, ever ever so close, and kiss your eyes, your ears, your cheeks, your lips...

When she grew impatient about how long it was taking her to settle things, Sachin would tease her and say, as she recounted in her letter of 8 May:

> Madam, the only thing I can suggest is to switch your mind off. Take it to soothe you to some mountain country, what about the Kulu valley?

Preoccupied with her own predicament, she barely referred to what was happening around her or in the world at large. In a rare instance on 8 May, she scribbled in the margins in one of her daily letters to him:

> Today [the] end of the war in Europe!! Germany surrenders! War in Europe ends! V day—victory for Russia, America and England! 1945.

In the hundreds of letters which travelled up and down, and the telegrams they sent each other, she hinted sensibly that the value of the shares she hoped to sell would drop if she left without the annual accounts being passed and holding a board meeting after that. She still had not disclosed to anyone that she was going away forever.

She had told Prahladrai Brijlal, who was a director at HIT, that she was going on a holiday due to persistent ill health, and to spend time with her mother, perhaps for six months. Unaware of the urgency, or of her desire to leave and marry Svetoslav, he was in no hurry to call the board meeting. She could not argue, but found the delays were 'killing' her. She was tense, and the heat was terrible. She said she had an 'awful feeling at my work, the dead feeling, the quiet feeling of knowing, being ready and not being able to act'.

She was aware that Prahladrai had a deep affection for her, and admired her for working so hard, despite being a widow. But being very conservative and old fashioned, if he learnt that a 'Hindu' widow was remarrying, and that too a Russian, she feared he would not help in any way after that. And he was essential to get the accounts passed and the new shareholder brought onto the board of HIT.

She had to wait, and wait patiently.

In any case, as far as Svetoslav and she were concerned, they were already husband and wife. She asked him to 'make the sign of the cross on me every night. I shall never forget the way you married your own wife in the Church. How like you! Absolutely arrogant, imperious, insistent. What you wish you will do...'

Svetoslav, too, recalled the church they had walked into—and the light that shone as they 'married' each other. Brought up in a far more spiritual fashion, he could read good portents into everything, and he had found that even their horoscopes were well matched. But there was nothing more he could do now, except fret over her absence. He wanted to be with her. The thought of an attack on her by men like 'Baby' worried him. But Devika refused to be frightened. She had worked hard on the studio and would not leave till she got her due—in terms of both money and recognition. She wanted people to remember that she had left behind a well-functioning and financially viable studio. She was working hard on a plan to go to the markets once more, to refinance the studio through a fresh stock offer. The studio had given her everything; she could not just walk away from it.

Letter from Devika to Svetoslav

I am very lucky with these men, they are real toughs, hard cruel gamblers, but to their partner they will never do a bad turn—they feel if they do, it will harm them! They have also been very kind to me, and trusted me completely and never said no. I don't take it from them of course and don't give them the opportunity but I like them, they have a certain something which is quite interesting & fresh, because it is their crude goodness. They are & have been the best business associates I had so far, and in their own way dearest have a love for me. I mean they are very fond of me, and laugh at me and they think I am a child—I don't mind so long as I get what I want for my work & workers. They also are afraid of me, that I fully know, because I never lied, or agreed to chat as they wanted, or did anything immoral. I kept myself free from any bad thing, or rather God and our Guru did—that fear and respect all of them have & I take good care to keep it up. I am not rich in money but I am happy and rich in my inner mind on these points. Once at a big fight, I said so—that I had the guts to fight them because I was stronger, because my wealth was in me, not in kind or how much money I had and I was not afraid of them not in the least. They could not buy me—never—and so what had I to fear? Having a majority share etc. meant nothing to me, they could not win that way!! It was funny the result—they all had tears in their eyes, and then asked my pardon!!…after that they were quite different men—kind, sympathetic, ever ready to help and then each got fond of me, they said they all felt better knowing me, which made me happy because it helped my work—and I lost none of my honour!

Bombay, 1945

17

CURTAIN CALL, 1944–45

If Svetoslav was getting impatient, the workers at the studio and the media outside were even more so. People knew that something was going to happen, but were not sure what it was and what its outcome would be.

To Devika's frustration, the three important meetings which could happen quickly and routinely were taking a long time to organise. The annual accounts for 1944 had not been reconciled as yet, so the General Body meeting could not be held. Devika was helpless, as she was dependent on others to put together the statement of accounts to present at the meeting. And it was only after that was done that she could sell her shares and resign.

Meanwhile, nothing could be announced about her and Svetoslav, or there might be turmoil at Bombay Talkies and the shareholders would be upset. If the share price collapsed, they could not issue fresh shares as they planned to do, in order to urgently inject more capital into the studio.

While she waited, questions were being asked all around.

Some had seen her with Svetoslav and wondered if they had got married, while others insisted she was still attending to work at Bombay Talkies. In the midst of all this, she was keeping an eye on their new production and was continuing to recruit actors and technicians. They still needed some new faces, since *Jwar Bhata*, with Dilip Kumar in the lead, had not done as well as she had hoped.

One possible option was Ranbir Raj Kapoor, the son of Prithviraj Kapoor, who had made a tiny appearance in *Jwar Bhata*. Devika wondered whether the good-looking, blue-eyed boy was ready for a bigger role.

She noted, from her files, that Prithviraj Kapoor had first contacted her about Raj on 27 January 1943. He had written:

> Dear Mrs Roy,
> This is just to introduce my son Raj—Ranbir Raj Kapoor. He has been working with one Kidar Sharma since March 1942 in the capacity of an assistant.
> He prays for an intern's work with yourself. Kindly grant him that and oblige.
> With Best wishes & regards
>
> Yours sincerely,
> Prithvi

She had agreed, and Prithvi, one of the stalwarts of Hindi cinema, had written back effusively. She noticed that his handwriting was very reminiscent of Svetoslav's. Did all handsome men write the same way, in this strong style with a sharp slant, she wondered idly.

The address on the letter said Navin Pictures, Kolhapur Cinetone, Kolhapur, and it was dated 12 April 1943.

> My dear Mrs Roy,
> Raj has come all the way to Kolhapur to tell me about your kind offer. He is very happy about it and I, grateful. I hope and pray that he proves worthy of this kindness, this affection, this trust.
> Wishing you the best of luck in anything and everything you do.
> With profound regards,
> I remain
>
> Yours sincerely,
> Prithvi

512-A College Road
Matunga
Bombay
27.1.43

Dear Mrs Roy,

This is just to introduce my son Raj — Ranbir Raj Kapoor. He has been working with Mr Kidar Sharma, since March 1942 — in the capacity of an assistant.

He prays for an interview with yourself — kindly grant him that and oblige.

With Best wishes & regards

Yours Sincerely

Prithvi

To
Mrs Devika Rani Roy

from Prithviraj Kapoor

That was two years ago, and Raj was doing well at Bombay Talkies in the production department. Perhaps they could do a screen test now?

She set the file aside so she could discuss it with Sachin and Amiya, then changed her mind. Perhaps she shouldn't get involved any more with production work. She would suggest it and let things be. There was no need to prove anything anymore, though she had a script in mind that might suit the boy. And since that pretty young girl, now called Madhubala would turn a teenager soon, she could be cast opposite him. Devika glanced ruefully at Himansu's photograph on the adjoining desk. Was he smiling at her? Who would have thought she too would hire young and barely educated girls as actresses? Heavens! She was doing everything that had annoyed her so much when Himansu was alive!

Sighing heavily, she got up. The pain in her abdomen had receded. She had taken 'something' to ensure her periods came on time, just as she had promised Svetoslav. She agreed with him that at their age, there was no point trying to become parents. They were both too old for it, though it would be nice to have a little child in her arms someday—a child who looked like Svetoslav, with his soft brown hair, grey-blue eyes and almost translucent skin. She had acted in at least two films that dealt with a woman's longing for a child. But this was the first time she felt the need to be a mother. She had considered it once with Amiya, but that was nothing like the desire that consumed her now. A few months ago, in March, she had written to Svetoslav when her periods were late by a few days, 'I have got something and there is no need now for worry. You were very worried in the car remember? It was the sign of the cross you [made] over me that protected us both. Dearest I did not tell you but it was late by 3 days so I took something which I will tell you about and anyway it is alright now—and I am very relieved so you should be too.'

The thought of 'their' child occurred to Svetoslav too. In June, he told her that he had dreamt about their baby. She wrote back to him, full of happiness, but also sorrow over what could not be. 'Yes what a wonderful Baby we could have had and even if we don't, the very thought that you would have like one, that you pictured our Baby—oh dearest is enough for me! It is the most sacred thought dearest husband.'

She pushed all such thoughts away now. They would only trouble her at a time when she needed all her wits about her.

Looking out of the window, she could see groups of people gathering in the evening, as they always did to discuss the next day's shoot. Once upon a time, she would have stepped out and joined them, as she had done occasionally after Himansu's death. But P. Jairaj was a competent director and she didn't want to interfere. She could see him talking animatedly with Amiya. Dilip Kumar, the hero of *Pratima*, was listening. She hoped he would get a better response with this film. Anyway, Hiten Choudhuri would soon be here to take over her office. She really had a lot to thank the two Choudhuri brothers for, especially now, as they would ensure a smooth transition after her departure.

Everything was in place thanks to her meticulous planning and management. Sachin was the manager, while Hiten would take over all her multiple roles, including that of sole producer. He was due back soon from America, where he was travelling partly on personal work, and partly to find new business opportunities for Gobindram Seksaria, Prahladrai's boss. Seksaria, a rich Marwari businessman, had deep pockets, and Hiten would need to stay on his right side to ensure that some of his funds came to Bombay Talkies. As of now, due to her good relations with Prahladrai, Devika had managed to get all her suggestions accepted. She would sometimes spend hours with him, trying to find solutions for the problems plaguing the studio. She was hopeful that Hiten, with his affable personality and charming manners, would enjoy the same relationship with Prahladrai, and through him, with Seksaria. Telegrams and letters flew back and forth between Devika and Hiten as she guided him on the matter of which businesses the Seksarias might be interested in representing in India.

But what she really wanted now was to have the board meeting, so she could sell her shares and join Svetoslav in their new life. She was surprised at her own detachment as she looked at the huge complex she and Himansu had built. There was nothing she wanted from it. Everything would remain here, just as it was, even Himansu's photograph.

She was confident that things would carry on the way they always had. Nothing ever changed, did it? There would always be new scandals and new worries to deal with—like the present one about Swarnalata, a rising starlet who had been recently employed by the studio.

Pratima had Swarnalata in the lead opposite Dilip Kumar. Devika had herself selected the fresh-faced Sikh girl who had gained many admirers with her earlier film, *Rattan*. Devika had noticed that she seemed a little headstrong and also that she was spending more time with her former leading man Nazir than perhaps she should. Then she heard from Amiya that Swarnalata's husband was behaving atrociously and physically abusing her. Exactly the sort of thing she had hoped would never happen again at Bombay Talkies, Devika thought grimly. But then, the studio is only a microcosm of society, isn't it, she asked Amiya. Why should it be any different? And who was she to say anything? Wasn't she constantly the focus of gossip as well?

The longer she took to leave, the more the rumour-mills churned, but she could do nothing about that. She was still the controller of production and the sole producer. The workers would become insecure if she tried to exit hastily. She could leave only after Hiten took over following his American trip. He was looking for some new trading agencies to add value to Gobindram Seksaria's company, as she had suggested. Once that was done, she hoped Seksaria would not object to him taking over from her.

As usual, Devika was two steps ahead of everyone else. What Manto and some others described as 'calculating' was a well-honed survival strategy. She had learned that being spontaneous and unthinking could land her into trouble. She had to plan and think ahead about the consequences of her actions to navigate the pitfalls of life. And one of the things that stood her in good stead was a simple understanding of human nature—if someone was obliged to you, it was unlikely that they would be nasty when you needed them.

And yet, the problems remained. Though she brushed any danger of physical attack aside, she had to be careful because Prahladrai did not want any disruption before the General Body meeting.

She wrote to Svetoslav:

> I feel more longing than you—the reason perhaps i say this is—you are free, you are not tied to anything like this, you more or less are able to do what you wish—it is in your hands. That is not my position, it is in my hands to push, to fight, never to waver, to lead them, to find a way out, but I have to get out of these things—carefully so that I can get my freedom forever and therefore the pressure, the strong longing is perhaps more. I feel desperate and yet with all my nerves I have to steer as if my brain was cool—and on top of it see that 475 men are in working order & see that a motion picture is completed and see the next one is started. All this is simultaneously with the "S" [Shiraz, who was to buy her shares] business so that after the General Body meeting no one can say "but you should complete this or that...

But Svetoslav was beginning to be worried about her meetings at home with men, even if they were Prahladrai or Sachin. He also wanted her to curtail her drinking. He was possessive about her and she indulged him.

'Your request that I should not drink my dearest, I never do—I keep it for the guests and even when I have guests in my house I never touch it.' She explained defensively that when he saw her drinking vodka at the house of a Russian acquaintance, it was just a sip. And only because they were raising a toast to Svetoslav and Russia.

'My one real sin, which I am going to leave slowly from next week is smoking—that is a definite habit and to give it up perhaps will be at first a little difficult but I told Mia today that I would start slowly to cut them.' It was not something she would be able to do, however, and would smoke for most of her life.

She knew Svetoslav was putting down all these rules because he was actually very perturbed over her safety. 'I can't stop rumours and prevent Baby from making a scene and this can only be helped and prevented if they hurry matters,' Devika told Svetoslav. She requested him to curb his impatience while she restrained her own. They had to be careful, she said, lest she, his 'Bengal Tiger', his 'Bundle', his 'Brown Fellow' suddenly burst out 'when it's supposed to be a perfect well mannered lady'.

She added:

Prahladrai swears he wants it [the share transfer] finished as it is getting on his nerves too & he knows that I mean it, as Shiraz has already signed that offer letter of ours. I don't want to be unpleasant or upset them because I am still under contract to them and they can be nasty if they want.

'Shiraz' was Shiraz Ali Hakim, who had agreed to buy Devika's shares and signed the offer letter.

Hakim was the extremely ambitious owner of Famous Cine Studio at Mahalaxmi. The studio had been constructed by Shapoorji, a wealthy builder. Everyone was impressed with its design and knew that Shiraz had the capacity to raise large sums of money. He could be a good partner to have on the board of HIT and Bombay Talkies.

Shiraz had also just begun work with K. Asif on an ambitious new production, *Mughal-e-Azam*. Sachin was in touch with him, and it was Hiten who suggested that their new actor, Dilip Kumar, could play the lead role in the film. The suggestion was rejected by Shiraz, who thought that D.K. Sapru was much better suited to play Salim. The young rising star, Nargis, was slated to play Anarkali. Then, in a twist of fate, Shiraz left for Pakistan after Partition, and K. Asif completed the film, with two Bombay Talkies stars in the lead—Dilip Kumar and Madhubala. The film would turn out to be one of Hindi cinema's biggest hits ever!

Both Prahladrai and his boss Seksaria had identified Shiraz as the best person to take Devika's shares since he would support them. Now that Seksaria had control of Bombay Talkies, with the young Prahladrai as chair, it was important that the board meetings and the studio continued to run smoothly even after Devika left.

A canny businessman, Prahladrai probably sensed that she would not return, though she kept reassuring him she would. They both knew there were still a few years left in her work contract with Bombay Talkies. If the board wished, they could stop her from leaving, or else withhold her payments. All kinds of worries spun around in her mind. How excited she had been to sign that contract. Now, it was like a chain that bound her. Annoyed, she lit a cigarette.

Her marriage with Himansu had taught her the hard lesson that women need to be financially independent. So, yes, she wanted the money from the sale of the shares and she wanted the board to give her the money that was due to her—even the fees she earned as a managing agent. She wanted to do what Sir Chimanlal and Keshavlal Mody had done—they had sold their shares to the next incumbent and then left. It was a neat deal, it gave the departing person some liquidity, and also ensured continuity in the studio. She did not want Bombay Talkies to collapse or the livelihood of the workers to suffer. Many of them had been loyal workers for over ten years.

She sat down and wrote a few notes for Sachin and Amiya. She also wrote to Hiten. But the stress, and a recent bout of fever, did not help. For Svetoslav she separately noted down what she had heard from different people at the studio:

> 1) I'm going to America, 2) going round the world, 3) selling my shares, 4) [someone [is] buying me out, 5) going to set up another studio, 6) going to be a government person, 7) going to act in a foreign film, 8) going to have a farm, 9) only going for a month's leave, 10) may make [a] production myself, 11) I

am buying them out, 12) I may leave films altogether, 13) I may make shorts, 14) may have lab of mine with Seksaria money, 15) very pally with big people, 16) may get foreign money, 17) may go to England and settle down there—these are today's rumours told [to] me at the studio.

At least this proved her versatility, she said nonchalantly at the end of the letter. Clearly, everyone thought she had a lot of options.

To complicate matters, Svetoslav had again told her that he wished to come to Bombay. Once more, using all her skills of lovemaking through long and romantic letters, she requested him to stay in Kulu. His presence would definitely reveal her plans to the board members. She could not risk it.

To get him to understand, in between paragraphs of passionate prose, she explained that she could not move on anything till the annual accounts statement was presented. It seemed like such a trivial matter, but she suspected that one of the auditors, N.M. Raiji, may have been paid to delay the task. He was not satisfied with the balance sheet, and did not approve of the expenditure of around ₹1.68 lakh on publicity. Devika had been adamant about the proper advertising of Bombay Talkies films and Sachin had personally supervised the activity. There was no question of rejecting the expenditure. It was essential—if they did not market the films, how would the audience come?

Prahladrai felt she should not argue about it and was a little annoyed that she was trying to bring the accounts meeting forward. To make peace, she presented him with a gilt-edged edition of the Gita. In these fraught times, at least someone was trying to help her!

She knew Prahladrai was already under pressure, having to arrange an income-tax payment of at least ₹2 crore, a vast sum of money at the time. This must be, she guessed without him spelling it out, tax on Seksaria's income. It was enough to preoccupy any man, so after a few requests, she stopped asking him about the meeting.

There was little that anyone could do till the auditors were satisfied. She realised that no one could hurry the pace. She could not speak to Seth Maneklal Chunilal Shah, who was now the chairperson, to call for the meeting of Bombay Talkies, because that would make him wonder why she was nervous about a routine accounting process which was to be presented on 5 July.

On 11 May 1945, Devika wrote:

> Sachin is at it again today. This accountant wants to put a note that he does not agree, so that the attention of the shareholders is drawn. This cannot be allowed—[Prahladrai] does not want to show his impatience, because he says he will on no account allow any of us to show that we are anxious for the G.B. meeting, as it may be that this accountant is being paid to trouble. If we hold tight, he may give in, really feeling there is nothing wrong whatever, [that] it was not true. P. Rai says any false step now is very bad and may ruin the issue of shares at par—and that is the first things isn't it [that we have to do]—and then the HIT shares?

Everyone was telling her to wait, including Sachin, and she felt like a 'caged tigress, wild, quiet, as if I could kill—or do something desperate'. Svetoslav teasingly told her that he had desired a Bengal tiger at the age of two, and now he had a tigress of his own.

While the tension mounted at Bombay Talkies, her romance flourished. According to Devika, her mother 'confessed' for the first time ever that she had always wished for her to have someone like Svetoslav in her life. If true, it meant that mother and daughter were becoming close again. In all the years with Himansu, she had barely met her family. In any case, the marriage had gone sour within seven years, and lasted only eleven. But this time around, she said, her mother was looking forward to meeting Svetoslav in Subuthu, where she lived. In her twenty-third letter to him, she wrote:

> But she lives very simply... we are simple country folk originally and are so now too. We are not rich either, and have nothing of value with us. Your Bunny and Bunny's mother are simple and have no big things, they can only love you with their life.

She was sure that her mother would worship him 'absolutely'.

However, this turned out to be just a face-saver, because Leela Choudhuri's letter to her prospective son-in-law was anything but effusive. This may have been because she remembered the earlier time when Devika had not even told her about her marriage to Himansu, and she had learnt about it from others. For many years after that, they had barely been in touch. Seeing how close Svetoslav was to his family, Devika wanted to connect with her own brother and mother. Perhaps she wanted Svetoslav to think well of her, and show him that her family and she shared a caring relationship.

Leela's letter on 10 July 1945, from Fife Lodge, House 24, Subuthu, in the Simla Hills, thanked Svetoslav for the photographs he had sent. Addressing him as 'Mr Roerich' she said:

> Devika is perfectly right in her description of you.
> It is so kind of you to think of sending me some fruit from your orchards. I am sure they are delicious! But I am writing to request you not to send me any, as they may be damaged or stolen in transit—Devika sent me a parcel last month and I have not received it! I do not know what it was as she did not tell me in her letter. The railway authorities do not seem to be able control these matters nowadays.

She said she was looking forward to seeing Svetoslav, but she was afraid he would find it 'muggy and warm after Kulu'.

The letter was not one excitedly welcoming a future son-in-law—there were no blessings of any kind for sure. However, Devika was at pains to explain to Svetoslav how close she was to her mother:

> [I] ever told Mother all my mistakes freely & she has been wonderful as a real friend & guide—about Rai's tempers or the real ugly things. She told me a really wonderful thing when I was 17 years old "Live & learn, but do not live my child to unlearn!! Death is better." [She meant that death is better than degradation.]

> Fifs Lodge. House 24
> Subathu
> Simla Hills
> July 10th 1945. Punjab —
>
> Dear Mr Roerich,
> Your letter of the 5th instant enclosing the photographs came yesterday — Ever so many thanks — I was delighted to receive them. Devika is perfectly right in her description of you — It is so kind of you to think of sending me some fruit from your Orchards. I am sure they are delicious! But I am writing to request you <u>not</u> to send.

As she waited for the final resolution at the studio, Devika kept up with her social commitments. The sexual banter in her letters to Svetoslav began bordering on the risqué, and may have been meant to keep her anxious fiancé engaged while he waited for their wedding day, but the letters also provide an insight into the swinging Bombay of the 1940s. Every night she would lie in bed, writing to him till 3 a.m., either about their own romance or about a city where cosmopolitan as well as conservative couples were rethinking the boundaries of their sexual life.

Being a widow gave Devika a chance to become the confidante of a wide variety of women, and much of what she heard made her tell Svetoslav frankly that this was definitely not the kind of married life she wanted. There was an awful lot of 'tolerance' in most marriages, according to her girlfriends:

> They say…that their husbands come to them, hardly talk to them & in a matter of fact way just do something or other and

then go to sleep. My friends say it is awful & they hate this part of married life, that's why some of them get a thrill by living with other men & some of them [are] disgusted.

She wrote about a pregnant friend who was angry that her husband still wanted sex, and another who enjoyed sex, especially when her husband was drunk. She told Svetoslav about her companion, Mia, who stayed with her off and on, that 'Brigette Masani & Mia had a funny night the other day—so Mia told me the next day.'

Brigette Masani, Dr Masani's Swedish wife, had unfortunately contracted tuberculosis. She invited Mia over one evening.

It was like this, Mia was invited to dinner and at bedtime, she was up in Brigette's room, there Brigette stays since her TB & she had a double bed—and at the end of the room there was a diwan made for Mia, and then they changed.

Both of them were in diaphanous nighties, when in came the husband, Dr Masani. Mia asked for a dressing gown, and was finally given one.

Then Brigette, Mia and he sort of lay…in the double bed. As Brigette asked Mia to come & have a last [cigarette] with her and she would read poems—1st was Brigette, 2nd Mia and 3rd Brigette's husband & suddenly as the poems were being read the husband started putting his hand over Mia & caressing her & Mia objected & then Brigette said 'Oh Mia he is lonely he wants just to be petted' & then turned to her husband & said 'Why do you keep your coat on', & he said 'Because Mia may not like so much hair on my chest' & then Brigette said nonsense, take it off & he did & and then put his head on Mia's chest.

Masani then tried to get more intimate with Mia, but she managed to get off the bed. But, as she told a somewhat bemused

Devika, 'They both, husband and wife, take all this quite in a normal way... strangely enough husband and wife are devoted to each other.'

Devika was taken aback as she had known the couple for years and had always found them 'awfully fond of each other'. She chastised Mia for becoming part of a menage-a-trois, saying that she had allowed herself to be violated. She told Mia that she would not have allowed a man to rest his head on her breast if she had known real love, because 'then is not even one hour of it, an inspiration to keep clear of dirt, to keep sweet, so that when [love] comes again and this time in all its power, you will give & give & give with all you have—sweet and clean.' It was as though, while discussing the affair with a 'saintlike' Svetoslav, she wanted to redraw the boundaries on acceptable behaviour, quite wiping out her own past flirtations and misdemeanours. She wanted that he thought of her as someone who respected the institution of marriage. Svetoslav assured her, over and over, that he adored her. Her past was irrelevant, and she should only focus on their life together. On her part, she had been truthful and honest with him—as much as it was possible to be.

Fortunately, Svetoslav, up in the mountains, had heard little and knew even less about these things, though some of his friends, such as Dhirubhai Desai (the Congress politician Bhulabhai Desai's son) had tried to give him a warning, and tried to raise questions about her which she angrily dismissed. She pointed out that these matters arose from 'Dhiru's' own frustration that she did not come to him to seek his help. Men like him could not tolerate an independent woman, while they themselves behaved differently.

She wrote with great sarcasm that did he think their relationship would impact Indo-Russian ties? When she was, after all, a 'well known actress', proud of her career. What a mistake it would be for 'you of old Russia, should you marry this thing—this actress—who has appeared for years on the screen, whose face is quite familiar with some of the public...' Shouldn't then Svetoslav 'meditate on the grave responsibility which will be yours'?

She continued in the same teasingly ironic tone, listing out the problems he was likely to face:

1. How are you going to put up with it?
2. What will be the social and other troubles?
3. Will your friends forsake you?
4. Will the British officials object?
5. Will the Muslim League object?
6. Will Congress object?
7. Will all the social and cultural societies on which you are President object or reject?
8. What will the Princes of States do—or rather the Princesses? Will they still want their portraits?
9. Then there are all the religious sects! including Bengal etc, in fact North South East West! the lot—my word it is stunning what they may think!
10. Will the name of your family suffer?
11. Will in any way your family suffer? Having an Indian Brahmin girl of Bengal as your little wife?

She told him not to be angry and to treat her questions as something she made up as she went along—just like she would spontaneously dance and sing in the car and then kiss him when they were together. She 'kissed' him now, too, in her letter.

Once again, she told Svetoslav that while she worshipped him, she was only sorry that she came to him so late:

> Scarred, not as I was as a girl, how I wish you could have taken me as I was then. My dearest my heart pains so when I think I am giving you who are so wonderful a broken thing like me—tainted, scarred, beaten, rough—oh dearest it is so good of you to take me like this…

She wished she could have been just a 'pure, sweet, flower girl, fresh and clean for you'.

However, certain things were still beyond her control.

Swarnalata, the heroine of *Pratima*, fell pregnant, and her husband refused to believe that the child was his. On 6 May, Devika wrote:

> Swarnalata is going to divorce her husband. She is pregnant, 3½ months, the husband says he does not know whose child it is, his or Nazir's, the man she is in love with. He beats her and during this she has lost blood and has held up our production. She will be alright by Thursday. She says her husband is a real brute, even when they were on good terms, he would force her all at once to submit to him, & immediately he was satisfied he would just leave her.... She is only 24 years old, and therefore suffers from nerves greatly. She told me this on Friday. She was feeling very ill then.

Soon after this, Swarnalata lost her child while the shoot was still going on. Devika said with the stoic tone of any producer:

> I just got a phone call that Swarnalata started bleeding badly and she is going to be operated, or rather cleaned up of the baby she had—that means she can't work for 15 days for sure which will hamper the finishing of our picture. But we will get through.

Eventually, Swarnalata married Nazir and changed her name to Sayeeda Bano. After Partition, they moved to Pakistan and carried on acting in films.

Devika herself had helped many women like Swarnalata—so many girls who had gone 'off' and were no good—which was another reason why she often felt she was no longer the 'clean, pure' girl she used to be. She said, 'I have washed and given douches to so many suffering kids, with doctors instructions, rubber gloves, Lysol, Dettol.'

She spoke of how difficult it was for actresses, even when they had their normal monthly period, surrounded by men who knew nothing of the agony they were going through. There was very little sympathy for them, though schedules were strenuous and there were few secrets. Many of the girls who joined were very young and sometimes, to their deep embarrassment, they would attain puberty in front of a crowd of men, not many of whom were understanding. Occasionally, Devika too would suffer cramps just before her period, but work carried on:

> And sometimes I had to act for long hours [and be] on my feet. Once it was for 14 days and nights. I acted & never slept and was bleeding all the time, glasses of blood, but carried on, acting, dancing till the 15th morning & my work was done. I came home and fell down unconscious and bleeding like anything. After that of course I had rest and good treatment—only injections.

Through these narratives, she also wanted to make sure that there was no question of Svetoslav wanting her to work anymore or asking her to stay on in Bombay. She had suffered enough, she was 'broken'.

The good news was that Hiten was ready to take over from her as the production controller. Both he and his brother shared one quality with the late Himansu—they loved to live well, and moved in the best circles, whether they could afford it or not. In 1940, after Himansu died (and possibly before he passed away as well) Hiten always helped her. His friends remembered how wealthy he became over time, eventually owning a large bungalow in Pali Hill. Unfortunately, most of his fortune dissipated, thanks to his tendency to befriend the wrong kind of people and his generosity with everything he owned.

By May 1945, Devika was looking forward to handing over the reins to Hiten. She said excitedly:

> He has to play a part in my leaving, he has to take over my job and has to like it!! Of course he knows something because I sent him a wire to America about the job. He will of course do anything for me—without question and without expecting anything—really speaking he is my best friend in India [all] of these years here.

Hiten was the same age as Devika, but she felt that he respected her, treated her like a sister and a 'pal'. He had always consulted her before doing anything, and she had never asked him for anything, apart from friendship. She said:

> He has of course a most charming nature, clean and honest, perfect manners, very good education, good experience of life, a good "mixer" in society, quite attractive to women because I suppose he keeps clean, you know these society ladies how they throw themselves about? I hear all about them from him (he seldom mentions their names and I don't ask) but he has often said just on the phone "Can I come and stay with you for tonight and the weekend? I have to be out of Bombay tonight, as someone is insisting I go to dine, please allow me to come."

She pointed out how much he was loved, and that he knew everybody, including directors in her company like Prahladrai. She added that he 'was a great favourite of the Poet [Rabindranath Tagore]' and that he came from the same sort of clan as she did. 'I came to know him 11 years ago, and strange to say, he felt he knew me so well.'

Lest their relationship be misunderstood, she added that he had been 'very unfortunate in love...the girl he so madly loves for years is his cousin and she loves him too, but she is married.' Similarly, she revealed that Sachin was in love with the journalist Margaret Pope.

Devika felt that Hiten had gauged how lonely she was. One evening, while they were having dinner, he told her:

> Mrs Rai, I wish only one thing. It is that you could love and be loved by a wonderful man, a really wonderful man who would marry you, care for you, give you peace, comfort, happiness. I do feel you need it so. You are the type who needs a home—you love beauty, home, all the gentle things. To go on as you do, with these rough people, to work as you do, it is slowly killing your

heart. I hope someday you may get to know some wonderful man, but he must be wonderful.

The brothers were able to give the two lovers, Devika and Svetoslav, some space in Sachin's flat whenever they wanted to hide from prying eyes. She remembered one day when Svetoslav and she had made love on the sofa in Sachin's flat:

> How happy we were! What does [anything] matter beloved when we are together, it's you I want absolutely!!
> You can't imagine what happiness you have given me. And what peace and what joy! Like a worn flower I was and you have picked it up from the road from the glare from being trodden on and given it life. It grows again your flower, its life depends on you entirely for life—yes dearest, it is true absolutely. I am and shall be what you make me, a model of yours, reborn in a new form, remoulded by you—entirely your creation, entirely given life by you...The great artist that you are of art, of love, of life...

She exclaimed to Svetoslav that his best creation would be his wife, whose heart would beat as one with his.

She was careful to send all her letters and telegrams to be posted by Yeswent, her driver, all the way to Bandra, as she was worried about the gossip if he was spotted. In the endlessly long, romantic letters, she said:

> [We will build] the most Perfect Life of harmony, unity, great achievements and we shall make all effort to reach that better glory of nirvana so that our souls as one will light the way while we live, and [in the] after life we shall join the light as one ray of perfection.

Instead of the very physical and somewhat tawdry life she had led at Bombay Talkies, now suddenly there were higher ideals to aspire to, and she began to recall her own roots, her family, especially her father. When she wrote to Svetoslav, she constantly referred to her inner world, and as she delved deeper and deeper into it, she found hidden links and meanings. Some of Svetoslav's mysticism began to rub off on her too. She wrote:

> Because of our suffering we have been given each other as a reward to be happy, really, and to better ourselves and attain that bliss which comes of love divine, as spiritual beings of higher attainment... two merged into one.

She was an actress, after all, and an intelligent one. It was almost as though she was re-scripting her life—as a higher spiritual being who had been trapped in a bad karmic cycle. She airbrushed out of it all previous entanglements—Himansu, Najam, Amiya.

Fortunately for her, with Svetoslav, she could paint the picture she wanted. Though a seasoned artist, he would not be able to scrape off what lay beneath each layer. Her life was already complicated enough to completely absorb him and make him sympathetic towards her. He could see that she was alone as she battled for 'honour'. He also understood how poorly women were treated at home and at work. The most important thing was that he believed her and in her—and respected her, not just as a woman, but for what she had achieved. And these words reassured Devika—she had, in her young life, rarely heard open appreciation of her identity as a working woman, and her work. Even when she told Svetoslav about her working as a 'make-up' girl on Bond street, he showered praise on her, saying that he admired all she had done, because it showed her spirit and her independent nature.

For his sake, she wanted her own spiritual evolution to be shaped in the right way. On 28 May 1945, she wrote that she wanted him to pray to his guru and to Lakshmi, with the appropriate rituals, to help speed up their marriage. He should ask his guru with complete 'poise & happiness'. She said:

> Please do this for us with purity, and only after your Bath at night or morning—one has to be completely clean & without shoes

or leather on, take a few flowers, one red rose, place it on a clean thali, a little rice, & kum kum and jasmine if you can get it, a little camphor, incense sticks or camphor will do, burn the camphor first, and just sit and watch the flame. This purifies the air, and then dearest, say OM, & his name & think of him & when you picture him clearly, then ask him. Don't think the flower etc. is heathen worship—it is not, these are only symbols of Lakshmi and creation and purity and it gives just that preparation to the mind and sort of attracts and attunes one to the best elements of creation and clears any evil mind nearby. By one's own mind one sends out a vibration of rhythm and harmony which travels and calls forth that which you want.

This was indeed very far from her life in the studio!

Despite their love and their professed modernity, Svetoslav wanted to see if their horoscopes matched. There were a stressful few days before she heard the result from him. She wrote with great relief on 28 May 1945:

> I am so happy to hear I have a good horoscope, and that we have stars and aspects alike, that shows we were meant for each other and shall build ever a wonderful life and that you have a "fine" wife.

At Bombay Talkies, meanwhile, things were finally beginning to move. All her problems seemed to pale before her persistence, but not without an occasional storm.

At last, on 5 July, the previous year's accounts were passed at a meeting at 6 p.m. at the registered office of Bombay Talkies at Readymoney Mansions. The meeting was chaired by Seth Maneklal Chunilal Shah and attended by Prahladrai, Devika, Girdharlal Karsondas Fozdar and D.R. Parker. It seemed the auditor, N.M. Raiji, who had caused the delay, had a change of heart and felt that the 'little lady' must be helped. He had withdrawn his objections to the amount spent on publicity and advertisements. Moreover, the company had achieved a turnaround, and a profit of ₹1,46,761. They were able to pay a dividend, as well as a bonus of around ₹35,000 to the workers at Devika's 'insistence'.

Devika's own performance at the meeting was fiery. She had wanted to put certain facts on the table and, after this endless wait for approval, decided to do so. She told Svetoslav the next day, 6 July:

> I am in rather a strange mood am I not? Like a caged tigress, hungry, without food & God help anyone who tries to do any funny business now!! Prahladrai said after the meeting "I never saw in your eyes that fire before. Anyone looking at your eyes alone would not dare say a word! That is why after you spoke to your ex-employee, no one had the courage. I, myself felt very timid!"

She had understandably pulled up the auditor and the accounts department for having needlessly delayed the meeting. She told Svetoslav that his love, God, and their destiny gave her immense courage. With all the years of experience behind her, she let the troublemaker have it 'good & strong':

> Point by point I slashed him for ten minutes in front of all, & they were surprised... every man I felt in my grip as one does on stage, the power over people one can feel it, isn't it? He just sat down & after I finished there was dead silence. I then broke it myself, & called the man to me—it was good, it made people feel that I had no ill will but merely discussed as a responsible director facts and after that all was forgotten!! & that broke the meeting & that made them all happy to agree quickly. How it all happened I don't know—but I am like that. I never know before, and don't try to. I always feel that God will help...
>
> I have practised for many years, as don't forget dearest I was alone & that developed this very strongly, this faith, and specially because of the extraordinary life I led.

Having established her reputation once again, very strongly, she left the men overawed by her performance. It was a good time to leave, she thought, while still on a high.

Actually, just a month before the balance sheet was to be presented, Devika had been thinking of a grand exit—with a wonderful new production called *The Day of Victory*, representing her own sentiments perhaps. In her letter to Svetoslav she said:

> Dearest today I got a perfect Title for the production, the one I shall start, the one [with which] I shall leave my career for good, and go to my new life with joy and perfect peace, victory and happiness—'The Festival of Dessara' is the happy link in the story and we have called it 'Vijaya Dashami', 'The Day of Victory' is it not fine? I shall be so at peace now—because all along I wanted a fine and apt title and like an inspiration it came to Narendra, that little man who you met and who is the 2nd best Hindi poet in the country.

As *Pratima* was almost finished, she said, she could now get the script written for the new film, and have it directed by Jairaj.

But this was not to happen. During a Bombay Talkies board meeting on 18 July 1945, it came out that perhaps the situation over the next three months was not so rosy. The directors who were present at the meeting were Seth Maneklal Chunilal, JP; G.K. Fozdar, Esq; D.K. Parker, Esq; and Devika Rani Rai. Also in attendance was Sachin Chaudhuri.

The company's bank balance, it turned out, was less than ₹5,000. The expected revenue for the quarter was ₹6,15,000, whereas the expected expenses were over ₹10 lakh. The estimated position for the next three months was presented, but no one on the board was overly worried. They were all businessmen and 'gamblers' who knew the situation could be turned around with just one hit film. The only creative person on the board was Devika, and she was not disheartened either. She had already been looking for ways to refinance the company. She had seen Himansu go through a financial crunch far too often. But what the others (except Sachin) did not know was that she would not be around for much longer to continue to steer the company's fortunes. Even Prahladrai was under the impression that she was going on a six-month vacation. Devika did not want to disturb the status quo till she had offloaded her shares.

The financial position over the next quarter was presented thus:

Cash in the bank	₹5,000
Minimum guarantee to be received for *Pratima*	₹4,37,000
Soviet Film Distributors for lab work	₹20,000
Government for royalty for films supplied	₹33,000
Receipts from old pictures for three months	₹1,20,000
Total receipts during the quarter	₹6,15,000

The expenses were:

Pratima publicity	₹1,00,000
Salary and overhead for 3 months	₹3,60,000
Bonus	₹45,000
Purchases	₹1,00,000
Income tax, 1943	₹1,17,000
Managing agents commission	₹3,40,000
Total expenses during the quarter	₹10,62,000

The expenses were finely balanced as long as the managing agents' commission and the publicity expenses could be kept in abeyance, and this must have been obvious to all.

As the company had already borrowed ₹5 lakh in March, it was decided that instead of borrowing more, the way forward was to allot preference and ordinary shares out of the company's remaining unissued capital of ₹10 lakh. For this, permission would be sought from the Government of India, for subscribing and allotting 300 cumulative preference shares of ₹100 each and 3,953 ordinary shares of ₹100 each. The minutes of the meeting stated:

> As this would be an allotment of the balance of the issued capital in terms of the Prospectus issued, it was resolved that the allotment should be made on the terms and conditions contained in the Prospectus.

This meant that, as stated in the Prospectus, it would be a private issue and each subscriber would pay ₹10 per share on application, ₹15 on allotment, and the remaining amount would be 'called up in sums not exceeding ₹25/- at such intervals as the Directors may fix'.

The managing agents were now instructed to take the matter forward with the government. The onus fell on Devika, and ever the trouper, she started the process. She was aware that once she left, the next steps would be up to Prahladrai—or Shiraz Ali Hakim, who would soon be invited to join the HIT board in her place.

Things were finally speeding up.

On 15 August 1945, a meeting of the board of directors of HIT was called to formally approve transfer of Devika's shares to Shiraz Ali Hakim, as had already been agreed by Prahladrai. On 18 August, at 5 p.m., there was another meeting of the board. The directors present, according to the minutes, were Prahladrai Brijlal, Seth Maneklal Chunilal Shah and Mrs Devika Rani Rai. Sachin Choudhuri was in attendance.

After the profit-and-loss statement of 1944 had been approved, the minutes stated:

> Mrs Devika Rani Rai handed over to the Board her letter dated 18th August, 1945, addressed to the Chairman requesting that she be relieved from her contract with The Bombay Talkies, Ltd, and from her post of Controller of Productions.

Her request was accepted. A resolution was accordingly passed:

> The Board greatly appreciated the handsome acknowledgement made by Mrs Devika Rani Rai of the consideration, co-

operation, kindness and sympathy she had received from the Chairman of both Companies and from their Directors. [The Board] took this opportunity of thanking Mrs Devika Rani Rai for the unfailing courtesy and co-operation extended to the Chairman of the two companies and their Directors by her all these years.

With this, and without regret, Devika ended her association with Bombay Talkies. She was richer than she had ever been. An amount of almost ₹40,000 was transferred to her account the next day, and more was expected to follow. She was free, and able to start her new life with some liquidity.

To add to her happiness, she received a letter from Svetoslav's mother, stating that the Great Guru, whom they believed in, had blessed her. She wrote:

> My Dearest Devika
>
> You are right in writing that the great aura of Love around you protected you during the meeting and somehow reached the participants and made them more human.
>
> Your loving call directed to the Great Guru certainly reached him and intensified the magnetism of your own.
>
> The Blessed Ones lend their ear to pure thoughts. Is it not said "The call of love will bring the answer from the beloved. There is no greater power than love."

Devika had already begun to pack, and as always, she shared the details in a long letter to Svetoslav. The trunk would be sent in advance. She was leaving a few things for Hiten at her home, since he would not only be taking over the job, he would also be shifting into 57, Dady Seth Road, where she had lived ever since she arrived with Himansu from London. So much had happened during this very eventful decade! Before she closed the trunk, she wrote:

> My beloved husband
>
> Today I did lots of work, I packed all things for my brother, books, silver, China, [a little] brass, all things which [are]

impossible to carry about and tomorrow I send also old embroidery linen, of our old times. There was not much, but it's nice only because it was used when we were young. My mother hasn't kept anything—she sent to my brother mainly… I sent mother a few things she wanted me to get for her too.

Just ordinary useful things I've kept for Hiten's use, poor fellow. It's not much or nice, but it will do—and all he needs anyway.

There was a separate box for Kulu:

I have packed my first box too for home—old photos, a few bits of silver, little plates etc., which I use, files since you asked me to keep any data which you want. It is not much, we threw lots of stuff away, it was too much carrying it about…

Beloved one… it is such a wonderful feeling & I felt so happy! To shut the box!! it's a steel one, my father put his regimental clothes in. It is quite ordinary but I like it because steel is strong and my father had it when he was 25!! It's awful the way things last with us—the family has that habit of keeping things well. I honestly get fed up, even my clothes dearest, they last and last!

When one is a widow in Bengal white is worn as you know—these my mother gave me—you know Rai never gave me clothes? I couldn't wear them, one or two yes, and ordinary petticoats and blouses I had to buy but other things all my mother sent every six months, even night suits, material, bangles, the smallest things. Anyway, let's see, I shall bring all my clothes and what you don't like me in, or what you don't want me to wear, we shall at once discard, and then you can dress me as you wish—all the things and the way you would consider best and graceful, and pretty for your wife. Simple things look best on me I feel, but I want you to decide. Being an actress for about 8 years, steady, one role after another, I can't fix my mind as to what to wear—it's got muddled you know? Because I really lived most of the parts and they were varied from a Bhil girl to an 'Achchut', to a Sati Savitri to Society to a dancing girl, to an old woman, heavens dearest so many lives they were! So I hadn't much time to concentrate anywhere else, only of that particular role, which as you know takes all one's time and energy.

She told Svetoslav that she would dress the way he wanted her to. She said she would wear whatever he wanted, become what he wanted. This would be her greatest role.

Excited that she was leaving Bombay Talkies forever, she picked up the small altar of St Anthony's and wrapped it carefully with her Lakshmi.

She couldn't wait.

Letter from Devika to Svetoslav

Your Bunny at any cost must be a completely well Bunny in every way, clean and sweet for you. Her body must be as nice as possible for you and she must smell sweet of sandal and be just what you will love—her whole self dearest is yours, completely dedicated to you, all faults must be therefore corrected and corrected properly. I am very strict with your Bunny now, and see she does only those things which may improve her—mentally, spiritually, bodily.

God in his Infinite mercy has given me my life, new, completely new. Never have I known such beauty, and now having his love, which is you my dearest heart, I must live up to it. I must live up to it and treasure it. I must build it, when I say 'I' it means we...one and together as sacred in our marriage in our church before Jesus our Lord, we shall make it our treasure. None shall come to know our Temple, our worshipping place, our bond, they can only be able to see the light which will shine as an inspiration. God has brought us together and married us because He wishes our love to shine and bring hope to many a lonely soul, to make many a broken heart feel that goodness is still in this world, love is still possible, marriage can still be a wonderful thing.

Bombay, 1945

EPILOGUE, 1945–1994

Finally, after the long struggle, having sorted out everything at Bombay Talkies and defeated her enemies almost single-handedly, Devika was free. She married Svetoslav on 23 August 1945, in Bombay.

Though Svetoslav was a well-known artist, the headlines were all about Devika—'Miss Devika Rani Remarried, Honeymoon in the Himalayas'.

The announcement had been carefully drafted by Svetoslav before being sent to the media. He knew that there would be a lot of interest around the world in this marriage between the families of the Tagores and the Roerichs.

The papers mentioned that the actress and the artist had got married on Thursday. 'Mr Roerich, who has established a considerable reputation as a portrait painter in this country, is a son of the world-famous Russian painter, Professor Nicholas Roerich, who for many years has made his home in the Kulu Valley.'

They said that Svetoslav had earned his reputation painting his father, and had held his first exhibition in New York, in 1923. He had later become the director of New York's International Art Centre, but 'had lately spent most of his time in India'.

Similarly, Devika's lineage was mentioned—as the daughter of the distinguished doctor, Lt Col M.N. Choudhuri, and a great grand-niece of Rabindranath Tagore. They said she was 'educated in England, where she had her first contact with the screen as a film architect. She appeared with her late husband, Himansu Rai, in her first film, *Karma* which was produced in English and Hindi.'

The papers also mentioned that from 1934, till Himansu's death in 1940, she had worked on the 'formation and conduct of Bombay Talkies...one of the first of India's modern film studios'. The brief report did not mention her life subsequently, up to the time she met Svetoslav—those crucial five years in which she almost lost everything and then rebuilt her life with grit and determination. This was a story that few would try to report or narrate, and now that she had left that world, Devika simply shrugged and left everyone to judge for themselves who she was and what she had achieved.

The announcement was brief and to the point, but that was the way they wanted it. Devika could not wait to begin her new life in the mountains, where she was greeted with garlands and love, and drawn into the folds of the eccentric and gifted Russian family. Overnight, from being alone in her struggles, she found a mother, a father, a brother—and a uniquely peaceful environment, where she could wake up, as she had dreamt of doing for so long, to the sound of a flowing river. During the day, she could walk hand-in-hand with

Svetoslav on the mountain pathways. Away from the pressures of Bombay Talkies, she could finally be in the arms of the man she loved.

And then there were the animals. Devika began to speak of herself as a country girl who had been temporarily dislocated to the big, bad world of cinema, but was now back in her real home. This was an image she maintained for the rest of her life.

There is nothin' to you —

> My dearest Devika,
>
> Your love so beautifully expressed in your letter made me feel happy for my son and brought you close to my heart.
>
> I have always admired in your epics the beautiful, the noble character of a Hindu wife and mother and I am happy that my son has found a loving heart and a real companion in my beloved India.
>
> My son's love and enthusiasm in speaking of you, his admiration of your moral strength, courage and achievements gladden my heart.
>
> Love him, trust him, my little Devika. He is worthy of a great love —
>
> His happiness is my happiness.
>
> Father and I shall love you dearly and Georgie will be a real brother to you — We are sending you our blessings —
>
> With love and tenderness
>
> your Mother

Earlier, in a letter written on 23 May 1945, she had said:

The trouble is, I love animals and if there are horses and cows anywhere, I go to them. I love the smell of a stable and goats too—kids are so sweet! You have got a still of mine carrying a goat or kid? Well he was from my stable. I originally had 4, and they became 19, and I supplied the kid from there for our picture. It knew me so well, its name was Bahadur. He was a fine chap and acted beautifully with me. People raved about him.

She was sorry when they lost some cows in Kulu.

How many died? Is there no way to keep them warm or shelter them from the cold? How I wish I were there. I would see them in milking time early in the morning and it would be wonderful.

She had written then:

Kulu should be our real resting place…I don't say in life one should be tied to things or property etc., but when one wishes to have a real peaceful place, I can think of nowhere really better than Kulu inasmuch as the complete quiet and really peaceful surroundings and the beauty of the mountains.

She also said in the letter that she was going to devote herself to Svetoslav and his art. Do everything in her power to see that he was not unhappy—even for a moment.

Explaining that she did not have the knowledge or the education to help him with his work, she said if she could, she would do anything he wanted her to. In her letter of 28 May 1945, she said:

[I will] clean the floor of your studio, keep things tidy, clean your paint brushes, clean the skylight, keep the windows clean, tidy your books, keep your newest ideas in sketches on the top, remember what you said about each sketch, remember the names of the colours you wished for them, remember your conceptions, remember what you want, all those things I would and could easily do with my whole heart and strength, nothing would make me happier.

She wanted Svetoslav to think and work towards building his own career. When they were making their wedding plans, she wrote to him on 28 May 1945:

> You are quite right beloved in saying that you should now do more for <u>your</u> self—in this sense it is not selfish. You know one should because it is a sin really to leave one's own work undone and be careless for nothing—all [that] help for others does it actually help them, don't they have to work out their Karma, yes, to be helpful yes, <u>always</u>, but to harm one's self and gifts from God is not right. It has the effect of one never completing. That is why I say, finish all you have to do and do it now really in earnest quite seriously.
>
> In my work here I am satisfied that here & in this work I can do no more...but I can truthfully now go with a free mind & it is destiny which is removing me from this field, completely at peace and have no worry on that issue.

Their life was peaceful for a few years, but Devika had already been warned by Svetoslav that the family would leave the valley sometime in 1947. Their departure had been decided even before she joined them as a new bride. With the Roerichs, who constantly spoke of spiritual guidance from another world, things could move in mysterious ways. Perhaps the Great Guru they believed in had willed it, but in 1945, they had already discussed their departure with a plan to re-establish themselves in Russia in a few years' time. By 1947, only Svetoslav and Devika were left in Kulu.

Devika had hoped for them to be together. She had said:

> I love peace, how I need a home, how I have lived in misery, how I long for love, warmth, kindness, how I shall be grateful, how I

am willing to be taught, & to learn—then she will know. I love her [mother]. Strange... how I love mother and father.

But the partition of India had created a terrible unrest in the mountains. Nicholas, perhaps unable to take the trauma of seeing the disunity—the opposite of what he had worked for—died the same year, in December, at the age of seventy-three. Svetoslav's mother Helena and brother George left soon afterwards, first for Delhi and then for Khandala, hoping to eventually leave for Russia via Bombay. Since the passage never came through, they went to Kalimpong, where Helena died in 1955. She was cremated on the top of a mountain facing Kanchenjunga, and her ashes were placed inside a Buddhist stupa which is in the compound of the Zang Dhok Palri Phodang Buddhist monastery. After a long and very interesting life, all that her epitaph said was 'Helena Roerich, the wife of Nicholas Roerich, thinker and writer, old friend of India'. Similarly, Nicholas Roerich's grave only has a very rough-hewn stone with his name on it, outside their home in Naggar, surrounded by the spectacular Himalayas he painted so often.

George settled in Moscow, finally having got permission to live and work there. Among his many achievements is an eleven-volume Tibetan–Russian–English dictionary. He died at the age of fifty-eight.

And so, the family life in the hills that Devika had envisaged was not to be—their peaceful, bucolic existence lasted less than two years.

With his parents and brother no more at Naggar, and Devika his only support, Svetoslav wanted to start a new life with her somewhere in the countryside, away from the hills. Their old friend Tara Ali Baig noticed that he no longer wanted to paint. The death of his parents unsettled him further. They began to explore living on a large farm that could pay for itself, especially if it were a little better connected than Naggar.

Using most of their resources, they bought around four hundred acres of land in Tataguni, outside Bangalore, where they would grow linaloe, the aromatic extract from which is used to make perfume and cosmetics—cosmetics were something that Devika had loved all her life. This became their main home, though they continued to visit their beautiful Naggar home occasionally.

According to Tara Ali Baig, who visited them at the farm in Tataguni, there were always rumours of 'strange things' happening there, of which she found no evidence. When she dropped in for tea, Devika asked her to do a puja and put some flowers in her hand, leading her to a beautiful little shrine 'nestling under a banyan tree'. Tara performed the rituals that Devika asked her to do, feeling an intense 'need to communicate with whatever unknown deity or force was focused on this sacred spot, some word of supplication to look after, protect and care for this gentle soul'. Tara recalled:

> It was indeed a hallowed spot. Why did I have this feeling? Part of it may be because Devika often speaks in riddles. They are uttered so softly, it is hard to tell whether she is playing a game or playing a part. Yet, I know she is far too genuine a person to play games in life itself. For one who has scaled such heights of fame, and more important still, achieved so much, why did she now need protection of a special kind?

When Tara looked back to see her standing at the doorway, she thought her 'great eyes [were] filled with pain. It was like a sorrow that came after me, poignant, unfathomable...her still womanly form mute but intense in that doorway. Are we never really fulfilled in life?'

Tara heard from Devika that it was she who had coaxed Svetoslav to begin painting again. She had even organised an exhibition for him in Delhi in 1960, which was inaugurated by Prime Minister Nehru. But things went awry after that. The paintings went to Russia, and upon their return, customs duty was charged on them— on his own paintings which he had taken to Russia! It appears that the very sensitive Svetoslav could not handle such setbacks or unfair practices. Between them, Devika would always be the strong one.

It was ironic that all these years, she had longed to be looked after. In all her relationships, she had wanted a mentor, a father figure to replace the one she had lost so early—but the men in her life would always lean on her, instead. Somewhere, then, did she always feel unfulfilled? Perhaps it was the loneliness born of this that Tara saw in her eyes.

Though Tataguni was also far away from the city, it had ample room for the treasures the couple began to acquire. Using all the skills she had learnt of conserving money and creating a profitable business, Devika ensured the linaloe plantation did well. Money was no problem now. Apart from an increasing number of paintings by Svetoslav, the Roerichs possessed a vast collection of art and artefacts, and Devika could at last display all these rich and wonderful pieces in their new home. The couple proceeded to buy more exquisite antiques, textiles, carpets, coins, art—visitors would remember an abundance of rare and beautiful pieces.

To compensate for all she had lost and pawned in the years with Himansu, she amassed vast quantities of jewellery and clothes. Every day, she would put on her make-up and dress elaborately in a silk saree accessorised with fine gold jewellery studded with expensive stones, regardless of whether they were staying in or—more and more rarely—going out.

The next four decades of their life were probably the most peaceful she had ever known. But visitors like Tara would wonder if she was truly happy. She shared with Tara her desire of 'contributing something of value to India. To me, and I am sure to you, there is no other country in the world like India.' She was depressed when she saw 'mundane' things around her; she wanted to soar higher and strive harder. She also jealously guarded their privacy, and while there were occasional requests for her to act again, it was Svetoslav she focused on.

In that sense, her entry into his life had been perfectly timed. The gentle and sensitive man that he was, and somewhat unworldly, it might have been difficult for him to survive on his own, without his parents and brother. In the past, he had suffered the occasional bout of overwhelming loneliness, which engulfed and depressed him, and there had been times when he toyed with the idea of death.

Devika constantly tried to build him up. He was charming, but at the same time quick to admit defeat. Protectively, she said:

> Dearest, you must never say you are "weak" or use any detrimental word for yourself to me. I worship you and will never allow you to—you are what Confucius said is a Superior Man in every way, in everything and together if you teach me I will be ever willing to learn the greater life. Together we shall join it and what infinite peace it will give us, my dearest heart.

For Svetoslav, this determined interest in his work and in him was unexpected and more than welcome. His family was so overwhelmingly talented that it had been difficult for him to take his own prodigious skills too seriously. Just as she was in search of a father figure, he was perhaps looking for a maternal touch. His own mother was clearly much closer to his brother, George, and possibly very busy with her own work as well. Devika helped him create art again, supporting him, occasionally roping in a friend to become a muse for him. She even brought a new sensuality into his art.

Their first discussions were about a painting that would become very famous—of a nude, plump, fair Eve, plucking an apple for a dark and supplicant Adam, who is on his knees, with folded hands, literally begging for the fruit. There is no 'temptation' in the form of the snake—in this depiction, there are overlays of sexuality, of need and hunger. But no sin, only desire.

Even without having seen his proposed painting *The Call Eternal*, Devika discussed it excitedly in her letter of 2 May 1945:

> Somehow I feel we are thinking the same—isn't it wonderful? And I can feel what you feel, what somehow you are doing, I picture it so clearly. And my love the best of all news is the

wonderful picture you describe The Call Eternal!! What a wonderful idea and what a subject! Dearest is it not? Don't you see it is not "High" in the sense you talk of? It is the very root of life, of human life, Man & Woman and of course if a great work like that is done, oh beloved it is the best possible thing—and with it of course the best idea, the highest is the simplest. It hits straight!...the ordinary man in the street can follow The Call Eternal. Instinctively I feel it will be a masterpiece.

Another well-known painting, titled *Awakening,* also done by Svetoslav in the mid-1940s, shows two women by the seaside, clad in sarees and gazing into the distance. The style and appearance of the women, and their clothes, is reminiscent of Devika. She recognised that it had been inspired by their meetings on the beach and the longing she had felt for him, but the mood in the painting is sombre, as is the palette.

After they were married, she did, for a while, become his muse as he entered his most prolific phase. The portraits he made of Devika were vibrant—in one, she is clad in yellow, with a pale green blouse, a string of bright orange coral pearls gleaming around her neck. The sketches he did are alive with splashes of yellow. She is young and glowing, looking at him with undisguised longing.

Surprisingly, the portraits from the 1950s, just a few years later, show her as much older. She has also gained weight. In her midforties, just seven years after their marriage, she is no longer impish or sexual, but far more reflective. In one of these, the colours glow bright red, and she is no longer the lover but a slightly more maternal figure. Yet another portrait shows her in shades of brown, looking into the distance, peaceful, pensive, calm.

With Devika by his side, Svetoslav had lost some of his reticence. His paintings were often more dramatic, and bolder. But she was no longer his lone muse. She had introduced to him someone younger than her who fitted that role well—Bharatanatyam dancer Rohan Vajifdar Ghose, whose sister Shirin Vajifdar was married to Mulk Raj Anand, the writer.

In one of these paintings, Rohan wears just a strip of cloth across her breasts, and a very low-slung saree. In other paintings, she leaves little to the imagination, with her bare back. This, for conservative Bangalore in the 1950s and 1960s, would have been very avant garde.

Devika knew that these portraits would connect widely with their direct and sensual appeal. Sure enough, Svetoslav's portraits of Rohan were published on the cover of the *Illustrated Weekly of India* and other popular magazines.

Another beautiful muse who appeared frequently in his paintings was Katherine Campbell, an aspiring American actress, who also helped them with the museum in New York.

Of course, by now, they were well settled on their farm and Devika was running a tight ship—just as she had run the studio.

Meanwhile, though she rejected all offers to act in films, Devika was not forgotten by the world of cinema. She continued to receive awards and occasionally attended functions. She received a Padma Shri, and Svetoslav a Padma Bhushan, both among the highest civilian awards given by the Indian government. She was also the first woman to receive the Dadasaheb Phalke award, for her contribution to cinema. The irony may not have been lost on her, given the number of attempts made to destroy her legacy.

Their enchanted life could have gone on much longer had they not become infirm and helpless as they grew older. In 1989, they abandoned their beautiful farm and moved to the far more mundane environs of Ashok Hotel in Bangalore city, along with their attendants.

Things started unravelling very fast after that. Some of the people they had trusted took advantage of their absence and their inability to supervise their vast estate or their incredible collection of textiles, shawls, sculptures and paintings, not to mention the invaluable gold jewellery and coins. As Svetoslav and Devika became increasingly frail, stories began to emerge about how their treasures were rapidly disappearing. Devika however, wore her heavy silk sarees and gold jewellery and insisted that their lives carry on as usual. Her lips were as bright as ever, and her eyes still lined with kohl, although her skin was sagging and the wrinkles on her face were starkly evident. It was her way of telling the world that she was eternal, unchanged, still the dazzling Devika. Only, now, the make-up was not subtle at all. The face was powdered almost white, like a kabuki mask.

People continued to visit them—and it is quite remarkable, the number of people they knew—even as they became less and less mobile. Svetoslav became increasingly withdrawn in the last years of his life, but Devika would smoke and imperiously stride about, controlling their world. It was only after her legs gave way that she was forced into dependency—not something she took to easily.

The vulnerable state of their health meant they barely visited Tataguni. Not only from their farm but also from the hotel, precious items kept disappearing. It was like tragedy repeating itself. Both the institutions that Devika had built with such care—Bombay Talkies and the Tataguni estate—would soon lie in ruins.

Instead of their last years being spent peacefully together, they got embroiled in a court case concerning the sale of a part of their farm, which a businessman claimed to have bought after transferring money to Devika. The government of Karnataka, ostensibly to preserve their heritage, began the process to take over the farm and their collections, while the Roerichs resisted, saying that they wanted to set up a trust of their own. They claimed to have approached, among others, the vice president of India, Shankar Dayal Sharma, the leader of the Congress, Sonia Gandhi, as well as the president of Russia, Boris Yeltsin. But before they could get any results, Svetoslav died on 30 January 1993, at the age of eighty-nine.

Devika had kept her promise to take care of him, till the very end. But after his death, she lost the will to live. She died the following year, on 9 March. She was eighty-six.

Tragically, the feisty Devika spent her last days not so differently from Himansu Rai—paranoid and fearful, living in a make-believe world, and looked after by someone who did it more out of duty than love. She told friends that her secretary and confidante, Mary Joyce Poonacha, wanted to kill her. She even showed one friend large blotches on her legs, claiming that Mary was forcing her to take some injections. And yet, she continued to be dependent on her. Like many other elderly patients, she became a hostage to those who were paid to attend to her. By the time she died, no one knew her better than Mary, who had been with her for twenty years, and many suspected no one had exploited her more.

Devika's and Svetoslav's graves lie on the estate in Tataguni, side by side. After a series of court cases, the state government had its way and took over the estate, since there were no legal heirs. But not before as many as five wills turned up. Mary Joyce claimed, after their death, that she had been named the heir to the property. The police, on raiding Mary's home, found huge amounts of gold, emerald and diamond jewellery, 'including a diamond studded armlet, a gold waistband besides Dr Svetoslav's collection of guns and papers referring to numerous fixed deposits and share certificates' according to a report by Bangalore-based journalist Sandhya Mendonca in *Sunday* magazine.

Devika died as she had lived, in the middle of controversy, and refuses to be forgotten. Even now, when one visits either the ruins of Bombay Talkies or the chalet at Naggar, where a rough-hewn stone has been placed in her remembrance, or the grand graves near an old spreading banyan tree in Tataguni, one can sense her spirit, wild and free, and her desire to create beauty all around her.

She had wanted her ashes to be kept both at Naggar and at Tataguni, where she lies next to Svetoslav, the only man to understand her and give her the freedom she needed to be herself. He was the 'reward' she believed she had been given for keeping faith in spite of all the abuse and humiliation she had suffered. And her restless passion seems to still hover over the graves.

In both places, the tombstones stand next to stone idols symbolising Shakti. A strange energy emanates from the idols—their sturdy, grey bodies, with their vivid red bindis and the shining zari on their dupattas. As you stand there, looking at them, you can almost hear Devika whispering the words she wrote to Svetoslav on 25 May 1945:

> Longing, yes beloved, longing to be with you, longing to see you and longing to love you. To just love you and be loved as only husband and wife can love, for I know what it means, this separation and the ache. The inner thirst can only be quenched to some degree, if I were near you, and could be yours, completely merged in you—completely to love and caress every bit of you and to hold you near me, so that we could feel deeply that mad rhythm, that complete oneness. Your tears beloved on your letter, dearest love—why? Why those tears? My heart bleeds for them. I cannot bear to think that those eyes I adore so shed such tears—please dearest why? Why do you let them? Don't you know I am yours? Your wife completely, body and soul? Can't you feel me ever with you? Can't you feel that love? And at night you ask me to think hard of you dearest husband of mine. I can't help it, I actually sometimes feel even in my sleep you take me in your arms, kissing my lips, waking me and softly saying "Bunny sweetheart come to me, I want you." Yes dearest I never wrote about it because you know how sacred that love of ours is, how infinite, how very overpowering. But actually every night I lie down, put out the light, think of you and feel the sign of the cross, you're doing it—and then oh dearest, then the terrible longing for you and your love overpowers me, I long for you and when I feel you go away, tears do come…

Her voice fades, and disappears into the sound of the wind rustling through the trees.

SELECT BIBLIOGRAPHY

Dilip Kumar, *Dilip Kumar: The Substance and the Shadow – An Autobiography* (Hay House India, New Delhi, 2015).

Hansa Wadkar, *You Ask, I Tell: An Autobiography*, edited and translated by Jasbir Jain and Shobha Shinde (Zubaan, New Delhi, 2013).

Khalid Hasan, editor and translator, *Bitter Fruit: The Very Best of Saadat Hasan Manto* (Penguin Books India, New Delhi, 2008).

Khatija Akbar, *I Want to Live: The Story of Madhubala* (Hay House India, New Delhi, 2017).

Kishore Valicha, *Dadamoni: The Authorized Biography of Ashok Kumar* (Penguin Books India, New Delhi, 1996).

Lubna Kazim, editor and compiler, *A Woman of Substance: The Memoirs of Begum Khurshid Mirza, 1918–1989* (Zubaan, New Delhi, 2005).

Niranjan Pal, *Such Is Life: An Autobiography* (Susmita Publications, 1997).

Susheila Nasta, editor, *India in Britain: South Asian Networks and Connections (1858–1950)* (Palgrave Macmillan, 2012).

Tara Ali Baig, *Portraits of an Era* (Roli Books, New Delhi, 1988).

FILMOGRAPHY
Devika Rani, Actress

1933
Karma
Dir: J.L. Freer Hunt
Starring: Devika Rani, Himansu Rai

1935
Jawani ki Hawa
Dir : Franz Osten
Starring: Devika Rani, Najam ul Hussain

1936
Mamta (Mother)
Miya Biwi (Always Tell Your Wife)
Dir: Franz Osten
Starring: Devika Rani, Najam ul Hussain, J.S. Casshyap

Jeevan Naiya
Dir: Franz Osten
Starring: Devika Rani, Ashok Kumar

Achhut Kanya
Dir: Franz Osten
Starring: Devika Rani, Ashok Kumar

Janmabhoomi
Dir: Franz Osten
Starring: Devika Rani, Ashok Kumar

1937
Izzat
Dir: Franz Osten
Starring: Devika Rani, Ashok Kumar

Jeevan Prabhat
Dir: Franz Osten
Starring: Devika Rani, Kishore Sahu

Savitri
Dir: Franz Osten
Starring: Devika Rani, Ashok Kumar

1938
Nirmala
Dir: Franz Osten
Starring: Devika Rani, Ashok Kumar

Vachan
Dir: Franz Osten
Starring: Devika Rani, Ashok Kumar

1939
Durga
Dir: Franz Osten
Starring: Devika Rani, Rama Shukul

1941
Anjan
Dir: Amiya Chakrabarty
Starring: Devika Rani, Ashok Kumar

1943
Hamari Baat
Dir: M.I. Dharamsey
Starring: Devika Rani, P. Jairaj, Suraiya

ACKNOWLEDGEMENTS

In June 1945, Svetoslav Roerich wrote to Devika Rani that before she left Bombay Talkies to marry him, she must look at her *'personal papers, documents etc etc.'* He told her, *'You must attend to those. There may be some that can be quite useful, others you may not want to keep. Have you gone over them, Dearest? I always feel it is a pity to destroy documents that may have some historical interest or throw some important light upon one's periods in Life. You are leaving your present place, you must think about it. Or have you already... ?'*

Because he encouraged Devika to keep all her personal papers safely, the first person I have to thank for this book is Svetoslav Roerich. His advice to her made it possible for me, eighty years later, to access her letters and archives.

I have to thank my publisher, the patient and brilliant Karthika V.K. It is fifteen years since she first heard of the book, and in the intervening period, I managed to collect 4,000 documents (running into 8,000 pages, stored in two large suitcases), apart from interviews, films and so on. I also thank Sanjiv Sarin for his careful edit. And I have to thank my family—especially my first reader and always encouraging husband, Meghnad Desai, who got used to being seated at the very edge of the dining table because the rest was perpetually covered with 'Devika Rani papers', as was most of the house.

ACKNOWLEDGEMENTS

I am immensely grateful for the early help from my daughter Mallika, who was then based in Washington—I was supposed to be on holiday with her, but frequently disappeared for research in New York. I am also very grateful to Veena and Philip Oldenberg, Amit and Bunty Sawhney, Deepa and Colvyn Harris and Usha and Ram Ramaswamy for their generous hospitality while I travelled around piecing the book together. On these travels in India and abroad, I encountered a lot of helpful people, and many had a 'Devika Rani story' to narrate. My only regret is that not all the conversations and documents could feature in the book because I had a page limit to work with.

I am grateful to the entire team at the National Film Archives of India and at the Nicholas Roerich Museum in New York, for helping me so thoughtfully with my research.

I want to thank my parents, Padam and Rajini Rosha, as well as Gaurav and Priyanka Ahluwalia for their constant support, and Om for his delightful appearance in our lives.

Writing this book was a process of discovery, and sometimes very challenging, as when a few people offered me information but only against payment, which I was forced to decline. But taking inspiration from Devika, I did not give up. Finally, I found what made the book special for me—Devika's own letters, and her voice, containing information not many knew about. The extracts from her letters have been very lightly edited so that the flow is retained.

My unfathomable interest in Devika continues. I have written a play about her and even given lectures on her, and each time, I learnt something more about her. I thank all those who have been part of this process, including Lillete Dubey, who produced the play, *Devika Rani: Goddess of the Silver Screen*.

I also want to thank Rinki Roy, Jayabrato Chatterjee, Ratnotamma Sengupta, Tripurari Sharan, Marika Vicziany, Poonam Saxena, the Dietze family, the late Russian ambassador Kadakin, the family and friends of Himansu and Devika Rai, the children of Sir Richard Temple especially Peter Temple, Niranjan Pal's family,

Rajeev Bhargava, Amita Baig, Amitabh Mattoo and Jawhar Sircar. All of you encouraged me, gave me a chance to discuss Devika and shared invaluable information that enriched the book.

This book has taken me on a very long journey of discovering Devika, and is the most exciting I have written so far, as I could unearth so much which was not in the public domain before. Thank you for writing those very detailed letters, and keeping your personal and professional papers so safely, Devika!

ABOUT THE AUTHOR

Kishwar Desai is an award-winning author and playwright who writes both fiction and non-fiction. She worked in television as an anchor and producer for over twenty years before becoming a writer. She is the chairperson of The Arts and Cultural Heritage Trust that set up the world's first Partition Museum at Town Hall, Amritsar. She also helped to install the statue of Mahatma Gandhi outside Westminster in the UK.

Kishwar is the author of *Darlingji: The True Love Story of Nargis and Sunil Dutt* (2007). Her novel *Witness the Night* won the Costa First Novel Award in the UK, in 2010, and was followed by two others: *Origins of Love* (2012) and *Sea of Innocence* (2013). The trilogy featuring Simran Singh has since been optioned for a web series.

Kishwar's first work of political non-fiction, *Jallianwala Bagh: The Real Story* (2018), won critical acclaim and inspired exhibitions on the massacre in India, the UK and New Zealand. She also wrote a play, *Manto!* which won the TAG Omega award for Best Play in 1999. Most recently, in 2019, her play, *Devika Rani: Goddess of the Silver Screen*, was successfully staged in venues across India.

30 Years *of*
HarperCollins *Publishers* India

At HarperCollins, we believe in telling the best stories and finding the widest possible readership for our books in every format possible. We started publishing 30 years ago; a great deal has changed since then, but what has remained constant is the passion with which our authors write their books, the love with which readers receive them, and the sheer joy and excitement that we as publishers feel in being a part of the publishing process.

Over the years, we've had the pleasure of publishing some of the finest writing from the subcontinent and around the world, and some of the biggest bestsellers in India's publishing history. Our books and authors have won a phenomenal range of awards, and we ourselves have been named Publisher of the Year the greatest number of times. But nothing has meant more to us than the fact that millions of people have read the books we published, and somewhere, a book of ours might have made a difference.

As we step into our fourth decade, we go back to that one word – a word which has been a driving force for us all these years.

Read.